Black Lambs & (

Women Travellers in the Balkans

Edited by John B. Allcock and Antonia Young

Berghahn Books
New York • Oxford

Women in War (I): the romanticised view of nursing work with the Red Cross offered to the readers of *The Graphic*, in 1912.

Second edition published in 2000 by **Berghahn Books**

www.berghahnbooks.com

© 1991, 2000 University of Bradford

First Published in 1991 by the University of Bradford

Library of Congress Cataloging-in-Publication Data

Black lambs and grey falcons : women travellers in the Balkans / edited
by John B. Allcock & Antonia Young. –2nd ed.
  p. cm.
Includes bibliographical references and index.
ISBN 1-57181-744-1 (alk. paper)
1. Balkan peninsula – Description and travel. 2. Women travelers –
Balkan Peninsula Biography. I. Allcock, John B. II. Young, Antonia.

DR11.5 .B58 1999
914.9604'559 – dc21   99-34760
                                                                 CIP

British Library Cataloguing in Publication Data

A catalogue record for this book is available from the British
Library.

Printed in the United States on acid-free paper

ISBN 1-57181-744-1

'I confess I am malicious enough to desire, that the world should see to how much better purpose the LADIES travel than their LORDS, and that whilst it is surfeited with male Travels, all in the same tone, and stuffed with the same trifles, a lady has the skill to strike out a new path, and to embellish a worn-out subject with variety of fresh and elegant entertainment.'

(The anonymous Preface to Lady Mary Wortley Montagu, *Letters During Mr Wortley's Embassy*, of 1724.)

Contents

List of Illustrations   xi

Preface to Second Edition   xiii

Acknowledgements   xix

Editorial Introduction: Black Lambs and Grey Falcons:
    Outward and Inward Frontiers   xxi
    John B. Allcock and Antonia Young

1. Two Victorian Ladies and Bosnian Realities, 1862–1875:
    G.M. MacKenzie and A.P. Irby   1
    Omer Hadžiselimović

2. Edith Durham: Traveller and Publicist   9
    John Hodgson

3. Edith Durham as a Collector   32
    June Hill

4. Emily Balch: Balkan Traveller, Peace Worker and
    Nobel Laureate   39
    Elinor M. Despalatović and Joel M. Halpern

5. The Work of British Medical Women in Serbia during
    and after the First World War   71
    Monica Krippner

6. Captain Flora Sandes: A Case Study in the Social
    Construction of Gender in a Serbian Context   90
    Julie Wheelwright

7. Rose Wilder Lane: 1886–1968   99
    Antonia Young

8. Rebecca West, Gerda and the Sense of Process   113
   Felicity Rosslyn

9. Margaret Masson Hasluck   128
   Marc Clark

10. Louisa Rayner: An Englishwoman's Experiences in
    Wartime Yugoslavia   155
    Anne Kay

11. Mercia MacDermott: A Woman of the Frontier   166
    Diane Waller

12. An Anthropologist in the Village   187
    Barbara Kerewsky-Halpern

13. Bucks, Brides and Useless Baggage: Women's Quest
    for a Role in their Balkan Travels   208
    Dea Birkett

14. Constructing 'the Balkans'   217
    John B. Allcock

15. Women Travellers in the Balkans: a Bibliographical
    Guide   241
    Jennifer Finder

The Contributors   257

Index   259

Illustrations

Frontispiece: Women in War (I): the romanticised view of nursing work with the Red Cross offered to the readers of *The Graphic*, in 1912.

Plate 1.   Mary Edith Durham, displaying an item from her own collection of Balkan costume.

Plate 2.   One of Mary Edith Durham's watercolour sketches of Albania costume.

Plate 3.   Emily Greene Balch (2nd from left) with Euphemia Abrams (centre) and Austro-Hungarian officials, probably during her journey of 1905.

Plate 4.   Emily Greene Balch in St. Petersburg, before the First World War (far right), in connection with her work with the Women's International League for Peace and Freedom.

Plate 5.   Women in War (2): the realities. A unit of the Scottish Women's Hospitals setting up camp in Macedonia, in 1918.

Plate 6.   Dr Alice Hutchinson, CMO of the 2nd Scottish Women's Hospitals unit, Valjevo, 1915.

Plate 7.   Flora Sandes' own photograph of her unit crossing the River Shkumbin during the retreat through Albania in the winter of 1915–16.

Plate 8.   Flora Sandes as an officer in the Serbian army.

Plate 9.   Flora Sandes in retirement, shortly before her death at the age of 80 in 1956.

Plate 10.   An Albanian family at Pultit from Rose Wilder Lane's Peaks of Shala. The young boy was her guide, Rexh Meta.

Plate 11. Louisa Rayner in her Belgrade apartment shortly before the Second World War.

Plate 12. An 'Albanian virgin', photographed by Mary Edith Durham. The subject is commented upon by several of our travellers.

Plate 13. Louisa Rayner in 1935.

Plate 14. Barbara Kerewsky-Halpern on the threshold of 'the old house', in 1953.

Plate 15. Mercia MacDermott and fellow students with Dimitrov in the summer of 1948. (Mercia is seated on Dimitrov's right.)

Plate 16. Barbara Kerewsky-Halpern with a woman of Orašac who was sixteen years old when they first met.

Plate 17. Margaret Hasluck

Plate 18. Margaret Hasluck's photograph of 'Mother and son, each appropriately laden'

Preface to the Second Edition

The first edition of this book appeared in 1991, and since that time a great deal has changed in Europe, and particularly so in the Balkans. Curiously, however, the changes which have taken place have served to add to its interest and relevance rather than to render it out of date.

Yugoslavia has disintegrated in a dreadful succession of armed struggles. As we prepare the text for the press it seems clear that the conflict in Kosovo has reached a pause rather than been brought to a conclusion. After witnessing in 1991 the toppling of the statue of Enver Hoxha in Tirana's Skanderbeg Square, Albania is now emerging very hesitantly from a period of chaos involving nothing less than the collapse of its economic and political structures. Although the problems experienced there have involved less drastic upheaval for their populations, Bulgaria is still striving with difficulty to move out from under the shadow of the former Soviet Union, and Greece has both been shaken by the controversies surrounding Macedonian independence and caught up in the backwash of disorder in Albania. For the 'rump Yugoslavia' there is still no evident way to break free from the morass into which the Milošević regime has led it.

Throughout the unfolding of these events there has been a general tendency in the reporting of the region to retreat into well-worn, stereotypical generalisations about the enduring characteristics of the Balkans. A late nineteenth century traveller described 'Eternelle Turquie' as follows.

What is Turkey? Turkey is the classic country of massacres . . . its history can be summed up as follows: pillage, murder, robbery, extortion – at every level – revolts, uprisings, repression, foreign wars, civil wars, revolutions, counter-revolutions, sediton and mutiny . . . (Arsène Pérlant, cited in W.E.D. Allen, The *Turks in Europe: a sketch study*. New York: Charles Scribner, 1920)

This assessment of the propensities of the region to violence and disorder might well have been compiled as a précis of media coverage of the Balkans since the publication of our first edition. This book can be read in part as a valuable corrective to this kind of reductionism. Certainly our collection features writing by or about women caught up in war. An important aspect of our anthology, however, is the diverse range of experiences of the Balkan countries and their peoples which are reported by our women travellers. The recent wars have no doubt seen the re-emergence of women as soldiers and as those who bear the burden of caring for the wounded and displaced. It remains essential, even so, to remind the reader of the tranquillity of village life, and the strength of family bonds, which have been equally characteristic of Balkan societies. The voices which can be heard in these pages do not only recount the pain and horror of war, but also reflect the patient pursuit of scholarship, or the effervescence of creative imagination. These are today, as much as they ever were, also typical of life in the region and of the response of the traveller to it. If it is true that the Balkan countries have not changed in their essentials over time, then this does not only apply to Balkan violence and disorder: it also obtains for the diversity and subtlety of the cultures of the region. We hope that in offering a new edition of this collection to the reader we will be able to challenge as much as confirm accepted images of life there.

Our first edition appeared at a time when there was a broad upsurge of interest in women travellers. Dea Birkett's *Spinsters Abroad* (1989), Jane Robinson's *Wayward Women* (1990), and Miranda Davies and Natasha Jansz's *Women Travel* (1990) might be taken as typifying this. Our book was interesting within that context, in part, because it provided a link between the anthologising and descriptive approach which was generally characteristic of this body of writing, and a more analytical, critical and academic emphasis. Work at this more general level of interest has come to fruition more recently in Maria Todorova's *Imagining the Balkans* (1997). As a historian she treats the general development of processes of representation through which the Balkan region has come to be known.

The work of Todorova, with its impressive breadth of scholarship, conveys well a sense of the systematic character of the patterns of representation through which the Balkans are made present in the imagination as specifically 'Balkan'. The volume and complexity of this material, which certainly has the advantage of challenging earlier and perhaps over simplified ideas about the representation of other peoples (such as those of Edward Said), tends to leave unanswered at least two questions which are posed by our own collection.

Attention to the broad sweep of ideological change can run the risk of mystifying the process of representation if it is not complemented by a corresponding awareness of the ways in which individual writers contribute to the general process of 'imagination' by giving expression to their personal experiences. The approach in terms of individual case studies, adopted by the majority of our contributors, does direct attention to the ways in which the diverse descriptions of Balkan life and history, penned by the writers in question, emerged from a range of entirely personal projects. If the idea of 'The Balkans' does have a specific place within our collective imagination, it is remarkable how this shared element of wider European culture has emerged as the product of such a diversity of intentions.

Our anthology cannot claim to bear comparison with the erudition, fluency and intellectual sophistication of Todorova's study. Nevertheless, there is a sense in which we can legitimately claim that it is worth returning to the essays collected here after reading her work. In doing so, it might help to make more readily apparent the need to see significant cultural movements as produced and reproduced by the working of the imaginations of concretely situated persons with individual voices.

A further question raised by our first edition may well be in danger of getting lost in the generality of theories of representation. What is it that *women* specifically bring to writing about their experiences of travel? At the time when our first edition appeared a good deal of the attention which was aroused by writing about women as travellers had to do simply with registering the fact that they did it. Acknowledgement of the fact that women could travel adventurously was one element of a wider aspect of the impact of feminism upon social consciousness, in which the boundaries of the prevailing perceptions of what it was both possible and acceptable for women to do, and aspire to do, were being pushed back. Julie Wheelwright's *Amazons and Military Maids* (1989) can perhaps be regarded as a benchmark of this kind of material. The emphasis upon enlarging our awareness of what it was possible to do and be as a woman, however, tended to push into second place the equally important issues of what women *meant* and *felt* in doing these things, and the forms in which they conveyed this subjective experience.

This kind of concern with the specific forms of feminine sensibility and their expression to some extent can be found in the essays which we collected, although often that is implicit rather than explicit in the text. Popular consciousness has not perhaps moved far beyond a somewhat sensational interest in what women might or might not be able to do, as the recent controversy surrounding the death on Mt Everest of Alison Hargreaves illustrates vividly. Nevertheless, it is no longer necessary for gender studies to remain fixated at that level. More complex and subtle questions can now find their place on the agenda concerning the nature of women's experiences, the meanings which they attach to these experiences, and the articulation of those meanings.

Perhaps a useful bridge to this newer level of interest is provided by the only additional essay to appear in this second edition – Marc Clark's study of Margaret Hasluck. In many ways Hasluck stands apart from other figures included in our study, in that she spent the better part of two decades in the Balkans (principally in Albania) as a resident as much as a traveller. Her motivation appears to have derived more from a commitment to anthropology than from any sense of adventure. She was not looking for a cause as much as an intellectual niche. Throughout the years of her residence in the region, and her writing about it, can be traced the thread of the difficulty of reconciling (and separating) the depths of personal involvement and affectionate attachment, and the demands of impersonal scholarship – usually at the cost of concealing the latter in her writing. In this respect her story can be read as an interesting contrast to that of another of our contributors, Barbara Kerewski-Halpern. Hasluck's achievements as a scholar were bought at the price of the obliteration of personal sensibility, whereas Kerewski-Halpern's essay is remarkable as a demonstration of the possibility of their synthesis.

To tackle those questions centrally would demand another book rather than a reissue of this one. Nevertheless, this is a suitable moment at which to publish a second edition, in that the early adumbration of these issues in the essays collected here can act as a signpost and an encouragement to those who are willing and able to pursue them further. History, scholarship and public sensibility have all moved on since 1991. The result, however, has been to permit our material to be seen in a new and different light rather than to render it out of date.

In preparing this new edition it has been possible to correct several errors which survived the editorial process in the first. June

Hill's essay has been revised to take account of the new museum coverage of the work of Edith Durham. Jenny Finder's bibliographical essay has been revised and brought up to date.

John B. Allcock
Antonia Young

Acknowledgements

Individual contributors to this collection have acknowledged their gratitude for personal assistance in connection with their own projects at appropriate points in the text. The editors want to place on record also their appreciation of assistance and encouragement rendered by the following persons or organisations during the preparation of the book.

The Royal Anthropological Institute has supplied the photograph of Edith Durham which appears as Plate 1. The Bankfield Museum in Halifax, West Yorkshire, has allowed us to reproduce the material from the Durham collection as Plate 2 and on the front cover. David Berryman, photographer at the University of Bradford, prepared both of these illustrations. The Smithsonian Institution provided Plate 3, Isobel Božić provided the photographs which accompany Anne Kay's essay on Louisa Rayner; and Mercia MacDermott the one which accompanies Diane Waller's essay. The British School at Athens has granted permission for the reproduction of Plate 17, and the Museum of Mankind provided Plate 18. Stuart Davidson and Jennifer Braithwaite, cartographer and graphic artist at the University of Bradford, kindly drew the maps.

The staffs of the J.B. Priestley Library at the University of Bradford, and the Leeds Library, have been most helpful throughout the project.

Valuable assistance has been given in the typing of the script by Beverley Toulson, Jeanette Stevens and Anne-Marie Robinson.

Permission is also gratefully acknowledged to reproduce brief passages from copyright works: Isobel Božić, for the use of passages from Louisa Rayner, *Women in a Village*; Century Hutchinson, for the excerpts from Dorothy Anderson, *The Balkan Volunteers*, and also her, *Miss Irby and her Friends*; Macmillan, for the quotation from *Rebecca West: a Celebration*; Oxford University Press, for extracts from E. E. Evans-Pritchard, *Witchcraft, Oracles and Magic among the Azande*, and, *Theories of Primitive Religion*;

the Peters Fraser & Dunlop Group Ltd., for sections from Rebecca West's *Black Lamb and Grey Falcon*; Routledge, for quotations from Edward Said's *Orientalism*; and Virago Press, for extracts from Edith Durham's *High Albania*.

John B. Allcock
Antonia Young

Oh dreadful is the check – intense the agony –
When the ear begins to hear, and the eye begins to see;
When the pulse begins to throb, the brain to think again;
The soul to feel the flesh, and the flesh to feel the chain.

Emily Bronte, **The Prisoner.**

Black Lambs and Grey Falcons: Outward and Inward Frontiers

John Allcock and Antonia Young

Tourism brings well over four million Northern Europeans and North Americans to Yugoslavia, nearly three and a half million to Greece, and more than a million to Bulgaria each year. While popular travel on this scale is a recent phenomenon, the Balkan countries have always held for travellers to that area a very peculiar magic. This is clearly not only because of the strategic or economic significance of the region, of which most people probably have little appreciation.

The images which motivate people to visit the Balkans are complex and multi-layered. The very word 'Balkan' in the English language has come to stand for confusion and fragmentation, and carries a definitely derogatory meaning. An article in *The Guardian* during the summer of 1988, on operating systems for micro computers, bemoaned the 'balkanised' state of the current market.[1] If the area has such negative connotations, how has it come at the same time to carry so many rich and attractive associations? Two general answers to that question might be offered.

In part it may well be the expectation of extreme contrast to their homelands that has enhanced the appeal of the Balkans for travellers there. Harry de Windt, describing his travels through 'savage Europe' at the beginning of this century, tells his readers:

'... the term accurately describes the wild and lawless countries between the Adriatic and the Black Seas'.[2] In 1912 the anonymous author of an article in the Magazine *The Graphic*, entitled 'Why the Balkans attract Women', asks the question:[3] 'Why should the Balkans, those rough, wild, semi-civilised and more than half Orientalised little countries appeal so strongly to some of our astutest feminine intelligence?' and answers it:

> ... it is not an attraction which the intellectual people reason about ... The Balkans are the gateway of the East, through which one catches one's first glimpse of the languorous land ... three quarters psychic, one quarter mystic, wholly sensuous ... the East attracts women because it is feminine to the core, just as the West is essentially masculine.

In the same year Edith Durham was reporting to the anthropological journal *Man* on head-hunting and nose-taking in the Balkans.[4]

The continuing importance of this aspect of the fascination of the region into more recent times is reflected by Olivia Manning, whose *Balkan Trilogy* has been adapted as a successful television series. Speaking through her fictional character Doamna Hassolel, she tells us that: 'These Balkan countries are wild'.[5]

The sense of otherness which is generated by this emphasis on savagery or wildness creates in us the impression that we confront the Balkans across a gulf as wide and deep as that conventionally separating the masculine from the feminine – and with an equivalent resulting fascination.

In spite of the superficially dismissive way in which the terms 'Balkan' and 'balkanised' are used, they do suggest at the everyday commonsense level the deeper reality of the complexity of the region. Perhaps this provides a further explanation for its attractiveness. The roots of this complexity are manifold, ranging from its physical geography to the strategic relations between the current super-powers. The fact which interests us above all others, however, is its multiple marginality. The Balkan countries stand at the overlapping edges of several different aspects or points of view from which the identity of the region might be constructed. The definitions of marginality may have shifted over time; but nevertheless, significant cultural, economic or political frontiers have met here at least since Roman times.

In a period characterised by a new sense of openness in the Soviet Union the sense of confrontation has eased. Throughout the post-war period, however, the principal feature of the relations between countries across the globe has been their distribution along the boundary between capitalism and communism. This divide, crossing the face of Europe like a livid weal, for a long time was represented to us by politicians as something definite, clear-cut and essential in the world. Even so, at the height of the Cold War the countries of the Balkan peninsula presented a constant challenge to that black/white representation. Yugoslavia was a by-word for its idiosyncratic amalgam of political and economic elements drawn from both systems.

Romania under Ceausescu was characterised by a bizarre mixture of caesarism and nationalism in politics, and state planning in the economy. Albania until 1990 was an enigmatic museum-piece of Stalinism laced with tribalism. Greece moved in a decade from being a fascist military dictatorship to moderate socialism. Only Bulgaria appeared to fit the conventional image of a 'normal' Communist state. In reference to the general picture of global division, the entire region was a confused liminal zone. As the supposed monolithic structure of a Communist bloc has collapsed, that sense of complexity and ambiguity has, if anything, been heightened. It may no longer be Communist in any agreed sense; but neither is it unambiguously democratic or capitalist.

In some respects the perception of the Balkans has not changed for centuries: but one key element is novel, and marks off our understanding from that of people in centuries past. The imagery which we now apply to the region is political and economic: that employed by former generations was basically religious. Through the Balkans ran the frontier between Christendom and Islam.

It is hard for us to recapture a sense of the way in which the world was understood before the middle of the nineteenth century. The modern cynic may claim that behind the pretensions that they were acting as the 'protector of the Christian subjects of the Sultan', advanced in turn by British, Austro-Hungarian and Russian statesmen, lay a thinly disguised interest in the possibilities for territorial or commercial expansion in the Balkans. While it does seem likely that religion might be regarded as a pretext rather than as a motive for action, it is worth noting that it was necessary for policy to be explained in these terms. There was no other available, convincing and acceptable rhetoric (or as Hans Gerth and C. Wright Mills put it, no 'vocabulary of motives') in which these covert ambitions could be decently dressed.[6] Consequently, when Prime Minister W.E. Gladstone took up the 'Eastern Question', it was in religious terms that he found it both most natural and most politically effectual to present his cause.

Although the terms of the discussion have changed over the centuries, and the imagery of religious confrontation has been replaced by economic and political frames of reference, this attribute of standing across a frontier has remained a constant feature of the appearance of the Balkan countries to their western neighbours. In this respect, a part of the problem that these countries has faced has been the difficulty that they have experienced in developing any kind of intelligible construction of themselves which might endow them with any distinctive or intrinsic value in themselves. Whatever they are, or claim to be, they are always incompletely, marginally, ambiguously, something else as well. Herein, perhaps, lies another root of the fascination of the Balkans for many of us.

Women and the Balkans

The idea for the present volume developed from the discovery that, of the large fund of writing about the Balkans which has accumulated over the past two centuries a very significant proportion of it had been written by women. Lady Mary Montagu Wortley's collected *Letters and Works,* in which she recorded her lively impressions as she travelled overland in the company of her husband, the Ambassador from the Court of St James to the Sublime Porte, were published in London in 1837 (though her first journey to Turkey had taken place in the previous century).[7] The first published tourist guide book to the Adriatic coast was also written by a woman – Ida Düringsfeld – whose *Aus Dalmatien* reflected on her travels in the region during the early 1850s.[8] From these early beginnings the quantity and diversity of writing about the region by women has become truly impressive (to which the bibliographical essay by Jennifer Finder, concluding this collection, bears witness).

In April, 1987 a conference was held at the University of Bradford to which papers were invited on this subject. The variety and interest of these spurred the editors to make them available to a wider readership, believing this to be a topic the attractiveness of which would extend well beyond its original academic frame. The book focuses on the processes of identification and interpretation of the Balkan region, through the eyes of these women travellers.

The women whose lives and work are the subjects of the essays gathered here do not form a coherent group in any sense. As personalities they are extremely diverse. As John Hodgson's essay notes, there was no love lost between Rebecca West and Edith Durham. Mercia MacDermott's romantic and somewhat uncritical identification with all things Bulgarian was poles apart from the cool and detached scholarship of Emily Greene Balch. Indeed, it is difficult to identify any common characteristics that they may have possessed. Although there is no attempt to diminish the variety of their characters and interests, and each is allowed to appear here in her full individuality, a number of broad themes are intertwined throughout the collection. These themes all relate in one way or another to our understanding of femininity and women's situation in contemporary society.

The enlargement of women's roles: travel, politics and war

To a large extent our major theme has to do with the ways in which, for several of the figures who stand at the centre of our interest, their travels in the Balkan peninsula either facilitated the adventurous expansion of conventional women's roles, or constituted a means of escaping from them. This idea, developed more fully in the essay by Dea Birkett, is conveyed touchingly but very clearly in this passage from Edith Durham's *Balkan Tangle*:[9]

> It was in Cetinje in August, 1900, that I first picked up the thread of the Balkan tangle, little thinking how deeply enmeshed I should later become, and still less how this tangle would ultimately affect the whole world. Chance, or the Fates, took me Near Eastward. Completely exhausted by constant attendance on an invalid relative, this future stretched before me as endless years of grey monotony, and escape seemed hopeless. The doctor who insisted upon my having two months' holiday every year was kinder than he knew. 'Take them in quite a new place,' he said. 'Get right away no matter where, so long as the change is complete.'
>
> Along with a friend I boarded the Austrian Lloyd steamer at Trieste, and with high hopes but weakened health, started for the ports of the Eastern Adriatic.

It is interesting how adventurous travel lay ready to hand for her purpose. The gentle-woman traveller could be said to be, in many ways, a familiar model which was already available: after all, the

Grand Tour as a component of genteel education was well established by the middle of the nineteenth century. In the hands of the women whose progress we will be following, however (such as the redoubtable Miss Irby and her companions) the ready-made role is redefined in the Balkan context with a passion and a radical edge. Far from simply conforming to a recognised role, people like Edith Durham were (often quite consciously) pushing back the boundaries of what it was possible for women to do.

It is worth reflecting upon just what is meant by 'travel' in this context, and in particular upon the distinction between travel and 'tourism'. None of the women whose work is considered in this book would have called themselves tourists: they were 'travellers'. Although Rebecca West's *Black Lamb and Grey Falcon* is still very popular with English speaking tourists in Yugoslavia, and still shapes significantly their perceptions of that country, she herself would surely have resisted the designation.[10] The difference may appear at first to be a trivial one; and historically it is true that tourists have followed in the footsteps of the travellers; but an important contrast of attitudes and purposes is at stake.

The word 'tourist' is not necessarily a derogatory one: but the essential character of tourism is that travel is undertaken for recreation. Even where tourism is sold as a commodity in the modern package tour, its purpose is defined first and foremost by reference to the individual needs of the tourist, whether this be for relaxation, education, or some other aspect of personal development. In this respect, tourism stands in direct contrast to the everyday world out of which one steps on a temporary basis to find the refreshment which travel might bring. The traveller, on the other hand (in the sense in which we use the word here) is engaged in serious business indeed. Travelling is an occupation: it is a legitimate end in itself.

This element of high seriousness is conveyed perfectly in two letters written in 1863. Georgina Muir MacKenzie, writing from Athens to Mr. Graham Dunlop, the British Consul in Greece, and anxious to present her credentials as a person who might legitimately seek to persuade Her Majesty's Government about the errors of its foreign policy in the Balkans, assures him that she and her companion have been 'assiduously travelling' in the region for more than twelve months.[11] Adeline Irby, approaching the same gentleman, contrasts the value of her own experience of the area as a basis for judgement with the claims of others less well qualified.[12]

Last year a book appeared on these countries by a young Artillery officer: – the title is (I think) 'Omer Pasha and the Christian Rebels', by
Lieut. Arbuthnot. He remained some time with the army of Omer
Pasha, and being taken ill soon after he entered Bosnia, traversed a portion of that country in a hospital cart – and paid a brief visit to Belgrade.

Her scorn is restrained, but nevertheless unmistakable. In contrast
to Arbuthnot, who is accused of being both superficial and of dis-
torting the information given to him by local people, her own experience, that of the serious traveller – is to be given due
consideration.

Tourism had begun its penetration of the Balkans well before the
opening of Adeline Irby's school for Christian girls in Sarajevo in
1870. Resorts such as Opatija and Bled had been in operation for
two decades, and the area was already given coverage in
Baedeker's guides.[13] Omer Hadžiselimović begins his contribution
to our collection with an anecdote about the Englishwoman who
visited the court of Prince Njegoš in Cetinje out of 'curiosity'.
Would curiosity alone have been enough for Adeline Irby and her
companions (or for most of the other figures who feature in this
book)? It seems unlikely. Although in our world the majority of visitors to the Balkan countries are unequivocally tourists, they
remained firmly located in another world, which perhaps we have
also lost – that of the traveller.

This contrast is important for our purposes in two respects. It
challenges the overdrawn and oversimplified suggestion that somehow women have a special affinity for the 'romantic' Balkans,
advanced by the magazine correspondent quoted above. The specific motivations which underlay the attachment of particular individuals to the area seem to have been very varied. In some cases
there was undoubtedly a streak of romanticism in their make-up.
Rose Wilder Lane's work hovers uneasily between the coyness
which seems to have been expected by the magazine readership to
which she addressed herself, and the obvious signs of her own
toughness of mind and body. Both she and Edith Durham plainly
relished the flattery of a succession of proposals of marriage from
Albanian chieftains. In the main, however, we are not offered writing which is either naive or sentimental. Their accounts are typically filtered through the prisms either of particular literary or
professional genres, which impose their own discipline, or more
significantly, their own needs to make a statement about the world.

It is important to note that in large measure the focal concern of these statements was political. It is essential to grasp the importance of politics to the majority of the writers in whose lives we are interested here if their fundamental seriousness of intent is to be appreciated.

The manner in which political engagement was expressed took several forms. Flora Sandes, Edith Durham, Adeline Irby, Georgina Muir MacKenzie and Rose Wilder Lane all at one time or another campaigned openly for the cause of particular Balkan peoples whose interests they espoused. The seminal work of Emily Balch, on the origin and culture of Slavic migrants to the USA, was quite explicitly directed by a desire to shape policy, and reflects her wider and life-long concern with social and political issues.

The character of Rebecca West's political expression was rather different. Her *Black Lamb and Grey Falcon* can be read as a sustained meditation on the theme of power which runs throughout the greater part of her writing, and is by no means confined to the journalistic efforts of her youth, or to works of criticism such as *The Court and the Castle*.[14] The fact that this intention is not always easy to recognise has to do with her tendency to subordinate her argument to rather metaphysical concepts. Felicity Rosslyn has drawn attention in her essay to one aspect of this political sense; but there are others. A reading of *Black Lamb* would be possible treating it as a reflection on the nature of Empire.

Mercia MacDermott's work in and identification with the fate and fortunes of Bulgaria are incomprehensible without an appreciation of her commitment to socialism. It is the depth of their political commitment which makes intelligible also the bitterness with which both Rose Wilder Lane and Rebecca West identified with anti-Communism in the post-war years, sensing the betrayal and loss of the causes for which they had argued.

The process of redefining the conventional roles and limitations of women is highlighted in particular by their experiences during periods of war. Shelley Saywell has noted that: 'Women have always been in battle yet (there is) little written in their own words about these experiences'.[15] In many ways war may be seen as a liberator for women, for whom it has offered opportunities both to travel more widely and to participate in domains otherwise restricted almost entirely to men. This is illustrated very clearly in the work of the various charitable organisations which were active in the region around the time of the Balkan Wars and the First World War.

From the founding of the British Red Cross, and its first practical operations during the Franco-Prussian War of 1870-71, nursing offered opportunities of this kind on a wide scale. With the support of such groups as the Scottish Women's Hospitals for Foreign Service, this hitherto unprecedented form of nursing career became both recognised and applauded. It provided a vital channel for the newly qualified women doctors and surgeons where their skills and dedication were fully used and appreciated. So we find large numbers of young women working as nurses and doctors in Montenegro during the Balkan Wars, with the Serbian forces during the retreat through Albania, and in Macedonia during the Salonika Campaign, and also working as educational missionaries in the mountains of Northern Albania under the Red Cross initiative after the war. Aspects of these experiences are explored in Monica Krippner's essay.

Julie Wheelwright's study of Flora Sandes takes us, in some respects, to the limits of this process in her exploration of a young woman whose encounter with the Balkans began as a nursing volunteer and ended as a commissioned officer of the Royal Serbian Army.

Several of the women who are the subject of our concern married and settled in the region. Their experience of war is a more private one, involving the attempt to hold together the personal significances of family life in a world overturned by war. In this respect, Louisa Rayner's book, discussed here by Anne Kay, may be considered among the most important examples of the expression of a feminine view of war. We see how, as an Englishwoman stranded in a Serbian village during the Second World War, she makes the best of her situation, and every effort to assimilate into Serbian culture, giving the reader a vivid view of life in that time and place. She points up the significance of the lives of the peasant women among whom she lives at very close quarters. Her own classical education enables her to see the simple activities which are carried out in the village as an important continuation of life as it has been lived there since Homeric times. She finds new and simpler interpretations of passages from the Odyssey by having lived through these same situations herself, for example, describing the ritual of personal washing, relating this to the mores of ancient Greece.[16]

The value of her account does not lie in the picture of women only marginally affected by war, but not actively engaged in it. In a very significant sense it is through the sustaining of this basic hope in the continuity of existence in the activities of its women that the village draws the strength which makes survival possible. Shelley Saywell has written that: 'The hope of peace is the special joy of war'.[17] In this case it seems that if war has brought about an enlargement of the traditional roles of women, it has not done so by redefining them, but by elevating and expanding their significance.

Women and writing

The individuals whose lives and work are examined here sought both to communicate their own experiences to a wider public, and to comment more generally on the life and history of the societies in which they found themselves. Our final particular interest, therefore, is in their writing. In many cases the literary vehicle which they used for conveying their experiences and observations was the travelogue – a piece of continuous narrative constructed around the journey itself. Typically, however, these volumes are of interest to us because their authors were able to use the conventions of the travelogue form to convey a range of ideas about a far greater set of issues.

Travel writing itself, as a genre, has been rather undervalued in the literary world until relatively recently, for reasons which remain puzzling. Perhaps literary critics find it too popular to be taken seriously. Maybe something of this is indicated by the fact that shelves of the Leeds Library (a public subscription library) are better furnished with original volumes of early travel writing than those of the neighbouring university libraries. It is useful to speculate about the reasons for this by placing the fate of travel writing alongside that of biography. Both forms seem to attract the creative energies of women, and also to be very popular among female readers. As genres however, they both appear to stand as poor relations to other types of writing: biography to history and the travelogue to geography. The difference in each case is that the more prestigious, more academically respectable form, is the more abstract and especially the more impersonal account of the world.

What we find here is a reflection of a wider pattern which has been observed by several important feminist writers in recent years, and that is the correspondence between gender roles and the division between the public and the private spheres in our culture. The public sphere, encompassing the state, the law, the church and the market place, is the world of men. The private sphere, above all that of the family and personal relationships, is the preserve of women's influence.[18] The public, or impersonal, account of society and its development emerges as history or sociology: a private or personal account, on the other hand, is expressed in the form of biography. Similarly, a public account of travel takes the abstracted, generalised and impersonal form of geography or ethnography: the private counterpart of this – the account of a personal journey – is the travelogue.

One of the things which we would hope to achieve in this book, is to suggest that travel literature can be a medium for communicating insights which are both deep and subtle, and above all, which deserves to be taken seriously.

Not all of the essays in this volume relate to travel. Anne Kay's portrait of Louisa Rayner, and Diane Waller's account of Mercia MacDermott are cases in point. Barbara Kerewsky-Halpern's piece also escapes this designation. In this sensitive meditation on her own experiences as an anthropologist working in a Serbian village, she is reflecting as much upon her own development as upon the culture of her hosts. She is an outsider: perhaps also a 'traveller': but her journey is an inner one of self-discovery achieved through the encounter with others, and above all, with their perceptions of her.

It is possible that reflexivity is a general characteristic of travel writing, and not one which is confined to women. One learns as much about Patrick Leigh Fermor as about pre-war Europe from his description of his epic walk to Constantinople.[19] Similarly there is a valid sense in which the subject of *Black Lamb and Grey Falcon* is Rebecca West's response to the Balkans rather than an account of her journey through Yugoslavia. The recognition of this fact, however, enables us to appreciate another level at which the material which is the subject of these essays is interesting and significant. It might be said that at the heart of this study is women's reflection upon their own experience and identity, framed by their encounter with Balkan cultures. To the extent that this is true, the value of the work of our travellers lies as much in their accounts of these inward journeys as in their crossing of geographical or social frontiers.

The image of the Balkans

The history of European understanding of the Balkans has been a largely spontaneous and unselfconscious interaction between a wide variety of features of European culture and society. Thus, the more obvious elements of domination (military and economic power) are entwined with – and often themselves crucially shaped by – philology, theology, literary and artistic studies, archaeology and anthropology, all of which have lent their weight to the formation of images of the East which are now so powerful and deeply rooted in European culture that they appear ineradicable.

In this process, the work of the authors to whom this book is devoted is interesting and relevant in part because of their portrayal of Balkan societies. Through their writing they have contributed to the development of a public opinion about the region and its peoples which continues to have important consequences. This process of opinion formation is complex and works at a number of different levels, from popular magazine writing to serious scholarship; from fiction to the political tract.

When it comes to writing a history of image-making in the Balkans, however, to deal with the contribution of women does not confine one to writing about a subsidiary contrapuntal theme to a major one played by men, for this historical process has been influenced to a truly remarkable extent by the writing of women. There have been men who have made vital contributions to our knowledge and awareness of the Balkans, as academics and as communicators to a more general audience: men such as Sir Steven Runciman and the Seton-Watsons in history; Irwin Sanders and Henri Stahl in anthropology; Fred Singleton and Frank Carter in geography; Lord Byron and Eric Ambler in literature. Drawing up a list of women who have shaped our appreciation of the region, however – and leaving aside entirely those people whose lives and work are remembered by contributors to this book, or who are themselves contributors to it – we could make reference to an even longer list: Phyllis Auty and Elizabeth Barker in history; Olive Lodge and Tone Bringa in anthropology; Doreen Warriner and Deborah Milenkovitch in economics; Sharon Zukin and April Carter in sociology; Nora Beloff and Hella Pick in journalism; Agatha Christie and Olivia Manning in literature. It is hardly the case that women have been 'hidden from history' (to borrow for a moment the phrase popularised by Sheila Rowbotham in her path-breaking study) in the story of image construction in the Balkans. Women in large measure are that history.

Notes

1. Jack Schofield, 'The ultimate way', *The Guardian* computer page, 11 Aug. 1988.
2. Harry de Windt, *Through Savage Europe: being the narrative of a journey, through the Balkan states and European Russia*, London: Fisher Unwin, 1907.
3. *The Graphic, 26* October 1912.
4. M. Edith Durham, 'Head-hunting in the Balkans', *Man*, No. 11, Feb. 1923, pp. 19-21.
5. Olivia Manning, *The Balkan Trilogy*, London: Penguin Books, 1985.
6. Hans Gerth and C. Wright Mills, *Character and Social Structure*, London: Routledge & Kegan Paul, 1954, Chap. V, 'The Sociology of Motivation', esp. pp. 114-9.
7. Lady Mary Montagu Wortley, *Letters and Works*, (ed. Lord Wharncliffe), 3 vols., London: Richard Bentley, 1837.
8. Ida Düringsfeld. Aus *Dalmatien*, 3 vols, Prague: 1857.
9. M. Edith Durham, *Twenty Years of Balkan Tangle*, London: George Allen & Unwin, 1920, p. 9.
10. Rebecca West, *Black Lamb and Grey Falcon: the record of a journey through Yugoslavia*, London: Macmillan, single vol. ed. 1967.
11. Letter from Georgina Muir MacKenzie to Mr. Graham Dunlop, dated Athens, 19 April 1863, Public Record Office, FO/78/1767, *Turkey: Consular Correspondence*, Jan-Dec. 1863, p. 129.
12. Letter from Adeline Irby to Mr. Graham Dunlop, dated Athens, 9 April 1863, *ibid.*, p. 126.
13. An account of aspects of the early development of tourism in the region is given in: John B. Allcock and Joan Counihan, *Two Studies in the History of Tourism in Yugoslavia*, University of Bradford, Bradford Studies on Yugoslavia, No. 14, 1989.
14. Rebecca West, *The Court and the Castle. a study of the interactions of political and religious ideas in imaginative literature*, London: Macmillan, 1958.
15. Shelley Saywell, *Women in War*, Harmondsworth: Penguin Books, 1986.
16. Louise Rayner, *Women in a Village*, London: William Heinemann, 1957, esp. pp. 52 and 57.
17. Saywell, *op. cit.*, p. 57.
18. Discussion of this idea, which has become quite extensive, seems to stem from the work of Jean Elshtain: *Public Man, Private Women: women in social and political thought*, Oxford: Martin Robertson, 1981.
19. Patrick Leigh Fermor, *A Time of Gifts*, Harmondsworth: Penguin Books, 1979; *Between the Woods and the Water*, Harmondsworth: Penguin Books, 1987.

CHAPTER 1

. . . the state of the refugees has been most deplorable. Small-pox and famine-typhus have wrought terrible ravages among the weaker portion of these unfortunates; and though the disease has now somewhat abated since October last, over 2,000 have died in this district alone. The arrival of the two English ladies has been, indeed, a godsend to the Bosnians in this part.

I have accompanied to the frontier village where I write this a relief expedition which the unflagging energy of the English ladies (Miss Irby and Miss Johnston) has dispatched to bear food and clothing to the hitherto terribly neglected Bosnian refugees of this part of the Croatian frontier; and I am sorry to have to add that I have been a witness to an act of official barbarity which has gone far to render the efforts of English charity unavailing.

There is nothing, indeed, that Miss Irby has more consistently aimed at in her system than to educate as well as feed the children. She has now established no less than twenty-one schools, and the Ragusa Committee has an additional seven.

Arthur J. Evans, *Illyrian Letters,* 1878.
From Letters I, VIII and XIV.

Two Victorian Ladies and Bosnian Realities, 1862–1875: G.M. MacKenzie and A.P. Irby

Omer Hadžiselimović

Petar Petrović Njegoš once told a group of English officers about a visit paid him by two English travellers in 1843. One of these was a woman. They had come to Cetinje after a hard climb through enemy ranks to see the Montenegrin ruler and poet. Asked by Njegoš what made her undertake such an arduous and perilous

1

journey, the woman replied: 'Curiosity . . . I am an English-woman'.[1]

One wonders, not knowing all the circumstances of that particular visit nor the personalities of the travellers, whether this was an overstatement or an understatement.

Two English women travellers a generation later, Georgina Muir MacKenzie and Adeline Paulina Irby, when they set off on their Balkan journeys which included Bosnia and Hercegovina, similarly did not lack curiosity – nor some other things. They had good education, good connections and were financially secure. Their Balkan experience was described in several texts which appeared between 1861 and 1877. Interestingly enough, Bosnia and Hercegovina, which were to become central to A.P. Irby's life, did not figure prominently in their writings of the 1860's. It was only in the fourth edition (or second, for all practical purposes) of their book *Travels in the Slavonic Provinces of Turkey-in-Europe*, published in 1877, when G.M. MacKenzie had been dead for some years, that Bosnia had been given fuller treatment.

The first edition of the book, which came out in 1866, describes only one of their journeys, that of 1863, when the two women toured northern Greece, Macedonia, Kosovo, northern Albania and Montenegro. However, some scattered references to Bosnia and Hercegovina and the trip from Belgrade to Dubrovnik via Sarajevo and Mostar they undertook the year before, in 1862, can be found there. Similarly, there is some scanty information on these provinces in their earlier book on the Balkans entitled *Notes on the South Slavonic Provinces in Austria and Turkey-in-Europe*. That booklet, published anonymously in 1865, contained the material presented by Georgina Muir MacKenzie in a lecture at Bath the previous year. The editor and writer of its preface was Humphrey Sandwith, a doctor who had travelled in the Balkans and Turkey and was a strong supporter of Slavic peoples. Georgina and Paulina did not want to put their names as authors of the book for obvious reasons – they were women, and young women at that, and felt they could not match a man's knowledge of the area. It is no wonder, then, that at the beginning of the book they 'beg to submit to those who may be interested on the subject the following notes.'[2] The young ladies' first travel book, *Across the Carpathians* (1862), was also published anonymously. (The unnamed author turns out to be a woman who says she was travelling with her aunt.) In much the same style, Georgina's and Paulina's article on Montenegro, which appeared in the collection *Vacation Tourists and*

Notes of Travels, in 1861 (1862), was signed by an enigmatic 'I.M.'. The authoress was again accompanied by her 'aunt'. This authorial self-effacement was discontinued by their *Travels,* which carried Georgina's and Paulina's full names on its title page. But Victorian feminine humbleness in intellectual matters was repeatedly expressed in their 'Introduction' to the book, notwithstanding the fact that this modesty was not necessary. Nor was it a mere accident that Paulina Irby should have asked such a man as W.E. Gladstone to write a preface for the 1877 edition. Just as she was desirous of the masculine stamp of approval for Georgina's and her political judgements, so Gladstone, on his part, wished to emphasise the significance of their characteristically feminine account of the Slavic parts of Turkey. Having praised the superior quality of the general information they provided ('no diplomatist, no consul, no traveller, among our countrymen, has made such a valuable contribution to our means of knowledge in this important matter')[3], he pointed out, with typical period pathos, their accurate and poignant description of the life of Christian womanhood in the Balkans – a life in which wife and daughter, the appointed sources of the sweetest consolation, were the standing occasions of the sharpest anxiety'.[4]

This objectivity in portraying Serbian and other South Slavic women was acknowledged with gratitude by Ćedomilj Mijatović, the Serbo-Croatian translator of *Travels,* which came out in Belgrade just two years after its publication in England. Unlike most earlier travellers, who had dealt only with the 'male half of [the South Slavic] society', Miss Muir Mackenzie and Miss Irby now provided a good depiction of its 'female half', a depiction enriched with a 'feminine perspective'.[5]

The ladies' 'feminine perspective' colours, naturally, their entire work as it did their actual contacts with the South Slavic people and Turkish officials while they were pursuing such a 'masculine' business as travelling in the mid-nineteenth century Balkans, where there were few roads and where, especially in Bosnia, people travelled mostly on horseback or on foot. However much Georgina, the principal author of the two of *Travels,* (observes Dorothy Anderson in her excellent book Miss *Irby and her Friends),*

... in writing their saga, might discount the evidence of their sex, it is obvious throughout that the fact that they were women had much to do with the way their journeys went; and that both women enjoyed their distinctive position. It was, to put it bluntly, much more exciting and much more gratifying to be two Englishwomen in the wilds of Turkey than to be at home in England, or attending a German spa, or making an Italian cultural tour. They had their independence and they had their achievements; they had won esteem, even some notoriety; they had faced up to dangers and discomforts and had enjoyed overcoming both.[6]

In a sense, Georgina and Paulina in the 1860s, and Paulina and her new friend Priscilla Johnston in the 1870s were at the same time more immune and more vulnerable as women travellers in the Balkans than were their male counterparts. They were well prepared for travelling and well equipped with necessities: they even carried with them such items of women's paraphernalia as a zinc-lined bathtub that could also be used as a table. They were furnished with powerful Turkish passports, the *bujurdi* and the *firman*, and with various letters of recommendation from one Christian family to another, so they could usually count on the best lodging available. But they had to spend long hours in the saddle, exposed to all kinds of weather, and frequently had to sleep at *khans*, which were sometimes little more than ordinary stables. (They took their own bedding with them and usually ordered cushions, carpets and mats to be taken out of the rooms before or upon their arrival. Sometimes, in limiting hygenic situations, they even pitched their tent inside *khans!*). The armed escorts that accompanied them were not always reliable.

Whereas *Notes on the South Slavonic Provinces in Austria and Turkey-in-Europe* devoted only a few pages to Bosnia and Hercegovina (mention of a bey who insists that all South Slavs speak the 'Bosnian tongue',[7] brief description of roads and the guide-book style information on the cities of Sarajevo and Mostar), and whereas the first edition of *Travels* subsumes the region under general considerations of Balkan history, geography and politics, the 1877 edition of this book included a vivid record of Paulina's and Priscilla's experience during their trip from the Austrian frontier to Sarajevo and back, and of the political situation following the outbreak of the Christian rebellion of 1875.

Paulina Irby, the sole writer of these three Bosnian chapters, expressed at the outset her attitude toward the Turkish rule over a country in which she had now become a part-time resident. (Her school for Serbian girls in Sarajevo was established in 1870.) The country was miserably poor after centuries of foreign domination and the Turkish yoke lay heavily on the Christian population. The Muslim element, though disliking the Osmanlis, oppressed and exploited the Christian *rayahs* and held them in contempt. But the

4

Muslim masters of the country, those 'offspring of an alliance between feudalism and Islam',[8] who used to be powerful guardians of Turkish western frontiers, were now a decaying, corrupt and fanatical class. 'The Bosnian Beg par excellence . . . is a chained monster with drawn teeth and cut claws.'[9] In the political near-anarchy created by the Bosnian-Hercegovinian uprising, passions were let loose and the position of Christian peasantry was more precarious than ever. There was arbitrary violence and killing on all sides and the *rayahs* were frequently the victims of Muslim vindictiveness. That was the Bosnian situation which Paulina and Priscilla witnessed or heard about after they had reached Brod on one of the Sava steamers in August of 1875. Paulina did not conceal her sympathy for the Bosnian Christians, especially the Serbians, whose age-long suffering under the Turks came to epitomise for her a most tragic historical destiny, a destiny that could now take a different, more propitious turn. In the years to follow she did everything she could to help them and tried in every way to identify with them.

Travelling across Bosnia in such disturbing and uncertain times presented itself as a more formidable task than ever. But the English ladies were resolved to get to Sarajevo and join their schoolgirls. Paulina was by nature strong-willed, proud and obstinate, and these characteristics certainly served her well during their trip.

Being English and being women – or vice versa – largely determined their way of seeing and of being seen. As women, Paulina and Priscilla could easily come in touch with Christian women (sometimes also Muslim), they had access to their houses and their family life. Paulina cites, for example, a Bosnian woman, apparently from Sarajevo, who told her about the changes which had taken place in the country during the previous decades, including the changes in the lives of Orthodox women in the city.[10] In Bosanska Gradiška ('Turkish Gradishka') Paulina and Priscilla were taken to the house of a Christian merchant and talked with his wife who served them 'coffee and sweetmeats'.[11] In Banja Luka the next day they again visited another Christian family and not only learned the latest about the political situation there, but also that the daughters of that family 'were beautiful girls' who 'had been educated by governesses from Austria and are now married to Serb merchants, living in Belgrade'.[12] From this family the English ladies also heard stories of Christian girls being kidnapped by Muslims in the vicinity of Banja Luka. And while in Sarajevo, they were informed that the wife of the Austrian consul was about to leave the now unsafe town, with her little boy, 'on the excuse of the illness of her mother'.[13]

Paulina's and Priscilla's women's eyes did not fail to notice other 'human interest' details, such as the food that was the typical fare of the Bosnian peasant ('the coarsest black bread, boiled beans, and maize'),[14] the contents of shops in the Gradiška bazaar, the interior of the *khans* by the wayside, or the looks of one of their drivers during their return journey from Sarajevo:

> This boy was after the worst type of Bosnian Mussulmans. He was lank and small, with colourless eyes, wisps of sandy hair escaped from the red handkerchief which was tied round a dirty white linen cap; his weazened boy's face was old with an expression of mingled cruelty, rapacity and cunning.[15]

This description, with its possible subconscious meanings, could hardly have originated from the pen of a male traveller. Another incident, though of a different kind, reveals also Paulina's and Priscilla's feminine vulnerability. It was a situation that, again, a 'Frank' (i.e. Western European) male traveller could probably not have experienced: while staying overnight at the *khan* in Kiseljak, the Englishwomen were awakened by bigoted Muslim women who were throwing charcoal through the window of their room.[16]

But because they were women, and because they were English, they could also feel and show a degree of superiority and courage that helped them pass through the Bosnian confusion in the summer of 1875. Thus they got rid of a *zaptie* (policeman) in Banja Luka who came to tell them to report immediately to the Turkish authorities there by answering that they were 'English ladies, and should do no such thing'.[17] Moreover, showing their passports, they ordered him to go to the local governor at once, with the message that he supply them with an escort for their journey the following day.[18] Sometimes, their feminine boldness – and Englishness – combined with their warm feeling for the Christian Slav cause, was basis for misunderstanding or even humorous situations, as when they heard, while on the Sava steamer, that insurrection had started in Bosnia. The news was told them by their friend Vaso Vidević, who, 'pale as death', and with tears in his eyes, implored them not to go to Sarajevo. 'We told him, encouragingly', writes Paulina, 'it might prove a very good thing for their cause if two English ladies were killed. To which he replied, 'Yes; but not you'".[19]

Paulina Irby's complete identification with Bosnia and its

downtrodden Christian population, to whom she was to devote her whole life's work – truly an errand into the educational wilderness – was not possible. She had enough pity and understanding and she possessed sound political judgement concerning the Balkans for her time, advocating freedom and independence for Southern Slavs and even disagreeing with mainline British policy towards 'European Turkey'. But her native culture was worlds apart from what she found in her adopted country and her Englishness asserted itself time and again in various ways. Bosnia was a 'rude land' for her,[20] 'the most barbarous of the provinces of Turkey in Europe', in which one felt like being 'in the wilds of Asia'.[21] (This echoes Georgina's earlier statement, from *Notes*, on the South Slavic countries as being as distant from the minds of Englishmen as if they were in 'the interior of Tartary or the centre of Africa').[22] The whole province, wrote Paulina, did not even have a book shop, 'excepting the depot of the British and Foreign Bible Society in Sarajevo which has been established for about eight or ten years'.[23] And the town of Gradiška, for instance, struck her as a veritable cultural frontier between East and West, the last 'line of the Asiatic encroachments into Europe'.[24]

Paulina Irby travelled to Bosnia with English travel guide-books, Murray's *Handbook for Travellers in Turkey*, and Bradshaw's *Continental Guide*, which basically offered advice to West Europeans regarding Turkish travel conditions and Oriental ways generally. Sometimes these guide-books reflected not only English culture but also British commercial and political interests; Bradshaw's *Guide*, for instance, traced the projected railway across the Balkans and further to the East – a railway which has never been completed. Paulina Irby mentioned it as an important line of communication which 'may some day become our main highway to India'.[25] Her sympathy with the Southern Slavs, especially Serbians, certainly did not exclude something of a patronising attitude towards these 'younger children of the European family', as she calls them.[26] The best hope for the Balkan nations, she was saying or implying, lay not only in retaining their cultural and religious identity and in winning their political independence, but also in their full reintegration into the European world. Symbolically, the European costume on the Bosnian girls from her Sarajevo school whom she was taking to Prague gave them a kind of political and cultural immunity and a safe passage out of the country at the frontier in Brod. Their crossing of the Sava, in Paulina's description meant much more than reaching another bank of a river. It was a change of civilisations: 'A peal of bells from the church in Austrian Brod sounded more cheerily than ever across the water, while we were waiting for the ferry-boat in a golden breath of evening sunlight'.[27]

Notes

1. (Anonymous), 'S Njegošem na bojnom polju. Beleške jednog engleskog putnika (1843)', *Politika* (Beograd), 18. septembra 1925, XX11, 6250, str. 3.
2. Humphry Sandwith, ed., *Notes on the South Slavonic Countries in Austria and Turkey in Europe*, Edinburgh and London: William Blackwood, 1865, p. 25.
3. G. Muir MacKenzie and A.P. Irby, *Travels in the Slavonic Provinces of Turkey-in-Europe*, London: Daidy, Isbister, 1877, 'Preface', p. IX.
4. *Ibid.*, p. XIII.
5. G. Muir MacKenzie and A.P. Irbi, *Putovanje po slovenskim zemljama Turske u Evropi*, Beograd: Državna štamparija, 1868, translated by Ć. Mijatović, 'Predgovor prevodiocev', no pagination.
6. Dorothy Anderson, *Miss Irby and her Friends*, London: Hutchinson, 1966, p. 39.
7. *Notes*, p. 24.
8. Muir MacKenzie and Irby, *Travels*, p. 6.
9. *Ibid.*, p. 8.
10. *Ibid.*, pp. 13-14.
11. *Ibid.*, p. 25.
12. *Ibid.*, p. 26.
13. *Ibid.*, p. 31.
14. *Ibid.*, p. 27.
15. *Ibid.*, p. 33.
16. *Ibid.*, p. 31.
17. *Ibid.*, p. 27.
18. *Ibid.*, p. 27.
19. *Ibid.*, p. 30.
20. *Ibid.*, p. 3.
21. *Ibid.*, p. 1.
22. *Notes*, p. 25.
23. *Travels*, p. 19.
24. *Ibid.*, p. 25.
25. *Ibid.*, p. 3.
26. *Ibid.*, p. 6.
27. *Ibid.*, p. 34.

CHAPTER 2

I'll walk, but not in old heroic traces,
And not in paths of high morality,
And not among the half-distinguished faces,
The clouded forms of long-past history.

I'll walk where my own nature would be leading:
It vexes me to choose another guide;
Where the grey flocks in ferny glens are feeding
Where the wild wind blows on the mountain side.

What have those lonely mountains worth revealing?
More glory and more grief than I can tell:
The earth that wakes one human heart to feeling
Can centre both the worlds of Heaven and Hell.

Variously ascribed to Charlotte and Emily Bronte, **Stanzas.**

Edith Durham: Traveller and Publicist

John Hodgson

Of the many British women travellers in the Balkans, Edith Durham is one of the most forceful, and perhaps the woman whose work had the most profound impact on the area she came to know and love. Rebecca West seems to have thrown off a gorgeous pageant of a book about Yugoslavia without being marked by a permanent imaginative commitment to the country. But Edith Durham appears almost to have found her purpose in life in her contact with the Balkans; her identification with their lands and peoples became ever more complete. It was also a dynamic commitment, in that her views changed according to historical developments. In the end the story of her Balkan life is perhaps even a sad one, and when the lands and peoples she loved were

9

overwhelmed by the violence of war, she too was in a sense irrecoverably crushed.

Durham was a person of vigorously held opinions, and her forthrightness made many enemies among Balkan specialists in England. Equally, she could awake extreme devotion, both among British people who worked alongside her, but also most memorably among the Albanians and Montenegrins among whom she travelled and worked. Those who remember her late in life describe her as 'queenly', in her stateliness, recalling the manners of the Edwardian era. Yet as her opinions developed on her travels she was led into positions at odds with her own society, particularly during the First World War, and she took with her the least baggage of British received ideas. She was free of prejudices for or against any particular religion, and if she found the Balkans strange and new, she was also fond of pointing out buried similarities between the tribes of northern Albania and those of her native North London. If the Albanian tribes foretold the future from the breastbones of fowls, there was palmistry and spiritualism at home. Above all Durham possessed the essential ethnologist's capacity to watch and wait. In her relations with her fellow-countrymen she was often brusque and intolerant, but her patience with the people of the Balkans was limitless. 'Their endless questions', the British Consul at Cetinje complained to her, 'drive a man mad. He loses his temper and then it is all up. These people require endless patience and women have a great deal more than men.'[1]

She is still remembered in Albania today. Enver Hoxha himself makes an honourable exception for Durham in a book whose title tells all – The *Anglo-American Threat to Albania*. The *Albanian Encyclopaedic Dictionary* published in 1985 gives her a warmly appreciative entry, remarking that 'she remained until the end a defender of the cause of Albania.' Yet the entry adds that in her books, 'alongside objective analysis and evaluation, there are also mistaken generalizations stemming from her ideological limitations.'[2] It is true that her seven tough, fluent, candid and opinionated books on the Balkans do not always make comfortable reading.

It has been difficult to find out much about Edith Durham's early life, before she began her Balkan travels at the age of thirty-seven. One archive which might be worth searching might be the Belgrade police files for 1902. The Serbian police plied her with countless questions.

I did my best to assist their plans, (she wrote) and have in fact provided them with the materials for a fairly accurate biography of myself, should one ever be required. Its excessive dullness went a long way towards soothing their agitated nerves.[3]

The point is, of course, that Durham herself felt her life had been dull.

Some facts are known. Her father's family was distinguished in the medical profession. On her mother's side, her grandfather William Ellis was a noted economist and friend of J.S. Mill. The Durhams were a large and prosperous family, and almost all of Edith's seven younger brothers and sisters achieved eminence – in medicine, engineering and the civil service. We know that she first trained as an artist, and illustrated several volumes of the *Cambridge Natural History* with drawings of a suitable precision, which look nothing like the vigorous sketches made at speed to entertain her highland hosts in the Albanian mountains. But there is every sign that Durham felt her life slipping away; she had been overtaken by her younger brothers and sisters, and given the duty of caring for her invalid mother. Her departure for a cruise down the Adriatic coast was a response to a severe nervous crisis.

The letters and diaries of Durham's first journeys, which survive in the library of the Royal Anthropological Institute, offer an evocative glimpse of the more advanced kind of tourism of the day. We are safely and precisely in the world of E.M. Forster's *A Room with a View*, in which novel it is regarded as a brave but not impossible adventure for the two elderly Miss Allens to travel down the Illyrian coast in a cargo boat. Durham sets out in the company of a friend with pleasurable expectation for Dalmatia, 'a land flowing with maraschino and insect powder', and is immediately dazzled with the loveliness of the landscape, and fascinated by the variety of tongues. There is one odd premonition during an afternoon's outing near Zadar, where the two women walked out 'to Erizzo, a so-called 'Albanian' village according to Baedeker. Couldn't see anything that came up to our idea of Albania,' which was at least one disappointment shortly to be remedied.[4]

The Montenegrin border, its desolate rocks bare from a distance, when close was found to be rich in wild pomegranates and aromatic herbs. The first sight of Montenegro was breathtaking – a vast desolation of impassable rock, crag over crag, an endless series of bare mountaintops, utterly arid and lonesome. After the grandeur of' the landscape, Cetinje was a comic disappointment, 'the baldest, barest, most ridiculous toy capital conceivable ...

just like Ladysmith or Mafeking (she wrote) barring the corrugated iron'. More picturesque were the Montenegrin people.

> The modern man never goes out walking without a Colt revolver in front and most frequently a modern rifle on his back. It strikes me as very odd and unnecessary but the men are purely ornamental nowadays & seem to have nothing to do except carry firearms & wear embroidery. The work, enormously hard, is all done by the women, who are consequently very worn and not as decorative as the peacocks.

Her descriptions combine a measure of frivolity and romantic fantasy with genuine accuracy of observation.

> The fellows who amuse me are the Albanians. An Albanian on the mash is almost exactly like the mediaeval swells of the Italian frescoes & the first ones we met quite startled us. They wear the tight-fitting trunk hose made of woolen stuff hooked up the back of the leg. It is white with long black stripes of embroidery down the leg & at the top in front the shirt is pulled through slashes. They are long slim chaps with dandy little moustaches & are most theatrical in effect.[5]

Durham responded warmly to the superficial operetta-like incongruities of Montenegrin life. 'It is like a dream or a cinematograph, (she exclaimed). It is as safe as an Earl's Court show and many times more respectable.'[6] Apart from the irony that in another seven years she would herself be organising Montenegro's show at Earl's Court, such remarks show how simply touristic her feelings were at the time. The Balkans were a place of colour and life where she could forget home miseries. In later life she would look back with some wistfulness and wonder to that time when she 'knew foreign lands only as places which received tourists with open arms and hotels gaping for guests.'[7]

Durham had the habit of copying poems into her diary – and after her first journey she copies Tennyson's *Lotos-Eaters:*

> Let us swear an oath, and keep it with an equal mind
> In the hollow lotos-land to live and lie reclined
> On the hills like gods together, careless of mankind.

At home she passed the long months deeply immersed in studying the Serbian language and reading Balkan history. It was on her second voyage that she so amazed the captain of the boat with her proficiency in Serbian that he summoned the crew to hear.

'Now listen,' said the captain, and he proceeded to ask me questions in Servian, pronouncing very carefully, to almost all of which I was able more or less to reply. Everyone was astounded and vowed that such a thing had never before been heard of as an English who knew Slav! . . . I sat on a coil of rope and recited the verb 'to be' to admiration.[8]

In Cetinje, Durham was now becoming a familiar figure. 'Cetinje is quite extraordinary, everyone salutes or talks to me. . . . The prince's tutor bows politely but I do not like to tackle him as in his position he is naturally shy of tourists.'[9]

Besides the curiosities of' politics, and the splendour of Montenegrin costume, Cetinje also offered theatrical life.

I went to the theatre instead of to bed and saw a wonderful piece. It had very little plot (as far as I could gather), was purely Montenegrin, of local manufacture and produced for the first time. It consisted entirely of fighting the Turks. There were consultations of warriors who sat cross-legged in a circle on the ground. When they had decided what to do (I don't know what it was) they all joined hands solemnly & danced round in a ring singing at the tops of their voices a song which I gathered was in honour of the Petrović's. Then a lady came in with a gourd of *rakija*, a very small one, out of which they each took a most enormous drink till the audience was overcome with laughter at the amount it contained and a very stout and decorative man near me made loud remarks, apparently decisive. The lady promptly went out and returned with the bottle supposed to be replenished. Then we had a scene between the Turkish Pasha & several advisers. An aged party with a beard, who spoke very clearly & whom I understood better than any of the others, came and made the Pasha a long harangue warning him of the bravery of Crna Gora. This was received with great applause. The Pasha however would not be advised but rushed on his fate. The result was the battle of Trijepca in which a whole stage of Turks was completely routed in 5 seconds by five or six Montenegrins with wild yells and most terrific firing. Hardly were the Turks all done away with when the lady appeared with more *rakija* & a brand new luncheon hamper & they all refreshed. Then we had a very long pause but were rewarded by a magnificent tableau entirely illuminated by red fire in which each Montenegrin was killing a Turk. The curtain was raised on this twice. The second time the victorious Montenegrins were so overcome with laughter that they could hardly keep their poses?[10]

In 1902 Durham also travelled through the Kingdom of Serbia, now consciously assembling material for a book. Serbia was, it seems, not used to visitors, and it was the town of Pirot which apparently first dignified Durham's travels with the name of science. In conversation with the curious inhabitants:

> I explained that I wished only to note things characteristically Servian, such as the costumes of the peasants, the houses, and so forth. 'In short,' said a gentleman, 'you are making geo-ethnographical studies.' This struck me as a remarkably luminous idea; I should never have thought of it myself. I said I was, and everyone was pleased.[11]

By the end of 1903 she had finished *Through the Lands of the Serb*. The book is a delight. It is her gentlest and most frankly pictorial, not yet clouded over by the political turmoils that darken her later books. There are even tones of broad comedy. In Serbia, for instance, Durham is pursued by large flocks of handsome, dashing, but quite impecunious army officers, any of whom, she is assured, would become her husband for an income of forty pounds a year.

Above all Durham delights in evoking the alien mentality of the peoples. Here again there is a great deal of humour at the incongruities produced by the clash of cultures, but it is a warm and understanding humour, in the long run both serious in intent and appreciative of the real harshnesses of Balkan life.

> 'Hast thou a father?'
> 'No.'
> 'Did the Turks kill him?'
> 'No.'
> This caused surprise.
> 'Hast thou brothers?'
> 'Yes.'
> 'Glory be to God! How many Turks have they killed?' For my male relatives were always credited with a martial ardour which they are far from possessing. The news that they had killed none caused disappointment. Then:
> 'Is thy vilayet (province) far off?'
> 'Very far.'
> 'Five days?'
> 'More.'
> 'God help thee! Are there many Turks in thy vilayet?'
> 'None.'
> 'No Turks? Dear God, it is a marvel!'[12]

Landscape, architecture, and costume are evoked in prose which resembles the vigorous and sure strokes of her drawings. The book

describes Montenegro, and the lands of the then Kingdom of Serbia, but the most lively and moving descriptions are reserved for
the most exotic parts of her journey, to Turkish territory in Shkodër
and to the monasteries at Ipek (Peć, Pejë) and Dečani.
For her next journeys, the most obvious destination was those
parts of the Balkans that were still under Ottoman rule. It requires
some effort today to imagine the feelings of a nineteenth century
western European towards the Ottoman Empire. Even Durham,
secure in Christian Montenegro, had looked across to the distant
north Albanian mountains and written of 'the land of the unspeakable Turk'. So many travel books of the nineteenth century evoke
the especial horror of approaching the Turkish frontier. Famously,
there is the opening of Kinglake's *Eothen* where travellers are fer-
ried across the Sava into plague-stricken Belgrade, knowing the
quarantine regulations forbid return, while vultures hover above.
In 1894, 'Odysseus' (Sir Charles Eliot), travelling to Skopje by train,
still found that:

> the Turkish frontier is peculiarly terrible, and I never cross it without a
> spasm of alarm. How many people have I seen there overtaken by
> some mysterious visitations of fate – some turned back, some sent on
> under arrest, some requested to wait a few days, inquiring spirits
> deprived of their guidebooks (on the ground that such literature is sedi-
> tious) and sportsmen robbed of the guns with which they had thought
> to shoot big game.[13]

On her first visit to Ottoman territory, in Shkodër, Durham was not
turned back at the frontier, but solemnly entered into the Customs
Book as 'Edith of London'. A second visit the following year turned
out to be a very pleasant experience. 'Scutari received me with
enthusiasm on the strength of my having spent a day there last
year with Dora. My having come alone on purpose to see them
touched them deeply as they have a bad reputation.' Despite the
warnings of local foreign consuls, Durham visited the bazaar
alone.

> The joke was that I met lots of wild weird folk who greeted me as an
> old friend. . . . They were mostly from mountain tribes & had seen me
> in Montenegrin markets the year before! Far from molesting me as the
> consul had feared, I was given roses & coffee & was shown how to
> make cartridges, shoe horses, make pottery, silver filigree, and all the
> other handiworks of the bazaar.[14]

Her trip to Ipek had aroused the admiration of the Montenegrins
themselves among whom the Albanians had a dire fame:

'Albanians behind every rock, and piff, paff, a bullet in your living heart'.[15] Durham acquired renown as 'one that could look death in the eyes', and on her return she was feted at Andrijevica: 'Now I have a reputation for *junaštvo*, which has its inconveniences, as it means that the other dobar junaks, of which there are many, all stand me drinks.'[16] But on her own account there was another aspect to her bravery.

> The danger I did not mind. My two months' liberty each year were like Judas's fabled visit to the iceberg – but they made the endless vista of grey imprisonment at home the more intolerable. And a bullet would have been a short way out.[17]

Nineteen hundred and three saw the 'Ilinden' uprising against the Turks in Macedonia, and the hideous reprisals of the Turkish army against the impoverished peasantry. Although Durham had only returned from Montenegro that August, she felt that despite her family obligations she could not turn down an appeal for her help from the Macedonian Relief Committee. 'I was now forty, and this might be my last chance.'[18] So in December she started on the five months' journey which is described in *The Burden of the Balkans*, and culminated in her journey through Albania from south to north. *The Burden of the Balkans* is extraordinarily frank in expressing Durham's distaste for her relief work in Macedonia. She was certainly shocked by the misery of her patients, and worked hard to help them. But she seems to have found it extremely hard to cope with her patients' efforts to subvert her efforts to heal them, their contrariness, claims for exclusive attention, and their refusal to obey instructions – characteristics one imagines not peculiar to patients in Macedonia. H.N. Brailsford, one of Durham's fellow-workers, whose own fine book on Macedonia appeared in 1906, wrote a very sharp review of *The Burden of the Balkans:*

> Miss Durham is an artist who went to Turkey in search of the picturesque. She found the Bulgarian peasants, who were cowering, broken and stricken, in the ruins of their devastated villages, anything but an attractive spectacle. Starving, downtrodden, hopeless, defeated, they were no subject for romance and but an indifferent foreground to a picture. She scarcely pitied them. She heartily despised them.[19]

Concerning Durham's subsequent enchantment with her journey through Albania, Brailsford raises a further accusation of heartlessness which Durham would have to face again, for the review describes her as travelling blithely through Albania, while:

the roadside was strewn with the graves of murdered men, and splendid creatures in gay costumes boasted of their prowess and talked of their 'honour', a word you will never hear in the Balkans on the lips of any race but the Albanian.

It is interesting to note that a friendship between Durham and Brailsford survived this drubbing. *The Times Literary Supplement* also deplored Durham's 'anti-Bulgar stance', which the paper felt had been rushed to on limited evidence. 'In a writer who seems otherwise so full of sympathy this attitude is difficult to understand.'[20] It is certainly true that through circumstances Durham came to know the Macedonians when their fortunes were at their very lowest, while in her trip through Albania, she had an altogether different kind of contact with the most advanced, vigorous and optimistic sections of society. It is not hard to see that her trip through Albania would represent an upswing.

She had as her guide Konstantin Sinas, a *colporteur* of the British and Foreign Bible Society, whose mission of the journey was not of course to guide Durham, but to sell Bibles. It is worth mentioning here that the Bible Society, for reasons quite apart from religion, played a quite exceptional role in Albanian history at the time. By a curious but typically Ottoman anomaly, the Society's books were the only exception to the Turkish government's ban on all printed books in the Albanian language. This exception had arisen because the Sultan had granted permission to the Society to sell its books on Turkish territory, little thinking that an Albanian Bible would be produced. So the Albanians, Christian and Muslim alike, crowded to buy the books, avid for any scrap of print in their own language.

The journey was still a perilous one. As the Society's agent in Constantinople, T.R. Hodgson, reported:

I am somewhat perplexed by the fact that an English lady, Miss Durham, a writer of books, has attached herself to Sinas for his journey through Northern Albania – without any reference to me. The lady will not be pleased if Sinas is stopped, and it makes the position a peculiar one for him. For the present I am inclined to ignore the fact that she is there.[21]

Durham could hardly have found a better guide. Bible House reports on Sinas' work praise him as 'probably one of the best

Albanian scholars of the day, and to him was entrusted the first draft of the transliteration of the four gospels and the psalms into the new Albanian character.' His own reports on his work still exist, in a meticulously exact hand and unnervingly correct English. Through the earnest Sinas, Durham came into contact with some of the leading intellectual figures of Albania at the time, at the height of the intense intellectual and patriotic ferment of the years of 'National Rebirth' which culminated in the declaration of independence in 1912. She attempted to learn the Albanian language herself, but the bizarre, as yet unstandardised alphabet and the then still unmapped grammar defeated her.

Her Albanian journey became the most physically demanding she had hitherto undertaken, and it was at one of the inns of the south that she contracted the malaria which was to trouble her for years. Yet in the towns separated by impassable mud she would come across small circles of intellectual curiosity, and practical schemes to rouse Albania from backwardness.

One of Durham's greatest pleasures on her travels was to emerge from the wilderness and astonish cautious stay-at-home spirits with tales of her feats. She had done this every year so far. Now she descended upon Scutari from the wrong direction, not by boat across the lake from Montenegro, but down from the wild mountains. She made straight for Cetinje, where the town was all agog to hear of her exploits. She was summoned by Prince Nikola and asked about her journey, in the first of many meetings in an acquaintanceship where each side appears to have regarded the other as impossibly irreformable. Nikola promised that whenever Durham was kidnapped by an Albanian tribesman, he would himself contribute to the ransom. Durham did not think such an eventuality would arise. On her 1904 journey, Durham had come to know a land which, though poor, deprived of education, and deliberately kept that way by the Ottoman authorities, nevertheless was acquiring a national identity and a vision of a better future. From now on Durham becomes fascinated by, and actively supports, the Albanian national idea. Montenegro, quaint and picturesque, is seen as a romantic anachronism, nourished by tales of past heroism, and a land of easy-going swagger and gorgeous embroidery.

Nevertheless Montenegro remained her base. At about this time Durham deserted Cetinje with its atmosphere of diplomatic intrigue, and went to live in the village of Njeguš, in the home of her guide, Krsto Pejović, who appears to have been an amiable rogue whose living came from smuggling tobacco. Durham had an outhouse to herself that had originally been designed to store contraband.

In this way Durham achieved an intimacy with Balkan village life not equalled, I think, by any other Englishwoman before Louise Rayner. This made her at times dismissive of students of the Balkans who relied more on books:

Seton-Watson for example took all his information presumably from ambitious politicians and lived himself in comfortable hotels. He had and has no idea what the peoples are like. He wrote the article on Montenegro in the *Encyclopaedia Britannica*, which infuriated the Montenegrins, after staying for a fortnight (so far as I have learnt) at the Grand Hotel, Cetinje. I never heard of him up country.[22]

Durham travelled through Montenegro, Bosnia and Hercegovina for three summers, but the ethnographical material she collected at this time did not reach publication until *Some Tribal Origins, Laws and Customs of the Balkans* more than twenty years later. Travelling was hard, and Durham describes the poverty of the land with uncompromising bleakness.

We went on through a land, the filth and poverty of which is unimaginable to those who never left England. The sterile waterless rocks made it impossible to live with any decency. The worst English slum is luxury in comparison. Barely enough water to drink. None to wash in. One day I had nothing but dirty melted snow out of a hole. Vermin swarmed and no one worried about them. 'If we had only as many gold pieces as lice,' said folk cheerfully, 'this would be the richest land in Europe.'[23]

For herself, Durham took such hardship lightly. Of one miserable inn she reported enthusiastically, 'a very lean affair, and the most insecty I have met. A perfect Zoo.'[24]

On these journeys, she was as much an object of study as a student herself.

Krsto Pejović, when I first went up-country with him, began to explain me as soon as we got off the highroad. He was the showman, so to speak, and I was the monkey to his organ-grinding. On arrival at a *han* he would begin loudly: 'She can read and write several languages. She can make pictures without a machine (i.e. draw). She can, etc.' According to Krsto there were few things I could not do. Moreover, the Montenegrin proverb says: 'Long hair, short wits, a woman's head,' and as

19

I wore my hair short, an uncommon thing in those days, the simple folk accepted the fact that my wits must be long. Krsto would point this out, and add, in an aside, to bachelors: 'She is not married, and God knows how rich'. When I protested, he declared this was the right way to conduct a tour, and he knew all about it. I had come to see real Montenegrin life, and I saw it . . . But how many times, when hoarse and exhausted, I have howled 'The British Grenadiers', or some such ditty, only to have it rapturously encored![25]

In Sarajevo, Durham wrote to Pauline Irby's school, and hoped to visit. But Irby was away in London at the time and the meeting between the two formidable women never took place. Perhaps this was a good thing, because the views of the two were now growing strongly divergent, with Irby a Slavophile of long standing, where Durham was growing increasingly critical of the Slav nationalist movement. Increasingly, Durham had her sights set on Albania, and in the summer of 1908 she set out from Cetinje to Shkoder and then on a series of journeys through the northern Albanian mountains, as described in *High Albania* – which is undoubtedly the most splendid of her books. It explores the wildest and most remote territories, and produces her deepest insights into the most alien people. Durham turned her back on Cetinje, saying that she wanted anthropology, not politics. *High Albania* does represent something of a holiday from the kind of great power intrigues which Durham found of such compelling interest. There is a mood of joy and celebration throughout the book, and a characteristic atmosphere of blinding heat which also gives it a literary unity, as Durham and her guide travel slowly over the harsh, sun-reflecting *karst*, with Durham pausing by the rare stream to fill her open umbrella with water, and pour its contents over her travelling companion.

The sense of celebration is a personal one, for Durham had never before achieved so much. 'I have in fact had an extraordinary glimpse (for it is only a glimpse) of the life of by-gone centuries. I feel as if I must have dreamt it, or be hundreds of years old.'[26] But the book is also full of the celebrations of the Albanians themselves, the welcoming of the 'Young Turk' Constitution, the return from exile of Prenk Bib Doda, the head of the Mirdite tribe, and most memorably perhaps of all, St. John's Day in the mountains.

The afternoon passed in paying visits-sitting on heaps of fern in dark dwellings, drinking healths in rakia, chewing sheep-cheese, and firing rifles and revolvers indoors; a noisy joy that peppers oneself and the refreshments with burnt powder and wads. In one yard two girls were slowly turning a whole sheep that, spitted lengthwise, was roasting over a large wood fire. It was stuffed with herbs and sewn up the belly, and of all ways of cooking mutton, this is the most excellent.

By night-time we were all too sleepy to do much sing-song. . . . We had passed a true Albanian day, said the Padre of Toplana:

Duhan, rakia.

Pushke, dashtnia.

(Tobacco, brandy, guns, and love). I suggested that dashtnia should come first, because 'maxima est caritas.' But they said not in Albania.[27]

The heady exultancy of *High Albania* persists in the face of the grimness of north Albanian life, its poverty, ignorance, and above all in the face of the horrors of the blood feud. Durham does not close her eyes to these things, or gloss them over. Above all she does not romanticise them.

She is particularly outspoken in her condemnation of the blood feud. She does however make a particular effort to understand its internal logic and morality, and she makes no moral distinction between the feud as carried out by an Albanian tribe and war as waged by a modern western nation. On the other hand, there is something in the very virulence of Durham's pacifism which uncomfortably suggests a suppressed violence in her own nature. *High Albania,* though, celebrates not violence but trust. Durham writes at length about the Albanian *besa,* or word of honour, and the famous Albanian traditions of hospitality, of 'bread and salt and our hearts' which the head of every house offered his guest. This quality of trust distinguishes her from many other contemporary writers who mention Albania in passing, whose books bristle with near escapes from bandit ambushes, nights spent clutching pistols, armed escorts, and the like. Even in the very rare instances where she was not warmly received, Durham could still cope.

We all sat on the ground out of doors and I was asked if I was sister to the King of England. I laughed at the notion and said, no, nor did my ragged and travel stained state encourage the idea. I gave them Scutari cigarettes which interested them vastly. The bajraktar's son said if he believed I was really the King's sister he would kill me at once as they would have no foreign (giaour) kings coming to the land – they did not even obey Sultan Hamid, much less a Giaour. He asked me if I were afraid. So, as I know them pretty well now, I said I was not, but would be happy to shoot him instead if one of his friends would lend me a revolver. This pleased everyone highly as it is their idea of a joke.[28]

Durham would never travel so far again, and certainly never with such joy. From this time on, her health deteriorated; she was forced to spend a year in England, and passed the winter of 1910 in Egypt, where she was shocked by what she saw of British colonial rule. But above all, after this time, the purpose of her journeys necessarily changed. As the Balkans drifted deeper into revolution and war, there was less time for ethnology, and there was the need for relief work.

Early in 1911 Halley's Comet appeared, and Shkodër looked up at the 'star with a tail' with foreboding. For those who could read them, there were the signs of blood and war in the bones of sheep and fowls. The Albanians feared Turkish reprisals for the Kosova rising of 1910. Durham had inadvisedly returned to Shkodër before fully recovering from illness, had suffered a relapse, and was prostrate in the Austrian-run hospital. But the Albanians urged her to write articles: 'Is it printed yet? Do the people in England know?'[29]

After the widespread disillusionment with the 'Young Turk' Constitution of 1908, there had been a number of regional Albanian uprisings, but the entire country had never risen together. In 1911 too, the rising misfired, and the highlanders alone, encouraged by Montenegro, rebelled and were severely crushed by Turkish forces. There was again all the misery of burnt crops and villages. Refugees poured into Shkodër. Durham, starting with her own money, did her best to supply basic food and clothing. One of the personally saddest aspects of this work was that some of the destitute were the same highlanders who had offered her such warm hospitality on her 1908 journey. There was a pathetic faith in her powers to help.

> The mere fact that I could read and write, and so communicate with the outer world, was a marvel. I protested vainly that I had no political influence; that a little help for their wives and children was all I could promise.

Durham acquired the popular name of *Kraljica e Malesorëvet*, (the Queen of the Highlanders), a title which subsequently gave offence to both Turkish and Montenegrin authorities.[30]

A helper in this work was the liberal journalist H.W. Nevinson, who describes one of their joint up-country relief trips.

> We rode on to Braga-Mati (the marshes of the River Mati), and so on to a large farmhouse at Gursi, strongly protected from the Evil One by skulls of horses and goats, some of whom were nailed to a cross. There

we found a vast swarm of fevered people, a thousand I suppose, for the priest had foolishly told of our coming. Stuffing the women in the kitchen because they were ashamed to be treated in the presence of men, we did what we could in distributing our poor fifty boxes of 50 tabloids apiece, and of course they would not anything like go round; for the sick longed to devour them by handfuls.[31]

On their return to Shkodër, Durham and Nevinson were promptly arrested by the Turkish authorities, but Durham entertained her captors by throwing shadows of animals on the wall with her hands, and the two were quickly released. Revolution was followed by the declaration of Albanian independence at Vlorë. But the provisional government could only command a shaky authority in the south. Shkodër was besieged by the Montenegrins, and Durham describes her personal response to the First Balkan War in that harrowing book, *The Struggle for Scutari.*

Perhaps her most moving comments on this period of violence and destruction are the simple notes pencilled into her own copy of *High Albania,* and which record the fate of some of her friends, such as the old man of Hoti who had told her the history of his tribe: 'died of pneumonia as a result of exposure in the winter of 1911–12 after the revolution – a good man.' And a priest, 'martyred by the Montenegrins for refusing to cross himself in the "Orthodox" manner.'

Working in Montenegrin field hospitals and behind the lines at Podgorica, Durham began to move toward the extreme pacifist position which would later lead her to refuse to work for the Red Cross in the First World War; she felt that 'by curing men to go back to the front I was not only prolonging the war, but aiding and abetting every kind of atrocity, and that I ought to cease to do so.'[32]

The end of the Balkan Wars brought the Ambassadors' Conference in London, and the definition of new Balkan frontiers by the major powers. An international commission was sent to Albania while the powers debated the choice of a king. Durham was dismayed to find the fate of Albania decided by people who knew nothing about the country whatsoever, and who were more concerned with maintaining the peace and balance of power among themselves than with the interests of the country itself. The powers appointed to the throne the anodyne Wilhelm zu Wied; his reign was brief and disappointing, though Durham expected little else from him.

I have little or no sympathy with the king. He is a blighter. Why or by whom he was chosen is a mystery. Surely those responsible must have known he was a feeble stick, devoid of energy or tact or manners and wholly ignorant of the country? They are very Royal, both of them, keep a court and keep people standing in their presence. It is all ludicrous. The Queen, the few times I have spoken to her, impresses me as a bright young woman, but her only idea is to play the Lady Bountiful, distribute flowers, put medals on the wounded, and make fancy blouses of native embroidery.[33]

Durham suspected that the powers had even chosen Wied for his very incompetence, so weak was their commitment to Albanian independence. The landowner Essat Toptani, the notorious 'tyrant of Tirana' attempted to seize power, and the Italians representing the international force in Durrës made half-hearted efforts to defend the town.

They built rubbishy barricades, and annoyed me by making one across the street near the hotel door. I pulled it down so as to be able to get in and out easily. The officer was very angry.[34]

With Albania sliding into anarchy, Greece invaded, and Durham travelled to Vlorë, where in the once comparatively prosperous south of Albania she did her best to relieve conditions of starvation and disease among refugees which were worse than anything she had witnessed even in the First Balkan War. She appealed to the Foreign Office for help; but her letter is dated 28 July 1914,[35] and with the outbreak of the First World War a few days later, Durham was forced to interrupt her work and return to England as soon as possible. She travelled home by ship via Biscay, surrounded by travellers who wondered whether the war would be over by the time they docked at Liverpool. But Durham knew that modern wars were not brief or heroic, for she had seen Montenegrin soldiers advancing against Turkish barbed wire and machine guns at the siege of Shkodër.

Moreover, Durham found herself deeply out of sympathy with British war aims. She considered the Sarajevo assassination as a state-sponsored crime, and since the First Balkan War had lost her sympathy for the Serbian state. Her one aim, she says, was to get as far away from the war zone as possible, and she achieved this by first working in a hospital in the Pyrenees. Durham passed the war usefully, but in some obscurity. She worked for the YMCA in Port Said, though not prominently enough to deserve a mention in

the YMCA's history of its Egyptian war work. The slaughter initiated by the great powers now made the blood feuds of the Albanian highlands seem very small. In 1917 a strongly militaristic and vindictive parliamentary candidate inadvisedly attempted to win Durham's vote. 'I told him he had better stand for the Cannibal Islands, or Dahomey.'[36]
Her last visit to Albania was in 1921, but lasted merely a month. She arrived in Durrës and travelled straight to Tirana, where she found the American Red Cross established. Things were greatly changed; 'I don't feel as if my Albania existed any more.' The Red Cross were 'very disagreeable – smoking, the gramophone. Can't make out what class of people they are ... stunned with the row, smoke, and folly. . . . Free and easy American manners are not a good example here.' The Albanians welcomed her, if anything, too warmly.

> I feel like a pet animal in a cage. Extreme hospitality overwhelms me. In the evening a great procession with lights and songs came to do honour to me. The street full of the poor grateful people all cheering. I was thunderstruck. Went on balcony and heard a speech in English by a young American Albanian. Was too overcome to reply properly. Thanked as best I could. It frightens me. They think that I have much more power and influence than I can ever aspire to have.

She travelled to Shkodër, this time not on horseback, from *han* to *han*, but in an American motor car. In Shkodër the heads of the Kastrati and Hoti tribes came to visit her, and 'expected me to start political work at once to get the Serbs out of Kastrati. Said I was powerless. They would not believe me. Said in vain I was now old and tired. They persisted till I promised to 'write something' ... God knows what.'
The next day she was forced to bed for almost a week. 'Got up better but very shaky. Must get away at all costs', she wrote in a faint and spidery hand.[37]
And there the Balkan diary ends. But there is a poem copied into its pages, and one very different from the dreamy languor of Tennyson's 'Lotos-Eaters' which she had copied twenty years before. It is Christina Rossetti's 'Mirage':

> The hope I dreamed of was a dream
> Was but a dream – and now I wake
> Exceeding comfortless and worn and old
> For a dream's sake.

Lie still, lie still my breaking heart,
My silent heart lie still and break.
Life and the world and my own self are changed
For a dream's sake.

If Durham could no longer travel, she could campaign on Albania's behalf at home. The first mention of her in a Foreign Office card index dates from 1908, and reads somewhat prophetically: 'Durham, Miss M.E.: Inadvisability of Corresponding With'. Certainly from the Foreign Office's point of view, she would be a persistent agitator and at times a plain nuisance. 'Miss Durham is a remarkable woman, with a great command of strong language.'[38] On the other hand, British diplomacy was often keen to make use of her intimate knowledge of the local situation in the Balkans, and was not always deaf to her pleas for help in fund-raising for relief work.

In 1918 Durham became honorary secretary of the Anglo-Albanian Association, with Aubrey Herbert, member of parliament and enthusiast for things Albanian, as its president. According to J. Swire, the historian of the development of Albanian independence, it was largely as a result of the efforts of this society that League of Nations recognition was won for Albania.[39] The Association was wound up after the early death of Aubrey Herbert, but also with a sense that its purpose of obtaining Great Power recognition for Albania had been attained.

But Montenegro had vanished in the post-war world. Durham had returned her Montenegrin decorations to King Nikola (as Prince Nikola became in 1910) after the First Balkan War. But she nonetheless took a kindlier view of the man in an article after his death in exile.

He was picturesque, he was kindly, he was courteous. He asked the peasant woman how her pigs were, and at Easter had red eggs in his breeches' pockets for the tribesmen. He was brave, and, according to his lights, he was very religious. Those of us who knew him can spare some moments of regret for the man who meant so well, but failed to cope with the rising tide of time, and has now died far from the grey mountains which he loved with all his heart.[40]

The situation in Albania was still precarious, with the aftermath of war and successive crop failures. There seemed hope for the country in the June revolution of 1924, which brought to power the democratically-minded Fan Noli, whom Durham knew well and greatly respected. Noli was a remarkable polymath, a poet and dramatist, and Albanian translator of Shakespeare, an Orthodox bishop and later founder of the Albanian Autocephalous Orthodox Church, and later even a composer of note. His presidency seemed to promise an end to the squalid intrigues among landowners which marked much of Albanian political life at the time. But this hope was extinguished in December when Ahmet Zogu returned to power. On her 1908 tour, Durham had found the reputation of Zog's home district of Mat so wild that she was deterred from visiting it. 'We are not so bad as Mat', tribesmen had said to her. Now, with Zog, later King Zog, in control, Durham felt there was little political hope for Albania:

> He was forcibly expelled by the Albanians in 1924, but was returned forcibly to the country with the support of Belgrade. . . . By first giving territory to the Serbs and then granting concessions to the Italians he has now put Albania into a difficulty, and she has become a bone of contention between Yugoslavia and Italy. In 1908, when all the tribes were eager for an independent Albania, no one could have foreseen its destinies could be thrown into the hands of the wildest and least educated of the tribes.[41]

It was against this gloomy background that Durham initiated the most acrimonious political discussion of her career. For her it was political, though others in the main interpreted it as historical. This was her research into establishing responsibility for the 1914 Sarajevo assassination. She leapt into battle at once with a letter to Ramsay Macdonald in November 1924 announcing:

> I have now quite incontrovertible proof that the Serbian Government of 1914 knew all about the plot to murder Franz Ferdinand some month or three weeks before the murder took place.[42]

The immediate occasion for this was the publication in Belgrade of some reminiscences of 1914 by Ljuba Jovanović, who had been Serbian minister of education at the time. 'I have watched like a cat at a mousehole (wrote Durham) for proof from the Serbs themselves. And have got it at last.' Her articles in *Foreign Affairs* of December 1924 and in *The Contemporary Review* of January in the following year contained material which she was later to build up into her book *The Sarajevo Crime* (1925), and provoked some discussion among politicians and diplomats.

The force of Durham's arguments was generally admitted – but not their relevance to contemporary British policy in the Balkans. Most readers detected a vein of malice in Durham's book, which also surfaced in her talks at the Royal Institute of International Affairs and the Near East Association. One member of the Foreign Office attended both these meetings and noted:

> Notwithstanding her extremely unattractive manner and her obvious partisanship, in both cases she made a very considerable impression. At the second meeting I thought I should be justified in making a few observations, and I took the opportunity of pointing out that the better the Austrian case against Serbia was, the more lamentable was her handling of it.[43]

Some writers commented that the causes of the Great War lay much more deeply than in the Sarajevo assassination. Others, more headily, accused Durham of always having been pro-German – and her publication of articles in the Berlin magazine *Die Kriegsschuldfrage* did not help here. It is important that on this occasion Durham was brought into conflict with such prominent Slavicists as R.W. Seton-Watson. Ever afterward she was to be regarded as a maverick in academic circles, and her opinions often taken as reflex prejudice.

Durham turned her attention back to her ethnographical work, collating notes from her travels into the book whose formal ungainliness is suggested by its awkward title, *Some Tribal Origins, Laws and Customs of the Balkans*. Durham confesses its incompleteness, again explaining that her plans, 'like so many others, were completely put an end to by the Great War.' The book is a wonderful treasure house of lore and custom. At least for the non-professional reader, the attraction of the book is heightened by its anecdotal quality, and it is also permeated by a personal nostalgia, both for travels which the writer will never undertake again, and more painfully for a society that has vanished.

In her seventies, her health declined. Durham did not take philosophically to a narrower way of life, and her letters are full of bitter complaints, rage and despair. Had her mother, one wonders, been a similarly fractious invalid? But Durham's writing on current affairs is if anything even more pungent and immediate. As late as August 1939 the Foreign Office was informed of her views on the question of Danzig.[44]

Durham appears to have relaxed her extreme pacifism in the case of Nazism, but it was still at this time that family tradition reports her dismissing from her doorstep a callow youth who was

distributing Christian pacifist tracts. 'If you read your Bible properly, young man, you will find that Jehovah was the greatest war
lord of the lot.'
It was inevitably the fate of Albania that interested her most.
Durham became a rallying-point for Albanian exiles in London,
and was encouraged to write and speak, which she did, in great
pain and discomfort. But the activities of the 'Friends of Albania'
were emphatically not encouraged by the Foreign Office, and
Durham and her colleagues were more than ever remote from
events in Albania itself. Half way through the war there was
another battle to fight:

> The novelist Miss West, (she wrote to the historian G.P. Gooch) has
> written an immense book on the strength of one pleasure trip to
> Yugoslavia, but with no previous knowledge of land or people.[45]

The Manchester Guardian had sent Durham *Black Lamb and Grey
Falcon* to review, and she was horrified to find some very scathing
references to herself on page 20. In the book, Durham is rather
loosely categorized as 'the sort of person, devoted to good works
and austerities, who is traditionally supposed to keep a cat and a
parrot,' and who 'had been led by her humanitarian passion to
spend nearly all her life in the Balkans.' There followed a report of
a conversation Durham is supposed to have had with some Serbian
officers, ending, wrote Durham, 'with a malicious sneer about my
gullibility'. Correspondence ensued, with West and her publishers,
and with Durham's solicitor, who held the passage to be libellous.
The publication of *Black Lamb and Grey Falcon* was delayed, and
eventually Macmillan agreed to reprint the 'offensive pages' without mention of Durham's name. At some time during recent years,
Durham's name has been restored, and a copy of the book bought
today will have her name in.
One source of satisfaction during her last years was the friendship and support of many Albanians who had been driven into
exile either by King Zog's regime or by the Italian invasion. One of
her last letters was to Fan Noli, who along with other Albanians in
the United States would send Durham parcels of dried egg, sugar,
tea, and coffee.

> Please give the kindly donors my very hearty thanks, not only for the
> delicacies they have sent me but also for their kind and generous
> thoughts. I am greatly touched. I little thought when I was distributing
> relief in North Albania in 1913 and in South Albania in 1914 that later
> on Albania would feed me.[46]

Durham died in November 1944, only two weeks before Enver Hoxha and the partisans entered Tirana, and Albania embarked on a path which not even Edith Durham's forty years of study of the country could have predicted for it. Albania has perhaps remembered Durham better than Britain. When she died, Durham implied in her will that her books would probably be forgotten. This would be undeserved. Besides their value as an ethnological record, they are imbued with a powerful depth of feeling and love for the Balkans which makes them still startlingly vivid. With every journey there is a sense of personal regeneration and renewal. Durham was often thanked for the work she did for the Balkans; it could also be said that the Balkans worked for her.

Notes

1. Royal Anthropological Institute MS: Letter to mother, 19 July 1903.
2. *Fialor Enciklopedik Shqiptar*, Tiranë: Akademia e Shkencave e Republikes Popullore Socialiste te Shqiperise, 1985, p. 215.
3. *Through the Lands of the Serb*, London: Edward Arnold, 1904, p. 156.
4. RAI MS: Diary, 10 September 1900.
5. RAI MS: Letter to mother, 10 September 1900.
6. RAI MS: Letter to mother, 24 August 1900.
7. *Twenty Years of Balkan Tangle*, London: George Allen and Unwin, 1920, p. 42.
8. RAI MS: Diary, 11 April 1902.
9. RAI MS: Letter to mother, 21 April 1902.
10. RAI MS: Letter to sister Nelly, 5 May 1902.
11. *Through the Lands of the Serb*, p. 186.
12. *Ibid.*, p. 289.
13. Odysseus, *Turkey in Europe*, London: Edward Arnold, 1900, pp. 353–54.
14. RAI MS: Letter to Uncle Ashley, Autumn 1902.
15. *Twenty Years of Balkan Tangle*, p. 87.
16. RAI MS: Letter to mother, June 1903.
17. *Twenty Years of Balkan Tangle*, p. 81.
18. *Ibid.*, p. 93.
19. H.N. Brailsford, review of *The Burden of the Balkans*, in *The Speaker*, 25 May 1905.
20. Review of *The Burden of the Balkans*, in *The Times Literary Supplement*, 31 March 1905.
21. Bible Society Archives, London: Letter of T.R. Hodgson, Bible House, Constantinople, 13 April 1904.
22. MS Letter to G.P Gooch, 13 December 1943.
23. *Twenty Years of Balkan Tangle*, p. 120–1.
24. RAI MS: Letter to sister Nelly, 7 July 1905.
25. *Some Tribal Origins, Laws, and Customs of the Balkans*, London: George Allen and Unwin, 1928, pp. 287–8.

26. RAI MS: Letter to sister Nelly, 13 June 1908.
27. *High Albania*, London: Edward Arnold, 1909, p. 177.
28. Public Record Office: F0371/560: Letter to Mr. McGregor, British Consul at Manastir, 5 October 1908.
29. *The Struggle for Scutari*, London: Edward Arnold, 1914, pp. 14-5.
30. *Ibid.*, pp. 101-2.
31. Henry W. Nevinson, *The Fire of Life*, London: Nisbet, 1935, p. 278.
32. *The Struggle for Scutari*, p. 238.
33. Margaret Fitzherbert, *The Man Who Was Greenmantle – A Biography of Aubrey Herbert*, London: John Murray, 1983, p. 126.
34. *Twenty Years of Balkan Tangle*, p. 270.
35. PRO. F0371/1895.
36. *The Man Who Was Greenmantle*, p. 216.
37. RAI MS: Diary, May 1921.
38. PRO: FO/371/560.
39. J. Swire, *Albania – The Rise of a Kingdom*, London: Williams and Norgate, 1929, p. 281.
40. 'King Nikola of Montenegro' in *The Contemporary Review*, vol. 119, April 1921, p. 477.
41. *Some Tribal Laws*, p. 31.
42. PRO: F0371/9835.
43. PRO: F0371/10794.
44. PRO: F0371/23025.
45. MS Letter to G.P. Gooch, 4 March 1942.
46. MS Letter to Fan Noli, 11 September 1943.

CHAPTER 3

I found yet another design that was purely abstract. Bars and squares of black with raised designs and touches of purple in the solid background depicted no natural object whatsoever, yet evoked certain exaltations. It appears doubtful whether Tolstoy ever saw a peasant. In the imbecile work What is Art? *he asserts that peasants only appreciate pictures which inculcate a moral lesson . . . and that only a person perverted by luxury can care for art which was created without a specific, didactic aim. If he had put his head out of his window and looked at his own village, he would have seen . . . that peasants, more than any other class in the modern community, persistently produce and appreciate art which is simply the presentation of pleasing forms. It was not improbably because Tolstoy was a bad man that he wished art to do nothing but tell him how to be good, and perhaps these peasant women can permit themselves their free and undidactic art because their moral lives are firmly rooted. They had been trodden into the dust by the Turks, condemned to hunger for food and to thirst for blood, but they had never forgotten the idea of magnificence, which is a valuable moral idea, for it implies that the duty of man is to make a superfluity beyond that which satisfied his animal needs and turn it to splendid uses.*

Rebecca West, ***Black Lamb and Grey Falcon.***

The clothing of the peasant women is warm and comfortable for winter wear, but must be found intolerably hot and heavy in summer Only the sturdy frame of a Bulgarian could, I believe, easily support the weight of the full gala costume, with all the ponderous silver ornaments worn on head, neck, waist and wrists. Indeed, I have never found it possible to wear for more than half an hour at a time the costume I had obtained at Salonika with the object of using it as a fancy ball dress.

Lucy Garnett, ***Balkan Home Life.***

Mary Edith Durham as a Collector

June E. Hill

When Edith Durham deposited her collection of Balkan garments and embroideries at the Bankfield Museum in 1935, she gave Halifax a legacy of international significance. Gathered during Miss Durham's travels between 1900 and 1914, the collection contains work from Croatia, Bosnia, Hercegovina, Montenegro, Dalmatia and Albania. Combined with her notes, photographs and drawings, the collection provides a vivid record of the life and traditions of the Balkan people during a time of unrest and before the area was affected by Western influences. As an entity, the collection is an invaluable aid to our understanding of the Balkans. It thus not only provides a material record of Edith Durham's travels, but also continues the work she began of increasing our awareness of the Balkans.

The collection held at Bankfield includes a range of embroidered garments and textiles produced in various regions of Yugoslavia and Albania for daily and ceremonial use. The bulk of the costume is typical of that worn by women and includes shirts, skirts, aprons, *jeleks*,[1] *giubbas, japangi*[3] and footwear. There are complete costumes worn by an Orthodox Bosnian, a Roman Catholic in Scutari and a Bulgar in Monastir. All of the pieces are elaborately decorated with patterns distinctive to each area. So unique is each design that it was said that an expert could tell a man's tribe by the pattern on his clothing.

This regionalisation of pattern is evident in the differing decorations used in the central and coastal areas of Yugoslavia and those found in southern Yugoslavia and Albania. The former areas are marked by their angular patterns. The latter region is noted for its use of curvilinear design and gold-work. This form of decoration reflects a strong Turkish influence: not surprising in view of the area's long history of Turkish rule. Gold braiding and embroidery features prominently on the *jeleks* and *guibbas* and was worked by Albanian male tailors. Such fine pieces of clothing were worn in the towns rather than the highland areas and the quality of the work was noted by Miss Durham: 'The superiority of the Albanian as a designer is marked. He is the artist of the Balkans'.[4]

In contrast to these pieces, other items within the collection are

33

utilitarian, and were produced by peasant women. Fragments
called 'oshvitza' were embroidered on panels of cloth and then
applied to shirt sleeves, collars and front openings to add strength
to areas subject to much wear. Made by young girls who often
worked them whilst minding sheep, the oshvitza were sold at market for 8d or a shilling. Although cheap to purchase, the quality of
the embroidery 'is so fine that it is a wonder the human eye can
stand the strain especially when subjected daily to pungent wood
smoke'.[5]
The decoration used in each region was traditional, passed on to
each new generation, their meaning often lost. Christian, Muslim
and folk religion themes were used but nature motifs predominate,
especially flowers, birds and animals. Such was the skill of the
embroiderers that designs were often worked freehand without
being marked out.

The significance of the Durham Collection does not just lie in
the quality of the textiles, however, but also in the time when the
material was gathered. The early 1900s was a period of unrest in
the Balkans with a revolt in Macedonia against the Turks in 1903–4
and the Balkan War in 1912–13. It was during these years that
Edith Durham undertook her travels in the Balkans, initially as a
visitor and later to give aid and succour to those caught in the conflicts. Throughout these travels Miss Durham collected material,
made notes, drew and took photographs. In doing so, she compiled
a unique record of Yugoslavia and Albania at a time of great
change.

References to the unrest recur throughout Edith Durham's notes
and several garments at Bankfield are directly related to the conflicts. Miss Durham purchased most of the textiles she acquired. In
some instances she bought items from people impoverished due to
the unrest and forced to sell their finest clothes to provide much
needed income. Describing a *jelek* Miss Durham notes:

> In the Balkan War of 1912–13 the Montenegrins took Ipek and treated
> the Moslem inhabitants with hideous brutality. Numbers fled with lit-
> tle but what they stood up in, and sold their garments to buy bread.
> This was sold by one of these poor victims who had been well-to-do.[6]

On other occasions, Miss Durham was presented with beautiful
garments in recognition of her work on behalf of the Balkan people.
Another *jelek* of outstanding design and workmanship, for instance,
was presented to her by the provisional government of Berat in July
1918. Edith Durham records the background to this gift:

Korcha was occupied by Greek troops in the Balkan war of 1912–13, and the Greeks claimed it. Along with Mr. H.W. Nevinson (the famous war correspondent), I rode three days over the mountains arriving at Berat early in the morning, and drafted a telegram to the Council of Ambassadors in London as a petition from the inhabitants of Korcha saying they wished to remain Albanian, and Korcha remains Albanian to this day as a result of that desperate ride.[7]

The *jelek* was given to her as a token of the gratitude of the people. Given such a history, articles like the *jeleks* acquire a historical significance of their own. Linked to specific events, such pieces provide an insight into the effect of social and political unrest on the Balkan people. Yet the importance of the Durham Collection is heightened further for it also represents a record of the material culture of Yugoslavia and Albania which saw much change during this period of upheaval.

During Edith Durham's early travels in the Balkans, dress and ornamentation was distinctive, varying between regions. After 1914, however, increasing Westernisation began to undermine the ethnic culture. Aniline dyes were introduced, replacing the natural ones, adding garish colours to embroidery designs. On a broader plane, Western dress began to be worn by the Balkan people. Franz, Baron Nopcsa noted that as early as 1912, international European dress had begun to be adapted, especially by men.[8] Young Catholics of Scutari, he recorded, had depreciated older styles and wore a combination of European garments and the older head dress, fez and shoes. At the same time, younger women had, to some extent, discarded the wide trousered skirt and veil worn by their mothers. Aware of these changes Edith Durham purchased examples of traditional costume. One knitted and beaded glove held at Bankfield is, she records, 'such as were worn by old men in the winter, although such elaborate ones were already becoming uncommon in 1907.'[9]

As knowledge of her collecting grew, Miss Durham was also proffered pieces illustrating work rapidly being abandoned. Given a sleeve in 1906 from Stjipanjica by an Austrian officer collecting specimens for the Sarajevo Museum, she writes that the work was considered antique and that 'the peasants had . . . ceased to do this fine form of silk embroidery'.[10] As she systematically acquired a range of traditional textiles, Edith Durham formed a valuable collection of ethnic dress when it had a distinct individuality. Combined with the detailed background notes she made of each new acquisition, she created an invaluable record of Balkan culture.

Indeed, the extensive background information that Miss Durham recorded about the Balkans and her collection greatly enhances the material itself. Using her notes, the textiles are carefully put within their social context. Without such a context, specimens can easily become mere curios, examples of 'antique work'. Placed within their context, however, each piece is given a historical setting. Edith Durham was meticulous in her notes, regarding the methods of production and occasions when items were used. To these she added her drawings and photographs. There is no condescension in her work. Her collection and notes reflect her immense knowledge of the Balkans, her love for the land and for its people. Through reading her works, even now, one is given insights into life in the Balkans during the early twentieth century and the pride of its people.

> When I was on relief work visiting large numbers of burnt villages where the inhabitants camped in holes in the ground and under rough hovels, one of my jobs was to deal out clothing material, as most people had only what they stood up in. We obtained a large quantity of shirt material. I cut it into lengths and dealt it out to the refugees who came to fetch it. After several weeks I visited a village expecting to see the women in new garments. Not a bit of it; they were in filthy rags as before. I asked what had become of the shirt stuff, it was, they said, such good stuff it would have to be for best clothes. They had got as far as outlining the embroidery patterns and were beginning to fill it in. But I was assured it would be months before the things were done.[11]

Edith Durham's collection of Balkan material is now held by five institutions. The bulk of her notebooks, diaries and manuscripts are kept by the Museum of Mankind, whilst her photographs are cared for by the Royal Anthropological Institute, both in London. The jewellery she acquired was deposited at both the Pitt-Rivers Museum, Oxford, and Cambridge Museum of Archaeology and Anthropology. The costumes and textiles with related photographs and drawings were given to the Bankfield Museum, Halifax. Exactly why Miss Durham donated the material to Bankfield in 1935 is uncertain. Unfortunately no documentation of the transaction has been kept. It is possible, however, to make an educated guess as to why Bankfield became the home of her garments and embroideries.

As Edith Durham has no obvious links with Halifax itself, it seems possible that Bankfield was chosen because of the strength of its textile collections. These had been built up by Ling Roth, curator of Halifax Museums from 1900–28. A renowned anthropologist and collector, Ling Roth travelled extensively and acquired a unique collection of British and ethnographic textiles, supplemented by examples of textile equipment. This collection was housed and displayed at Bankfield. Like Edith Durham, Ling Roth was involved in the work of the Royal Anthropological Institute and a contributor to its journal. It is known that Ling Roth was familiar with the work of Miss Durham and he refers to her work in his own notebooks.

Given her contacts with ethnographers developed during her involvement with the Balkan States Exhibition at Earls Court in 1907 and her work at the Royal Anthropological Institute, it seems fair to assume that Miss Durham was also aware of Ling Roth's work. Although Ling Roth retired as curator of Halifax Museums in 1925, his work was continued by his successors who added to the textile collections. It was probably her knowledge of this collection, its curators and the continued interest in ethnographic material that influenced Edith Durham's decision to deposit her own collection at Bankfield.[12] Another possibility is that the material was given to Bankfield as a result of the friendship between Edith Durham and Hilda Carline. Hilda, a painter and wife of the artist Stanley Spencer, was the sister of George Carline, curator at Bankfield between 1925 and 1932. He also had a keen interest in Balkan culture; and another brother, Sidney Carline, painted a view of the old bridge at Mostar, now on display in the museum. Whatever the reasons behind her decision Edith Durham gave Halifax a glorious collection and a rich resource.

The bulk of the Durham Collection is on display in the 'Bread and Salt in our Hearts' gallery at Bankfield.[13] The gallery provided an opportunity to include, for the first time, objects on loan from each of the other institutions with Durham material. The reserve collections at Bankfield are available for research, and can be viewed by appointment. Please contact the Keeper of Costume and Textiles at the Bankfield Museum, Akroyd Park, Boothtown, Halifax, West Yorkshire HX3 6HG. (Tel. 01422 354823/352334, Fax: 01422 349020).

Notes

1. A sleeveless small jacket worn by both sexes.
2. A sleeveless coat with a circular skirt, part of the indoor dress of women and girls of Scutari, both Christian and Muslim.

3. An out-of-door cloak worn by married women and presented as a wedding gift from the groom to his bride.
4. E. Durham, 'Some Embroidery Patterns', *Man*, May 1923, No. 40.
5. E. Durham, *ibid.*
6. Edith Durham, Notes, quoted in *The Durham Collection*, Halifax: Bankfield Museum, 1939, p. 52.
7. Durham, Notes, quoted p. 50.
8. Franz, Baron Nopcsca, *Albanien, Bauten und Gerate*, Berlin: 1935.
9. Durham, Notes, p. 68.
10. Durham, Notes, *ibid.*
11. Durham, Notes, *ibid.*
12. Durham, Notes.
13. P.J. Mackenzie, *Bread and Salt in our Hearts*, Halifax: Calderdale MBC, 1997 (catalogue).

CHAPTER 4

In reality Europe is already, in normal times, one single society. Yet perfectly artificial national boundaries are made to signify collective greeds and hatreds, and only a few miles off the fields are permanently ruined, and the countryside is poisoned with corpses, and all the decent thrifty little homes are smashed to dust, and the irreplaceable beauties of the cities are destroyed, and living, thinking men are deliberately killing one another. The soldiers in the hospitals say to their nurses: 'We don't know why we are fighting. Can't you women help us? We can't do anything.' That is the very question we are trying to answer.

Emily Greene Balch, the concluding words of her report from the International Congress of Women at The Hague, May 1915.

Emily Greene Balch: Balkan Traveller, Peace Worker and Nobel Laureate

Elinor Murray Despalatović and
Joel M. Halpern

It can be safely said that there are only two women in this volume – Rebecca West and Emily Greene Balch – whose lives have truly international significance, in that their primary distinction lies outside the field of Balkan and East European studies.[1] Virtually everyone familiar with twentieth century English literature knows the name of Rebecca West, while Emily Greene Balch, who won the Nobel Peace Prize in 1946, is almost unknown to the literate general public. Balch was the second and, to this date, the only other American woman to be so honoured. Her good friend Jane Addams of Hull House first received the Prize in 1931. There is an Immigration History Institute in Philadelphia that bears the name of Emily Greene Balch, and, as her biographer Mercedes Randall notes, her accomplishments are and were 'well known and admired – in the peace movement – both in the United States and abroad; among Quakers, Unitarians, American historians and economists, and among advocates of international organization.'[2] Emily Greene Balch went to the Balkans in 1905 to do field research for her classic study of American Slavic immigrants, *Our Slavic Fellow Citizens*, a 536-page volume published in 1910. As she writes in her Preface, her book was:

> based upon first hand inquiry both in Europe and in America. Acquaintance with any immigrant people in America . . . is not enough. The naturalist might as well study the habits of a lion in a menagerie or of a wild bird in a cage. To understand the immigrant we should know him in the conditions which have shaped him . . . in his own village and among his own people; we should study the culture of which he is a living part. . . . Convinced of this, I spent the greater part of the year 1905 in Austria-Hungary, studying emigration on the spot, and over a year in visiting Slavic colonies in the United States, ranging from New York to Colorado, and from the Upper Peninsula of Michigan to Galveston.[3]

This volume has not been surpassed in its comprehensiveness and keen sense of vital social issues.

Like Rebecca West, Emily Balch had a long life (1867–1961) in which her study of the Balkans represented a temporary focus. Balch, like West, did her work in Eastern Europe as a mature professional bringing to the task both a trained mind and a background of professional writing and accomplishment.

To fully understand Emily Balch and the level of sophistication of her writings it might be useful to begin by contrasting her approach with another American woman traveller of the same period – Frances Kinsley Hutchinson. They travelled in the same regions of the Balkans, Balch in 1905, Hutchinson in 1908. Hutchinson writes:

> What a charming little valley we ran into, this one of Vinodol! A dancing stream, a rustic bridge, overhanging oaks, young elms in winged blossom, and people so gay, so friendly! Imagine women being gay when carrying baskets of rocks from a quarry to a wagon! Imagine being on good terms with life on thirty-two cents a day! Imagine women who really seem to enjoy the making of roads! One balanced a heavy table on her head as she climbed the hill. A tiny child of five running beside her already had her bundle strapped upon her back, in imitation of her elders. Here at the mill where we bought the gasoline, we found

that the overseer had been in America; he had worked in the mines of West Virginia and Pennsylvania, he said. Now he was home again, very much looked up to, evidently, as a traveled personnage.[4]

On parallel topics Balch notes:

The original occasion of emigration from the back country seems to have been the opening of the first railroad to the coast, built in 1873 from Karlstadt to Fiume, which started emigration from Modruš-Rijeka county. Previously freight and passengers had come over the mountains on wheels or on pack animals, and this gave occupation to a large part of the mountain population. An eighteenth century traveler says that this traffic then brought $16,000 or $20,000 into circulation, and he tells of women carrying heavy burdens on their shoulders for a four or five hour climb up the mountains, spinning as they went.[5]

(The returned emigrant) . . . is less docile, less contented, perhaps less religious, often self-assertive and rough in manner. Sometimes he gives himself airs as an 'American', displays the silver dollar that adorns his watch-fob, and turns the heads of the boys with his big talk. I was asked in Croatia why it was that men who came back from America refused to take off their hats in the bureau of an official . . .[6]

Clearly the former is the example of the ethnocentric, romantic and banal views of a casual traveller, while Balch's observation is that of a trained scholar, based on evidence and analysis. But how did Balch arrive at this point? How did she acquire her values? Which specific sorts of academic and intellectual training did she bring to her writing? To fully understand these matters it is necessary to look at her background in some detail.

Emily Balch was born in 1867 to an upper class Boston family, in local terms 'Boston Brahmins'. She spent her childhood in the prosperous Boston suburb of Jamaica Plains, in what the historian of Boston Sam Bass Warner, Jr. described as '. . . a community composed of an unusual proportion of people of the energetic and enlightened New England stock, generally well-to-do, but no worshippers of money, with a fairly clear sense of the values of life, much devoted to their institutions of education and religion.'[7] Emily belonged to a large warm family. She had four sisters and one brother at home and grandparents, aunts and uncles and cousins living nearby. In her words:

Mine was a simple happy suburban home. Grass underfoot and a sky overhead were part of my birthright. It was a shock to me when I went through settlement experience when I realized many children have never spent a night in the dark, have never spent a night in silence.[8]

Theirs was not a typical neighbourhood. The Balch neighbours were people of distinction: the President of Harvard, distinguished professors, scientists, lawyers, historians.[9]

Emily Balch came of old pioneer New England stock on both sides of the family.[10] Her paternal ancestor John Balch, who came to America from England in 1623, was a founder of the town of Beverly. His house, still standing in 1964, was known as the oldest documented house in Massachusetts.[11] By the nineteenth century the Balch family, originally farmers, had moved into business and the professions. Emily's paternal grandfather Joseph Balch was president of a large marine insurance company, and her father, Francis Vergnies Balch, was a distinguished lawyer. Francis married his first cousin Ellen Maria Noyes, the daughter of a respected Newburyport physician. The Noyes family had come to Massachusetts from England in 1633. From the very beginning they tended towards the professions producing a series of ministers, doctors, lawyers, even an inventor. Harvard was, of course, the university for the males of both families.

The Balch and Noyes families were community leaders, people who espoused issues and acted according to their consciences. Just as John Balch had fought for religious toleration and sheltered people who fled Puritan religious persecution, many of Emily's parents' generation were active opponents of slavery. For two years during the American Civil War (1863-4), Emily's father served in Washington as secretary to Senator Charles Sumner, one of the political leaders of the Anti-Slavery Movement. Emily was raised in an atmosphere of what she herself called 'NeoPuritanism', which was Puritanism:

> . . . without its rigors, narrowness or introspection, but colored through and through by complete acceptance of the role of conscience and by a warm and generous sense of the call to service . . .[12]

The Balch family attended the local Unitarian church. Although Emily became a Quaker in later life, she was much influenced in her youth by the Unitarian minister Charles Fletcher Dole. She writes:

> His warm faith in the force that makes for righteousness and the challenge of his whole conception of Right commanded my allegiance and became, so far as I can judge, the chief of all the influences that played upon my life. He asked us to enlist . . . in the service of goodness, and . . . to meet the demands of this service whatever its cost. In accepting

this self pledge . . . I consciously dedicated myself as genuinely as a
nun taking her vows, and in spite of endless weakness, wrong doings,
blunders and failures, I think I never abandoned in any way my desire
to live up to it. . . .[13]

Dole underlined Emily's family tradition that people should serve
others, but with a twist. He told his congregation that they must
take responsibility for the world outside of their families and community. They must try to understand the social and economic
problems spawned by this new industrial age and the new ideas
and organisations which have sprung from them – socialism, anar-
chism, labour unions.[14]

The Balches were people who loved books, good company and
lively talk. Emerson, Whittier, Lowell, Holmes and Longfellow
were part of the world they knew, Longfellow in fact was a professional associate of her father, and the writings of Thoreau and
Hawthorne were 'familiar teachers'.[15] Emily's values – a mixture of
New England literary optimism and conscience combined with a
strong sense of service – were formed in this post-Civil War world
of the socially and intellectually privileged. This old American elite
have played an important role in American history and in a major
political sense still continue to do so. We need only mention pres-
idents of upper class origin such as both Roosevelts and Bush.

Emily Greene Balch was given what was considered a fine education for a girl, first at local private schools, then from thirteen on
at Miss Ireland's school in Boston. Miss Ireland's was not a college
preparatory school, women were only then beginning to go to college, but it offered a challenging curriculum which focused on
modern languages and literature. Emily in later life referred to her
education through high school as 'scrappy'.[16] Francis Balch took
pride in Emily's developing skills and in her bookishness. He supported her decision to attend the new Quaker women's college at
Bryn Mawr Pennsylvania, and even suggested that she study law
and join him in his practice.[17]

Emily Balch entered Bryn Mawr College in 1886 and graduated
in 1889. Bryn Mawr, founded in 1885 to give women as good an
education as their brothers received in schools like Yale and Harvard, had a distinguished young faculty which included Edmund
Wilson, Woodrow Wilson, Carey Thomas and Charlotte Angus
Scott. Emily concentrated on literature and classics in her first two
years but saw this as 'pure self-indulgence'.[18] It was in an economics course in her senior year with Franklin H. Giddings that

Emily suddenly found her focus. She read Charles Booth's massive *Life and Labour of the People of London*, Jacob Riis's study of New York's immigrant poor, *How the Other Half Lives*, and studies by Christian Socialists such as Charles Kingsley and the Fabians, and:

> . . . I felt that this was no time for 'idle singers of an empty day' but for efforts to study and better conditions. This is interesting not as the development of one woman but as characteristic of my generation.[19]

Upon graduation Emily Balch was awarded the first Bryn Mawr European Fellowship. She spent a year in Paris (1890-1) working with Emile Levasseur, the well-known economic historian, demographer and geographer. During that year Balch wrote *Public Assistance of the Poor in France*, which was published in 1893 by the American Economic Association. Dorothy Canfield Fisher, a pupil at an American school in Paris where Emily boarded while at the Sorbonne, provides a brief portrait of Emily at that time:

> She was a tall, slim girl in her early twenties, comely with youth, with a magnificent smooth forehead, and gleaming young hair which she wore in classic simplicity. . . . Her great eyes were clear, intelligent, calm, as few eyes ever are. She dressed simply and unobtrusively. . . . The whole school was proud to have her there. . . . She was called 'The Intellectual', with an accent of warm admiration.[20]

The research for Emily's monograph on public assistance in France was done entirely from books, and she was determined upon her return to Boston to go into the slums, meet the working class, see things for herself. She became one of the pioneers in the social work profession. Emily worked with Italian children in a Home Library programme in Boston's North End, served on the board of a children's home, and, in keeping with her skills and interests, compiled a manual on juvenile delinquency.[21]

In the summer of 1892 she attended the Summer School for Applied Ethics in Plymouth Massachusetts, a programme designed for settlement house workers. This was a high-powered group: Jane Addams, fresh from her first three years at Hull House, Felix Adler, Vida Scudder, Katherine Conant, Franklin Giddings, Helen Dudley, Emily Balch. That December Emily and several others from the Plymouth groups founded Denison House, a small settlement house in South Boston which served as a meeting place for working girls from the neighbourhood. Most of them were in the tobacco, laundry or garment industries, and through these women

Balch was brought into the labor movement. In 1894 Emily Greene Balch joined the Federal Labor Union. Emily's social work brought her into contact with others concerned with social reform and helped to confirm her orientation toward a lifelong career uniting research with public policy.

During the fall semester of 1891–4 Balch took courses in sociology at the Harvard Annex (later Radcliffe College), then spent the spring semester of 1894–5 at the University of Chicago studying economic theory. In 1895–6, she went back to Europe with her friend Mary Kingsbury, this time to take courses at the University of Berlin.[22] Since women were not regularly admitted for study at the University they had to get special permission for each class. Among Balch's professors were the 'armchair' socialists Adolph Wagner, Gustav Schmoller and the sociologist Georg Simmel. In Wagner and Schmoller's classes Emily became exposed to the theoretical side of socialism, and in meetings of the student *Verein* she met fellow students who cared passionately about workers' and women's rights, and politics. She wrote home: 'I don't know when politics has seemed more interesting as now – here, in England and at home and above all internationally.'[23] After classes ended, Balch and Kingsbury went to London where, with international press passes, they attended a stormy meeting of the International Socialist and Labour Congress.[24] There, these gently bred New Englanders heard Liebknecht, Bebel, Ferri, Kier Hardie, the Fabians, and various other European labour leaders argue heatedly about many issues, but most particularly about the ways to meld democracy with socialism.

Emily had hoped to complete work on her doctorate at the Massachusetts Institute of Technology, but M.I.T. required a background of chemistry for admission, and she had never studied chemistry.[25] Therefore in 1896, instead of working on a Ph.D., Emily Balch began her teaching career at Wellesley College. She offered courses on economics, sociology, the labour movement, immigration, the history of socialism, statistics and social work, and many of these courses involved field work in the Boston area. Balch has been credited with organizing the first undergraduate courses in the United States on social work and immigration.[26]

In the early 1890s, as the number of immigrants from southern and eastern Europe began to swell year by year, white Anglo-Saxon protestant Americans began to worry that these 'alien hordes' were not assimilable, that an 'English' core group was essential to American democracy, and that unrestricted immigration would tip the balance, ethnically, politically, culturally. This was especially acute among the social and intellectual elite of Boston. As Warner explains:

> ... they imagined a kind of human flood drowning their formerly virtuous republic. They focused all their disappointments and fears on one target - the immigrant. With their inability to speak English, their wrongheaded religion, and their inappropriate culture, the new immigrants were the source of all difficulties - unsanitary, overcrowded housing, low wages, shoddy work, vulgar entertainments, ignorance, promiscuity, unruly children, lawlessness and political corruption .[27]

The prevailing stereotype was that immigrants were 'the scum of Europe'. Therefore free immigration must be stopped.

In 1894 the Immigration Restriction League of Boston was formed, an organisation which soon rose to national importance, and many of the founding members were personal or family friends of Emily Balch, or professional colleagues. These included Senator Henry Cabot Lodge, Franklin Giddings (sociologist), John Fiske (populariser of evolutionary philosophy), Robert A. Woods (social worker), A. Lawrence Lowell (Harvard President from 1909 to 1933), and David Starr Jordan (President of Stanford University). Emily was part of the small but vocal opposition to these views. Her allies included William James (philosopher), Charles W. Eliot (President of Harvard University 1869–1909) and Josiah Royce (Harvard philosopher).[28]

Balch responded to the critics of immigration with facts in her book *Our Slavic Fellow Citizens.* She decided to focus on the Slavs, for they were the most recent and least known immigrant group, and on the Slavs of Austria-Hungary, for that was the empire of origin of the vast majority of Slavic immigrants.[29] Balch spent her sabbatical leave of 1903–4 studying Slavic immigrants in the United States. In the autumn she lived in a New York tenement with a Czech worker's family. There she picked up some rudimentary Czech, which would help with other Slavic languages as well. She spent the rest of the year travelling all over the country visiting Slavic immigrant colonies, collecting statistics, observing living conditions, interviewing immigrants, labor union people, social workers and priests.

In 1914 a large fire at Wellesley College destroyed College Hall and almost all of Balch's records.[30] Included were not only the notes on which *Our Slavic Fellow Citizens* was based, which judging by the final text must have been very extensive, but also all of the associated documentary material which she collected. Our knowledge of her Balkan trip, therefore, must be based upon the book, a travel article on Bosnia and Montenegro, personal letters, and some fragmentary diary records.

In January of 1905, Emily Balch set off for a year of travel and research in Austria-Hungary. Her travelling companion was Euphemia Murray Abrams, a resident of Greenwich Settlement House in New York City. Abrams was quite young, only twenty-three, and they had met only briefly before the trip. Emily's family must have raised some questions about Miss Abrams' ethnic origins, for Emily reassured them in one of her first letters home that Miss Abrams was a Protestant from 'old' American stock.

> On her father's side they have been in the US for five or six generations and before that came from Germany with as far as they can make out no Jewish affiliations. . . . On her mother's side she is Scotch and that is what she looks like with her retroussé nose and blue eyes with dark lashes . . . her grandfather was the son of a Lord John Murray. . . . She has large wide open loveable blue eyes, round cheeks with a nice complexion and pretty color. . . . Brown hair much pompadored, a pretty figure and a very neat well groomed person. Her expression is friendly, alert, honest and humorous.[31]

Euphernia was not a 'Boston Brahmin', but she came from the small socially-active, educated elite in which Emily Balch circulated, and later married Walter Ernest Clark, who would become the President of the University of Nevada.[32] Euphemia seems to have been an easy companion, hard-working, practical and efficient. By February Balch reported home: 'She (Euphemia) is a perfect treasure and about doubles my available time and more than doubles my pleasure.'[33]

Not only was it useful to have someone along for company as Emily Balch travelled in areas where single women rarely went alone and where there was often no one who spoke her language, but also it was good to have a younger person who could run errands, pack, and take care of Emily when she had an accident or was sick.

Emily Balch and Euphemia Abrams docked in Trieste on 2 February 1905. They stayed a few days, then spent the next six weeks in Vienna and Hungary, returning to the Balkans in late March. For the next two and a half months, they travelled from north to south, from Carniola and Istria through the regions of the former Croatian Military Frontier, to Dalmatia and its islands and back to Zagreb.

They also made an overnight trip to Cetinje, the capital of Montenegro, and took a week of vacation in Bosnia-Hercegovina. The bulk of the travelling was done in April and early May, and on 14 May when back in Zagreb Balch noted:

> When we came to sit still a little we found ourselves unexpectedly tired. It was a month in which we had not slept over three nights running in one place, and we had only done so once in six weeks.[34]

Emily Balch comes through in her letters and writings as an extremely intelligent, witty, and adventuresome woman. She was 40 years old in 1905 and in good health, and in her letters and the descriptive parts of the book and article one has the feeling she was simply having a wonderful time:

> At the outset I had warned her (Euphemia) that this was a journey for business not for pleasure, and lo, no pleasure journey that I have ever taken compared with this for pure joy of travel.[35]

They travelled by ship and small boat along the Dalmatian coast, by railroad between Dubrovnik, Sarajevo and Zagreb, by carriage, and by foot. Emily writes of the beauty of forests, flowers, birds, small villages, colourful peasant costumes, white beaches against the blue Adriatic sky, terraced hillsides. They stayed in comfortable hotels and pensions and in simple inns, coped with rough food, rain, and occasional bedbugs.[36]

Emily Balch was fluent in German, and Euphemia seems to have spoken German too, as well as a little Italian.[37] German was useful for Croatia, and Italian for Istria and Dalmatia, and both picked up some necessary phrases in Croato-Serbian. They also had opportunities to speak English, for many Southern Slav emigrants who had learned some English in the United States had returned to their homeland.

Emily Balch was surprised and humbled by the interest officials and the educated elite of the Southern Slav areas took in her project and she was constantly aware of the immense task before her. In Vienna when suffering from a bad cold: '. . . I feel so much invested in me. This seems such a big opportunity and I feel so little before it'.[38] In April:

> We are as great curiosities in these out of the way places as a circus parade and people are very considerate and helpful. Our Senj friend put a paragraph in a Croatian paper and while this notoriety was

uncomfortable and disagreeable, it had its good side also and helps smooth the way and explains us a little in Croatia.[39]

She never let the attention 'go to her head', as we see in a letter home about a visit to an exhibition of the works of young artists in Zagreb:

You would have laughed heartily to have seen us at the show this afternoon, old Herr K. Kršnjavi, (former Minister of Education) leading us from picture to picture, criticizing and telling us about the artist and his work, and we and him the center of a crowd of people, the galleries almost emptied to crowd around us. We felt like visiting royalty at least. It is very funny to be considered a distinguished foreign visitor, for whom nothing is too g(oo)d. I laugh at their kind delusion, but it is useful to us, if sometimes a little hard to live up to.[40]

Upon arrival in Trieste on 2 February, Emily Balch and Euphemia Abrams began a pattern they would follow throughout the trip. They set off with a letter of introduction to the editor of a local Slovene newspaper. He was away from his office since it was a holiday, so they went sightseeing instead, but went back to see the editor the very next day, and from that point on were involved in a busy round of interviews and social occasions.[41] Emily Balch came prepared with letters of introduction from American and European scholars, priests, journalists and emigrants. Once these were presented in Ljubljana, or Rijeka or Trieste or Zagreb, she and Euphemia were '. . . introduced from one person to another in a sort of endless chain . . .'[42] and by the time they returned to Zagreb the chain had almost become unmanageable:

Agram (Zagreb) is quite a city and a pleasant one, it is the capital of Croatia and there is an appalling amount of information here – statistics – history – literature and people. I had quite a lot of introductions and one leads to another so that the difficulty is to being swamped with social duties. . . .[43]

Through these letters and contacts Emily Balch met officials and members of the educated elite in Croatia-Slavonia and Dalmatia, and her understanding of emigration issues is heavily dependent upon these people for data. She did not have the language skills or time to undertake detailed interviewing of peasants. Her knowledge of village life was based primarily on observation, as she rode or walked through the villages, and on information from those in the elite who knew the villages well. Wherever Balch travelled, with letters of introduction or not, she sought out priests and officials and schoolteachers who could tell her about conditions and customs and reasons for emigration.

Emily Balch came from the American equivalent of the gentry class, and she carried herself with dignity and self-possession. She was, as well, a female academic, a scholar and a social activist, a rarity in America, an even greater rarity in Eastern Europe. The majority of females in the Balkan areas of Austria-Hungary in 1900 were illiterate: 62 per cent in Croatia-Slavonia and almost 90 per cent in Dalmatia, although conditions must have been better for Slovenes.[44]

Very few of the girls who went to elementary school went further, except to train as schoolteachers, and the universities were all male. Men dominated political and intellectual life, and played the major role in the arts as well, although Balch noted that women seemed to win acceptance more easily in the arts, for she met some gifted women poets and artists.[45] Finally, Emily Balch was an American – few Americans came to Croatia-Slavonia and even fewer American women, but many Croats and Serbs were in America, and here was an American who wanted to write a book on Slavic immigration, a subject of real concern to the politicians and educated elite at home. Therefore it is not surprising that Balch and Abrams were treated as colleagues not 'women'. Almost all of their official informants were men, and these men seem not have hesitated to share statistics, observations, documents with them.

Balch and Abrams sometimes got special treatment just because they were women. Their carriage drivers seem to have taken 'fatherly' care of them. In the major cities, Balch and Abrams were gathered into the social life of the middle and upper class women, invited to dances and teas and other social occasions. In Dalmatia and Bosnia-Hercegovina girls and women invited them into their houses and showed them their babies and their handicrafts, and often, pictures of relatives in America.[46] Balch notes again and again how the Balkan women were always working – spinning or knitting as they walked, carrying heavy loads, weaving textiles, working on their gardens. Some of the most poignant information about the effect of immigration in Balch's book comes from women, especially the short essay written by a young woman schoolteacher from a Croatian village with most of its young and strong members away in America.[47]

There were also things Balch and Abrams could not do because they were women. They could not linger in the tap-rooms of little inns, listening to the men talk as they drank and smoked, or in small kafanas. They could not go fishing or hunting with the men or sit with them after dinner over brandy and cigars. Emily Balch's work on Slavic emigration broke new ground. It is still an indispensable source for anyone working in Slavic immigration history. She describes the process and the reasons for emigration, talks of the experience of the Slavs in America and the impact of their emigration at home. The book is based upon her field research and on a wide variety of printed materials including basic works on Slavic history, language and literature, geography, economics, customs and beliefs.[48] Each chapter on a specific Slavic nationality begins with a brief history of the nationality, its language, and its position within the Austro-Hungarian Empire. The historical material was relatively easy to find, the statistical data were not. Balch had hoped to find well-organised figures on emigration from Austria-Hungary at the Central Statistical Office in Vienna, but 'most of the facts are known only through our own American statistics'.[49] Yet American statistics simply blurred the figures on Southern Slav immigration, for they put the Slovenes and Croatians together in one category, Dalmatians, Bosnians and Hercegovinians in another, and the Bulgarians, Serbians and Montenegrins in a third. Therefore Balch collected statistics wherever she went, and her final estimates are based on a number of sources: published official statistics, local figures or estimates, figures from ports of embarkation and arrival, and American census data.[50] She also includes unique material on the number of dollars sent from America to the home provinces each year, and estimates on numbers of returnees.

Balch and Abrams focused their travels on the areas of highest emigration. For the Slovenes that meant the district of Carniola, for Croatia-Slavonia the counties of Modruš-Rijeka, Zagreb, and to a lesser degree Lika-Krbava and Varaždin, as well as Dalmatia with its islands all the way to Boka Kotorska. On the way back they visited Cetinje and took a week's holiday in Mostar and Sarajevo. They most often used the major cities of the area as their headquarters – Ljubljana, Trieste, Rijeka, Zagreb, Split, and Dubrovnik, as well as a few smaller towns. They did not set foot in Slavonia, which Balch refers to as the 'rich eastern counties of Slavonia',[51] although emigration was beginning to come from this region by the late 19th century, and no reasons are offered for the omission. It may have been that Slavonia was an area of lesser migration, because Balch lacked introductions there, because much less was known about it, or because travel in Slavonia presented more difficulties for travellers. The small towns of Croatia and Dalmatia were used to tourists and had adequate hotels or inns. Slavonia, except for Osijek, had tiny cities, few tourists, lots of villages, and railroads only at its edges.

What image, then, does Balch give of the Balkan Slavs? Since her book is about all of the Slavs of the Austro-Hungarian Empire, we should start with her description of the general 'Slavic' type, then look at the Balkan variations.

> This type as it has shaped itself in my mind is short, thick-set and stocky . . . not graceful nor light in motion. The face is broad, with wide-set eyes and marked cheekbones; the nose broad and snub rather than chiseled or aquiline, the forehead rather lowering the expression ranging from sullen to serene but seldom animated or genial. The eyes are of a distinctive shade, grey inclining to blue. The whole suggestion is of strength, trustworthiness, and a certain stolidity, until excitement or emotion lights up the naturally rather unexpressive features.[52]

But the Croats and Serbs were different:

> As a race they strike the observer as darker, more graceful and more gracious than their northern kinsmen . . . and their language is more liquid and southern in character.[53]

She notes the thinness of the men: '"The Croatians look as if they were dying of consumption, but they are tougher than wire", said a doctor in the immigration service. . . .'[54] and their extreme height, especially those who lived along the coast.[55]

Since the Slavic emigration from Austria-Hungary was primarily one of peasant males, and agricultural labourers Balch attempted to explain to her American readers what a peasant was. Peasants were not from the poorest layer of society as many Americans assumed but people who owned land, in an economic sense much like the American farmer.[56] Culturally, however, they were very different, for they lived in a world of traditional peasant culture. The peasant may seem more 'coarse' than a townsman, for peasants '. . . have to deal with nature not mainly as a source of aesthetic emotions, but of a good litter of pigs and proper production of manure'.[57] But their traditional visual, verbal and musical culture is rich-textured:

... the Slavic peasant has created a world of fancy, of song, of tradition, of a whole code of dress, manners, morals ...[58]
The gift of the Slav for color and for music touches the whole life with poetry. Every occasion and act, every wood and hill and stream has its adornment of custom, superstition and legend, which with its glamour veils to the sentimental traveler at least, the hard and sordid sides of lives often close to actual want. . . . The old village life may not always be sanitary or clean or moral, but it is harmonious, complete, self-consistent. Lying aside from beaten routes of travel, many Slavic districts retain to an amazing extent an old-world aspect which gives them unspeakable charm. The beautiful costumes, fixed by tradition, but differing from village to village, ornamented with exquisite embroidery, hand-made lace, rich braiding or leather work, are still in many country places the ordinary and general dress. They are seen at their best at the weekly market, in the crowded church during mass, or at a wedding or a dance on the green.[59]

Not only is this a vivid description, but Balch catches some of the pulse of village life. Traditional peasants, she continued, lived in an economy where value was determined by utility to the owner rather than by market price:

If you wish to respect the peasant's purse, try to buy clothes or furniture like his. If you wish to respect his disregard of money, try to buy them of him. It is amusing to see how comprehensible this latter characteristic is to a commercial-minded Jew. 'Silly geese', said a shopkeeper, as some women refused his offers on our behalf for some embroidered caps that they were wearing. 'Silly!' – They were refusing to sell when a buyer was willing to pay more than the market price. . . .[60]

Peasants identified with their family, village and region, but not necessarily with their nationality.[61] In fact, as Balch notes, it was often in emigration that the Slavic peasant was first exposed to a sense of modern nationalism.

Balch sees clearly that in many regions this traditional peasant culture was adapting to the money economy and the beginnings of modernisation. Railroads took jobs away from those involved in carting and river trade and forced men to emigrate, yet railroads made emigration easier. Education taught the peasants to think differently and expect more. Rising taxes, sub-division of land, tight credit, and unexpected bad harvests caused by drought or plant and animal disease sent hundreds of thousands of Slavic peasants to the United States to make money to preserve their farms. The Slavic emigration was not an emigration of families who planned to settle in America, but a chain of men who went to America, lived with relatives or people from their village or region in tightly packed boarding houses, worked at dangerous and high-paying jobs, and planned to return home once they had accumulated enough money. Most of these men sent money home regularly to their wives and children or parents.[62] This money was used to restock vineyards destroyed by phylloxera, pay back taxes and debts, buy land, build better houses and farm buildings. It raised the living standards of the emigrant's family, and sometimes of the village as well. They also sent money to repair churches and build small roadside shrines. Such a shrine was seen in the village of Hrnetić on the edge of Karlovac; the inscription reads 'St. Nicholas pray for us. Gift of members of the parish in America, 1906.' Balch is not only interested in those who emigrate, she also looks at the 'returnees', those who have come back to stay. Has the experience in America changed them? Some, she writes, are unable to readjust, and leave for America again after a short while; others take up their village and family life once more but they are different.

> The man who has been to America, (from Croatia-Slavonia) we were told, is easily recognized. He carries himself more independently, he works better, he is more interested in education, but he is unfitted for the old life.[63]

Chapters VIII through X of *Our Slavic Fellow Citizens* deal specifically with the Southern Slavs. Chapter VIII is about the Slovenes, or 'Griners' as they were called in the United States. They were a bit too modern for Balch's taste.

> . . . among the Slovenes one does not get the impression of a living pulsating national tradition as one does, for instance, among the Slovaks, the Little Russians or the Croatians. This may be in part because the national costume has almost passed away. Certainly the people appear more assimilated to the Germans, and so to the general European type.[64]

Along the Slovene parts of the Istrian coast there is a triple overlay of culture:

> The situation (in Trieste) is curious – A Slovenian population (the villages about mainly such) molded by many centuries of Italian dominance, topped by a few generations of Austrian (German) rule.[65]

Slovene nationalism must then combat two enemies – 'So much strength is dissipated in this national jarring.'[66] Although the Slovenes lived in mountainous areas they seemed to live relatively well in the Chernembl district of Carniola where 12 per cent of the population had emigrated in the decade between 1890 and 1900.[67]

> My sharpest impressions are . . . of a village where we waited to bait our horses-its little pond, its comfortable looking houses with their stucco walls trellised with grapevines, its big church, and the women in long sleeveless coats (the only bit of costume I saw in Carniola) hurrying to Mass; and then the flowery fields, the vineyard slopes with little storehouses for wine shining white on the hillside . . .[68]

The Slovenes from this region migrated because phylloxera had devastated their vineyards in the 1880s and 1890s, and, according to Balch, they were too used to good living to cut back so got into debt. Even the karst region along the coast of Istria 'seems a mild affair' when compared to the stony mountains of Dalmatia or Montenegro.[69]

Balch and Abrams focused their Balkan trip on Croatia and Dalmatia. Balch seemed almost surprised by the bustling small Croatian capital of Zagreb (53,000 inhabitants), especially the new part of the city with its parks, museums, theatres, educational institutions and modern apartment houses. It was a typical Austro-Hungarian provincial capital with yellow stuccoed buildings, an old and a new town, broad tree-shaded streets, lively cafes. The view from the railroad station was 'worthy for some distance of Paris or Vienna'.[70] Balch was also fascinated by the open market on the main square where the colourfully costumed peasants from nearby villages sold their fruit and vegetables and eggs and cheese:

> The market scene itself is like a bed of flowers, and the prevailing colors being the white of linen garments, and the orange scarlet of ribbons and necklaces and dangling garters, of aprons and embroideries.[71]

Not far from Zagreb were the regions of heaviest migration. First the tiny overcrowded villages around Karlovac, then the mountainous and thickly wooded Gorski Kotar which merges into karst limestone mountains as it slopes down to the coast. Balch was especially struck by the rugged stark karst near the coast:

> Great stretches lie almost bare of any green things, a mere exposure of broken rock surface. . . . In many places there are depressions in the

stony ground, into which soil washes, and one sees such spots, perhaps fifteen feet across, walled around and carefully cultivated.[72]

Since Balch and Abrams spent the majority of their time in the karst regions along and behind the Istrian and Dalmatian coasts, they saw the most marginal and least developed agricultural area of Croatia-Slavonia and Dalmatia.[73] Balch does not seem aware of this. She comments: 'In general, Croatian living is primitive, with the charm and the drawbacks that implies.'[74]

Not only was the land of the karst region rocky, pitted with craters and regularly subject to flood and drought, for a long time it had been the end of Europe – the border with European Turkey. Until the 1870s almost half of Croatia-Slavonia was part of the Austrian Military Frontier, a region of peasant-soldiers where men were more used to fighting than farming, and where the incentive to farm efficiently was missing since the Imperial Authorities could always issue extra rations and stores in times of want. In times of war or defence, men spent most of their time waiting for something to happen, then fought furiously when necessary: 'On this account it is said that many Croatians have never acquired habits of steady industry, using their great strength for a few days, perhaps, then idling.'[75]

The area of Croatia in which Balch and Abrams concentrated their travels had been part of the Croatian Military Frontier. It had been settled for logistic rather than economic reasons, and agriculture had been chiefly for subsistence. This was, as Balch comments, 'poor preparation' for the economic demands of modern life.[76] After demilitarisation the peasant-soldier became a full-time farmer. He had to get used to marketing more of his goods, to increased taxes, to farming more efficiently. The few towns of the former Croatian Military Frontier were very small as was the middle class of merchants and artisans. Senj, for example, one of the larger towns, had only 3,177 inhabitants in 1900.[77] The professionals (officers) who had served as the doctors, teachers and administrators left when the army pulled out. There were no noble landlords. What was left, then, were peasant communities, priests and merchants. Life in the inhospitable lands of the former Croatian Military Frontier was difficult at best and it is no wonder that these were regions of high migration. It was an area of dispersed villages with houses often huddled for safety at the edge of the forest, low quality arable soil which was flooded over at regular intervals, and rocky pastures.

On the road from the coast to Otočac:

> The houses have very steep shingle roofs wh(ich) shelter family and beasts at once with just a partition between. Few have chimneys and in winter the smoke hold is closed for good. The ground is hopelessly stony except here and there in the valleys.[78]

In poorest houses:

> ... there may be simply a fire of twigs and branches on the floor and a baby wrapped in rags lying in the ashes. . . . The family sleep in one room, sometimes on straw, covered with thick wool blankets.[79]

Even the animals were poorly housed and fed:

> The poor cows, as we saw them, emerging after their long winter into the spring sunshine were pitiable objects, with the dirt so caked on their flanks as to tear the flesh and make sores. One official told us of his efforts to get the people to bring their cattle to market clean.[80]

There were indeed houses in the economically 'passive' areas of Croatia-Slavonia without chimneys, and homes where people slept on the floor on straw, but many peasant houses in Croatia-Slavonia by 1900 had chimneys and most peasants slept in beds on corn shuck mattresses.[81] The image Balch gives of Croatia is unintentionally one-sided, just as it would be to talk of the American South today only in terms of Appalachia. Balch does make some comments about the region around Zagreb and the Croatian Zagorje, but the bulk of her descriptive material comes from the countries of Modruš-Rijeka and Lika-Krbava. What is most serious is the total omission of Slavonia, for Slavonia, both Civil and former Military sections, would have introduced her to quite another kind of peasant life. Slavonia was an area of broad river valleys, large villages, enterprising peasants, rich food and well-tended cattle.

Another unique institution which Balch believed held back modern capitalist development was the *zadruga*, the traditional extended family farm. Balch, as a trained social scientist, looked into the *zadruga* in some detail, read the basic works available on the topic, talked with scholars in Zagreb about *zadrugas* and even went to visit one near Zagreb.[82] This *zadruga* was quite large, with sixty members, and prosperous.

In the main homestead the living room opened off a gallery or veran-
dah raised a story from the ground. One room was set apart for unmar-
ried girls, in the main room was a row of beds along each side, and at
one end stood the table at which all the men eat together. The women
eat afterwards. In the yard was a well, and about it a variety of farm
buildings and also small houses where some of the married couples
live. They eat, however, with the others.
This was quite a wealthy zadruga with money in the bank, and the
old man at its head was likewise the head of the village.[83]

Balch was impressed with the *zadruga* because work was shared,
taxes were low, and the property was passed intact from generation
to generation. 'It makes possible a varied and highly social household life, and is, moreover, a training in co-operation, toler-
ance. . . .'[84] She seems unaware of the practical reasons for the
zadruga in the Military Frontier – as a labour pool which allowed
most of the mature men to be away for long periods of army service, and as a method of social and economic control. What interested Balch was the relationship between the *zadruga* and
emigration. This was a period of rapid transformation of household
structures. Most of the large *zadrugas* were dividing into smaller
ones and single family farms. When one subdivided, everything
was divided: the land, animals, farm tools, seed, farm buildings,
even the planks of the house. This created:

> . . . a number of poor if not actually insolvent families . . . There are not
> ploughs enough to fit out all the separate undertakings, and they have
> not sufficient capital and must resort to loans. Moreover, the individual
> members lack experience and perhaps capacity for conducting an inde-
> pendent enterprise, and it is said that the disastrous result of the dis-
> solution of Zadrugas is one of the causes which drive Croatian peasants
> to emigrate to America.[85]

Her observations were apt, and *zadruga* division is still cited as
one of the major catalysts of change in rural Croatia in the decades
preceding World War I.[86]
Balch sometimes accepts uncritically the information given her.
She had heard, for example, that the women in the Slavonian counties:

> . . . which are much richer than the western part of the country, are
> much addicted to luxury and beautiful clothes and in order to gratify
> these tastes, limit their families and conduct themselves loosely. . . .[87]

She is referring here to the 'White Plague', the very low birth rate found in parts of Slavonia. This was an extremely complicated situation tied to traditional property rights of women in the area, the existence of many single family farms which would divide with each generation, fertile land, and social custom. The decision to limit families was usually not made for the woman's pleasure, but to limit population, and many women died or were maimed by crudely induced abortions.[88]

Balch praises the educational reforms which have brought elementary education to the majority of villages, but notes that there is still widespread illiteracy among peasant children and men in the poorer areas and among peasant women everywhere. But:

One must remember that illiteracy does not necessarily connote either stupidity or lack of desire to learn, and that it is compatible with such culture as can be transmitted orally. The printed page was not necessary to the composition of the Illiad or the Odyssey nor to their circulation.[89]

In her long chapter on the Croats, Balch shows a great deal of understanding for the problems of a small nationality trying to keep its identity and autonomy while under foreign rule. The introductory section on Croatian history and present problems is very carefully written. In her letters she describes the excitement among the gifted Croatian artists and writers she met in Zagreb.

Life (here) . . . seems so full of . . . promise and the very fact that the nation is so little, and is in political tutelage to Hungary, gives more significance to each individual achievement in art and literature.[90]

The peasants of Croatia-Slavonia were also, writes Balch, a gentle people:

. . . I doubt if one could find a safer country than Croatia. I remember one late evening in Gospić, the county town of Lika-Krbava, where we walked through oak woods, purple with a carpet of spring crocus and lit with the sunset, and through roads along which peasants were returning from the long market day and its following carousals, driving home in tipsy excitement. Though we were two women without escort we felt no fear. . . . In this once wild frontier no case of highway robbery is remembered for forty-five years. . . .[91]

Balch and Abrams were asked by peasants if the tales of violence in America were true, that emigrants were sometimes robbed of their wages as they walked home, 'and that they had to walk in groups of ten and twelve and carry revolvers.'[92]

Balch and Abrams found Dalmatia to be quite different than inland Croatia. It was a fertile strip of coast, backed by bare rocky mountains, with many islands. The Dalmatians had more possibilities to earn money for they were farmers and fishermen and sailors and 'unlike most Slavs they are capable traders'.[93] The Dalmatians seemed much more aware of the outside world, more enterprising and were quite striking in appearance:

> Physically the Dalmatian is a splendid type. Ethnologists note with some surprise the exceptional height of the Dalmatians, and still more of their neighbors of Bosnia-Hercegovina. They are among the tallest men of Europe, and not only tall but sturdy and markedly fine in their carriage. They are darker than the more northern Slavs, but very often the honest blue eyes of the Slav look out of the swarthy of olive face of the southerner. Greek blood too seems to have left its traces.[94]

Balch and Abrams visited Split and Dubrovnik and little Dalmatian towns and villages. People had told them of one village near Dubrovnik where most of the population had gone to America, but warned them against going there because it was a 'wretched hole',[95] but they visited it anyway. The railway had just reached the village two years before, and no other foreigners had been there:

> . . . we clambered down what was certainly not a path to the settlement which consisted of 16 houses . . . all built of stone . . . and it all seemed as deserted as a dream place. Then we met someone and greeted in our best Croatian and passed the time of day and mentioned we were Americans.[96]

This was the 'magic' word:

> The native population quickly gathered with smiles and gestures . . . we were offered bread and wine then led through houses and various rooms to an upper room with a bench covered with homespun woolen rugs all around it and a lovely view over all the wide valley. . . . [97]

When the visit was over the entire village accompanied Balch and Abrams to the railroad station and waited with them until the train arrived.

Balch with her classical training was fascinated by the ruins of Diocletian's palace in Split, which was honeycombed with streets and shops and churches and houses, but she never lost sight of her reason for coming—emigration. She noted the tiny plots of land cultivated by peasants. Some survived on an acre and a half of vineyards, others on a few olive trees, supplemented by fishing and jobs on the boats for men. Recently many of these sources of income had dried up: phylloxera had hurt the vineyards and a recent Austro-Italian treaty had depressed the price they received for their wine, and even the sea could not guarantee stability:

> On the shores of the Bocche [Boka Kotorska] one sees towns of dream-like streets with deserted villas and in Zeng [Senj] the proud row of warehouses built to shield the harbor from the Bora [wind] now out of proportion to the needs of trade, tell but the same story of the victory of steam over sails as the decaying merchant homes of Salem or Newburyport in New England.[98]

Emigration from Dalmatia began in the mid-nineteenth century and was quite different in pattern from that of the other Slavs:

> It has been . . . a long-continued dripping of individuals, not a mass movement growing as a snowball does like that among the Slovaks and Croatians. . . . The men go alone, often making the journey as sailors, and simply leaving their ship in port. . . .[99]

The women stayed behind and tended the farms. They had the reputation of being more faithful to their husbands than the women inland, perhaps because it was a region where the men were often away at sea and there were long-standing rules of behaviour for women whose husbands were away:

> In some places it is the custom that a woman shall go to no dance or festivity while her husband is on the sea, but when he is in port she knows that he is alive and probably having his share of amusement, and she goes with the rest.[100]

The only reference to immoral behaviour by the wives of emigrants in the inland areas is quite veiled:

> throughout Croatia, as in some other emigration districts, one hears a good deal of sporadic complaint of the injury to morality through emigration. Though cases where the husband has deserted his family appear to be rare, wives left alone at home sometimes misuse their freedom, and I have heard it said that infanticide has increased.[101]

It is very difficult to make any generalisations on this topic although contemporary newspapers and *Sabor* (Assembly) debates mention 'immorality' as a byproduct of emigration, and village studies from the period allude to it.

The southernmost point of their trip was Cetinje, capital of the tiny kingdom of Montenegro. Although a sizeable number of Montenegrins emigrated each year, most went to Alaska. Balch did not discover any Montenegrin colonies in her research in the United States but: '. . . I did run across traces of a party of 35 of them in a Colorado mining camp, where they had left an unenviable reputation for a low grade of living.'[102] Balch suddenly began to understand why, when on the trip to Cetinje she saw: '. . . low huts of unmortared stone, with roofs of grass and filled with smoke and children, . . . on the naked mountain sides.'[103]

Montenegro was stark and poor and, to Balch, it still seemed close to the Middle Ages:

> I thought of the still frequent newspaper accounts of the clashes with the Turks on the frontiers, and how close they stand to the heroic age in which the woman alone labors, since the man must fight and hunt. I recalled the Homeric figure of the blind gusla player singing epic songs on the square in Cetinje . . . and I did not wonder that the Montenegrins cannot meet the standards at once of the tenth and twentieth centuries.[104]

Wherever they travelled in the Southern Slav provinces of Austria-Hungary, Balch and Abrams found people who had relatives in America or knew of people who had gone to America, or had gone themselves. For some, the two American women were a personal link with those overseas. In the large *zadruga* Balch visited near Zagreb:

> Three of the sons were away, two in America and one in 'Spittsburg' (Pittsburg) and the old man seemed to be seized with the sudden sense of yearning, for he twice smoothed his worn hands down my cheeks and said 'Greet Janko for me if you see him in America'.[105]

Even in Cetinje, which seemed so removed from the modern world, a soldier on guard duty asked them how one went about emigrating to America, and:

> . . . a beautiful girl, with the rare, stately beauty of the Montenegrin woman, walking home with her knitting through the early twilight to her home on the mountains an hour away, told us that her brother was in New York.[106]

Doors opened for them because they were Americans: the office doors of bureaucrats, and doors of peasant houses. Balch and Abrams were both investigators and informants, for just as they asked local people about the reasons for emigration, they were quizzed about life in America.

On the way back from Dalmatia, Emily Balch and Euphemia Abrams took a week of vacation in Bosnia-Hercegovina. This is described in an article published in the *Bryn Mawr Alumnae Quarterly* in 1908.[107] They visited Mostar, Jajce, Sarajevo and Banja Luka. This was a week of rest without interviews or gathering of statistics. The tone of the article is quite different from that of *Our Slavic Fellow Citizens*. It is clearly a travel piece, filled with descriptions of costumes and scenery and chance meetings. The two provinces which had passed from Ottoman control to Austro-Hungarian administration in 1878 seemed:

> . . . a curious blending of East and West. One notes the signs of active progress; order and safety, religious tolerance, business activity, handsome school buildings, railroads, excellent highways, and other public works, postal service, good hotels. Yet the East is not less present. The closely veiled figures on the street, the thronged and sounding lanes of the bazaar, the muezzins calling to prayer . . . the secluded homes with their bayed and latticed windows, all speak of the Turk and the Orient.[108]

Balch includes a brief introduction to the complicated history of Bosnia-Hercegovina, and its present status and religious diversity.

Throughout the article, there is a feeling of distance. Balch clearly felt herself a stranger there. She describes a visit to a harem, the womens' quarters of a Muslim family, arranged by a Croatian woman who taught in a school for Muslim girls:

> The old lady, our hostess, was decidedly grande dame despite a certain shabbiness of aspect as she squatted on her heels and smoked. Her pretty young daughter-in-law, in all her finery, brought us Turkish refreshments and showed us her heavy forehead adornment of gold coins, which was her dowry, or part of it. . . . Our visit, which seemed to have a background of curious and amused maids and children, was as interesting an experience to our hostesses as to ourselves, but as a purely social occasion even our kind introducer and interpreter could not prevent its being somewhat meager and embarrassing. I think we were all glad to have seen one another and relieved to part.[109]

It was harder for Balch and Abrams to get to know people in Bosnia-Hercegovina than in Croatia or Dalmatia; time was limited, they went without letters of introduction, and neither spoke more than a few basic phrases of Serbo-Croatian. In addition, since this was not yet an area of emigration, the fact that they were Americans meant almost nothing to the people they encountered. They were able to talk with a few acquaintances in German, but much of the time they reverted to sign language. Perhaps that is why this article is so filled with visual observations, as for example when Balch reflects on the meaning of the various color schemes of the costumes of the women:

> I could not help speculating on the curious contrast in the color scale affected by Christian and Mohammedan Slavs. Where the former delight in robust though skillfully combined reds, whites, blues, greens and blacks, with a rare use of orange and yellow, all very pure and bright, these trousered women make much use of turquoise blues, purple pinks, emerald greens and such tints. Does the difference go back to industrial grounds – home-dyed stuffs versus manufactured? Is it a question of imitation through fashion of a different racial taste, that of the Turks? Or has it conceivably some psychological relation to the contrast between days of out-of-door labor and open sun, and stifled artificial lounging indoors?[110]

Emily Greene Balch returned to the United States at the end of 1905 to take up her teaching duties once more, and she wrote her book on the Slavic emigrants over the next three years while teaching full time. Her book, once published, became the basic work on Slavic Americans. It made her famous, but did not make her rich.

> For this work of two and a half years, I think I received seventeen dollars in royalties besides a generous number of gift copies. I spent thousands of dollars preparing for it. It was well worth it if only in the pleasure it gave me, and I hope it has been of service.[111]

Balch's experiences in Austria-Hungary pushed her in another direction as well. In December of 1905,[112] she wrote in her diary:

> . . . I have decided to call myself a socialist and accepted appointment at Wellesley only on condition of the President knowing this. It will lead to some misunderstanding of course, but I hope to get some better understanding too.[113]

Balch had wrestled with whether or not to declare herself a socialist since her student years in Berlin, but it was the poverty of

Eastern Europe which finally sparked the decision.[114] Balch was never a Marxist, for she could not as an economist accept Marx's theory of surplus value, but she was opposed to the exploitative nature of modern capitalism. Balch identified primarily with the Fabians and Christian Socialists of Great Britain and the revisionist social democrats on the Continent. After World War I, she stopped calling herself a socialist, not because her beliefs had changed but because she disliked the statist aspect of Leninist socialism, and because she distrusted 'labels'.

In 1913, Emily Greene Balch became a full professor of Political Economy and Economic Science at Wellesley. She also served as Chair of the Department. Her professorship was terminated by the Wellesley Board of Trustees in 1918 after twenty-two years of service. The reasons given were Balch's protracted absences (she had taken a series of unpaid leaves and a sabbatical in order to participate in peace work), and her radical economic beliefs and her involvement with pacifism in World War I.[115] We must remember that 1918 was the year in which the 'Red Scare' began to grip the United States.

While her dismissal from Wellesley clearly violated academic freedom, Emily Greene Balch chose not to make a *cause célèbre* out of the affair. Instead she turned her energies to work associated with the Women's International League for Peace and Freedom (WILPF), of which she was a founding member. The WILPF, established in 1919, had its headquarters in Geneva and worked closely with the League of Nations. Jane Addams was elected International President, and Emily Greene Balch as International Secretary-Treasurer. Thus, at the age of 52, Balch began a new career. In her words:

> Here (in Geneva), for a dozen years or so, I spent much of my time absorbed by the peep show that Geneva afforded of the events of that fateful period during which there was a complete failure to make any intelligent or adequate effort to check the growing aggression that began in Manchuria and swept on its triumphant way to Pearl Harbor and beyond; during which the noble experiment of the League of Nations failed, so far as its function as preserver of the peace went, because the governments were not in earnest in using it to that end.[116]

Balch became an active international spokesperson for peace and freedom. She envisioned a 'new age' for the world:

> The new age must be a social age, an age of more fraternal relations between men, an age in which exploitation of class by class is

outgrown, an age in which brutal and greedy rivalry of nation with nation is outgrown, an age in which the unlikeness of other races will be conceived to be as much of an asset as the unlikeness of wind and string instruments in a symphony.[117]

Balch worked to involve Eastern European women's groups with WILPF activities, headed a delegation to investigate conditions in Haiti in 1926 after the US Marine occupations, spoke and wrote in favour of the Kellogg-Briand Pact and of disarmament in general.[118] She warned of the dangers of Manchurian crisis, called for a mediated peace in Spain, called for international control of the polar regions. It was in Geneva that Balch joined the Society of Friends. She saw the United States enter World War II with mixed feelings; as a confirmed pacifist she opposed all wars, yet the Fascists had so clearly broken all rules of international law that they had to be stopped. During the War when so many of the countries in which Women's International League members lived were under Axis control, Balch kept the organisation alive and helped publish a newsletter with whatever scraps of information came from overseas. She turned the attention of the Women's League, of which she was now honorary President, to the problems of refugees, the internment of Japanese-Americans and to the massacre of the European Jews. As the War neared its end she turned her energies to winning support for the United Nations and bringing the Women's International League back to full life. Emily Greene Balch was once more elected honorary President by the WILPF in their first post-war meeting in 1946, and received the Nobel Prize for Peace in November of the same year.

Emily Greene Balch died in 1961. In one of her last autobiographical fragments she wrote:

I am bringing my days to a close in a world still hag-ridden by the thought of war . . . and it is not given to us in this new atomic world to know how things will turn out. But when I reflect on the enormous changes that I have seen myself and the amazing resiliency and resourcefulness of mankind, how can I fail to be of good courage.[119]

Notes

1. Some of the research on which this was based was undertaken when Elinor Murray Despalatović was the recipient of an International Research and Exchanges Board fellowship in Yugoslavia in 1985–6.

2. Mercedes M. Randall, *Improper Bostonian: Emily Greene Balch*, New York: Twayne Publishers Inc., 1964, p. 7.
3. Emily Greene Balch, *Our Slavic Fellow Citizens*, New York: Charities Publication Committee, 1910, p.v. (Henceforth noted as OSFC).
4. Francis Kinsley Hutchinson, *Motoring in the Balkans: Along the Highways of Dalmatia, Montenegro, the Hercegovina and Bosnia*, Chicago: A.C. McClung and Co., 1909, p. 42.
5. Balch, OSFC, p. 175.
6. *Ibid.*, p. 61.
7. Sam Bass Warner, Jr., *Province of Reason*, Cambridge, Massachusetts: Harvard University Press, 1984, p. 92.
8. Emily Balch, autobiographical fragment, as cited in Randall, p. 38.
9. Warner, p. 91.
10. Randall, pp. 25–30.
11. *Ibid.*, p. 27.
12. Balch as cited in *Ibid.*, p. 48.
13. *Ibid.*
14. Warner, p. 93.
15. Randall, p. 37.
16. Randall, p. 53.
17. Warner, p. 94.
18. Balch, as cited in Randall, p. 69.
19. *Ibid.*, p. 70.
20. Dorothy Canfield Fisher as quoted in Randall, pp. 79–80.
21. Emily Greene Balch, *Manual for Use in Cases of Juvenile Offenders and Other Minors in Massachusetts*, 72 pp. (1895, revised 1903 and 1908).
22. Mary Kingsbury Simkhovich went on to have a distinguished career in social work as the founder and headworker of Greenwich House in New York City. Her husband. Vladimir Simkhovich, whom she met in Berlin in 1895, was professor of economic history at Columbia University.
23. Randall, p. 93.
24. *Ibid.*, pp. 97–9.
25. *Ibid.*
26. Mercedes M. Randall, (ed.), *Beyond Nationalism: The Social Thought of Emily Greene Balch*, New York: Twayne Publishers, 1972, pp. xxiii, and 52. (Henceforth cited as BN).
27. Warner, p. 98.
28. Randall (ed.), BN, p, 51.
29. Balch, OSFC, pp. 3–6.
30. Randall, p. 124.
31. Swarthmore Peace Collection, Swarthmore, Pennsylvania. *Papers of Emily Greene Batch* (1875-1961), Series II, Correspondence, Box 6/F1dr.7 Letter from Emily Greene Balch, 24 January 1905. (Henceforth SPC/II/)
32. Randall, p. 118.
33. SPC/II/7, Letter from Emily Greene Balch, 8 February1905.
34. *Ibid.*, II/8 Letter from Emily Greene Balch, 14May 1905.
35. Emily Greene Balch, 'A Week in Hercegovina and Bosnia', *The Bryn Mawr Alumnae Quarterly*, Vol. II (1908), p. 5.
36. SPC/II/8 Letter from Emily Greene Balch, 27 April1905.
37. *Ibid.*, II/7, Letter from Emily Greene Balch, 24 January 1905.

38. *Ibid.*, Letter from Emily Greene Balch, 10 February 1905.
39. *Ibid.*, II/8, Letter from Emily Greene Balch, 16 April 1905.
40. *Ibid.*, Letter from Emily Greene Balch, 14 May 1905.
41. *Ibid.*, II/7, Letter from Emily Greene Balch, 8 February 1905.
42. *Ibid.*, II/8, Letter from Emily Greene Balch, 27 April 1905.
43. *Ibid.*, Letter from Emily Balch, 14 May 1905.
44. Balch, OSFC, pp. 167, 197.
45. SPC, II/8, Letter from Emily Greene Balch, 14 May 1905.
46. *Ibid.*, Letter from Emily Greene Balch, April 27, 1905, Balch, 'A Journey', p. 12.
47. 'Notes from my Village', in Balch, OSFC, pp. 183-190.
48. See the extensive Bibliography in OSFC, pp. 483-512.
49. SPC/II/7, Letter from Emily Greene Balch, 16 February 1905.
50. Balch, OSFC, Appendices I-V, XII-XIII, XVII-XXV, XXVII.
51. *Ibid.*, p. 178.
52. *Ibid.*, p. 11.
53. *Ibid.*, p. 156. Her reference to racial types were typical in the literature of the time. She would later study with the anthropologist Franz Boas at Columbia University who spent a major part of his career distinguishing cultures from biological attributes.
54. *Ibid.*, p. 157.
55. *Ibid.*, p. 192. Overall, however, her impressions were favourable.
56. *Ibid.*, p. 37.
57. *Ibid.*, p. 45.
58. *Ibid.*
59. *Ibid.*, p. 57.
60. *Ibid.*, pp. 44-5.
61. *Ibid.*, p. 34.
62. See *Ibid.*, pp. 181, 182, and Appendix XXIII.
63. *Ibid.*, p. 181.
64. *Ibid.*, p. 150.
65. SPC/II/7, Letter from Emily Greene Balch, 8 February 1905.
66. Balch, OSFC, p. 150.
67. *Ibid.*, p. 153.
68. *Ibid.*, p. 154.
69. *Ibid.*, p. 152.
70. *Ibid.*, p. 175.
71. *Ibid.*, p. 172.
72. *Ibid.*, pp. 158-9.
73. This is the same region the Croatian economist Rudolf Bičanić described in 1935, in his *Kako Živi narod*, English trans. edited by Joel M. Halpern and Elinor M. Despalatović, *How the People Live: Life in the Passive Regions*, Amherst, Massachusetts: University of Massachusetts at Amherst, 1981, Research Report 21.
74. Balch, OSFC, p. 163.
75. *Ibid.*, p. 160.
76. *Ibid.*, p. 161.
77. Royal Statistical Office in Zagreb, *Statistički godišnjak kraljievina Hrvatske i Slavonia*, Vol. I (1905), p. 32.
78. SPC/II/8, Letter from Emily Greene Balch, 16 April 1905.
79. Balch, OSFC, p. 165.

80. *Ibid.*, p. 165.
81. In the village studies made between 1895 and 1914 for the *Zbornik za narodni život i običaje južnih Slavena*, of the Yugoslav Academy of Arts and Sciences, only one, the village 'Gage' in the former Croatian Military Frontier near the Bosnian border reports people without beds. See the collection of studies in Yugoslav Academy (JAZU) – Arhiv odbor za narodni život i običaje (ONZO), Stara zbirka (sz). A few of these studies are published in *Zbornik*. The study of Gage is JAZU/ONZO/sz 127c.
82. Look under *Zadruga* in the Bibliography of OSFC.
83. Balch, OSFC, pp. 161–2.
84. *Ibid.*, p. 162.
85. *Ibid.*, p. 163.
86. See for example Bogedan Stojsavljević, *Povijest sela: Hrvatska-Slavonija-Dalmacija*, Zagreb: Školjska knjiga, 1973, ch. 11.
87. Balch, OSFC, p. 170.
88. See Nada Sremec, *Nismo mi krive*, Vol. III of *Kako živi narod*, Zagreb: Tipografija D.D., 1940.
89. Balch, OSFC, p. 169.
90. SPC/II/8, Letter from Emily Greene Balch, 14 May 1905.
91. *Ibid.*, p. 172.
92. *Ibid.*
93. *Ibid.*, p. 192.
94. *Ibid.*, p. 193.
95. SPC/II/8, Letter from Emily Greene Balch, 27 April 1905.
96. *Ibid.*
97. *Ibid.*
98. Balch, OSFC, p. 194.
99. *Ibid.*
100. *Ibid.*, p. 196.
101. *Ibid.*, p. 170.
102. *Ibid.*, p. 201.
103. Balch, OSFC, p. 200.
104. *Ibid.*, p. 201.
105. *Ibid.*, p. 162.
106. *Ibid.*, p. 200.
107. Balch, 'A Week in Hercegovina and Bosnia', *op. cit.* pp. 5–22.
108. *Ibid.*, pp. 5–6.
109. *Ibid.*, p. 19.
110. *Ibid.*
111. Balch, as cited in Randall, *Improper Bostonian*, pp. 120–1. Balch did have a grant of $300 from the Carnegie Institute to help support her research, but 'it was not to be paid in advance or during the progress of the work, but on her return and only if the work seemed valuable.' *Ibid.*, p. 122, note.
112. See *Ibid.*, p. 123. Randall dates this as 1906. However, the diary entry says that Balch was just back from Austria-Hungary and we know that she returned in 1905 not 1906.
113. *Ibid.*, p. 123.
114. *Ibid.*, pp. 123–5.
115. *Ibid.*, pp. 246–55.
116. Balch, as cited in *ibid.*, p. 284.

117. Emily Greene Balch, 'What it means to be an American', in Randall (ed.), *Beyond Nationalism*, p. 39.

118. See Emily Greene Balch, *Occupied Haiti*, New York: Writers' Publishing Co., 1927, 186 pp.

119. As cited in Randall, *Improper Bostonian*, p. 445.

CHAPTER 5

The brother of one of the hospital sisters wrote today of the great lack of food, and several nurses were weeping over the news from Jambol; but I fear before long now tears still more bitter will be shed. An officer, hearing of my intention of working with the Red Cross, told me to prepare a heart of stone, otherwise the scenes would be too terrible to bear.

A Red Cross volunteer from England,
The Graphic, October 1912.

The Work of British Medical Women in Serbia during the First World War

Monica Krippner

Introduction

Since the end of the 1939–45 war most people in Britain have heard something of the exploits of members of British military missions who fought alongside various resistance movements in the Balkans, especially in Greece, Albania and Yugoslavia. Yet, few people are aware of the extensive aid given to Serbia by British people during the First World War.

Because this aid was not military or economic it has rarely been mentioned by historians. In fact it was medical relief undertaken by numerous British women and a few men volunteers – doctors, nurses, orderlies and ambulance drivers. Though unfortunately so little is known about them in Britain, they are remembered and revered, in Serbia.

During the 1914–18 World War, especially in the first disastrous phase in Serbia, 1914 to the end of 1915, Allied military aid, including that of Britain, was negligible. There were reasons, of course, some valid others less so, for this apparent neglect – the Gallipoli campaign for one; but in the calamity facing Serbia this seeming desertion by her Allies was a severe blow.

When at the end of July 1914 the Austro-Hungarian armies invaded, Serbia was sorely pressed economically, militarily and, as was to emerge, medically, after the previous two years during which the short but devastating Balkan Wars had resulted in heavy army casualties. In addition, endemic diseases such as typhus, typhoid, relapsing fever, and malaria in the south, had reached epidemic proportions in some areas, especially among the civilian population which had been totally neglected.

The limited means of communications – railways, roads and telegraph services – had been destroyed or severely damaged, causing an almost total breakdown in distribution. No medical help had reached the countryside, and few food supplies reached the provincial towns. Finally, heavy casualties had occurred among the doctors and nurses, owing chiefly to overwork and infectious diseases; there had been no reorganisation of even the most rudimentary medical services throughout the country, and no time to train a new cadre of medical personnel.

Because of new and deadly weapons – especially land mines, shell shrapnel and hand grenades – limb and head injuries were very widespread (also among the civilians) and delayed treatment meant gangrene, which ended in death or, at best, amputation. Supplies of anaesthetics were minimal.

The Relief Units

As the Austro-Hungarian forces invaded Serbia at the end of July, and Britain approached her state of war with Germany on 4th August, three very different people were engaged in activities that would soon merge to have a profound impact on Serbia and her people.

The first of these was Robert Seton-Watson, the historian, who knew the country so well, and who had contacts with many politicians and academics of the day in both Britain and in Serbia. As soon as Austria attacked, realising the gravity of the situation, he went into action to obtain immediate support for Serbia, especially medical aid. Thus, Seton-Watson was one of those instrumental in helping set up the Serbian Relief Fund (SRF), based in London, with the Queen as patron and supported by many prominent people of the day, among them Lord Curzon, Sir Arthur Evans, Bonar Law and the Archbishop of Canterbury. Seton-Watson was on the SRF committee.

The second person to take action was Mabel Grujić, wife of *America* Slavko Grujić, Secretary-General of Serbia's Ministry of Foreign Affairs, both close friends of the Seton-Watsons. At the end of July 1914 Mabel Grujić undertook a short intensive appeal campaign in Britain, arousing the sympathy of the public and genuine concern in the ministries. Her tireless efforts bore fruit, helped considerably by her friendship with Seton-Watson, and with Lady Paget, wife of the British minister to Serbia, who had herself recently been involved with medical relief during the Balkan Wars. Serbia became news and contributions poured in. On 10th August Mabel Grujić, with a small pioneer band of women volunteers – nurses and VADs – including Emily Simmonds, a theatre sister, and Flora Sandes, left for Serbia via France, sailing from Marseilles to Salonika. They travelled third class all the way to save precious funds. On reaching Serbia the volunteers immediately began work under appalling conditions in Kragujevac.

The third person was Dr Elsie Inglis, a brilliant surgeon and well-known personality in Edinburgh, active in the suffrage movement, but now aged 50, in poor health and planning to retire, she was galvanised into action by the advent of war. Dr Inglis conceived a double-edged plan, born of her profession as a doctor and her mission as a suffragette – to collect voluntary contributions to establish a medical unit, staffed completely by women, and offer it, fully equipped, to the War Office for service with the British forces. Thus was born the Scottish Women's Hospitals for Foreign Service, to give the full title, but always referred to as the Scottish Women's Hospitals (SWH). (The 'Scottish' in the title arose because the SWH was founded in Scotland. Its many unit members came from Scotland, England, Wales and Ireland, however, and from many corners of the Empire – Australia, Canada, India and New Zealand.)

Dr Inglis's rebuff at the War Office was curt and to the point – 'My good lady, go home and sit still', she was told. Undaunted, Elsie Inglis then went to the embassies of Britain's Allies where her reception was very different. The French, Belgians and Serbs warmly accepted her offer. The first SWF field hospital was established at Royaumont in France where it remained under Dr Frances Ivens, caring for the French wounded until it closed in 1919.

Elsie Inglis had hoped for sufficient funds to equip and staff one SWF unit; but the massive contributions enabled many units to be dispatched to various fronts before the end of the war.

As the SWH units were being formed Flora Sandes and Emily Simmonds returned to Britain for leave after three months in Kragujevac and immediately engaged upon an intensive publicity campaign for the Serbs. For the first time the press and the public had first-hand accounts of the frightful conditions in Serbia, and of the heroism of her people. It was Balaclava all over again, one newspaper wrote. What emerged was that the hospitals had few medicines, limited surgical equipment, no beds or bedding, no motor ambulances, only ox-wagons to transport the wounded, and a terrifying incidence of gangrene because of untreated wounds – sometimes the wounded only received attention as many as ten days after being in action. There was no sanitation, no hygiene, and unreliable power and water supplies. Such horror accounts had their effect and helped swell the contributions to the various relief organisations.

Meanwhile Elsie Inglis had got in touch with Robert Seton-Watson, who gave her every encouragement to get a SWH unit out to Serbia without delay. And so things began to move. On 17th November the first Serbian Relief Fund unit, under Lady Paget, arrived in Skopje to set up a large hospital, at first with 350 beds, later because of typhus expanded to admit over 600 patients. This unit had a staff of 50, including four doctors under Dr Morrison, a professor of medicine at Birmingham University. Except for about six all the staff were women.

The next unit to arrive was a fully equipped SWH field hospital with four doctors and Dr Eleanor Soltau as Chief Medical Officer (CMO), which reached Kragujevac on 15 January 1915 with beds and bedding for 100 patients. Within a week they were treating 250 patients, and by March were responsible for three hospitals they had set up – one for surgical cases, one for typhus, and one for relapsing fever and typhoid. Together this meant over 600 patients under their care.

That 1914–15 winter was one of the worst on record in a country renowned for its severe winters. Thousands of wounded came in daily from the three successful engagements the Serbian army had had with the Austrians: but the price had been high in casualties. In addition, 70,000 Austrian prisoners had been taken, many of them wounded or ill with typhus.

Typhus

Makeshift unheated hospitals were set up in commandeered houses, schools, halls, even barns and stables. Wounded were lying three to a bed, even bedless on the stone floors in the corridors, while walking wounded remained outside in the ox-wagons. Such were the conditions in mid-winter when typhus became a raging epidemic throughout Serbia and Macedonia. Dr Soltau wired desperately for fever nurses and Dr Inglis sent ten immediately, enabling a typhus hospital to be set up.

At Valjevo, where Flora Sandes and Emily Simmonds had been sent on their return from England, the situation was even worse. Being nearest to the front line the hospital had borne the brunt of the worst army casualties, and had been badly hit by typhus. Eventually Emily Simmonds, the trained theatre sister, was doing amputations herself since shattered limbs, chiefly from land mines, worsened by gangrene and frost-bite, comprised the majority of operations. Emily never lost a patient.

The Serbian medical staff had suffered terribly, particularly at Valjevo – 30 per cent had died on duty of typhus and the remainder were ill. Medicines had run out and supplies of anaesthetics were almost exhausted. Forever afterwards the British women would remember the courage and stoic endurance of those wounded Serbs.

In Skopje Lady Paget's SRF hospital had been on duty longer than any of the volunteer teams, and they were paying the price. At one time eighteen of the unit, including Lady Paget and two of the doctors, went down with typhus. They all recovered to resume their duties. In early spring, while the epidemic was still severe, the Wimbourne unit with a fresh group of doctors, nurses and orderlies arrived from England to reinforce Lady Paget's exhausted staff. Fortunately, since Christmas, the fighting had only been spasmodic. The Austrians had not resumed their offensive, but everyone knew it was only a matter of time.

Dr Elizabeth Ross, like a number of others, had come out independently to Serbia where she had joined a Serbian medical team in Kragujevac. She worked herself to a state of total exhaustion, fell ill with typhus and, despite the care given her by Dr Soltau's unit, died. Her grave is in Kragujevac beside those of Mabel Dearmer and Lorna Ferris, who died during the summer.

In Vrnjačka Banja, at the end of January 1915 the Berry Unit arrived, led by a husband and wife medical duo from the Royal

Free Hospital in London. James Berry was a surgeon and his wife an anaesthetist. A niece of Dr Inglis was a doctor on the staff. This well-equipped unit had the good fortune to be given a pleasant sanatorium as their hospital so their situation was vastly better than that of their fellow-nationals further north in Kragujevac and Valjevo, or south in Skopje, since Vrnjačka Banja was, and still is, Serbia's best-known spa.

Spring/Summer 1915

In April 1915 Mrs St Clair Stobart arrived with the second SRF unit – it was 75 strong with 15 doctors, all women except for four orderlies including Mrs Stobart's husband, the unit treasurer. Mrs Stobart was a strange and controversial woman, but brilliant, incredibly brave, and very experienced since she had led the first-ever all-women medical unit when she had taken her 'Women's Sick and Wounded Convoy Corps' to Kirk-Kilisse in Bulgaria during the first Balkan War, where they did a superb job, again under atrocious conditions. Some of the people with her, and with other units in Serbia, had served under her at Kirk-Kilisse.

Mrs Stobart's unit arrived as typhus was being brought under control, and it was she who initiated the idea of establishing roadside dispensaries at strategic points around northern and central Serbia. All units shared in this plan, chiefly to tend the neglected civilian population and thus stop them coming into the overcrowded town hospitals for medical treatment. A dispensary consisted of one doctor, one nurse and one orderly.

As the warmer weather approached and typhus was brought under control, a special Royal Army Medical Corps team of 30 under Colonel Hunter and Lt. Colonel Summers came up from Salonika and were given *carte blanche* by the Serbian authorities to do what they felt necessary to prevent further outbreaks of typhus. They applied draconian measures. All army leave was stopped; road blocks prevented the movement of the local population – another reason why Mrs Stobart's roadside dispensaries were so valuable – and a drastic disinfection programme was enforced. Railway carriages were scrubbed and disinfected, the seat coverings ripped out and burned; cafes and inns were similarly scrubbed and disinfected three times daily for two weeks. By the end of May the controls were lifted, the warm weather had arrived, and typhus had vanished.

In May 1915 Dr Inglis came to Kragujevac to relieve Dr Soltau who had been invalided home with diphtheria. With her Dr Inglis brought Mrs Evelina Haverfield as the SWH unit administrator. In no time Dr Inglis established a rapport with the Serbs – their tough stoic courage touched her deeply. The love and respect were mutual. The Serbs were practically to canonise her. Later they said: 'In Scotland they made her a doctor, in Serbia we would have made her a saint.' Soon afterwards Dr Inglis brought out another unit, which was sent to Mladenovac under Dr Beatrice MacGregor. Then, at the end of May Dr Alice Hutchinson arrived with the large third SWH unit, entirely under canvas and based in Valjevo. Also in May a British Red Cross unit came out to Vrnjačka Banja, not far from the Berry's hospital. Finally, in August the fourth SWH unit under Dr Edith Hollway set up its hospital further north in Lazarevac. By the end of 1915 an estimated 600 British women including 60 doctors would have served somewhere in Serbia or Macedonia.

In Belgrade there was a British Fever Hospital, chiefly for the use of the small international Anglo/French/Serb force commanded by Vice-Admiral Troubridge. This force, 90 strong, harassed the Austrians over the Danube at Zemun. They had a small home-made torpedo boat, some artillery on the heights of Kalemegdan, and a couple of aeroplanes flown gallantly and effectively by French pilots. Also in Belgrade were two hospitals run by private British relief organisations, the 'Young Farmers' and the 'Wounded Allies'. Both were staffed mostly by British doctors and nurses and supported by voluntary contributions.

Little military action took place in Serbia that summer. The staff of the various units spent the time treating the wounded, relaxing a little sometimes, preparing for the inevitable enemy offensive, and hoping desperately that the British and French would come to the aid of the Serbs, and that the Bulgarians would keep out of the war. During that summer lull the grateful citizens of Mladenovac built and dedicated a drinking fountain to Dr Inglis and her SWH units. Apart from being a generous tribute it was also an acknowledgement of Dr Inglis's gentle insistence on the necessity of hygienic water supplies – she continually drew attention to the hazards of open canals and drains in a land where typhoid and dysentery were rife.

Invasion

Then the lull was over–the massive Austro-Hungarian attack began. On 5th October Austria began shelling Belgrade; on 8th

October Belgrade fell; on 12th October Bulgaria attacked Serbia without a formal declaration of war; on 19th October the Bulgarians seized Vranje, virtually cutting Serbia in two. To quote *The Times:* 'It was as if Serbia's backbone were broken.' The Serbian army resisted fiercely but the odds were impossible. The familiar deadly pattern began again with wounded pouring into all the hospitals. On 22nd October Skopje fell to the Bulgarians and Lady Paget's SRF unit was the first to fall to the enemy.

Sir Ralph Paget, acting as British commissioner for all the British units, struggled from place to place to confront the unit chiefs with their choice – to remain and be taken prisoner, or to join the retreat which had already begun but which, with winter coming, would be an extremely hazardous undertaking over the mountains of Montenegro and Albania. He advised the few men of military age to leave to avoid being taken prisoner for the duration of the war, while the women had the chance of being eventually repatriated. Sir Ralph's mission was a delicate one – he could only advise since he had no jurisdiction over the units, all of which, except for the British Fever Hospital in Belgrade and the British Red Cross hospitals, came under the command of either the Serbian Army Medical Corps or the Serbian Red Cross.

Lady Paget's unit had chosen to stay and were already in Bulgarian hands. Dr Inglis, Mrs Haverfield and most of the SWH staff also chose to remain with their Serbian patients. Some individuals, with family and/or responsibilities in Britain, decided to join the retreat. Of the Berry unit most decided to remain, including the Berrys, but others such as Jan and Cora Gordon, left with the retreat.

Mrs St Clair Stobart took the controversial decision to divide her unit in two – the main part to remain at the base hospital in Kragujevac as long as possible, and the remainder to come with her 'flying field hospital', as she called it, to set up dressing stations behind the lines. This gallant attempt failed because of the chaotic situation at the front and the rapid disorderly retreat of the army – her mobile unit was pushed hither and thither with little time to receive casualties. Finally she was forced to join the retreat but was first put in charge of an entire Serbian army medical corps – Colonel Genčić, CO of the Serbian Army Medical Service, gave her a temporary commission with the rank of major. Mounted on a black cavalry horse, she was eventually to lead this medical corps and her flying field hospital over the mountains of Albania and Montenegro to Durazzo. She did not lose a single person, a considerable achievement in view of the thousands of casualties on that terrible winter retreat.

The Albanian Retreat

The 'Albanian' retreat, as it is known throughout Serbia – there is even an 'Albanian' medal for those who took part in it and survived – was one of the most tragic events of the war. As the Serbian army made a six-day last-ditch stand on the plains of Kosovo, awaiting the Allied help that never came, the Serbian government and general staff leap-frogged from one provisional capital to the next from Niš to Kraljevo, then to Peć and Prizren, after which they escaped individually as best they could. Their ageing King Peter and the old gallant but asthmatic Field Marshal (Vojvoda) Putnik, CIC of Serbian forces, were carried in sedan chairs. Behind, abandoned and disorganised, streamed the remnants of the army, the civilians, the Serbian boys – bands of schoolboys and cadets, urged by their elders in the hysteria of the moment to escape to avoid conscription into the Austrian army or imprisonment (disastrous advice as it transpired) and about 70 members of the British medical units. Dr Ćurćin, the Serbian medical liaison officer, who accompanied the British women, later sang their praise for their uncomplaining endurance and their courage.

Everyone had to manage as best they could with no assurance of provisions or refuge. Thus began the great retreat of the Serbian nation through the mud of the plains of Kosovo and the deep snows of the mountains of Montenegro and Albania in a freezing early winter. Weeks later the survivors reached the Albanian ports of Durazzo and Valona from which they were eventually evacuated to Corfu and Brindisi.

Flora Sandes, who had been recuperating in England after being ill with typhus, had reached Monastir (Bitola) on her return just in time to find Serbia collapsing and no way for her to rejoin her hospital. This led her to take the extraordinary step of joining a Serbian regiment at first as a medical orderly, later as a fully combatant soldier. Her regiment retreated via Struga, fighting a rearguard action against the pursuing Bulgarians until they reached Elbasan in central Albania. Later, after having reached the coastal plains her regiment was evacuated to Corfu.

Casualties

When ordered to retreat, the Serbian army was about 200,000 strong; 130,000 reached Corfu; thus, about 70,000 perished on the way. The toll of civilian losses can never be known, but it must have run into many thousands. Of the unescorted bands of Serbian boys an estimated 6,000 to 10,000 died of exhaustion, cold and starvation.

Prisoners of War

Back in Serbia, now overrun in the north by the Austrians and in the south by the Bulgarians, the unit women were managing as well as possible. The units of Dr Alice Hutchinson from Valjevo, Dr Beatrice MacGregor from Mladenovac, and Dr Edith Hollway from Lazarevac had all been forced to withdraw with great difficulty south to Kraljevo, Kragujevac and Vrnjačka Banja where they joined the remaining units to help in the overcrowded hospitals.

Dr Inglis and all her SWH staff, the Berry Unit and the British Red Cross hospital, were at first allowed by the Austrians to continue running their hospitals and given considerable freedom of movement. Later, controls were tightened and the Austrians took over the main Kragujevac: hospital. Eventually, in 1916 the units were repatriated through the International Red Cross in varying stages via Hungary, Austria, Switzerland and France, most arriving in England by spring or early summer.

In Skopje the SRF unit did not fare so well. An appalling winter had set in; they had no fuel; 600 patients crowded the wards; the food supplies were meagre, worsened by the Serbs' scorched earth retreat; and the Bulgarians were suspicious and difficult. Above all, the unit staff were very exhausted, some of them ill. Lady Paget proved to be an excellent leader who eventually managed to establish a working relationship with the Bulgarians, hoping that the unit might soon be repatriated. But this only became likely after the Germans under General Mackensen arrived and tried to commandeer the hospital for themselves. This infuriated the Bulgarians, who then connived with Lady Paget to hand over the hospital to them, much to the fury of the Germans, especially since Lady Paget in fact continued to run it. Finally, at dawn on 17th February 1916 the unit's tortuous repatriation began via Bulgaria, Romania and Russia. They at last reached England on 3rd April, seventeen months after they had arrived in Skopje.

Rehabilitation

During the months that followed, in Corfu and elsewhere the evacuated Serbian army survivors were rehabilitated, retrained and re-equipped before being transferred to Salonika to await the expected Allied offensive north to liberate Serbia. The SRF and SWH units continued looking after the Serbs in Corfu, Corsica, Bizerta in Tunisia, and in Sallanches. In Bizerta the SRF ran a centre for blind and crippled soldiers who were taught crafts and skills that might help them later in civilian life. At Sallanches in the Haute Savoie a 100-bed sanatorium was put at the disposal of the SWH by the French for the many Serb TB cases. It was run by an experienced doctor who had had her own hospital in India, Dr Matilda Macphail. In Corsica the CMO of the main unit was Dr Mary Blair. Also based in Corsica were three other women who would later become particularly well known in Serbia Dr Katherine Macphail, Francesca Wilson and Olive Lodge.

Also, survivors from the bands of Serbian boys were cared for in Corsica and many sent to families in France and Britain. Twenty-five went to the famous Herriot School in Edinburgh and some later went on to Cambridge.

Salonika

Attached to the French Expeditionary Force in Salonika was the SWH Girton and Newnham Unit under Dr Louise McIlroy. Based just outside the city they had a comprehensive hospital with an X-ray unit . . . the only one in Salonika . . . under Edith Stoney; an orthopaedic wing to treat crippled soldiers; and a supply of' artificial limbs, crutches, and even massage facilities. The administrator was Mrs Harley, sister of Field Marshal Lord French. Another SWH hospital, the America Unit, so named because the voluntary funds had come from the United States, was based at Ostrovo, west of Salonika. Its CMO was Dr Agnes Bennett, an Australian – in fact most of the 60 unit members came from Australia and New Zealand.

Among the first Serbian troops to arrive in Salonika was Flora Sandes' 2nd Regiment, and the attractive woman sergeant aroused considerable interest in the city. Sporadic fighting continued along the Macedonian front between the Bulgarians and the British and French forces, which meant a constant flow of wounded to the base hospitals but, until the real offensive began, the main enemy was malaria, a very virulent form of which was prevalent in Macedonia. In 1916–18 the total admissions to hospitals of malaria cases was over 160,000 for the British and French armies, and many members of the SRF and SWH units were victims. Mrs Harley left the Girton and Newnham Unit to form the first SWH Motor Ambulance Column with its own ambulances and a staff of 18 – all women. This unit, which was to be of immense help to the Serbs, was based at Ostrovo and attached to the American Unit.

In early autumn 1916 the long-awaited offensive began with the French and Serbian forces advancing north to Monastir over the Moglena mountains, while the British headed for the Vardar valley. In the second half of September 1916 the great Battle of Kajmakčalan look place. The Bulgarians had entrenched themselves in formidable fortifications near the summit of this 8,000 foot mountain, which dominates the frontier region between Greece and Yugoslavia. The battle lasted two weeks with heavy casualties on both sides, and a victory for the Serbs. This ferocious battle put tremendous pressure on the base hospitals, and magnificent work was done by the Motor Ambulance Column.

Flora Sandes' regiment took part in the Battle of Kajmakčalan and later, in an attack to capture a strategic point, Hill 1212, Flora was severely wounded, taking her out of action for six months.

On 19th November the Serbs recaptured Monastir – they were back in their homeland. Then, for political and military reasons, much to the disappointment of the Serbs, the advance was halted, not to be resumed until 1918.

On 7th March Mrs Harley was killed by shrapnel at her base in Monastir. There was an impressive funeral at the Allied military cemetery in Salonika where she was buried with full military honours, the only woman among thousands of army dead. In July 1917 the Serbs unveiled a memorial they had erected over her grave.

At the end of November 1917 the women's units were shocked to hear of the death of Dr Elsie Inglis, the day after she had returned from Russia. A year earlier, after her repatriation from Serbia, Dr Inglis had responded to a Serbian appeal to send two SWH units, together with their own transport columns, to the aid of two volunteer divisions comprising Serbs, Croats, Slovenes and Bosnians from Austrian territories, which were engaged on the Dobrudja front in Romania. Again these gallant SWH women did phenomenal work under atrocious conditions, often just behind the front lines. Elsie Inglis took part in three retreats in the Dobrudja. Eventually, after the Russian Revolution had begun and the Russian armies were in disarray, Dr Inglis secretly connived with some British diplomats and Serbian officials from Odessa to alert the London War Office to the gravity of the situation for the Serbs, and to urge their evacuation to Britain. Dr Inglis feared that these volunteer divisions would increasingly take the brunt of the fighting, given the uncertain military situation in Russia.

On 14th November the SWH units with Dr Inglis, now terminally ill, and the remainder of the volunteer divisions, made the long journey north to Archangel where they embarked on a British troopship which reached Newcastle on 26th November. The next day Dr Inglis died. The moving funeral that followed in Edinburgh was attended by huge crowds, and reputedly every Yugoslav in Britain.

Allied Offensive

Suddenly, in mid-Septernber 1918 the main Allied offensive began on the Vardar and Struma fronts, while the Serbs concentrated on advancing north of Monastir. It was almost a rout. The Serbs swept northwards, taking the lead. They took the strategic Babuna Pass in Macedonia, then Veles, Skopje, Vranje and Niš. Hard on their heels was the SWH Motor Ambulance Column, and not far behind the SWH and SRF field hospitals. On 3 September 1918 the Bulgarians surrendered: but determined Austro-German forces were still ahead.

Dr Agnes Bennett had been invalided home with severe malaria and Dr Isobel Emslie had taken her place as CMO of the America Unit which now moved north to Vranje to re-establish their hospital in a huge, neglected filthy army barracks, where hundreds of Allied wounded – French, Serbs and British – awaited attention. Soon the hospital was in action – scrubbed, disinfected, and equipment installed. The unit would remain at this base hospital until well into 1919.

In charge of a hospital in Skopje was another SWH unit, the Elsie Inglis Unit, named in honour of the founder, under Dr Lilian Chesney. Later it was transferred to Sarajevo, where it also remained on duty until after the end of the war.

Post-war Misery

On 11th November the war ended, but not the misery and suffering in Serbia. Many unit members write how they hardly noticed the war's official end, since their own war against disease and terrible injuries went on. Then came the influenza epidemic with thousands of weakened malnourished victims dying each week throughout the country.

In early 1919 the units began to disband and the members leave for home, but some individuals stayed on. Dr Louise McIlroy came up from Salonika with her superbly equipped Girton and Newnham Unit which, together with the equipment from the other SWH units that were disbanding, was handed over to the Serbs to form the basis of the Dr Elsie Inglis Memorial Hospital, founded in Belgrade in 1919, and supported by funds from Britain, Serbia and the United States of America. Later, this hospital became part of the large Dedinje Railway Hospital complex, but the building is still there with the memorial plaques for all to see. Nearby is a small street, the Lady Paget Ulica. In 1916, in another context, Robert Seton-Watson had written in *New Europe:*

> History will record the name of Elsie Inglis, like that of Lady Paget, as preeminent among that band of women who have redeemed for all time the honour of Britain in the Balkans. Among the Serbs it is already assuming an almost legendary quality. To us it will serve to remind us that Florence Nightingale will never be without successors among us.

Staying on

Perhaps some of those who stayed on now qualify more as Balkan travellers women who remained to continue doing important work, and learning more of the country they had served so gallantly.

Dr Isobel Emslie and her staff remained at the large hospital in Vranje until the end of 1919. Some years later Isobel Emslie spent six months in Albania to help set up an anti-malaria commission, supported by that great friend of Albania, Lady Carnarvon. She married Lieutenant General Sir Thomas Hutton but never abandoned her medical career, and wrote two books on her wartime service.

Olive Kelso King was one of the very few women awarded a medal by the Serbs for bravery under fire. She was the daughter of a generous Sydney millionaire who financed her running of relief canteens for several years throughout the devastated provinces before she returned to Australia.

Hon Mrs Evelina Haverfield, daughter of Lord Abinger, returned from Russia where she had been with Dr Inglis, and came again to Serbia. In 1919 she opened a hospital for children at Bajina Bašta. A year later she died there of double pneumonia and exhaustion. Her grave is in the small churchyard.

Sister Jean Rankin and Florence Maw, who had served in Skopje and in Kragujevac with the SRF units – Florence Maw had taken part in the retreat – opened an orphanage at Niš. In 1941 this was taken over by the Germans and the two women interned in eastern Serbia for the duration of the war. They remained in Serbia until their deaths in Dubrovnik in 1953.

Dr Katherine Macphail remained to open three children's hospitals, the last one, a hospital for tubercular children, at Sremska Kamenica, which is still there today, part of a larger hospital complex. She remained in Serbia until 1940, and again after the war until the early 1950s. She died in 1974.

Olive Lodge, author of *Peasant Life in Yugoslavia*, who had served in Corsica with a SWH unit, eventually became a true Balkan traveller.

I travelled as the peasants travelled – on horses or mules, sometimes even astride a donkey. . . . Many times I footed it from village to village, *apostolski*, like the apostles, as the Serbs still say.

Cora and Jan Gordon, who had served with the Berry Unit, became known for their popular and charmingly illustrated travel books, among them *Two Vagabonds in the Balkans* and *Two Vagabonds in Albania.*

Dorothy Brindley, later Milić, who served with Mrs Stobart's unit and took part in the retreat, returned with the SRF to Monastir, and then took part in the advance to Belgrade. She was another who, like Olive Kelso King, was decorated by the Serbs for bravery under fire. She married a Serbian officer and remained in Serbia until 1940 when she and her husband were taken prisoner by the Germans. Only in 1945 was she freed in Germany and returned to Belgrade where her husband died shortly afterwards. Then she returned to England where she died in 1984, aged 92.

Flora Sandes remained in the army, was commissioned, and then she married. In 1922 she left the army but remained in Yugoslavia until 1945 when, by then a widow, she returned to Britain. She died in 1956 aged 80.

Miles Franklin was attached to the SWH unit in Salonika. This Australian author, well known in her own country, is probably best known outside it through the Australian film, *My Brilliant Career*, made from her first book. She wrote a number of articles and poems about her time with the Serbs. Professor Cvetkovski of the University of Skopje is at present researching her work and the links with Macedonia.

Postscript

Seventy years later, in June 1985, the Mladenovac fountain, erected in 1915 as a tribute to Dr Elsie Inglis and her Scottish Women's Hospitals, was renovated and rededicated in a moving ceremony. In the same year, in October, a similar ceremony was held at Vrnjačka Banja when a memorial to the British medical women and their staff was unveiled in the lovely city park. In Sremska Kamenica, also in 1985, another memorial tablet was mounted in the main hospital building as a tribute to its founder, Dr Katherine Macphail, and the street leading to the hospital has been named after her. Recently, in June 1988, at the invitation of the local medical authorities, and in the presence of the British Ambassador, a bust of Dr Macphail was unveiled by her niece, Mrs Elspeth Biggs, in the hospital forecourt.

A final comment: since by 1914 women had only been allowed to qualify as doctors in Britain for around twenty years, it is perhaps appropriate to end this brief account of their remarkable war work in Serbia by noting that over 60 British women doctors served with the Serbs during World War I. These medical travellers, together with their staff of nurses, ambulance drivers, pharmacists and orderlies, forced to be mobile by the exigencies of war, have left an impression throughout Serbia and Macedonia that has become part of the traditional epic memory of these nations. The curious British traveller of today in Serbia and Macedonia may chance upon scattered evidence of these women's graves in quiet provincial cemeteries, occasional street names and memorial tablets, the fountain of Mladenovac and, above all, the legendary quality they have assumed with the local population – 'naša Evelina', the young priest said to me as he led me to the grave of Evelina Haverfield in Bajina Bašta.

References

I. Secondary Sources

BALFOUR, Lady Frances, *Dr Elsie Inglis*, London: Hodder and Stoughton, 1919.

BERRY, James et. al., *The Story of a Red Cross Unit in Serbia*, London: Churchill, 1916.

CORBETT, Elsie, *With the Red Cross in Serbia*, Banbury: Chaney, 1964.

DEARMER, Mabel, *Letters from a Field Hospital*, London: Macmillan, 1915.

EMSLIE HUTTON, Isabel MD, *With a Women's Unit in Serbia, Salonika and Sebastopol*, London: Williams and Norgate, 1927.

JONES, Fortier, *With Serbia into Exile*, New York: Century Co., 1916.

KRIPPNER, Monica, *The Quality of Mercy*, London: David and Charles, 1980.

LAWRFNCE, Margot, *Shadow of Swords. A Biography of Elsie Inglis*, London: Michael Joseph, 1971.

McCLAREN, Mrs Eva Shaw, *The History of the Scottish Women's Hospitals*, London: Hodder and Stoughton, 1919.

St CLAIR STOBART, Mrs Mabel, *The Flaming Sword, in Serbia and Elsewhere*, London: Hodder and Stoughton, 1917.

SANDES, Flora, *An English Woman Sergeant in the Serbian Army*, London: Hodder and Stoughton, 1916.

STANLEY, Monica, *My Diary in Serbia*, London: Simpkin, 1916.

WILSON, Francesca, *On the Margins of Chaos*, London: John Murray, 1944.

II. Primary Sources:
(IWM–Imperial War Museum: FL–Fawcett Library: PRO-Public Records Office: P-private).

Introduction

IVENS, Dr Mary H. Frances, MB, MS (London), 'The part played by British medical women in the war', *RMJ*, 18 August 1917 (IWM).

The Relief Units

SETON WATSON, R.W., Telegram to Dr Inglis, 8 November 1914 (SWH Box: IWM).

GROUITCH (GRUJIĆ), Mabel. Letter (copy) to Lady Paget, 28 September 1914 (SRF Box: IWM).

SCOTTISH WOMEN'S HOSPITAL, Letter (copy) signed by Dr Inglis, and sent to their Excellencies, the Ambassadors of Belgium, France and Russia, 20 August 1914 (SWH Box: IWM).

INGLIS, Dr Elsie Maude, Letter to Mrs Fawcett, 9 August 1914 re setting up SWH units, and the use of 'Scottish' in the title (FL).

INGLIS, Dr Elsie Maude, Letter to Mrs Fawcett 13 October 1914 re. terms of contract for SWH unit recruits (SWH Box: IWM).

INGLIS, Dr Elsie Maude, Letter (copy) to the Editor of the *Times*, 27 October 1914 (SWH Box: IWM).

PAGET, Lady, *1st Serbian Relief Fund Report: With our Serbian Allies*, November 1914-February 1915 (SRF Box: IWM) 48pp.

MORRISON, J.T.J., MA, MSc, FRCS, 'Experiences in Serbia, 1914–1915', *The Lancet*, 6 November 1915 (PRO: FO 372/881).

SCOTTISH WOMEN'S HOSPITALS, Forms, contracts, conditions of service, acceptance notices etc. concerned with joining an SWH unit (FL).

SCOTTISH WOMEN'S HOSPITALS, Reports from: America Unit (Dr Bennett), Girton and Newnham Unit (Dr Mellroy); 1st SWH Unit (Dr Soltau) etc. SWH Box: IWM).

Typhus

SCOTT, Flora. Letters from Skoplje (Lady Paget's SRF Unit), plus a long hand-written article, 'The Hospital' 1915 (SRF Box: IWM).

Spring/Summer 1915

FRASER, L.F., 'Diary of a dresser in the Serbian unit of the Scottish Women's Hospitals', *Blackwoods Magasine*, June 1915 (SWH Box: IWM) 21 pp.

HANSON, Dr Helen, *A Serbian Diary*, Church League of Women's, Suffrage, July-November 1915 (P).

SQUIRE, Harry (with Lady Paget's SRF unit in Skoplje), Letters and Diary, 1914-1915 (SRF Box: IWM).

Invasion: The Albanian Retreat. Casualties: Prisoners of War

TROUBRIDGE, Vice-Admiral C.T., Official Diary while Head of the British Naval Mission in Serbia. 21 January-27 December 1915 (IWM).

LORIMER, Craigie, Letter to her brother, Alec. 24 October 1915 (IWM).

PAGET, Lady, 2nd. *Serbian Relief Fund Report: With our Serbian Allies*, February 1915 until repatriation in 1916 (SRF Box: IWM).

PAGET, Sir Ralph, *Retreat of the British Hospital Units in Serbia*, October-December 1915 (SRF Box: IWM).

PHILLIPS, Captain E.F., British Military Attaché (Serbia), Letter from Scutari, Albania. Describes chaos of the retreat and is very critical of the Serbian authorities, military and government (PRO: OW 107/55).

de SALIS, Count (British Consul in Cetinje, Montenegro), Decoded message expressing concern for the British women about to embark on the retreat, 26 November 1915 (PRO: FO 383/88).

St CLAIR STOBART, Mrs Mabel, My Diary – Serbian Retreat, 9 October–28 December 1915 (IWM).

INGLIS, Dr Elsie Maude. Letter to Miss Mair reporting on 1915 Serbian retreat 5 November 1915 (SWH Box: IWM),

ASKEW, Alice and Claude, 'Vivid story of the great Serbian retreat', *The Great War: The Standard History of the Conflict*, (H.W. Wilson, Ed.) Part 85, Vol. 6, Ch. CIV (Ch. XCIX gives a full account of the retreat of the Serbian army). I include this as a 'primary' source because it was given to me by Mrs Milić (née Brindley), who features in my book, and I have never found it elsewhere! (P)

BRINDILY, Dorothy (Mrs Milić), *Our flight from Serbia*, Church League of Women's Suffrage, March 1916 (P).

ČURĆIN, Dr M., 'British Women in Serbia and the War'. *The Engishwoman*, September 1916 (P).

FOREIGN OFFICE: Correspondence and Memoranda regarding Serbian students and schoolboys, in Britain after surviving the retreat (PRO: FO 371/289K).

FOREIGN OFFICE: Dispatches regarding fate of units in the retreat and those taken prisoner, 1915 (PRO: FO 371/8 and 9).

GOODEN, Captain R.B., British-Serbian Liaison Officer with the British Adriatic Mission: Papers, Diaries and Reports from Corfu and Salonika 1916–17; and Casualty List of the Serbian Army to 1 August 1917; and Field State of the Serbian Army at Salonika, 1 August 1917. (IWM: File 73/137/15).

Rehabilitation: Salonika (also Monastir and Ostrovo)

BOSANQUET, Professor. Patterson and Fitzpatrick, Joint Report on SRF work in Corfu, 12 March 1916 (SRF: Box: IWM).

MACPHAIL, Dr Katherine, Letters to her mother from Corsica, 1916 (SWH Box: IWM and P).

McNEILL, Dr Mary, Girton and Newnham Unit, Diary 1916 (SWH Box: IWM).

ROYDS, Kathleen F. Letters to her mother from Salonika and Corsica, 29 October 1916–26 October 1917 and Corsica: MS of an article (8 pp). (SWH Box: IWM).

SERBIAN RELIFF FUND, *Report, year ending 30 April 1917* (SRF Box: IWM) 20 pp.

INGLIS, Dr Elsie Maude: Obituaries in: *The Lancet, 8* December 1918; The *Times* 28 November 1917; *Daily Telegraph; Morning Post; Scotsman: Evening News; The Globe;* etc. (FL).

HAIGH, Dr W.E., Report of the Work of the Monastir Ambulance, 1917 (SRF Box: IWM).

Allied Offensive: Post-War Misery

RENDEL, Frances Elinor, Letters to her mother from the SWH Elsie Inglis Unit in Salonika and Sarajevo, 1918–1919 (FL).

CHAPTER 6

(Rosalind)   *Were it not better,*
Because I am more than common tall,
That I did suit me all points like a man?
A gallant curtle-axe upon my thigh,
A boar spear in my hand; and – in my heart
Lie there what hidden woman's fear there will –
We'll have a swashing and a martial outside,
As many other manish cowards have
That do outface it with their semblances.

William Shakespeare, *As You Like It*, Act 1, Scene 3.

Captain Flora Sandes: A Case Study in the Social Construction of Gender in a Serbian Context

Julie Wheelwright

The story of Flora Sandes, an English woman who became a Serbian Army officer in 1916, captures some of the essential contradictions thrown up by the social construction of gender. Her seven years as the only woman officer serving in an all-male regiment reveals the particularities of how gender operated within a given historical period. Although Flora Sandes began her military career as a Red Cross nurse, the problems that a female soldier posed to prevailing concepts of masculinity were overlooked by potential critics because Sandes was fighting for an Allied cause. She used her position as an unofficial ambassador to promote the Serbians' position and to raise much-needed funds for her adopted country. In the British press she provoked an intriguing debate about the appropriate role for women at the front and in positions of' 'masculine' authority. Privately she articulated the fundamental dilemma of being biologically female but being socially accepted as a man. The following paper will explore both her private and public reflections on her experience within the Serbian army and their relevance to current issues about the social construction of gender.

Sandes, who was born at Poppleton, Yorkshire in 1876, was raised as the youngest daughter of a large family of an Anglican rector. She grew up in a society which believed that a woman's central and most significant role was that of mother and wife; that male and female spheres were clearly delineated by their presumed biological functions. Men, it was believed, belonged to the world of commerce, activity, action and public power while their wives were expected to find contentment in the domestic realm. This theory was brought home to Flora when her two elder brothers became the only family members whose university education was funded by the Reverend Sandes.

The tightly controlled, hierarchical world of Edwardian England, however, had its rebels. There were middle-class women who fought against the restrictions imposed upon them and envisioned liberation by literally adopting male social privilege for themselves. As Flora Sandes wrote of her childhood:[1]

> When a very small child I used to pray every night that I might wake up in the morning and find myself (transformed into) a boy. . . . Many years afterwards when I had long realized that if you have the misfortune to be a woman it is better to make the best of a bad job and not try to be a bad imitation of a man I was suddenly pitchforked into the Serbian army and lived for seven years practically a man's life.

Rather than recognising her frustrations in the suffragettes' struggle for women's entry into the wider political sphere, Flora Sandes fostered her ambitions for change privately. Like many other women of her class, she secretly dreamed of joining her male counterparts in their pursuit of a life beyond the stifling confines of Edwardian Britain. Flora Sandes shared with the Victorian women travellers like Mary Kingsley, Edith Durham and Isabella Bird a desire to reinvent herself in a place where her gender would play a secondary role to questions of class and race.[2]

When war began in August 1914 thousands of British women eagerly volunteered for service overseas and in almost equal numbers the War Office turned them down. Flora Sandes, who had trained with the Ladies' Nursing Yeomanry, was among the first to volunteer. But Sandes was considered too inexperienced for the

Volunteer Aid Detachment nurses and instead chose to sign on with Madame Mabel Grouitch's Red Cross Unit, destined for Serbia. Sandes knew little about the country when she left London on a three-month contract on 12th August, on the first boat to follow the British Expeditionary Force across the English channel. She was 38 years old and considered her life was just beginning. She had shed her identity as an eccentric spinster who lived with her retired father, working as secretary during the week and spending her weekends exploring the English countryside in a French racing car.

At the end of her first contract Flora returned home to Britain, and with her friend Emily Simmonds, known affectionately as 'Americano', went to New York to raise money for medical supplies in Serbia. When they returned in early 1915 with packing crates full of much-needed materials, the president of the Red Cross at Niš asked them to continue on to Valjevo – then known as the 'death trap of Serbia'. The war-torn country was now deep in the grip of a typhus epidemic and Valjevo was almost completely cut – off. Sandes and Simmonds ignored dire warning from an American doctor that they would die within a month if they did not turn back, and resolved to continue.

When Flora Sandes delivered a lecture about her war-time experiences to an Australian audience in 1920 she mentioned a visit to the British consul that influenced her decision to push on to Valjevo. The consul handed her a letter from British Foreign Minister Sir Edward Grey addressed to all nurses working in Serbia. Whatever assistance they gave Serbia, he wrote, 'was helping Britain and the Allies and was of inestimable benefit to the common cause.' Grey, however, changed his position, and clarified his earlier statement by claiming that it was intended 'in a political and not a military sense'. This left the Serbs without the support of supplies they had anticipated so that the British nurses became at least a highly visible sign of Allied concern and support.

Flora and Emily Simmonds were both stricken with typhus but survived to work ceaselessly throughout the winter. By the spring of 1915 the epidemic had abated and Sandes began to enquire about joining a regimental ambulance unit. As she explained in her 1927 autobiography, it was a position usually barred to women. As the only first aid dressing station it was frequently shelled therefore nurses were required to live with the regiment. When her first attempt to get an ambulance position were thwarted, Sandes returned home to England.

Her stay, however, was brief; and on 18 October Sandes left London to return to Serbia. On this journey she was befriended by Dr Isabel Emslie Hutton who was also destined for relief work in a Serbian hospital. When Dr Hutton wrote about her war experiences she remembered vividly a conversation with Sandes that belies Flora's public protestations that she had no intention of going for a soldier when she left London in 1914. When Hutton saw Sandes again in 1916, now a sergeant, she wrote in the diary.[3]

She has got what she wanted without too much difficulty for I remember on the Moussoul she told me that she had always wished to be a soldier and fight . . . she got caught in the retreat, however, shouldered a gun and was made a soldier . . . she looks well and in good spirits.

After much wrangling Flora had been attached to the Ambulance of the 2nd Regiment in Southern Macedonia as a dresser, which was undoubtedly a reward for her services in Valjevo and a sign of trust from the Serbs.

Flora commented later on the seemingly incongruous shift from her role as nurse to soldier, 'Looking back I seem to have just naturally drifted, by successive stages, from nurse into a soldier'.[4] The change was gradual, but the Serbs' point of view completely reasonable. There were other women in the army; the Serbs were in retreat and needed all the military support they could muster and enlistment was often haphazard. Sandes also possessed extremely valuable skills – she could shoot and she could ride and she was English.

When the regiment pulled back to within a few miles of Monastir, Sandes was transferred to the regimental field unit attached to army headquarters. Sandes' friend Dr Nikolić warned darkly that the journey through Albania would be terrible and the army's difficulties experienced so far nothing compared with what lay ahead. Undaunted, Flora told him she would stay with the regiment unless she was asked to leave. Her regimental commander Colonel Milić said it would be better for Serbia if she stayed but it would be better for Flora Sandes if she left. Nikolić said she would encourage the soldiers as she 'represented England!'[5] Equipped with her violin, three cases of cigarettes, jam and warm helmets (gifts for the soldiers) Flora Sandes, now the living promise of Allied rescue, motored back to her regiment's camp. Along the way she breathed a sigh of relief; 'for me it (was) too good to be true, having been fully expected to be ignominiously packed back to Salonique as a female encumbrance'.[6] A hurried line to her family at home, and in half an hour she had disappeared into a howling blizzard, en route for Albania.

Sandes' awareness of her political importance and her unique position provide another explanation for her motives and for the Serbian military official's acceptance of her. Grey's promise of military aid had been sadly lacking, and each night when the 2nd Regiment sat around the camp-fire Sandes was asked 'when are the British coming to help us?'[7] Considerations of sexual difference were overridden by larger questions of social position and the politics of war. Sandes' comments about a Serbian woman soldier in another battalion, Milunka, underlined the importance of being English. The 17-year old Milunka had a reputation for extraordinary bravery and for having shot a man in her village who insulted her sister. But according to Sandes, Milunka was always in trouble and 'being a peasant like themselves the men did not treat her at all the same way they treated me.'[8] Sandes was neither Serbian nor a peasant but an English *lady*, and thus an invaluable asset.

Like Edith Durham, the English woman traveller who became an unofficial but extremely important representative of Albania before and during the Great War, Flora Sandes served an important function in the Balkans.[9] By 1915 Sandes had already shown her flare at fundraising for the Serbian cause, and wrote her first autobiography to publicise her cause. When she returned home on leave a year later, fresh from the front line where she had lived with and fought alongside the Serbian soldiers as a comrade, she spoke as the irrefutable voice of authority. In the English press she was catapulted from Red Cross nurse to the 'Serbian Joan of Arc', stopped in the street by cab drivers, dined with British generals and lunched with Royals. Her 1927 autobiography was hailed as 'important to students of Balkan affairs and to those diplomats whose duty is to preserve the peace of the Near East.'[10] Her ventures were phenomenally successful in raising funds and in publicising the plight of the Serbs.

Sandes became a minor celebrity while home on leave; she proved that her gender did not prevent her from becoming a publicly recognised heroine. While the impact of her achievements was not part of' a revolution in social understanding she did represent an alternative image of a powerful woman. Through her, issues concerning the acceptability of women entering traditionally male-dominated occupations, were brought to the fore. The reception she received in England, France and Australia bears this out. In Britain she was described in the press as the 'new woman' in a period when there was much speculation about the impact that female combatants might have on changing definitions of gender. A review of Sandes' 1916 autobiography from the *London Graphic* commented that:

> The adaptability of the new English woman comes out in every line of Miss Sandes' fascinating story . . . affirming in her own plucky person those qualities of our race usually passed on by women to their sons.

And the *Glasgow Herald* labelled Sandes 'the model of the modern girl', while in America the increasing numbers of Russian female soldiers prompted experts to question whether this phenomenon would change 'our ideals, our chivalry and all that has grown out of them'.[11]

When Sandes received her Royal Command for an audience with Queen Alexandra in 1918 she was 'smitten with consternation in case she disapproved of women in breeches and I had nothing but my uniform with me.'[12] The Queen, however, proved understanding. Sandes returned home on leave in 1917 and 1918 to find that she was a celebrity because of her officer's status and as a representative of Serbia. This combination of factors allowed the press to portray Sandes as an anomaly: the *London Globe* notes in September 1916:

> Her adventure is not a resolution which in the ordinary way we would commend and most commanders would, we think, be extremely embarrassed if her example had many imitators; but in this case, it was certainly justified by the results.

The report added that as a Serbian spokeswoman Sandes was extremely valuable to England and 'it is not easy to exaggerate the good she has affected in this area.' In Australia in 1920 she was hailed as a 'superwoman'.

Although Flora Sandes never cross-dressed out of uniform, she shares with women who masqueraded to enter male occupations many of their experiences. Within her regiment she felt accepted as 'one of the men' but could only achieve this by denying any connection with other women. A vivid example of this was her decision to accompany her Serbian comrades on a visit to a local brothel in Bizerta, Tunis. At a 'sort-of-café' a young woman came and planted herself on Sandes' knee and put her arms around her neck and soothingly said, 'he doesn't look so stupid, but he's very shy'. Sandes, 'kept it up for a while' but gave herself away when the woman attempted to kiss her. This incident, described in Sandes' 1927 autobiography was probably intended as a humorous anecdote playing on the ambiguity of her position. However, it also reinforced Flora's identification with her comrades rather than a woman she happened to meet. In her uniform, working for an important cause, hailed as a war hero, Flora Sandes felt she had no more in common with the woman sitting on her lap than any other woman in her café did. If she or any other female soldier in a similar position allowed herself to empathise with women who served the military in other capacities, her credibility was threatened. Her acceptance was based on her status as an exception even a mascot – but not as part of a trend. Despite this elevated status, Sandes realised it was only the exceptional circumstances of the war that allowed her to become a comrade and even then her 'manhood' was frequently tested.

Like all retired soldiers, the women who fought in the dubious battle for King and Country soon faded from public sight. But unlike their male counterparts, once these women resumed a female identity, they were barred from the male society that might have eased their transition back into civilian life. Coming home to the 'softer sphere of womanhood' could be the most brutally isolating experience because there was often no comforting companionship and little public recognition beyond their short-lived value as curiosities. Even the intense friendships formed with fellow soldiers in the heat of battle vanished when the larger world intruded and the men suddenly became conscious that their mate was not, after all, one of them. When Flora Sandes left the Serbian army after its demobilisation in 1922, her painful metamorphosis back into womanhood unalterably changed her relationships. 'It lost me all my old pals', she wrote in 1927.[13]

> Though still quite friendly they were now quite different. Never again could it be quite the same. As long as I had occasion to notice men are never quite so naturally themselves where there are women present, as when among themselves. Formerly they had been so used to me that I did not count.

It was not true that Flora Sandes had not counted, but that her femininity had been unobtrusive. Without her uniform, however, plucked out of a military environment, her comrades were suddenly highly conscious of her female presence.

It was more than seven years since Flora Sandes had first haphazardly enlisted with the 2nd Regiment during the Serbian army's retreat into Albania. According to her friend, Dr Katherine MacPhail, after the war Sandes became a familiar sight in Belgrade, 'marching with her soldiers through the streets in the early morning and drilling them in the barracks at the fortress.'[14] But after demobilisation in 1923 the sight of Sandes in a dress deeply disturbed her comrades who felt they could no longer treat her as an equal. When she visited her former commanding officer in southern Serbia after the war, he threw up his hands in horror when Sandes appeared on his doorstep in a newly purchased dress and hat. He ordered Sandes to change into one of his old uniforms before her would talk with her. 'He didn't know where he was with me nor how to talk with me,' she wrote.[15] Flora Sandes had experienced equality within the Serbian army and was bound to respect its social and sexual hierarchy. She was accepted as an individual who posed no fundamental ideological challenge to the military's structure. Upon her retirement she relinquished her claims to the male world without protests but mourned the loss for the rest of her life.

Sandes proved that in exceptional circumstances considerations of gender could always be over-ridden for political expediency. The war gave Sandes access to a newfound power; it allowed her to develop skills that might have lain dormant if she had remained at home during the conflict. But her acceptance within the Serbian army was dependent on her status as a representative of an important Allied nation. While her insightful and often passionately articulate autobiographies brought questions about the definition of gender into the public arena, she could do little to challenge the prevailing concepts of sexual difference. In fact, Sandes had a vested interest in maintaining her status as an exception, not the precursor of a trend. Women like Flora Sandes must merit the attention of contemporary social theorists because they can illuminate a vast, neglected sphere of female experience. However, it must be recognised that the freedom they found in the military was gained at great cost. As Antonio Gramsci has argued, 'people negotiate their own terms of domination' and this English woman-sergeant was no exception.

Notes

1. Flora Sandes, The *Autobiography of a Woman Soldier*, London: H.F.G. Witherby, 1927, p. 9.
2. For further information about Victorian women travellers see, Dea Birkett, *Spinsters Abroad*, Oxford: Basil Blackwell, 1989.

3. Dr Emslie Hutton, *With a Women's Unit in Serbia, Salonika and Sebastapol*, London: Williams and Norgate, 1926, pp. 67–8.

4. Sandes, *op. cit.*, p. 12.

5. Flora Sandes' diary, November 28, 1915, in the Flora Sandes Private Collection, Orford, Suffolk.

6. Sandes, *op. cit.*, p. 13.

7. *Ibid.*, p. 13.

8. Flora Sandes, *An English Woman-Sergeant in the Serbian Army*, London: Hodder and Stoughton, 1916, p. 47.

9. Edith Durham, *High Albania*, London: Virago, 1985, p. xii–xv.

10. 'The Autobiography of a Woman Soldier', *Times Literary Supplement*, 20 May 1927, p. 378.

11. 'When Women Fight', *The New York Times Magazine Section*, 2 September 1917, p. 3.

12. Sandes, *Autobiography*, 1927, p. 116.

13. *Ibid.*, p. 230.

14. Jean Bray, *Biography of Dr Katherine Stuart MacPhail*, unpublished, Imperial War Museum manuscript, p. 48.

15. Sandes, *Autobiography*, 1927, p. 221.

Mary Edith Durham, displaying an item from her own collection
of Balkan costume.

One of Mary Edith Durham's watercolour sketches of Albania costume.

Emily Greene Balch (2nd from left) with Euphemia Abrams (centre) and Austro-Hungarian officials, probably during her journey of 1905.

Emily Greene Balch in St. Petersburg, before the First World War (far right), in connection with her work with the Women's International League for Peace and Freedom.

Women in War (2): the realities. A unit of the Scottish Women's Hospitals setting up camp in Macedonia, in 1918.

Dr Alice Hutchinson, CMO of the 2nd Scottish Women's
Hospitals unit, Valjevo, 1915.

Flora Sandes' own photograph of her unit crossing the River Shkumbin during the retreat through Albania in the winter of 1915–16.

Flora Sandes as an officer in the Serbian army.

Flora Sandes in retirement, shortly before her death at the age of 80 in 1956.

An Albanian family at Pultit from Rose Wilder Lane's Peaks of
Shala. The young boy was her guide, Rexh Meta.

Louisa Rayner in her Belgrade apartment shortly before the
Second World War.

An 'Albanian virgin', photographed by Mary Edith Durham. The subject is commented upon by several of our travellers.

(above) Louisa Rayner in 1935. *(right)* Barbara Kerewsky-Halpern on the threshold of 'the old house', in 1953.

Mercia MacDermott and fellow students with Dimitrov in the summer of 1948. (Mercia is seated on Dimitrov's right.)

Barbara Kerewsky-Halpern with a woman of Orašac who was sixteen years old when they first met.

(right) Margaret Hasluck.
(below) Margaret Hasluck's
photograph of 'Mother and
son, each appropriately laden'

CHAPTER 7

We never knew why she came to our country nor what her motives were while she was here. . . . Also, I was interested in the little madame. She was too thin. She walked like a man and it was impossible to understand the language of her eyes. If all the women of America are, like her, per Zoti! I pity the men! . . . But why should an American madame come here? Americans are rich; they can go anywhere. She was young; scandal could not already have driven her from all the civilized cities. But she was deep, that one. She lied with a skill which would have made even Abdul Hamid envious. Perhaps she was an agent of some secret service? Perhaps of the American oil companies? But she offered no one any money, and her talk of politics was all about Leagues, and peace, and land for the peasants. One would say it was the caprice of a woman weary of civilized love, seeking a new adventure.

Rose Wilder Lane, 'The Blue Bead', **Harper's Monthly Magazine,** June 1925.

Rose Wilder Lane: 1886–1968

Antonia Young

Rose Wilder Lane's family history, whilst remote from the Balkans, is nevertheless fascinating. She was born in South Dakota in 1886. At the age of seven she journeyed with her parents for six weeks joining the lines of covered wagons that were fleeing the drought-stricken Dakota plains to the Ozarks. In those six weeks they travelled 650 miles to Mansfield Missouri where Rose's parents remained until they died more than 50 years later. Rose stayed with them there for ten years until she finished school, and returned for long periods in her later life.

Rose Wilder Lane was the daughter of Laura Ingalls Wilder, known for her authorship of the 'Little House on the Prairie' books (serialised and distorted at great length for TV in recent years). The first in the series of nine children's books came out in 1932. Each book describes in detail the eventful lives of the pioneer Ingalls family as they encounter all kinds of difficulties and disasters in the form of fires, locust plagues, droughts, storms and intensely hard winters on their move across several states, during the decades of the 1860s to the 1890s, always building their own new house. The last book tells of Rose's birth at a time of financial depression and great personal disaster of her parents in the late 1880s, and then her long-term separation from them, leaving the reader wondering what became of her.

From other sources it has been possible to trace that when Rose left home, school and De Smet, Missouri, at the age of 17, she went to work at the Western Union in Kansas City. This was in 1903, when such a move for a young, single girl was considered both dubious and unusual. With enormous energy she worked double shifts, learned to type in her evenings and moved from promotion to promotion in different cities, reaching San Francisco in 1908. There she took up real estate selling, where she found herself the only woman with such a position and felt a great deal of antagonism directed towards her. With the outbreak of war, the real estate business folded and Rose turned to a new career – writing for the women's page of the *San Francisco Bulletin* – the start of a prolific writing career. She was soon to become the highest-paid woman writer in the USA, writing short stories for women's magazines. It was through her success as a writer and her encouragement, that her mother, Laura Ingalls Wilder (by then aged 60) started recording her own childhood experiences and is now the better known of the two.

Rose Wilder Lane's first book was published in 1917.[1] By this time she had been married and divorced and was ready for change, ready to accept a job offered her by the American Red Cross and Near East Relief investigating and reporting on conditions in Europe and Asia for the US press in order to raise more American money for their relief work.

For her first trip outside the US, Rose started work in the Red Cross offices in Paris. From there she travelled to Italy, Greece, Yugoslavia, Albania, Egypt, Armenia, Arabia and Persia. But it was Albania which held her lasting interest. She first visited Albania almost by chance, and was shortly to move on from the refugee camp she was visiting in Scutari (now Shkodër) when another American Red Cross worker, Frances Hardy, persuaded her to join a small party who were about to embark on an expedition in the northern Albanian mountains for the purpose of setting up three schools in this extremely underdeveloped area.[2] In other parts of Albania over 1,000 schools had already been founded since 1912, with teaching in the Albanian language, which had been forbidden for the thirty years prior to the revolution of that date. It was this trip in 1921 which inspired her book *Peaks of Shala,* in whose introduction she explains that:

> It is not an attempt to untangle one thread of the Balkan snarl, (but) to send back by a traveller to those who stay at home, a fragment of this large, various and romantic world.[3]

Hers is a very personal narrative, unlike Edith Durham's more objective reporting. For example, after her first night in an Albanian home, she relates:

> It was as though I had returned to a place that I knew long ago and found myself at home there. I had forgotten that these people are living still in the childhood of the . . . race and that I am the daughter of a century that is, to them, in the far and unknown future, twenty five centuries had vanished for me as though they had never been . . . even now I wonder, about the value of the centuries that had given us civilization.[4]

At the time of Edith Durham's first several visits to Albania, it was part of what was then known as 'Turkey-in-Europe'. This was before Ismail Kemal Bey raised the flag of independence in 1912. Independence from Turkey after five centuries only put Albania more at risk of being overrun by the Balkan alliance of Greeks, Serbs, Montenegrins and Bulgarians, all of whom claimed to have interest in ending Turkish domination over Albania. In fact each had more selfish motives; Albania's only real support came from Austria-Hungary through whom their independence was taken up at a conference of ambassadors of the great European powers in London, and their independence recognised. In 1913 these same powers drew up the frontiers granting Kosovo to Serbia. Rose Wilder Lane comments on the arbitrariness of this changed borderline, made by bureaucrats who had never visited this area, which with a mark of the pen had cut off markets for dozens of the northern Albanian villages.

In 1914, the First World War facilitated occupation by Greece of the southern provinces of Albania. Only two months later Italy took over the port of Vlorë. The next year Serbian and Montenegrin troops overran northern and central Albania. Austro-Hungarian troops ousted the other nations, and worked to help Albania build schools, obtain higher education abroad. The defeat of Austria-Hungary in the war, and Italian occupation, lost Albania the only European power which had genuinely come to her defence.

By 1920 a new atmosphere of national unity provided the necessary impulse for a popular uprising to bring about the withdrawal of the Italian army; and once again independence was declared. Albanian acceptance into the League of Nations in the same year gave the country recognition, and its first real elections were held in 1921. As a result of these elections Ahmet Zogu became prime minister in 1922. There was a brief overthrow of Zogu's government by Bishop Fan Noli and his moderately liberal and reformist administration. Zogu in exile in Yugoslavia gathered an army of Albanian mercenaries with Yugoslav military and financial assistance, however, and with these and Yugoslav government backing, took back power in Albania late in 1924. He claimed the Albanian throne in 1928 as King Zog I – dropping the 'u' from 'Zogu' in order to Europeanise his name.

The party which Rose Wilder Lane, Frances Hardy and a Miss Alexander took into the northern Albanian mountains in 1921 (following closely in the footsteps of Edith Durham's earlier ones), also included Rexh Meta, a twelve-year-old refugee child from Kosovo who had walked 250 miles to Scutari after his whole family and village had been killed by Montenegrins at the time of the border changes.[5]

This lad took charge of the six men with pack horses who carried the needs of the party. Finally, as interpreter, came Rrok Perolli who was secretary to the Albanian Minister of the Interior, and who had recently escaped a death sentence in a Serbian prison. This man of course was not proud to make known his government affiliations amongst the north Albanian tribes who were still antagonistic to the relatively new government. Located in Tirana, this was seen, not as an *Albanian* government, but rather as a *Tirana* government. Furthermore, many felt that it might be in league with foreign governments as too often in history had Albania been treated as a pawn amongst larger, stronger nations. Rose's autobiographical story 'The Blue Bead' relates how she shared with Edith Durham the disapproval by local authorities over the undertaking of such an expedition as theirs amongst the interior tribes of northern Albania .[6]

There are other parallels of Rose Wilder Lane's to Edith Durham's journeys. They both set out on these adventurous trips in their late thirties, Edith Durham on doctor's advice to 'get right away, no matter where, so long as the change is complete'; Rose attributed her restlessness to the war in Europe: 'the real trouble is that the war overshadows everything', she wrote in her diary.[7] Both developed a tremendous love for the country, a respect for what they saw as an independent, unique, brave-spirited people; were fascinated by the working of the Laws of Lek which intricately prescribed behaviour concerning blood-feuds, and which in turn dictated all social behaviour. In fact, both were protected by these ancient laws which guarded women at the cost of the lives of men – if any man dishonoured a woman in any way at all, it was considered correct that such man should be killed.

A Greek woman, Demetra Vaka, described in 1917 her recent travels with her diplomat brother and other officials.[8] One of these officials – a Frenchman by the name of M. Gaston Decourt – wore a flower which belonged to a certain woman with whom he had been seen conversing. By its wearing it was considered that he had insulted her family and tribe. He was shot dead for this wrongdoing. But the Laws of Lek forbade anyone ever to shoot to kill in the presence of a woman. Similar respect was given to any guest, even if the guest was the strongest rival of the host. No host would shoot such a guest until he had been hospitably treated and escorted off the tribal land and was thus no longer a guest. Hence the delight of the Shala guide who purposely took Rose off her route into many homes of the rival Shoshi tribe, revelling in the hospitality his enemies had to show him in the presence of a woman.[9] Had he been alone they would have shot him.

Young boys were equally vulnerable to being shot for no greater crime than being of the family or even the tribe of a woman who had declined to marry the man chosen for her (and paid for) at, or even before birth. For this reason it was often considered too dangerous for boys to walk the long distance to any form of school. Very young boys, boys who were too young to have their hair cut, were exempt, hence many wore long hair as protection.

In *Peaks of Shala* we also get a description of the *besa* (the inviolable oath of peace between tribes or families) which confirms Edith Durham's descriptions, but disputes her contention that more modern methods of dealing with blood-feuds had evolved.[10] Rose Wilder Lane gives plenty of evidence that little had changed in the intervening ten years. As does Edith Durham, so also Rose Wilder Lane gives wonderful descriptions of her climbs into the Chafa Bishkasit[11] (one of the high ranges of mountains in northern

Albania) and of the system of 'telegraphing' across mountains, which the Albanians did not by shouting or singing, but by means of long shrill continuous high notes ending with three fired shots to indicate the end of a message. The almost constant use of shots to register welcome or farewell persisted from the time of Durham's visits, but such exuberance was never given for the benefit of solely female company, there had to be men present where there was shooting.

A further, perhaps consequent parallel between Rose Wilder Lane and Edith Durham was that their involvement in the country led them later to pursue relief work in the area.

These travellers underwent terrific ordeals. They were unaccustomed to the local manner of travel, and they found the trails (they could never be called roads or even paths) very rough, steep and hazardous and the distances extreme (measured only by the hours or days it took for nimble Albanians to walk).[12] The conditions were not improved by the almost constant rain which both describe. Rose tells of fording rivers sometimes on the shoulders of men who shifted them from shoulder to shoulder mid-stream, like sacks of produce. Many of their mountain climbs were on extremely precarious routes. Their progress contrasts vividly with that of a native woman of Shoshi of whom she tells:

> Up the trail came a woman of Shoshi. . . . On her back, held by woven woolen straps that crossed between her breasts, was a cradle tightly covered by a thick blanket; in one hand she held a bunch of raw wool, and from the other dangled a whirling spindle. Her feet were bare and as she came up the trail which had exhausted me, she sang softly, dexterously spinning thread from the bunch of wool . . . (yet) . . . her hands and feet would have been madness to a sculptor, in Paris she would have been a sensation.[13]

These Western women had further to contend with being special guests and the bearers of news, and as such great feasts were prepared in their honour. But the preparation for the feasts only started upon their arrival, which was always late at night when they were already cold, wet and tired. Upon arrival, whether in private homes, monasteries or schools, they were given, as traditional all over Albania, overwhelming hospitality; but hospitality which was hard to enjoy. Instead of a chance to get dry and warm and to rest, the travellers were always expected to sit in their wet clothing and sociably discuss current events; to await the festive meal which usually took several hours to prepare, often served at one or two in the morning, by which time these weary foreign visitors were too tired to get pleasure from it. In one home where they stayed, a young lamb, a young kid and a chicken, all very used to human company and much fondled by the children, were first shown for admiration to the guests, then all taken out, killed, skinned, cooked and finally consumed. It was considered impolite to show any signs of either tiredness or hunger. Furthermore, many mornings' journeys started at around 3.30 or 4 a.m. with only a cup of black coffee for sustenance before the start of the day's trek. These details comply exactly with Durham's descriptions.

John Hodgson tells that Edith Durham was known as 'Queen of the Mountain People', and William Anderson notes that Rose Wilder Lane also became a national hero. The northern tribes-people translated her name literally as 'Flower of the Road'. Reputedly King Zog asked Rose Wilder Lane to marry him. As with all marriages in Albania at that time, this would probably not have involved romantic attachments, but rather it would have been regarded as for the good of his people. Perhaps he felt that as an American she would have advice as to how to modernise Albania; and he did in fact take her advice in the placement of an airport near Tirana. The tribal chief Lulash of Thethi made an offer also to marry her, putting her value at the equivalent of $2,000 for the benefits that he felt his tribe would gain. He did not consider how it would affect him personally, as he said: 'people do not expect happiness in marriage; happiness comes from other things'. When asked why he had chosen Rose of the three American women, it transpired that the other two had long hair and Lulash had surmised thereby that they were already married. Rose with short hair, and wearing trousers, symbolised to Lulash her equivalence with an 'Albanian virgin', a woman who, refusing to marry the man to whom she was betrothed in childhood or before, promised never to marry anyone.[14] Such women in Albania then led the life of men, cut their hair short, dressed as men, did men's work, and carried rifles. Thus her betrothed man did not lose his honour, and therefore did not need to seek vengeance upon her family. However, Lulash felt he would be safe from the wrath of Rose's original betrothed since America was so far away.[15]

It does not appear that Rose Wilder Lane met Edith Durham or even read her books. She makes only passing reference to them; recording that the Catholic Bishop at Pultit had met Durham ten years earlier, had heard that she had written a book and wished he could have afforded to acquire a copy.[16]

There were many aspects of Albania that especially appealed to Rose Wilder Lane. She admired how the tribes she visited had avoided being conquered by either the Romans or the Turks, even if they had been influenced by both. She also admired how they lived as a 'simple communistic society, without private property or any organized government, the only law is the moral law, enforced by tradition, by custom, by consent'.[17] She became very excited by the outlandishly unusual demand made by one woman of Pultit who, having built a house with her husband, felt that upon his recent death she and her two sons should be allowed to be the sole occupants of that house. Rose wrote: 'I was seeing with my own eyes the invention of private property'.[18] The outraged village members engaged her in long argument concerning this issue; for they had put the woman's brother-in-law and a total of sixteen family members into that house, telling her that she was most welcome to either remain there with them or to take her two sons and live with any other family in the village. Rose tried unsuccessfully to explain the American system. The theme reappears in her book *Discovery of Freedom*, some years later.[19]

Rose Wilder Lane found a strong sense of national pride amongst all the Albanians she met – she was told that throughout history the northern Albanian tribes had, often with much fighting and great sacrifice, managed not to fall under the rule of any other country. Even though Albania's boundaries may have been diminished, never had the country been submerged into another nation, as had been the case for so many other Balkan peoples. She heard stories of world famous men who were believed to have been of Albanian origin. For example, Philip II of Macedonia wanted his son (now known to us as Alexander the Great), who was born in Emadhija, to be taught the wisdom of Greek learning, but in the hands of an Albanian.

Such a one, it was claimed, was Aristotle, born of an Albanian merchant living in Macedonia who sent his son to Greece for schooling.[20] Cicero was reported to have spent much time (and money) in the merry wicked city of Durrës – he had been forced to send back to Rome for money. Rose tells of heroic songs sung of:

> the men who have been driven . . . to become the khedives of Egypt, pashas . . . of Turkey, political leaders in Italy, great surgeons of France. From all these countries men are coming back now to make the new free government of Albania.[21]

Whilst the tribes of northern Albania claimed mostly to be Roman Catholic, many of their customs and habits were either Muslim or pagan. For example, turbaned and fezzed men were often seen in Roman Catholic processions. Eastern-dressed women often went unveiled whilst some, otherwise in European clothing, were seen veiled. The Bishop of Pultit observed that, while they attended Mass regularly, the Church had not greatly altered the ancient customs of the people. He was tolerant of the fact that the basis of many tribal ceremonies was fire-worship.[22] Religion amongst these tribes was completely subordinate to the working of the Laws of Lek, so that for instance, blood-feud killings could never be seen as murder.

Other spiritual beings also featured frequently in the lives of these people who watched for signs from the *ora* (spirits of the forest, souls of trees or rocks). We are told that the Greeks called the Albanian *ora* 'oreads'; and one of the tales Rose heard she recognised as one which she had heard as a Greek myth. This was the tale of the man of Mali Sharit who wanted to marry a water *ora*, and achieved his wish with the help of a wise woman, only to lose her and their three-day-old child when he tried vainly to break her year-long total silence.[23] Even the European-educated Perolli believed in the powers of the *ora* and told of a man he knew 'who called the large magpie to watch him bury his treasure' for the protection of the spirit of that native bird.[24] The travellers were shown a place where *ora* love to sit, where 'no human person lives' in the ruins of the old town of Pog, which was built 'by men of the land of the Eagle ... before men began to remember'.[25] Throughout *Peaks of Shala* there are references to people who have been in touch with the *ora*, including a man from Ipek who married one, and had *ora* children. (His wife and children were never visible to other mortals; but his home was well kept and he was happy.)[26] Rose herself describes feeling a presence in the Wood of the Ora:

> I ... felt an uncanny sensation while going through that narrow dark defile between gray cliffs. The trees stood thickly there, climbing the bowlder-strewn slope; they were cut, like all the trees of the mountains to mere limbless stumps, and they were very old. They seemed for centuries to have writhed under the blows of shepherds' axes; they were contorted as if in pain; their few half-amputated branches were like mutilated arms. Beyond them rose rocks, perhaps five hundred feet high, evil-looking cliffs contorted like the trees, and these faced, above our heads, a smooth sheer wall of tilted grey limestone that overhung the trail. Our men stopped singing. . . . How do we know that there are *ora* in the Albanian mountains? Because all the Albanians who live here have heard them, and many have seen them.[27]

Rose Wilder Lane found northern Albania rich in folklore. Weather could be explained by the behaviour of the *drangojt* (dragons with wings) which would cause rain and thunder storms and could also dispel these.[28]

She often tried to find reasons for observed habits, but was too often answered: 'it is the custom'. However, she found this a useful explanation herself sometimes, especially in explaining their apparent need to wash daily:

> 'We do this every morning – it is American custom – every morning we wash the children and the babies all over, from head to foot.' 'Yes?' said the (Albanian) woman indifferently, 'Here babies stay in their cradles. Children go into the water when they are old enough to swim. Then only in the summer, when it is not cold'.[29]

In the same way Edith Durham could only satisfy the curiosity of those she met concerning the wheat she wore on her head (her straw hat), by explaining that it was a British custom.[30] Both these writers commented on the use of the breastbone of a chicken which had lived all its life in one family, to tell the fortune of those in the family.[31] The tales she heard and the experiences she had during these years in Albania helped supply Rose Wilder Lane with themes for some of her many short stories in years to come.[32]

Rose Wilder Lane ended her first trip to Albania rather abruptly, feeling a sudden urgency to return to Paris at a moment when the physical conditions in which she had been living were making her ill. The following year she returned with a photographer friend, Annette Marquis who took the photographs which illustrate her *Peaks of Shala*. One photo is captioned: 'Once a day she comes walking over 15 miles of mountain trails', and shows a woman carrying her wares to market 'knitting on the way'. Another shows a bandit whom they met in a cave. He sang to them, and discussed life as a bandit. In the Postscript to *Peaks of Shala*, written after this later visit with Annette Marquis, Lane tells of the revolution that surrounded them, and which brought Zog to power. A picture of the 'fighting men who came into Tirana to defend the government' shows men from seven tribes, distinguishable by the pattern of their trousers.

Rose's last visit to Albania was planned as a very long stay. By this time (1926) she had learned Albanian, had contacts in Albania and invited her friend, the author, Helen Dore Boylston (whom she first met on a train from Paris to Warsaw) to join her. Helen Boylston the daughter of a physician, had considered a medical career, balked at the long study necessary to become a doctor, and trained instead as a nurse. She volunteered for service with a medical unit from Harvard in a field hospital in Europe, 1917–18, and with a mobile unit outside Tirana in 1920, at the time of national uprising when Italian forces, then occupying Vlorë and other parts of Albania, were driven out.[33] Like Rose Wilder Lane, Helen Boylston felt unsettled by the effects of war in Europe and an urge to take on an active role in world affairs. When a friend suggested to her that she should go on this assignment to the Balkans, she was ecstatic.

> Daddy wants me to settle down, but I'm young! I'm young! Why shouldn't I live? What is old age if it has no memories except of 40 years or so of blank days?[34]

William Holtz explains the eagerness of Lane and Boylston to leave the US:

> The initial European experience had in fact alienated them from their homeland, which in the boom years of the 1920s struck them as hectic, provincial and crassly commercial. Albania with its Mediterranean climate and its people still unspoiled by modern ways, began to glimmer in their imaginations as a Shangri-la.[35]

So, on 20 August 1926, these two women and their reluctant French maid, Yvonne, set off by car. The adventures of the trip are described in Holtz's book of edited letters from the women to their relatives and friends in the US.

The trio arrived in Durrës in two weeks, travelling through Italy and across from Brindisi – this would be no mean feat even today. The plan was to have a villa built and to live there on the earnings of the two writers, sending material back to the US for publication. But life was not as idyllic as they expected. They began to see Albania as:

> trembling in a kind of primal innocence, on the verge of a corrupt modern world, it seemed to be a final sanctuary, where its leader, King Zog, struggled to unify warring factions . . . and to develop a rudimentary foreign policy.[36]

It seems that after only one and a half years family complications in the US called them back; and thereafter political developments made any return to Albania both harder and, to them, less desirable.

Rose had difficulty maintaining contact with those she knew in Albania after she left, although she did manage to send Rexh Meta (the twelve-year-old of her first trip) to Cambridge University in Britain, and to keep sufficiently in touch with him to learn that, in spite of his unusual education he returned to Albania to marry into traditional society.

The excitement and romanticism which Rose Wilder Lane obviously attached to her adopted country turned sour on her as she saw the political upheavals develop by the late twenties. The disillusionment which she must have felt as she saw Zog's regime ineffective in countering the stronger outside influences, especially from Italy, allowed her no possibility to return to Albania. Her writing during the thirties returned to the more mundane stories depicting life in small town America: 'Woman's Place is in the Home',[37] 'Object, Matrimony',[38] and 'Pie Supper'.[39]

After her father's death in 1949, Rose devoted much time to her mother until Laura's death in 1957, when Lane became involved in turning her parents' home into a museum: The Laura Ingalls Wilder Home Association of Mansfield, Missouri. Rose Wilder Lane died in 1968 at the age of 81 on the eve of a planned trip around the world.

Notes

1. Rose Wilder Lane, *Henry Ford's Own Story*, Forest Hills, NY: E.O. Jones, 1917.
2. This project was funded through efforts of Frances Hardy and Miss Alexander (known in *Peaks of Shala* as Alex), but there is no mention which were the other two schools besides the proposed one at Thethi.
3. *Peaks of Shala*, New York and London: Harper and Brothers, Publishers, 1923, Introduction.
4. *Ibid.*, pp. 65 and 86.
5. He was one of the 25,000 refugees in Scutari at the time, but being neither female nor under 12, was given no help, instead had taken it upon himself to care for five younger refugees.
6. Rose Wilder Lane, 'The Blue Bead', *Harper's Magazine*, Vol. 151, June, 1925.
7. 8 August 1918, quoted in William Holtz, ed. *Travels with Zenobia. Paris to Albania by Model T Ford*, Columbia and London: University of Missouri Press, 1983.
8. Demetra Vaka (Mrs Kenneth Brown), *The Heart of the Balkans*, New York and Boston: Houghton Mifflin, Co., 1917.
9. *Peaks of Shala*, p. 245.
10. Detailed documentation of the existence of blood-feuding into the 1930s may be found in Margaret Hasluck's *The Unwritten Law in Albania*, Cambridge University Press, 1954.
11. *Peaks of Shala*, pp. 7-8.

12. *Ibid.*, p. 46. More recently, Dymphna Cusack also encountered this method of measuring distance. See her, *Illyria Reborn*, London: Heinemann, 1966.
13. *Peaks of Shala*, pp. 12–13.
14. M.E. Durham, *High Albania*, London: Virago, 1985, p. 156.
15. *Peaks of Shala*, pp. 207–8.
16. *Ibid.*, p. 25.
17. *Ibid.*, p. 29.
18. *Ibid.*, p. 107.
19. Rose Wilder Lane, *The Discovery of Freedom*, New York: John Day Co., 1943.
20. *Peaks of Shala*, p. 186.
21. *Ibid.*, p. 89.
22. *Ibid.*, p. 26.
23. *Ibid.*, p. 171.
24. *Ibid.*, p. 48.
25. *Ibid.*, p. 44.
26. *Ibid.*, p. 65.
27. *Ibid.*, pp. 94–6.
28. *Ibid.*, pp. 215–7.
29. *Ibid.*, p. 85.
30. *High Albania*, p. 258.
31. *Ibid.*, p. 64; *Peaks of Shala*, p. 132.
32. The following are a few of her stories relating to the Balkans: 'Padre Luigi of Kiri', *Harper's Magazine*, Vol. 147, June, 1923. 'Edelweiss on Chafa Shalit', *Harper's Magazine*, Vol. 147, November, 1923. 'The Blue Bead', *Harper's Magazine*, Vol.151, June, 1925. 'Nice Old Lady', *Saturday Evening Post*, 6 July, 1935. 'Song Without Words', *Ladies' Home Journal*, Vol.54, August, 1937.
33. 'Everyday Life' in *Atlantic Monthly*.
34. Quoted in Holtz, *op. cit.*, p. 6.
35. *Ibid.*, p. 10.
36. *Ibid.*, p. 27.
37. *Ladies' Home Journal*, Vol. 53, October, 1936.
38. *Saturday Evening Post*, Vol. 207, September, 1934.
39. *American Magazine*, Vol. 118, October, 1934.

Bibliography

Anderson, William, *Laura's Rose*, Mansfield, Laura Ingalls Wilder Home Association, 1976.

Anderson, William, *Rose Wilder Lane Lore*, Vol. 12, No. 2, 5 December 1986.

Anderson, William, 'The Literary Apprenticeship of Laura Ingalls Wilder', in *South Dakota History*, Winter, 1983.

Boylston, Helen Dore, 'Everyday Life' in *Atlantic Monthly*, 136, September-November, 1925, quoted in Holtz.

Cusack, Dymphna, *Illyria Reborn*, London: Heinemann, 1966.

Durham, M. Edith, in J.A. Hammerton (ed.), *Peoples of All Nations*, London: Educational Book Co. Ltd., n.d.

Durham, M. Edith, *High Albania*, London: Virago, 1985.

Hasluck, Margaret, *The Unwritten Law in Albania*, Cambridge University Press, 1954.

Holtz, William (ed.), *Travels with Zenobia. Paris to Albania by Model T Ford*, Columbia and London: University of Missouri Press, 1983.

Lane, Rose Wilder, *Discovery of Freedom*, John Day Co., 1943.

Lane, Rose Wilder, *Diverging Roads*, New York: Century, 1919.

Lane, Rose Wilder, *Peaks of Shala*, New York: Harper and Batters, 1923.

Logoreci, Anton, *The Albanians, Europe's Forgotten Survivors*, Boulder CO: Westview Press, 1977.

MacBride, Roger Lea, *Rose Wilder Lane: Her Story*, Stein & Day, 1977.

National Geographic Magazine, October 1980, p.539.

Swire, J., *King Zog's Albania*, New York: Liveright Pub. Corp., 1937.

Vaka, Demetra (Mrs. Kenneth Brown), *The Heart of the Balkans*, New York and Boston: Houghton Mifflin, Co., 1917.

Wilder, Laura Ingalls, *On the Way Home*, New York: Harper Trophy, 1962.

Wilder, Laura Ingalls, *West from Home*, ed. Roger Lea MacBride, New York: Harper Trophy, 1974.

The author would like to acknowledge the help of:
William Anderson, editor of the Laura Ingalls Wilder and Rose Wilder Lane papers
Bill Bland of the British Albanian Society
Susan Buckley, Birmingham, England
William Holtz, Prof. of English, University of Missouri, Columbus Mo.
Irene Licty-Le Count, curator of the Laura Ingalls Wilder Museum, Rocky Ridge Farm, Mansfield, Mo., 65704
Dwight Miller, librarian, Herbert Hoover Library, West Branch, Iowa

CHAPTER 8

They defended the customs that suited them as savagely as they would attack anyone who tried to take from them lovers that suited them. Many of them were ugly, a certain number of them looked cruel, they wore dark clothes with an air of murderous thrift and contempt for lightness. But they were all splendidly themselves, having been compelled by the extreme degree of their aggressiveness to throw aside everything that was not real and necessary to them and worth the trouble, which in their case was apt to be furiously inordinate, of defending. 'What an amusing people to live among!' Isobel thought affectionately.

Rebeeca West, *The Thinking Reed,* Ch. 10.

Rebecca West, Gerda and the Sense of Process

Felicity Rosslyn

Rebecca West's relations with Yugoslavia in the 1930s were nothing short of a love affair, with a period of rapturous discovery, rising to a generous climax in the writing of *Black Lamb and Grey Falcon,* followed by bitter post-war recrimination, lawsuits and silence. The relationship had another characteristic of passionate affairs: one party saw in the other a solution to a central problem that had preoccupied them from long before, so that the violence of the break-up reflected a philosophical shock as well as a human betrayal: the solution was no solution, one would have to build the world anew. I do not imagine anyone mistakes *Black Lamb and Grey Falcon* for a mere travelogue, but unless one knows all the rest of the author's work, it is not so clear what the central thesis is, that Rebecca West was pinning on Yugoslavia. And unless one knows Yugoslavia, it is not so clear how the thesis came unstuck; so I should like to explain what I take to be the inner mechanism of this love affair, the hope that powered it, and the shock that ended it; in the expectation that, along the way, we will touch on truths of central importance to both parties.

One can trace a fascination with the interrelations of large powers with small, both in the work of Rebecca West and in her biography; and in this sense she was looking for Yugoslavia before she found it. She saw one potential configuration in the history of Finland, and learnt Finnish in preparation for writing about it:

> as a wonderful case of a small nation with empires here and there . . . But then, when I went to Yugoslavia for the British Council, I saw it was much more exciting with Austria and Russia and Turkey, and so I wrote that. I really did enjoy it terribly, loved it.[1]

We can see that the resulting book could never have been a factual record, capable of verification, from an illuminating comment she makes on D.H. Lawrence's travel writing. She once met him by chance in Florence, in the company of Norman Douglas, who had already told her about Lawrence's habit on arriving in any new place of going 'straight from the railway station to his hotel and immediately sit(ting) down and hammer(ing) out articles about the place, vehemently and exhaustively describing the temperament of the people. This seemed obviously a silly thing to do, and here he was doing it' in a 'small, mean room' at the rear of a hotel on the Arno.[2] But after Lawrence's death she looked back on her response as naive, and made handsome amends:[3]

> I know now that he was writing about the state of his own soul at that moment, which, since our self-consciousness is incomplete, and since in consequence our vocabulary also is incomplete, he could only render in symbolic terms; and the city of Florence was as good a symbol as any other. If he was foolish in taking the material universe and making allegations about it that were true only of the universe within his own soul, then Rimbaud was a great fool also. Or to go further back, so too was Dante, who made a new Heaven and Hell and Purgatory as a symbol for the geography within his own breast, and so too was St Augustine, when in *The City of God* he writes an attack on the pagan world, which is unjust so long as it is regarded as an account of events on the material plane, but which is beyond price as an account of the conflict in his soul between that which tended to death and that which tended to life. Lawrence was in fact no different from any other great artist who has felt the urgency to describe the unseen so keenly that he has rifled the seen of its vocabulary and diverted it to that purpose.

'If (Lawrence) was foolish in taking the material universe and making allegations about it that were true only of the universe within his own soul, then Rimbaud was a great fool also': and so, we may add, was Rebecea West. I cannot think of a better description of her method than that she 'rifled the seen of its vocabulary and diverted it' to the purpose of describing the unseen; or a better explanation for the kind of intellectual joy we may feel in reading *Black Lamb and Grey Falcon* at being given a vocabulary for discussing matters normally very hard to describe, yet of surpassing urgency, for us as well as the author. There is another remark she makes about Lawrence's greatness which is relevant here: we should rejoice, she says, 'that our age produced one artist who had the earnestness of the patristic writers, who like them could know no peace till he had discovered what made men lust after death'.[4]

'What makes men lust after death' is the central theme of *Black Lamb and Grey Falcon*. Indeed, if we decode her symbolism, it is really the book's title: the black lamb is offered by a gipsy for blood sacrifice on St George's Eve, in illustration of what she calls 'the repulsive pretence' of Western thought 'that pain is the proper price of any good thing';[5] and the grey falcon is the epic bird who offers Tsar Lazar a choice between an earthly kingdom and a heavenly one before the Battle of Kosovo. He, of course, chooses the heavenly one, and loses his earthly one to the Turks in consequence. 'So that was what happened', she remarks dryly, standing on the empty plain of Kosovo: 'Lazar was a member of the Peace Pledge Union'.[6] Rebecca West, like Lawrence, travelled in pursuit of herself and everything else she had left behind.

We can understand this in several different ways. As with this remark about the Peace Pledge Union, Yugoslavia helped her focus her thoughts about the political situation in Europe at the end of the 1930s. She found herself on the opposite side from the liberal and enlightened spirits who were for appeasing Hitler, thus subtly preparing a future for their civilisation as barren as the plain of Kosovo. Yugoslavia offered her a vocabulary in which to express the limitations of Western rationalism, and expose its underground links with the will-to-die. Beyond the immediate political crisis, however, Yugoslavia offered her scope for the widest possible speculation about the interrelation of small cultures and empires, a subject that seems to have preoccupied her since her schooldays at George Watson's Ladies College. There, she was imbued with a Roman culture which had flourished by suppressing or deleting many others; and the young Cicily Fairfield (half-Irish, living in Scotland) had the liveliest curiosity about the Carthaginian view of Rome. In Yugoslavia she was privileged to watch a young culture struggling into autonomy after a long history of domination, commented on by 'Constantine' (Stanislav) Vinaver, one of its most enlightened spirits, and with 'the quality of visibility that makes the Balkans so specially enchanting'.[7] And lastly, and most privately, she found in Yugoslavia her equivalent of Augustine's City of God-living proof that the love of life can prevail over the love of death. Rebecca West did not merely love Yugoslavia, she believed in it: and here we come to the delicate area where the potential pain and betrayal of her love affair are located; for no-one understood or annotated more scrupulously than Rebecca West the discrepancies between the spiritual and the material planes of existence, but here she finally abandoned precaution and proclaimed the belief that they were one. I shall return to the price she paid for that faith at a later stage, but here I will sum up all these considerations in the simplest way, with a quotation from a speech made by (or put in the mouth of) her husband: 'If Europeans have not the virtues of the Macedonian peasant, our life is lost, and we are the greenfly on the rose tree that has been torn up and thrown on the rubbish-heap.'[8]

This remarkable statement comes at the end of a long exposition of the meaning of Constantine's German wife, Gerda – which explains my title, 'Gerda and the Sense of Process'. For here, in the space of a few pages, we have a concentrated analysis of the nature of the German threat to Europe and the only possible antidote to it, which Henry Maxwell Andrews calls 'the sense of process'; and if I had to point to a single thesis at the heart of the book, to which all its other theses were related, it would be this; for it manages to be at once historical, mythical, and visionary, as you see from the language of the remark that precedes the one I have just quoted: 'But the Turks are here, for Gerda is here, and Europe is in her soul Macedonia.'

'Gerda is here' in the sense that she had invited herself to be the guest of Rebecca West and her husband as they travelled through Macedonia with Constantine, generating ugliness, shame and embarrassment with the assiduity of a moral somnambulist. But politically speaking, 'Gerda is here' in the sense of the German presence in the centre of Europe; and this was equivalent of saying 'the Turks are here' because the empire Gerda threatened to establish had all the hallmarks of the Turkish one, not least in marrying rapacity with the inability to generate its own wealth. The exposition of Gerda's meaning comes while Constantine is seeing her off on the Belgrade train, and the others sit outside their hotel with a drink, feeling 'weak but contented, like fever patients whose temperature has at last fallen':

> My husband bought some guelder roses from an Albanian, laid them on the table, contemplated them for some moments, and said:
> 'Gerda has no sense of process, That is what is the matter with Gerda. She wants the result without doing any of the work that goes to make it. She wants to enjoy the position of a wife without going to the trouble of making a real marriage, without admiring her husband for his good qualities, without practising loyal discretion regarding his bad qualities, without respecting those of his gods which are not hers. She wants to enjoy motherhood without taking care of her children, without training them in good manners or giving them a calm atmosphere. She wants to be our friend, to be so close to us in friendship that we will ask her to travel around the country with us, but she does not make the slightest effort to like us, or even to conceal that she dislikes us. She is angry when you are paid such little respect as comes your way because you are a well-known writer, she feels it ought to come to her also, though she has never written any books. She is angry because we have some money. She feels that it might just as well belong to her. That our possession of this money has something to do with my work in the City and my family's work in Burma never occurs to her. For her the money might as easily have been attached to her as to us by a movement as simple as that which pastes a label on a trunk. As she has no sense of what goes to bring people love, or friendship, or distinction, or wealth, it seems to her that the whole world is enjoying undeserved benefits; and in a universe where all is arbitrary it might just as well happen that the injustice was pushed a little further and that all these benefits were taken from other people, leaving them nothing, and transferred to her, giving her everything.'

With the eye of the banker he was, Andrews notes the connection between this bewilderment, economic weakness and the threat of aggression wherever this type of personality emerges:

> 'It seems to me that it appears wherever people are subject to two conditions. The first condition is that they should have lost sight of the importance of process; that they have forgotten that everything which is not natural is artificial and that artifice is painful and difficult; that they should be able to look at a loaf of bread and not realize that miracles of endurance and ingenuity had to be performed before the wheat grew, and the mill ground, and the oven baked. This condition can be brought about by several causes: one is successful imperialism, where the conquering people has the loaf built for it from the wheat ear up by its conquered subjects; another is modern machine civilization,

where a small but influential proportion of the population lives in towns in such artificial conditions that a loaf of bread comes to them in a cellophane wrapper with its origins as unvisualised as the begetting and birth of a friend's baby. The other condition is that people should have acquired a terror of losing the results of process, which are all they know about; they must be afraid that everything artificial is going to disappear, and they are going to be thrown back on the natural; they must foresee with a shudder a day when there will be no miraculous loaf born in its virginity of cellophane, and they will have to eat grass . . .

Gerda is bourgeoise and town-bred. She is proud because her family are all professional men; it is of importance to her that she cannot bake a loaf, she likes to buy her cakes in a shop. Her theory of her own social value depends on her being able to put down money and buy results of processes without being concerned in the processes themselves. And she is enormously afraid that she will not be able to go on doing this. The war made her afraid; the depression has made her still more afraid. It does not occur to her that what she and her kind must do is to reorganize the process of state life 'till there is some sort of guarantee of a certain amount of artificial goods for all of us. It does not occur to her that she had better learn to bake bread instead of buying it, for since her social value depends on her not doing so, she regards this as a sentence of death. Therefore she wants to take results that belong to other people: she wants to bone everybody else's loaf.'[9]

I must not dwell on the meaning of Gerda for the Second World War, fascinating as that is, or the value of this economic analysis, which gives the term 'alienation' a richer significance than Marx himself gave it. Our subject here is not the immediate political context, but the mythological value of Gerda, whom Rebecca West had been looking for, so to speak, before she found her. Gerda is the epitome of one of her obsessions: the human being without discipline, who brings destruction in her wake not through malice, but pure ignorance.

Gerda's problem is that the mystery of process is so hidden from her that the universe seems purely arbitrary. She is like a child born deaf, surrounded by movements of lips she cannot interpret: her frustration rises to a crescendo of tantrums and violence, in the effort to snatch what she cannot otherwise obtain. The mystery she has not fathomed is really the mystery of creativity; for the reason Rebecca West dwells on the phrase 'the sense of process' is that it stands for the means by which we can all become artists – capable of exploring the universe by collaborating with its processes. Hence the horror with which she draws the various characters in her novels who are not disciplined, who do not submit themselves to external reality. There are two of them, significantly, in a novel called *The Thinking Reed*, which she wrote just before her first journey to Yugoslavia. One is the appalling Aunt Agatha, who bullies her servants, her family and her guests with animal brutality, yet is viewed in her aristocratic circle as a magnificent *grande dame*. She has her counterpart in *Black Lamb*, in the Archduchess Sophie who poisoned the existence of the Empress Elizabeth, and of whom Rebecca West sardonically remarks, 'She was the kind of woman whom men respect for no other reason than that she is lethal, whom a male committee will appoint to the post of hospital matron.'[10] The other character, who is dismayed by Aunt Agatha, yet sees 'she is terribly like what I might be in my old age, if I do not alter my way of living', is the beautiful heiress Isabelle. What frightens her is precisely that she has never had to submit to the discipline of any process; and she ends the novel clinging to the two things that offer her her first discipline, childbirth and the loss of a large part of her income in the Wall Street Crash.

It might seem a large and rather loose assumption to make, that we are all capable of being artists: but Rebecca West can justify it by the wide meaning she gives to the term art. Art, she says, 'is not a plaything, but a necessity, and its essence, form, is not a decorative adjustment, but a cup into which life can be poured and lifted to the lips and be tasted.'[11]

Thus every 'form' we make is a means of inquiry into the nature of life itself – an inquiry which is not a pastime but an urgent necessity, just as it is urgent to eat and drink in order to sustain life. The illustration of Gerda's sterility through her attitude to baking is not the triviality it might appear, either in Henry Maxwell Andrews' remark about the 'miraculous loaf born in its virginity of cellophane', or the episode in Belgrade which foreshadowed it, when Gerda had her guests to tea:

> Contemptuously she told us that when a Serbian family expected guests to tea, the housewife would put herself about to bake cakes and biscuits; but, as we would see, she said with a shrug of the shoulders, indicating the food on her table, which had obviously been bought from a shop, she was not so. Her cool tone drew a picture of how she would like to dispense hospitality. One could go down, well dressed, with a full purse, and all one's debts paid, to Kranzler if one lived in Berlin, to Dehmel if one lived in Vienna, to Gerbeaud if one lived in Budapest, and one would greet the assistant, who would be very respectful because of one's credit, and would choose exquisite pastries

and *petits fours*, which would not only be delightful when crushed against one's friends' palates, but would also be recognizably from Kranzler, or from Dehmel, or from Gerbeaud.

She was assuming that my husband and I would share her feeling, that we would be with her in upholding this cool, powerful, unhurried ideal against the Serbian barbarians who liked a woman to get hot over a stove, as if she could not afford to pay other women to work for her, which indeed was probably the case. It would have been difficult for us to explain how wrong we thought her. We like the *Apfelkuchen* of Kranzler, we have never gone to Vienna without buying the *Nusstorte* of Dehmel, we have been shamefully late for a friend's lunch in Budapest for the reason that we had turned into Gerbeaud's to eat meringues filled with cream and strawberries. But we knew that when one goes into a shop and buys a cake one gets nothing but a cake, which may be very good but it is only a cake; whereas if one goes into the kitchen and makes a cake because some people one respects and probably likes are coming to eat at one's table, one is striking a low note on a scale that is struck higher up by Beethoven and Mozart. We believed it better to create than to pay.[12]

Even a home-made cake is a 'form', a wrestling with the mystery of process, from which we are bound to learn something of value. If the cake should be a failure, it is an addition to our sense of the mystery; and even if it is a success, the wonder remains at how things material are transmuted into immaterial meaning – how a cake may strike a low note 'on a scale that is struck higher up by Beethoven and Mozart.' Compared with this, the 'cool, powerful, unhurried' detachment Gerda seeks is pure weakness, and quickly revealed as such by the inflation of the Deutschmark. She lacks, we may say, the peasant virtues: which returns us to our starting point some minutes ago; the statement that 'If Europeans have not the virtues of the Macedonian peasant, our life is lost.'

By 'the Macedonian peasant' Rebecca West means not merely the submission to natural processes which all peasant life, as a matter of definition, involves, but the transmutation of that into intelligence. Again and again in Macedonia she was struck by the fullness of knowledge in the peasant faces she encountered, and the wisdom implicit in the artistic forms they excelled in – embroidery, dance, church ritual, which all had their roots in Byzantium, and continued to express the great truths that culture had discovered about life and death.

It is somehow inevitable that Gerda should behave worst in Macedonia, and supply Rebecca West with a scene that sums up her thesis with a precision that lies somewhere between pleasure and pain. This is one of the occasions one is devoutly glad not to have been present at, and is very glad to hear of: a church feast at the end of the Easter celebrations, at the centre of which is the character who carries Rebecca West's central meaning about process and creativity on his magnificently broad shoulders, Bishop Nikolai of the Orthodox Church. The Bishop is a supreme artist in the sense I have been struggling to give the term: that is, he is a genius at casting life into 'form' and 'lifting it to the lips to be tasted'. This is, of course, what church ritual does, both literally and metaphorically, when it makes large gestures with the wine and chalice: but it is not every Bishop who can make the magic of the ritual prevail, or who can recreate it out of commoner materials – hard-boiled eggs and sheep's cheese, at a table to which unwelcome guests have invited themselves. Rebecca West perfectly knows that the Bishop 'was not at all glad to see us. I was aware that he did not like Constantine and that he was not sure of me, that he thought I might turn and rend any situation at which he permitted me to be present by some Western treachery' – but:

> He struck me now, as when I had seen him for the first time in the previous year, as the most remarkable human being I have ever met, not because he was wise or good, for I have still no idea to what degree he is either, but because he was the supreme magician. He had command over the means of making magic, in his great personal beauty, which was of the lion's kind, and in the thundering murmur of his voice, which by its double quality, grand and yet guttural, suggests that he could speak to gods and men and beasts. He had full knowledge of what comfort men seek in magic, and how they long to learn that defeat is not defeat and that love is serviceable. He had a warm knowledge of how magic can prove this up to the hilt. He had a cold knowledge, which he would not share with any living thing, of the limited avail of magic, and how its victories cannot be won on the material battlefield where man longs to see them. He was so apt for magic that had it not existed he would have invented it. He saw all earth as its expression.[13]

Bishop Nikolai's magic is a sublime version of the Macedonian embroideries which dilate on the process of existence with such authority. But what they achieve in the sphere of matter, he achieves in time and space: the continual meaning of the resurrection, which means the annihilation of death through love. His 'sense of process' is so complete that he cannot be said to *have* such a sense – he *is* the process, just as his love embraces the scene as a whole, in spite of his personal dislike of these Western unbelievers. The ritual distribution of eggs shows Rebecca West's theory about the value of home-made cake at work on a celestial plane. The eggs are meat, symbol of generation, and life eternal:

> Bishop Nikolai stood up and cried, 'Christ is risen!' and they answered, 'Indeed he is risen!' Three times he spoke and they answered, and then they stretched out their hands and he gave them eggs from a great bowl in front of him. This was pure magic. They cried out as if it were talismans and not eggs that they asked for: and the Bishop gave out the eggs with an air of generosity that was purely impersonal, as if he were the conduit for a force greater than himself. When there were no more eggs in the bowl the people wailed as if there were to be no more children born into the world, and when more eggs were found elsewhere on the table the exultation was as if there were to be no more death.[14]

But the Bishop was quite right to look at his Western visitors askance: for this magic by which an egg both is and is not an egg, which any child could understand, is too baffling for Gerda. With materialist treachery, she wrenches the scene on to the plane of the real, where magic cannot prevail, and takes another bowl of eggs to distribute to the waiting children.

> This was the moment that we all fear when we are little, the moment when some breach of decorum would put an event into a shape so disgusting that nobody who saw it could bear to go on living, Later we learn to disbelieve in this moment, so many of the prescriptions laid on our infant mind are nonsense, but we are wrong. There are things that shock, other than crimes. We did not feel any special shame at Gerda's action because we had come to the feast with her, we had not got to that yet, it was to come later. For the moment we simply participated in the staring horror that was shown by everybody at the table. The children to whom she held out the eggs took them awkwardly, not knowing what else to do, and then withdrew their attention from her, like animals turning from one of their kind who is sick.[15]

Gerda's action is monstrous because 'it denied the validity of magic' and asserted 'that an egg given by a human hand must be the same as an egg given by any other human hand,'[16] and it is all the worse because of the Bishop's own knowledge 'of the limited avail of magic, and how its victories cannot be won on the material battlefield where man longs to see them.' It is as though she had called out to a tightrope walker to tell him that the rope he was treading was alarmingly thin: and we cannot suppose that she does so in innocence, though she defends herself by saying, 'But some of the children were crying' – for her action is, in its own way, a protest. It is a protest against the creativity that can turn eggs into meaning, against a mystery whose secret she cannot fathom, and an assertion from the midst of her own frustration that hunger is real, hunger is eternal, and cannot be satisfied, not by all the *Apfelkuchen* of Europe's bakeries. Gerda is famished in the midst of plenty, like the two-headed calf they are taken to see the following day, which was incapable of drinking the milk that would have kept it alive, and spat out through one mouth what it took in at the other. Her action is such a terrifying assertion of the reality of such famine that there seems no possible response to it, until a blind beggar taps his way into the garden. He greets the Bishop, throws back his head, and bursts into an ancient hymn:

> It proceeded from the classic age of faith, before the corruption of masochism had crept in, before the idea of the atonement had turned worship into barter. It adored; it did not try to earn salvation by adoring; it adored what it had destroyed, and felt anguish at the destruction, and rejoiced because death had been cheated and the destroyed one lived. Again the sunshine seemed part of a liberated radiance.
>
> He ceased, crossed himself with a gesture not of self-congratulation but of abandonment, and the Bishop called him to the table, gave him his blessing, and filled his hands with bread and lamb and garlic and eggs . . . The occasion was entirely restored.[17]

'He crossed himself with a gesture of abandonment': the beggar, like the Bishop, has the secret of abandonment to life's processes, both physically, as a creature old and ill and dirty and blind, and spiritually, as one who accepts that man destroys goodness and goodness cannot be destroyed. He is validated by his own conviction, the opposite of Gerda's, that magic 'keeps all its promises': for he comes to the table hungry, but he leaves it with the Bishop's blessing on his head, and bread, lamb and eggs in his hands.

I dwell on this scene with great respect, because I do not think Rebecca West ever gave a better account of what she called (with reference to Dante) 'the geography within her own breast'. Macedonia is her Paradise, where poverty is fullness and the lust for destruction exposed and overcome. Bishop Nikolai in particular is central to her beliefs: the possessor of great natural power, whose force is all turned to creativity – a kind of private prayer of her own, as a woman of enormous natural power with great scope for destruction. I am also moved by this scene because she tells a truth here she went on to forget, in the sleepwalking manner of the artist: she admits the Bishop's knowledge 'of the limited avail of magic, and how its victories cannot be won on the material battlefield where man longs to see them.' The poignancy of this remark, properly translated, is that the magic of the entire scene belongs to the realm of art, and not to the realm of matter where we would long to find it. Here we return to the question of what gave the break-up between Rebecca West and Yugoslavia its particular taste of wormwood: she did not merely love Yugoslavia, as I mentioned before, she believed in it – and she never forgave it for being other than she believed it was.

What did she leave out of account, to make the nature of post-war Yugoslavia seem such a betrayal? I asked myself this question on the shore of Lake Ohrid, after driving to Macedonia in that state of exaltation that seizes so many readers of *Black Lamb and Grey Falcon;* only to find that if the lake remained one of the loveliest bodies of pearly water in the world, Macedonia was as spiritually vacant as a car park, whose presiding genius (descended doubtless from the Internal Macedonian Revolutionary Organisation) was a rapacious brand of tourist exploitation. I have asked myself very often since, and arrived at two partial answers I should like to offer here. The first, which I suspect Rebecca West would prefer, has to do with Marxism; the second, with Gerda and the sense of process.

The Yugoslavia she believed in could not have become Marxist; and when it did, she struggled to believe that this was for external reasons, like Britain's support for the Partisans rather than Mihailović. Tito himself she believed to have the remotest connection with the country; a Comintern agent merely, whom she heard at the Trepča mine (where he had been an agitator) to be son of a Czech Jew and a Hungarian mother.[18] Her confidence in Mihailović was not blind, but grounded in his ethnicity, which seemed to her the best guarantee for Yugoslavia's future, as she wrote to Sir Orme Sargent in 1944:

> My feelings about the situation are influenced by the fact that Mihailović is obviously a typical Serb officer-and by great effort I did once make myself realise what that meant. It is to live in a world where 2 + 2 = 5, and a blend of lawlessness and discipline and impiety and piety and cruelty and universal love work out to something that in the end harmonises pretty well with the English world where 2 + 2 = 4 and either/or as the operative principle. I feel the only safe guide for dealing with Yugoslavia is always to trust the worst elements in Serb life. It somehow works out right for them.
>
> But the professional revolutionary seems to me to harmonise with no

world, to work out at nothing but death and damnation. And surely Tito is the professional revolutionary.[19]

If 'the worst elements in Serb life' produce a giddy equation of $2 + 2 = 5$, then the worst elements of Communism produce one more like $2 + 2 = 1$ and it was by dint of minimising the ethnic conflict among the Partisans that Tito's forces swelled.

Modern Yugoslavia persists through a kind of homogenisation helped by the very fact that Tito was not a Serb; and Comintern agent as he was, he managed his own brand of ethnicity in breaking with Stalin over Yugoslavia's right to self-determination. But this would have been cold comfort to Rebecca West – for the idea that Yugoslavia might have to be much less than it could be, in order to survive, is the one idea she does not entertain in all her speculations. The idea that such a culture might consent to dull its sense of reality for the sake of a reality Serb, Croat and Slovene could share, is a treachery she never contemplates. Fond as she is of remarking: 'It is sometimes very hard to tell the difference between history and the smell of skunk', this is a trick of history she does not anticipate, for it is inconceivable to her aristocratic standards.

My other thought about what Rebecca West left out of account in her faith is this: that peasant virtues are the most perishable virtues of all. However imbued with them the peasant is, he is very unlikely to know that he has them – or to know how to retain them or to know why he should. To unite so much wisdom with his unconscious virtues, the peasant would need to have lived both on the land, and in a town, at his craft and at a machine, to have read Ruskin and Marx and Morris and heard Henry Maxwell Andrews dilate on alienation and the sense of process. He would, in short, have to be several hundred years old (as old as our industrial society) – and even so, he would probably not be wise enough. For what sustains the peasant virtues is primarily lack of choice. Once choice exists, he must exercise positive judgement; and he is more than likely to exercise it in favour of the machine, for as Andrews remarks, 'everything which is not natural is artificial and artifice is painful and difficult.' The machine is man's response to the pain inherent in process, and it would take the wisdom of Solomon to renounce it. The Macedonian women who wrestled thick white felt and home-dyed thread into folk costumes of Byzantine handsomeness were also capable, in response to Western imports, of 'the most frightful designs that could ever be found in an art

needlework shop in Brighton . . . the crudest naturalist representations of fruit and flowers in vile colours on drab backgrounds';[20]
a little more wealth, and they would be buying the materials they
were imitating, and transferring the *mana* once inherent in the traditional clothes to the new, precisely because they were machine-
made, and not the product of the human hand. One generation
later, and their children would be wearing Western fashions, and
occupying their gifted hands with that genteel obsession of modern
Yugoslavia, crochet.

When Henry Maxwell Andrews observed that one cause of
Gerda's alienation was machine civilisation, 'where a loaf of bread
comes . . . in a cellophane wrapper with its origins as unvisualised
as the begetting and birth of a friend's baby' he was really admit-
ting that the gulf between Gerda and the peasant was not impassable. Yugoslavia after the War bridged it very rapidly; and this, I
suspect, was the deeper cause of Rebecca West's revulsion. Communism certainly hastened the process, with its passion for heavy
industry, inorganic materials and team labour; but no-one can suppose that the modernisation of Yugoslavia would not have been
accompanied by most of the same phenomena, no matter what the
regime. In Belgrade, Rebecca West was repelled by the lack of
everything that made Yugoslavia so interesting in this, the most
modernised centre; 'urban life takes a deal of learning',[21] she
observes, on seeing how little peasant wisdom adapts to city
environments. Someone with a more cautious temperament might
have extrapolated from pre-war Belgrade what a Yugoslavia would
look like whose 80 per cent rural population had become 70 per
cent urbanised, as now.

And someone with dreadfully steady nerves, of a wholly logical
disposition, might have foreseen that it was not impossible that
Gerda should come to be the presiding spirit of Yugoslavia, when
once the conditions that produced her were repeated. Gerda's nerve-
lessness resulted, said Andrews, from the combination of mechani-
sation and economic collapse, when people developed a terror of:

> losing the results of process, which are all they know about; they must
> be afraid that everything artificial is going to disappear, and they are
> going to be thrown back on the natural; they must foresee with a shud-
> der a day when there will be no miraculous loaf born in its virginity of
> cellophane, and they will have to eat grass.

Something like this 'shudder', it seems to me, accompanies the
present economic crisis in Yugoslavia – a country infinitely richer,

in absolute terms, than it was before the War. But it is possible to starve in the midst of plenty, like Gerda, and to suffer from a famine of the mind as well as the body; and as the relation of the dinar to real value becomes ever more fragile, and the car needs repairing and the fridge ceases to function, the urban Yugoslav is prey to terrors of regression not unlike Gerda's, though he shows no signs of turning it to her aggressive uses. If this is an irony Rebecca West found too cruel to contemplate, we may not be very surprised.

Notes

1. Interview with Marina Warner, in *The Paris Review*, 79, 1981.
2. 'Elegy' in *Rebecca West, A Celebration*, London: Penguin, 1978, p. 388.
3. *Ibid.*, pp. 392–3.
4. *Ibid.*, pp. 394.
5. *Black Lamb and Grey Falcon*, N.Y.: Viking, 1941, p. 827. (Hence forth, *BL*.)
6. *BL*, p. 911.
7. *BL*, p. 202.
8. *BL*, p. 805.
9. *BL*, pp. 799-802.
10. *BL*, p. 5.
11. *BL*, p. 55.
12. *BL*, p. 622.
13. *BL*, pp. 720-1.
14. *BL*, p. 722.
15. *BL*, p. 722.
16. *BL*, p. 724.
17. *BL*, p. 723.
18. Letter to Sir Orme Sargent, 21 February 1944 (F0/371/44269). I owe this information to Dr M. Wheeler.
19. *Ibid.*
20. *BL*, p. 716.
21. *BL*, p. 474.

CHAPTER 9

Entreat me not to leave thee, or to return from following after thee: for whither thou goest, I will go; and where thou lodgest I will lodge: thy people shall be my people, and thy God my God: where thou diest I will die, and there I will be buried.

Ruth Ch. 1, vv. 16–17.

Margaret Masson Hasluck

Marc Clark

She was both extremely intelligent and very foolish.

Lady Helen Waterhouse on Hasluck.

I like to think of her defiant at G.H.Q. That was just our Margarita contra mundum.

'JMR' in the Aberdeen University Review, Autumn 1949.

On the face of it, few woman travellers in the Balkans should be better known than Margaret Hasluck. She spent 30 years in the southern Balkans, spoke at least three local languages, travelled incessantly, and wrote about it. She was the first west European scholar, female or male, to do systematic, sustained, ethnographic work in large parts of Macedonia and Albania. By temperament she was outrageously colourful and colourfully outrageous: it was nothing for her to boast that in the First World War she smuggled secret messages between Athens and London in her garters. In the Second World War she set up and for two years ran the Albania Section of the Special Operations Executive, Churchill's pet project to raise insurrection and put occupied Europe in flames.

Today she and her work are little read, even by Albanologists. This is surprising. Albanology is an esoteric field, and the pantheon of great foreign Albanologists is a small hall indeed. By any rational measure, Hasluck belongs in it. She travelled the length and breadth of Albania and lived there for sixteen years (1923-39). Edith Durham, by comparison, spent barely a tenth as much time in the country, never mastered the language, and did hardly any field work outside the Catholic enclave of the northwest. Yet Durham's works are required reading for Albanologists, while Hasluck's major work, *The Unwritten Law in Albania*, is the sort of book that academics cite but don't read.

It is worth considering how Margaret Hasluck lived and worked, and how she so quickly slipped into obscurity.

Early Years

Margaret Masson Hardie was born in 1885 in the village of Drumblade, and grew up in the Moray countryside near Elgin in northern Scotland. Her father was a farmer who achieved a modest prosperity. Margaret, the first of nine children, was sent to her grandparents. Family lore has it that when she returned at the age of six, she was reading Shakespeare for pleasure.

She had a strict Christian upbringing. Her father John Hardie experimented with various sects, all of them severe. Education and self-improvement were god-ordained tasks, relaxation was wicked. An uncle became a celebrated surgeon, went to Australia, and was knighted. A sister ran a ladies' college in Hyderabad and became one of the first European women to see Tibet. Many family members went to America where, among other things, they helped found a town in Texas which bears the name of the ancestral home: Dallas. Margaret is buried in the Dallas churchyard, beside her parents.[1]

She flourished as a student, winning various honours at Elgin Academy, then at Aberdeen University, then at Newnham College, Cambridge, where in 1911 she earned a First in the Classical Tripos. In 1910 the Vice-Chancellor of Cambridge nominated her for a studentship at the British School at Athens, the first time a woman had ever been nominated to the BSA. Margaret got her studentship, and the next summer she joined a dig in Anatolia under William Ramsay.

The BSA was an elite institution, a pillar of classical scholarship and the base for legendary excavations of Knossos and Sparta. It has also been called 'the best academic club in Europe.'[2] At the age of 26 Margaret Hardie, the farmer's daughter from northern

Scotland, found herself surrounded by glittering intellects and the scions of genteel English families.

One of them was the BSA's assistant director, Frederick William Hasluck, a brilliant archaeologist and orientalist seven years her senior. Photos depict a model Edwardian, someone who is patient, urbane, and self-controlled: everything that Margaret was not. In 1912 they were married at her home in Scotland.

Together they travelled extensively in the Balkans, despite Frederick's dislike of what he called, in the gently mocking style of Edward Lear, excessive 'roorality'.[3] In 1915 he quit the BSA and joined the Intelligence Department of the British Legation. In fact, the two institutions had largely merged. The scholars of the BSA were a priceless war asset, given their knowledge of regional languages, customs, personages, and geography. Equally important, they belonged to the social class that ran the Empire, so they were readily absorbed into its machinery of war. Much the same thing would happen in 1939–40.

Margaret worked for British Intelligence in Athens and in London, apparently in a minor capacity (notwithstanding her message-in-my-garters boast).[4] Her husband played a more significant role, compiling (along with Compton Mackenzie) a counter-espionage catalogue of suspect persons.[5] But his health was declining. In November 1916 the problem was diagnosed as tuberculosis. Margaret believed that he contracted the disease on a trip to Konia in 1913. The trip had been his wedding present to her: she had chosen the destination. Ever after, she would blame herself for his premature death.[6]

Frederick Hasluck died in a sanatorium in Switzerland in February 1920, aged 42. He had published some 50 articles and a monograph (together with H.H. Jewell) on church architecture. Margaret spent much of the next few years assembling and editing his notes and manuscripts to produce several books under his name, including a dense two-volume study of folk custom and cross-cultural links, *Christianity and Islam Under the Sultans*, which is still a standard in the field. In the footnotes she announces plans for future work under her own name, including a book on ethnic types and traditions in Macedonia.[7] The book never appeared.

Much of her early work shows the influence of her husband (although an article on traditional games of the Turks does not feel weighty enough for Frederick; a bibliography of Hasluck's known work is appended). Her work on Christian borrowings among

Balkan Musllms is a direct extrapolation of his. More importantly, her interest in Albania probably had its source in his interest in the Bektashi, a dervish sect based in Albania. But his influence should not be overstated. If he pointed out the direction, she chose to take it. Margaret Hasluck was, if nothing else, a woman with a mind of her own.

Independent Work

In 1921 Hasluck received the first of two Wilson Travelling Fellowships from Aberdeen University (1921–23 and 1926–28). Money would always be a problem, and the fellowships would help to sustain her. Despite deep February snow, she set off immediately. She would spend most of 1921 and 1922 in remote villages. 'I am the first to work West Macedonia,' she proclaims. Her letters and three reports to her sponsors[8] could be taken for the work of Edith Durham; if anything they are even more exuberant, with a breathless, almost girlish excitement. After a horrific war and four years of watching her husband slowly die, Hasluck clearly exulted in freedom and adventure.

With 500 marbles purchased in Athens, she bribed local boys to write down folk tales. 'Unfortunately I had underrated the Macedonian boy's passion for marbles and to the utter ruin of my peace a trail of children as long as eager as the Pied Piper's beset my footsteps from dawn to dusk.' 'As a rule I don't pay, even with marbles, for information, but I make an exception with witches.' For five days she was snow-bound in Kozani. Moslem women fled at the sight of this tall European in dark wool, thinking her a man. Crowds of women entered her room before dawn to watch her dress. She followed Moslems closely to see if they truly kept the Ramadan fast, because 'there's a considerable gulf in the Balkans between hearsay and experience' (she saw no fast-breaking). Villagers near Mt Olympus refused to hire her a horse and sent her off on a donkey, 'as being less useful to brigands.' When the donkey smashed her water bottle, 'I was perched so high on the wooden frames they use for saddles that I could not even kick him satisfactorily.' After a winter 'up country' she returned to Salonika where 'I turned on both taps in my room for the sheer pleasure of hearing [running water] and knowing there was lots of it, all mine to use as I pleased, without fuss. It was ten minutes before I realised that I was thirty-six and put away my childish things.'

The reports and letters also contain adult talk about local dialects and nominative etymology, ancient coins and botanical samples to be sent to Aberdeen, her photographs,[9] curious variations in lake levels, head-measuring of the locals – anthropometry was in its heyday – and a long list of folk customs (the evil eye, spells and exorcisms, dirges). And she wrote of 'the Book-that-is-to-be', which never was.

This would become a pattern. Almost every topic listed eventually found its way into an article, and in many of those articles Hasluck refers to forthcoming books. But, with the exception of her Albanian grammar and a slim wartime phrasebook, they never appeared (*The Unwritten Law* was published posthumously, much of it written from Hasluck's notes by a literary executor). She was a fussy writer who belaboured papers literally for years. She never enjoyed organising information and she was not particularly good at it. But she loved field work.

In truth, she was a born traveller. Until recently few if any travellers to Albania ventured into the hinterland for more than a few days or weeks at a time (soldiers and Zog's English gendarmes[10] excepted). Albania is a compact place – one can walk across the country in a matter of days – and, even without roads, it was too easy to scuttle back to the relative civility of Tirana or Shkoder. But Hasluck spent whole seasons up country. By 1922 she was convinced that 'I ought to stay three weeks in each village in order to do it justice.' Nicholas Hammond recalled in an interview that, when he met Hasluck in southern Albania in 1932, she had already extended her stay in the area for several weeks (to help a young woman who had been severely beaten by her father; Hasluck feared that if she left, the father might finish the job).

Her earliest writings go on at length about the difficulties of travelling to remote places; like any neophyte, she was thrilled at her ability just to get there. But over time, stories of travel troubles take on a boring sameness; the veteran traveller eschews them. In Hasluck's later writings there are no recalcitrant donkeys, no horrid wooden saddles, no storm delays, no wobbly canoes, not even any brigands. It's all taken for granted. In her 1937 review of Ronald Matthews' *Sons of the Eagles*, 'the third book on Albania which has passed through the reviewer's hands within as many months,' she gives weary thanks that there is 'not a single sentence that aims at making the reader say what a hero the author must be to venture into such a wild country.'[11]

She disdained swashbucklers' claims of tripping lightly through the Balkans, always staying with the locals. She knew what it was to sleep ten to a room, to smell cattle beneath the floorboards, to wake covered in red welts from insects unseen. She knew that it was possible to put up with this for a few days or even weeks–but not for months. 'Discomfort, however picturesque, only wastes one's strength.'[12] Her first long trip taught her that she had to pace herself, to limit her daily working hours and generally husband her strength. After that, she travelled with tinned food, a tea-basket and thermos, a folding chair, a camp bed and, in summer, a sturdy Whymper tent.[13]

In effect, she set up her own home in each village she visited. It gave her a place of rest and escape; but it also emphasised her oddity, her otherness. Albanian custom required travellers to stay in local homes – but Albanian travellers travelled on (as did most of the Europeans); they did not hang around for a month. Once, her tent cost her the services of a gendarme employed as a helper and bodyguard. 'The first evening we pitched it, a peasant called. 'I could not think what sort of Gypsies had a tent like this,' he explained. Next day the gendarme, unable to bear the thought of being taken all summer for a Gypsy, gave notice.'[14] At the end of an extended stay, Hasluck would sometimes throw a lavish party to thank local people, roasting a whole sheep and borrowing large pots to make gallons of soup and mountains of rice pilaf.[15]

By 1923 Hasluck had decided to focus on Albania. She was a widow with no income, but a first-class education. Like any professional scholar, she sought a niche. She chose Albania because of the 'scientific interest of European scholars in a little known country.'[16] There is no indication that she was impressed by the Albanians she had met in Greece and Macedonia; if anything, she found them dour.

It is unclear when she made her first trip to Albania. Frederick Hasluck went there in the spring of 1915 in search of Bektashi, but it is not clear if Margaret went with him. By her own account, she moved there in 1923, but she had no permanent address until 1935 because she was 'constantly travelling to collect material.' In 1935 she rented a house in Elbasan, in central Albania. The next year she bought land there and built a house, of which she was immensely proud. She chose Elbasan because, first, the local dialect was the standard form of Albanian; and second, Elbasan was the home of Lef Nosi, 'the Albanian specialist on my subjects, who gave me invaluable assistance and lent me otherwise inaccessible books.'[17]

Nosi became an integral part of Hasluck's life. The son of a well-to-do Orthodox merchant, he had been a leader of Albanian resistance against the Ottomans, a signatory of the 1912 declaration of independence, and a cabinet minister in Albania's first government. He was also a respected amateur archaeologist and ethnographer. Durham said he was the only Albanian who understood the value of folk lore.[18] For Hasluck, he was a knowledgeable collaborator, a cultivated friend in an uncultivated environment, and more. Enver Hoxha called her Nosi's mistress.[19] Whether they were lovers is impossible to say; but it is clear that she loved him.

The Loneliness of the Long-Distance Scholar

Lef Nosi was perhaps the only person in Albania with whom she could discuss her work. Once or twice a year she returned to Britain to visit family and colleagues and give the odd lecture, usually at the Folklore Society. She visited only because 'compelled by circumstances. . . . *How* I used to pine when shut up in London!'[20] But back in Albania she felt intellectually isolated. She worried that, while working up articles, she 'could not always avoid arguing *a silencio*, a dangerous method.' She suggested that *Folk-Lore* carry a page for the queries of far-flung researchers.[21] She asked Sir John Myres at Oxford for direction, but he refused to give it, saying that he would not bias her in any way.

Hasluck sent scores of artefacts – 'specimens,' she called them – to the Marischal Museum in Aberdeen: aprons, shoes, and a partridge net from Macedonia; bed curtains and bread stamps from Greece; head scarves and embroidered fragments from Kosova; carved cradles, embroidered socks, and iron dog collars from Albania.[22] Her letters in this period, particularly to Myres,[23] give insights into the difficulties of her field work.

The Albanians are extremely self-conscious, the Vlachs sharing this defect. Consequently they are terrified of being laughed at by foreigners, and they think – most disastrously – that all Albanian ways and beliefs are inferior and ridiculous in European eyes. . . . [The Catholics in the northwest] think they should be subsidised for everything they say to a foreigner. I am afraid to pay them – it tends to make them invent information after their stock of genuine material is exhausted – but I do often pay them. And so often their stuff is worth about 2d. (27.6.30)

They [the Catholics] hope expressly to *sell* their collection to some rich American or Englishman. In my possession are several letters from priests asking (a) how much will I pay them for their stuff and (b) whether I can make 'my university' buy the material. . . . I've tried every trick I know and nothing except paying answers. . . . I collect what I can, and make sure that everything told me by one person is checked by another. (1.7.30)[24]

This is tantamount to scoffing at one of Albanians' most cherished self-conceptions, namely that the highlanders, Catholic or Muslim, gave proudly and generously to visitors. Hasluck mocked this and other cultural givens, such as the notion that many Albanians could infallibly recite their ancestry for generations back. Most such pedigrees, she told Myres, were demonstrably bogus. Even the pedigree of John Markagjoni of Mirdita 'is false to my mind in the early branches, though it is based on church records.' Her willingness to challenge these icons of identity suggests genuine intellectual rigour and self-confidence, but also arrogance and insensitivity. One does not attack the fortress of national myth lightly, especially with a people who are 'terrified of being laughed at'.

Hasluck and Durham

Many of those myths were created by Edith Durham, the most celebrated Albanologist of Hasluck's time, and perhaps all time. Not surprisingly, Hasluck and Durham knew each other well. They occasionally attended the same meetings of various societies, notably the Folk-Lore Society, and they were in contact by letter (Durham's last visit to Albania was in 1921) until at least 1930, when Hasluck wrote to Myres: 'She was long one of my ideal women – none of these swashbuckling, chattering creatures who write modern books of travel – but of recent years she did and said some very queer things to me. . . . I was sweet to her for years – or thought I was – but latterly I had to stop. She shouldn't live alone; a boarding house has its disagreeables, but it's healthier for one's mind than a solitary flat.'

After that, Hasluck's references to Durham were double-edged. 'Miss Durham is a wonder. . . . I love the vim and humour of her writing – only get upset by her theorising. I'm sending in a little commentary [to *Man*] on her bride-price article; she has imported ideas from the South Seas that won't do.' Regarding tribal lists and maps, she told Myres that 'Miss Durham is completely wrong except for the N.W. and Mirdite,' then inserted as an afterthought: 'investigation *much* easier for me.'

One wonders if they ever compared their experiences as women in the Balkans. Neither were feminists in the contemporary sense, but both wanted – demanded – to be taken seriously. In the Balkans, they were. They were allowed into the society of men, and rich men at that, giving them more social power than they could dream of in Britain. Durham liked to boast that she ran with the 'buck crowd'. Hasluck was frequently mistaken for a man. Once, when a gypsy saw her, 'a tall foreigner dressed in a coat and skirt of soldiers' khaki . . . she thought I was an Albanian officer.'[25] Unlike Durham, Hasluck liked to think of herself as feminine and did not disdain the company of Balkan women, although she did agree with Durham that anyone sequestered in a Balkan harem did not make a great conversationalist.

Both evidently had some interest in Albania's sworn virgins. Durham, and later Rose Wilder Lane, explicitly acknowledged the parallels with their situation: women given the social standing of men. Hasluck took numerous photos of sworn virgins but she appears to have written nothing about them. This is unfortunate, as the photos of women she identifies as sworn virgins depict a huge variety of dress – from full male regalia to full female – and body language and demeanour – from an exaggerated, hips thrust forward, more-man-than-the-men swagger to an almost coquettish shyness. This wealth of images raises tantalising questions about the simple definitions of the custom bequeathed to us by Durham and others.

Of Hasluck's private life in Albania, other than her closeness to Nosi and her pride in her new home in Elbasan, we know little. A niece recalls that she arranged for shipment of some farming machinery from Scotland to Albania, but the exact purpose has been forgotten. As a farmer's daughter, she knew better than most how backward Albanian agriculture was, and was interested in improving it. In her will she set up a fund which she hoped would eventually provide scholarships for Albanian studies 'of a linguistic, folklore, historical, sociological, or agricultural nature.'[26]

She continued to travel much and write little. Her backlog of material grew and grew. 'I only hope I don't die before I get all my observations down,' she wrote to Myres in 1930. Five years later she had given up that hope. She had conceived a book on 'Customs and Customary Law in Albania' and won a two-year Leverhulme Fellowship to cover costs, but in 1935 she was still writing articles on Lake Ostrovo, based on field work from Macedonia in 1923. She posited new work to Myres – 'not that I shall live to write up all that I have already collected. Especially after I will go after strange gods like this lake.'

Her three articles on the geological and archaeological history of Ostrovo display the range of her curiosity and scholarship. But they amounted to intellectual doodling, a finer kind of procrastination. It was not her professional focus, and she knew it.

Flight from Albania

In April 1939, just days before Italian troops invaded, Hasluck was forced to leave Albania by Zog's government because, she claimed, the Italians demanded it.[27] Evidently they believed that she was a British spy. Hasluck would not have helped her case by claiming, as she often did, to have high-level contacts and influence, or by telling people of her earlier work with British Intelligence. Given her travels, she was indeed well positioned to spy. There is, however, no evidence that the Foreign Office formally employed her as such. There was probably no need. She liked to gossip, and she had an obvious interest in staying on good terms with British officials. During their occasional meetings she probably told them everything she knew.

Hasluck fled to Athens, leaving her home and her 3000-book library in the care of Lef Nosi. She took her notes and working material, including the manuscript of what she was then calling *The Unwritten Law in Albania,* but little else. Evidently she either had little time to prepare, or she believed that she would soon return. Six months later Germany invaded Poland. She never saw Albania, or Nosi, again.

She returned to the familiar halls of the BSA. At this point the records of her correspondence dry up for several years. But the BSA provides a mine of anecdotes; everyone associated with the school has a Hasluck story.

When Hasluck first came to Athens, the story goes, she more or less systematically interviewed prospective husbands. During a quiet moment with one candidate, she contrived to faint into his lap. The young man, presumably an upright Edwardian, grabbed a glass of cold water and splashed it in her face. (He was struck from the list.) That tale may be apocryphal, but there were plenty of witnesses in 1934 when Hasluck, then 49, walked into a gathering of mostly young males and announced loudly that 'there isn't one of you dear boys I couldn't marry.'

In the summer of 1939 Helen Waterhouse, on her way back to the BSA from London, was asked by the school secretary to take two corsets for Hasluck. She went to Hasluck's apartment with Tom Dunbabin, the BSA deputy director, expecting to meet a dowdy old lady. Then she heard Hasluck say, 'What I like about you, Mr Dunbabin, is that you always speak to me as to my husband's widow.' Sixty years later Waterhouse would shake her head at the memory of that splendid ambiguity and confess that she still wondered how Hasluck meant it.

When she was exiled to Athens Hasluck immediately went to a British official and insisted that he put her to work. He asked for her qualifications and she replied: 'I am the best-educated woman in the Balkans.' This tale shot around town (one wonders at the indiscretion of the official involved). But Hasluck soon had a job in the Press Office; in fact she was establishing contacts with potential Albanian resistance leaders.[28]

As more Balkan nations slipped into the Axis orbit, the BSA became a holding tank for evacuated British ex-pats. One of them was Olivia Manning, who was billeted briefly in the school's hostel alongside Hasluck. *Friends and Heroes*, the last volume of Manning's Balkan trilogy, is set in this Athenian limbo. 'Mrs Brett', a prominent character, is clearly based on Hasluck.[29] Brett bustles through the book organising social events, talking loudly and rudely, gossiping and expounding, denouncing her enemies and celebrating her friends. Clearly Manning abhorred this garrulous whirlwind of a woman,[30] but she is gracious enough to add that 'Mrs Brett's aggression covered nothing worse than unhappiness.'

Brett's husband, like Hasluck's, was an official at the Athens school who died young. 'It was my fault,' says Brett. 'I brought him here, and he got typhoid.'[31] The book makes no mention of Albania or Albanians; Brett is linked instead to Australians. She tells Harriet Pringle (Manning's alter-ego) that she is 'stimulated by contact with men who were 'wild in such a natural way'.' In a telling passage Brett is with a padre when three drunken Australian soldiers stagger into the tea room, each carrying a potted plant. One of them asks Brett to dance. The padre points out that there is no music and no dance floor, to which the Australian replies, 'Shut up you pommie bastard.' Brett takes charge.

'Of course I know how to deal with men in that state', Mrs. Brett said. 'I've had experience of all sorts. . . . I said: "Sit down, there's a good fellow, and I'll order you some tea"'. . . . 'We had a nice long chat and he showed me all the photographs in his wallet – Mum and Dad and Sis and so on. D'you know, he became quite attached to me. It was my evening at the canteen, but *could* I get away! No, I could *not*. . . . At last I said, nicely but firmly: 'I have to go now. You come tomorrow and have tea at my flat and you can tell me all your troubles.'. . . I can't tell you how much I'm looking forward to seeing him again.'[32]

Brett's courage and vitality, her taste for adventure, her eagerness to tell the tale, her fascination with 'wild' people, her vanity and flirtatiousness, her aggressive curiosity and determination to probe others' lives – these qualities are routinely attributed to Hasluck by family and colleagues. *Friends and Heroes* ends in 1941 with the British fleeing Athens as panzers sweep down the Balkans. Brett and the Pringles board a ship for evacuation to Cairo and find that the bunks are just wooden shelves, without mattress or bedding. 'Like coffins,' Brett says, then adds: 'Still, it's an adventure.'[33]

Hasluck at War

Hasluck's last great adventure began in February 1942 in Cairo, when she was recruited by the Special Operations Executive to she set up an Albanian Section. For more than a year she was acting head of the section. In fact, she was the only person in it. Albania was a low priority for GHQ, and her job was essentially a watching brief. In March 1942 she went to Istanbul under an assumed name, her grey hair dyed, to meet Albanian exiles, but was called back when reports reached MI6 that the Italians were aware of her activities. After that her principal roles were, first, to sift the available information and write fortnightly situation assessments; and second, to brief and advise SOE operatives about to be parachuted into Albania.

She called them 'my boys.' They in turn called her 'Fanny' Hasluck, a tongue-in-cheek reference to the hundreds of much younger FANYs, women in the First Aid Nursing Yeomanry, who supported SOE. On most mornings she lectured them about Albanian customs and culture. The value of those lectures is debatable. Reginald Hibbert found them largely irrelevant. Hasluck could answer any number of questions about Albania, he said, but they didn't know the right questions to ask. Hasluck, for her part, was also frustrated. She complained that her 'boys' were just that – very young men, utterly ignorant of Albania, 'with gallantry and social charm as their only assets'. She compared this with the mature talent available for operations in Greece, especially the

139

Balkan experts of the BSA.[34] 'A Lawrence of Arabia just can't be made out of a gallant youngster who has no pre-war background, and alas! there were only such available for my country.' Nonetheless, she liked her boys, and for the most part they liked her.

From Cairo Hasluck watched her adopted homeland disintegrate. Civil war compounded the misery of occupation. Hasluck believed that SOE's best option was to arm and co-ordinate tribal leaders in the north of Albania. She never understood or fully accepted the rise of the communist partisans. In her Albania there had been no communists, and she insisted communism was a foreign weed planted and sustained by Yugoslav or Soviet agents. Herself a virulent anti-communist, she consistently underestimated the partisans' strength in her situation reports.

In 1943, with the North African campaign won, the military began to show interest in the Balkans. Hasluck's stream of reports had at least kept them aware of Albania's existence and provided a base of information. That spring the first SOE operatives parachuted into Albania. At least 120 followed over the next 18 months. Officers began sending contradictory reports, often based on the slimmest of experience. Hasluck was left to reconcile these reports with her own vast, but somewhat dated, knowledge. The section split quickly and bitterly between those who wanted to support the communist partisans, and everybody else. There were accusations of incompetence, even treachery. Backers of the partisans argued that SOE's job was to kill Germans, and the partisans appeared to be the group most able and inclined to do so. The others, including Hasluck, accused them of being at best ill-informed, at worst communists themselves. Reading histories of SOE's Albania Section one sometimes gets the impression that they fought one another harder than they fought the Germans.[35]

Meanwhile, the Germans installed Lef Nosi as one of four elder statesmen on a Council of Regency. Hasluck defended the council,[36] but her links to Nosi inevitably brought charges of bias. Her battles with the new head of the Albania Section, Major Philip Leake, came to a head in January 1944 when he demanded that she give up control of the fortnightly situation reports and take a nebulous job as general advisor. She responded, typically, with an ultimatum. 'I cannot give unthinking loyalty and that is what working under Major Leake would mean for me.' 'He does not suffer correction easily, and I think he needs a little. I am afraid I think stubbornly that, if there is to be one voice in B8, it had better be mine.'[37] In February she left the section.

In Hasluck's personal file is an HQ minute stating that she left 'owing to the fact that her very intimate acquaintance with Albania led her to follow, perhaps somewhat too closely, her own ideas when they did not happen to coincide with HMG's [His Majesty's Government's] policy.'[38]

Margarita *contra mundum.*

Last Years

By May 1944 Hasluck was back in London and extremely ill. The diagnosis was advanced leukaemia. Given little time to live by doctors, she wrote to Aberdeen University to offer various Balkan artefacts (taken to Britain before the war). She hoped to go to a sanatorium in Switzerland, and 'if Switzerland doesn't revive me, they would be at the Museum's disposal in a comparatively short time. Please let me know your decision fairly soon.' But the disease went into remission and Hasluck went to Cyprus, where she could find the meat and milk recommended by doctors.

Her life was effectively shattered. Communists had taken over her adopted country, and with it, her one real financial asset, her home in Elbasan. Her beloved Lef Nosi was in prison. Her war work had ended in fiasco. She had little money, no job, and hefty doctors' bills. And she was dying. She worked as much as she could, especially on her 'big book', *The Unwritten Law,* knowing that much of her life's work would go unrecorded. Yet her letters from this period are brisk and business-like, with a minimum of bitterness and self-pity.

She sought Foreign Office help to go to Elbasan, if only for a few weeks, promising that, 'if allowed to travel in Albania, she would not let her anti-Partisan feelings run away with her.' She pleaded with them to intervene on behalf of Lef Nosi (they did not). She tried to get compensation from the partisans for her home.[39] Foreign Office records contain her detailed description of the twelve-room house and its furnishings, the brick stable and servant's quarters, the gardens and pergolas, the irrigation system for the 200 fruit trees, 150 vines, 250 shrubs, and 350 roses.[40] When a British officer brought her a rose from her garden, she wept.

Lef Nosi was shot as a traitor in 1946. 'With him died my best friend and the man who gave all my work what cachet it had.'[41] Hasluck wrote to a communist official in Elbasan to ask that someone cut roses from her garden and put them on Nosi's grave. She also asked 'In what year did he [Nosi] box the ears of the Turkish governor for insulting Albania? In what year, and for how many months, was he jailed by the Turks successively in Elbasan, Monastir, and Salonica, and how long was he exiled in Brusa?' and so on.[42]

She shuttled between Cyprus, London, and her family in Scotland, depending on the season. She continued to work on articles and on *The Unwritten Law*, which had been one-quarter finished when she was exiled from Albania. An article on a bust was 'not in finished condition,' she wrote to Myres, 'but must go in as it is; I can't be fussy nowadays.' She asked him to edit undone portions of *The Unwritten Law* (he agreed, although his own health was failing). In her last works she cited Nosi assiduously. Her grief reached a silent crescendo in *Oedipus Rex in Albania*, where on the last two pages Nosi's name appears seven times. Her will provided for a bequest of £500 to the Taylor Institution of Modern Languages in Oxford to set up a fund under the name of 'Lef Nosi of Elbasan, Albania Memorial'. The fund was to be used to purchase books on Albania and, if possible, to provide a scholarship for Albanian studies.

She maintained contact with a few of her 'boys' from SOE and some friends, mostly from the BSA. For the wedding of David Smiley she sent Albanian socks and an embroidered Albanian apron. Frank Stubbings, whose fiancée had a tenuous Scottish family connection, was surprised to receive from Hasluck a coin from the time of James I/James VI, the king who united the crowns of England and Scotland. It had been given to her by her husband Frederick, as a symbol of their union.

In the summer of 1948 she went to Dublin, evidently in search of a cool climate, but one without food rationing. She died there on 18 October. Her last known letter, dated 5 October, was a note to Aberdeen providing details of a bequest, a superb antique dining tray of beaten copper. The letter ends: 'I often think of how many of my treasures are housed in the Wilson Museum. I hope they will give pleasure to the discerning few.'[43]

Margaret Hasluck was awarded an MBE (Civil) in September 1944. The recommendation noted that 'she was solely responsible for briefing and advising the officers who were initially infiltrated into the country [Albania]. Mrs Hasluck's work has been of the highest order, and distinguished by her outstanding gifts of intellect and personality.' The MBE was posted from London to Cairo to Cyprus and back, but never delivered.[44] It is almost certain that she died knowing nothing of it.

The Unwritten Law

Articles under Hasluck's name would continue to appear in journals for two years after her death, but the task of completing her 'big book,' *The Unwritten Law in Albania,* was left to a woman named Jessie Alderson (J.H. Hutton is the editor of record, but his contribution appears to have been minimal). Alderson told Hasluck's family that she found it hard going, but she persevered. The result was a unique contribution to Albanology and to the study of customary law. Whatever its flaws, it is the closest we have to a summary of sixteen years of field work, and therefore should be taken seriously.

The unwritten law of Albania's mountains was (and still is) one of the most romantic social institutions in all the Balkans, a source of endless fascination for Durham, Hasluck, Rose Wilder Lane and many other travellers. Some claimed that its core was as old as Homer; others said it was merely mediaeval; all agreed that it was the distilled essence of the mountain spirit, a barbarous and splendid anachronism on the fringe of modern Europe.

Today there are two principal sources of information about the law, or more specifically about the regional variant called the Canon of Lek Dukagjini. The first is Edith Durham. The unchanging, all-encompassing, all-powerful Canon of Lek surges through Durham's 1909 classic, *High Albania.* The second source is a stylised text of the canon based on research by a Kosova-born priest, Shtjefën Gjeçov, published in 1933 by Franciscans in Shkoder.[45] Durham's writings on the canon, especially in *High Albania,* are largely anecdotal and eminently readable. The Franciscan text, by contrast, was constructed to look like a law code in the western understanding of the term. This latter text has acquired a near-sacred status in Albania, where it is regarded as a true depiction of the mountain law as it was, and by inference, of the people as they were.

Both sources are invaluable, but deeply flawed. Durham's work is typical of late 19th-century ethnography. When Europeans suddenly realised that tribes also had laws – 'that hypertrophy of rules rather than lawlessness is characteristic of primitive life'[46] – 'ye heathen' went overnight from lawless savage to primitive (but proud) democrat. Battalions of imperial bureaucrats fanned out to the dark valleys of the Caucasus, the plains of East Africa, and other 'peripheral' lands to collect and codify customary laws. In this vein, as in everything else, Durham did her best to boost

Albanians into first place: far from being lawless, she wrote, 'there is perhaps no other people in Europe so much under the tyranny of laws.'[47]

The Franciscans, for their part, had a clear social and political agenda. They saw themselves as enlightened Albanian patriots. As they worked over Gjeçov's notes (for his canon, like Hasluck's, was published posthumously) their overarching goal was to strengthen and unify a new nation; and, not incidentally, bolster the standing of the Catholic church.[48] Where there was variety in the unwritten law, they would set a standard; where there was diversity, they would show unity. They would iron out contradictions as if they were ironing out the mountains on a map of Albania. Their goal was not to record the law, but to improve on it.

Hasluck's great contribution is to show that variation was the essence of the unwritten law. Indeed, her book is an exhausting catalogue of variation. No sooner does she give a law than she gives the manifold regional variations, then the exceptions to the variants; then she goes on to say how people actually lived. Hasluck's unwritten law refuses to be a single, coherent set of rules. 'What chiefly precluded modern Albanian governments from adopting the unwritten laws,' she said, 'was their diversity.'[49] Not 'primitiveness' or 'bloodthirstiness,' but diversity. She attributes this diversity to geographical isolation.

While much of *The Unwritten Law* is trapped in the 'ethnographical present', that curse of anthropological writing, the book periodically points out sweeping social change over time. Gjeçov's and Durham's law codes are essentially timeless; they acknowledge that the law did change, but imply that the changes were minor pleats and tucks in the cloth of the law.[50] Hasluck, on the other hand, suggests profound change over time. Importantly, she relates these alterations to broader currents of change in highland society. Her unwritten law adapts to life, and not the other way around.[51]

Anthropology changed radically in the 1920s. Bronislaw Malinowksi, the father of functional anthropology, pointed out the futility of simply asking natives, 'What is (or was) your law regarding this matter?' The inevitable result, he said, is a 'mere recital of a fictitious native *corpus juris*. . . . The true problem is not to study how human life submits to rules – it simply does not; the real problem is how the rules become adapted to life.'[52] *The Unwritten Law* illustrates this admirably. Hasluck was deeply sceptical by nature and by training. Much as she loved Albanians, she found them particularly untrustworthy. In the same way that she had followed Muslims in Macedonia to see if they kept the Ramadan fast, she refused to take her Albanian informants at their word. The book constantly compares law-in-theory with law-in-practice.

In doing so, it subtly undermines another cherished idea of Durham's generation, namely that in tribal societies, the clan is everything. For Hasluck's mountaineers, family and *fis* are indeed central facts of their lives; but not the sum of it. Incredibly, given the flat, 'scientific' style in which *The Unwritten Law* is written, individuals begin to emerge. Mountaineers scheme and manoeuvre for power and prestige. They have goals and are vengeful in their own right. They are not slaves to the Canon of Lek. While they cannot break Hartland's 'chains of immemorial tradition', they stretch them mightily. Even the vaunted unity of the Albanian family – something promoted by Catholics and communists alike – begins to look suspect. Hasluck understood the value of myths of unity. She writes approvingly that 'the community sense was fostered by every art the mountaineers knew.'[53] But she doesn't shy away from the messy reality.

In short, Hasluck (or her editor) refuses to simplify the story. *The Unwritten Law* is sometimes bewildering in its variety and maddening in its refusal to force artificial conclusions. But after reading it carefully, the Franciscan (Gjeçovian) text appears sterile, while Durham's all-embracing Canon of Lek, so satisfying in its power of absolute compulsion, begins to take on a two-dimensional, cartoon quality: 'super code' and 'super savage' are colourful, even heroic, but finally unbelievable. Hasluck's unwritten law is messy and confusing, and her mountaineers are often greedy and cruel; yet despite this, or more likely because of it, they emerge more three-dimensional, more human, more believable and ultimately more interesting than Durham's tradition-driven noble savage.

Hasluck's Legacy

It is commonplace for anthropologists to say that they will be judged ultimately by the quality of their field work, that 'the 'ethnographic facts' are indeed our golden fleece.'[54] If so, Hasluck's reputation should be secure. In fact, her impact on Albanology has been negligible. Standard histories of Albania, all of which discuss the unwritten law, make no mention of her work.[55] The fact is that almost nobody reads it. There are several possible explanations for this.

For one, it is simply hard to read. *The Unwritten Law* is indeed an empirical gold mine, but a relentless stream of facts and examples exhausts any reader. The author (editor) seldom pauses to organise the information at some meta-level which would help the reader see larger patterns and meanings. There is no narrative structure, no ranking or hierarchies to anchor the examples. Even time is absent. This makes for hard going.

Such a bloodless style could be blamed on an unsure (or bored) editor. But there are indications that Hasluck thought it proper.[56] She saw herself as a professional scholar, and in her day social studies were struggling to get on the same ground as natural sciences. Part of their answer was to adopt a flat, mechanical style of presentation. The new model anthropologist was not an escapist travel writer but a sober, rigorous recorder. As Lévi-Strauss put it, 'If this was "escape", I was one of escape's bureaucrats.'[57]

Durham hadn't faced such cultural restrictions. In 1909 she was free to serve up information in a glorious, anecdote-laden and opinionated travelogue. *High Albania* is by far her best-read work, and with good reason. Twenty years later Durham put much the same information in *Some Tribal Origins, Laws and Customs in the Balkans* in the new, more 'scientific' style, and created a dull book. It is questionable how far her reputation would extend if readers had only *Some Tribal Origins* to go on.

Hasluck was in fact not a bad writer. Her letters were lively and colourful. Even her wartime fortnightly reports were well-written. And when she wrote for an 'unscientific' audience, she relaxed:

A solo by a young Gypsy girl of Elbasan lives in my memory as one of the most beautiful things I have seen. She was dressed in a gala local costume of bolero and wide-sleeved chemise of white silk, with voluminous trousers of filmy white lawn. A triangle of heavy gold embroidery at each ankle lifted the lawn enough to show her high arched feet; bolero and chemise, like the silken square draped over her trousers, were aglitter with gold and silver spangles; softly coloured lace flowers nodded and danced on her kerchief at each movement of her head. To soft music from tambourines she daintily pointed her heel and toe once, twice, thrice, pirouetted, and stepped lightly to one side. At each pirouette the trousers swung out like white wings, at each step the golden anklet flashed and the wings half closed. Out the trousers swung again in a pirouette so light that the girl seemed to float in the air. As she came full face, she sank gracefully to the ground and bowed her head between her knees as a sign that the dance was over.[58]

Hasluck's instinct seems to have been for colourful pieces, like her articles on gypsies and on Turkish games. But she craved academic kudos, and when she wrote for a serious audience, she was deadly serious. Arguably, her superb education and scholarly rigour held her back.

Other factors have contributed to Hasluck's obscurity. She spread her written output among several academic disciplines, so she built a body of work in none. And her timing as an Albanologist was not the luckiest. Durham had arrived in Albania when the unwritten law was a living, exotic thing and the 'Eastern Question' engaged readers; but in Hasluck's day, the unwritten law was fast disappearing, while Albania had already lost its novelty (for west Europeans). By the time *The Unwritten Law* was published in 1954, the country was itself a closed book. Cambridge University Press sold just 130 copies in the first year. A few years later the title was dropped from their catalogue. As a result, the book is extremely hard to find.

On a personal level, Hasluck did herself few favours. She could be kind and giving. As Jan Morris wrote of Gertrude Bell, another gifted Edwardian traveller, 'one feels with a pang of sympathy that she was often fonder of other people than they were of her.'[59] But Hasluck was undeniably arrogant, brittle, obstinate and impatient. She alienated potential supporters in academia, in the military, among Albanians, even in her family. After her death, nobody championed her work.

Finally, Hasluck was and still is out of step with the prevailing view of northern Albania and its traditions. A romanticised view of the highlanders and their unwritten law prevails in and outside Albania. Durham is revered partly because her view of Albanians was so favourably blinkered as to border on reverse racism. Hasluck was genuinely fond of Albanians and Albania – she chose to live there – but she would not blind herself to their faults. She refused to simplify the complexity of their lives or gloss over the difficulties. This 'unpatriotic' questioning of national myths simply was not and still is not acceptable to many Albanians.[60] Still, there is no getting around the fact that until the second half of the 20th century, no scholar, Albanian or foreign, so thoroughly studied Albania's mountain peoples. If Albanologists don't make the effort to read Hasluck's work, the field will be poorer for it.

M.M. Hasluck's Known Published Works

The titles reflect changes over time in Hasluck's disciplinary and geographical focus. Her first publications extend her classical education; then there is a broad shift to ethnographic work, first in Macedonia and Greece, then in Albania; then a 1939–45 wartime hiatus; and finally her post-war attempts to salvage work from Albania. For a time after her husband's death in 1921, she began again to use her maiden name, publishing as 'Margaret M. Hardie (Mrs F.W. Hasluck)'. After 1924 she was simply Margaret Hasluck. The 1924 article in *The Times* was unsigned (this was normal practice); it is possible that Hasluck wrote other unsigned articles for newspapers.

1912

Dionysus at Smyrna, *Annual of the British School at Athens*, No. XIX, 1912–13, 89–94.

The Shrine of Mên Askaenos at Pisidian Antioch, *Journal of Hellenic Studies*, Vol. 32, 111–50.

1923

The Evil Eye in Some Greek Villages of the Upper Haliakmon Valley in West Macedonia, *Journal of the Royal Anthropological Institute*, Vol. LIII, 160–72.

The Significance of Greek Personal Names, *Folk-Lore*, Vol. 34, parts 2–3, 149–54 and 249–51.

1924

Christain Survivals Among Certain Muslim Subjects of Greece, *Contemporary Review*, February 1924, Vol. 125, 225–32.

Macedonian Muslims: A Vanishing Folk, *The Times*, 19 September 1924.

1925

The Nonconformist Moslems of Albania, *Contemporary Review*, Vol. 127, May 1925, 591–906.

Ramadan as a Personal Name (Correspondence), *Folk-Lore*, Vol. 36, 280.

1926

Letters on Religion and Folklore by F.W. Hasluck, M.M. Hasluck (editor), Luzac and Co., 1926.

A Lucky Spell From a Greek Island (Correspondence), *Folk-Lore,* Vol. 37, 195–96.

1927

The Basil-Cake of the Greek New Year, *Folk-Lore,* Vol. 38, 143–77.

1928

Traditional Games of the Turks, *Folk-Lore,* Jubilee Edition, 137–59.

Witchcraft in the Western Balkans, *Illustrated London News,* 3 March 1928.

Queries to Readers of Folk-Lore (Correspondence), *Folk-Lore,* Vol. 39, 182.

1929

Christianity and Islam Under the Sultans (2 vols) by F.W. Hasluck, M.M. Hasluck (editor), Clarendon, 877 pages.

Measurements of Macedonian Men (with G.M. Morant), *Biometrika,* Vol. 21, 322–36. This paper includes a map of the ethnic distribution of villages in southwest Macedonia which is still used as a standard. See for example, page 107 in J. Nandris: The Enduring Identity, Social Being, and Material Culture of South-East European Latinity, *Journal of the American-Romanian Academy of Arts and Sciences,* Vol. 19, 1994, 74–111.

Minorities in Serbian Macedonia, *The Fortnightly Review,* Vol. 125, 1 June 1929, 788–97.

An Unknown Turkish Shrine in Western Macedonia, *Journal of the Royal Asiatic Society,* April 1929, 289–96.

1931

Nomad Shepherds of the Pindus Mountains, *Illustrated London News,* 18 July 1931, 100–1.

1932

Albanian-English Reader: Sixteen Albanian Folk-Stories Collected and Translated, With Two Grammars and Vocabularies, Cambridge, 122 pp.

An Albanian Ballad on the Assassination in 1389 of Sultan Murad I on Kosovo Plain, *Occident and Orient,* 1932.

Physiological Paternity and Belated Birth in Albania (Correspondence), *Man,* February 1932, No. 65, 53–54.

1933

Childhood and Totemism (Correspondence), *Man,* August 1933, No. 148.

Bride-Price in Albania: A Homeric Parallel, *Man*, December 1933, No. 203, 191–95.

1935

Pearls as Life Givers (Correspondence), *Man*, July 1935, No. 125.

1936

A Historical Sketch of the Fluctuations of Lake Ostrovo in West Macedonia, *Journal of the Royal Geographical Society*, Vol. 87, No. 4, April 1936, 338–47.

The Archaeological History of Lake Ostrovo in West Macedonia, *JRGS*, Vol. 88, No. 5, November 1936, 448–57.

1937

Causes of the Fluctuations in Level of Lake Ostrovo, West Macedonia, *JRGS*, Vol. 90, No. 5, November 1937, 446–57.

Review of 'King Zog's Albania' by J. Swire, *JRGS*, Vol. 90, July 1937, 69–70.

Review of 'Sons of the Eagle' by R. Matthews, *JRGS*, Vol. 90, November 1937, 469–70.

1938

The Gypsies of Albania, *Journal of the Gypsy Lore Society*, Vol. XVII, No. 2 (April) 49-61, No. 3 (Jubilee Number) 18–30, No. 4 (October) 110–22.

1939

Couvade in Albania, *Man*, February 1939, No. 18, 18–20.

1944

Albanian Phrase Book, 100 pages. Published for military use. The publisher and publication date are not inscribed. The copy in the British Library is marked '1944 (?)'.

1946

The Bust of Berat, *Man*, March–April 1946, No. 29, 36–8.

The Youngest Son (Correspondence), *Folk-Lore*, Vol. 57, 93–4.

1947

Head-Deformation in the Near East, *Man*, October 1947, No. 143, 130–31.

1948

Untitled (Correspondence), *Folk-Lore*, Vol. 59, 95–6.
On ex-King Umberto of Italy (correspondence), *The Times*, 14 January 1948, 7.

Posthumous Publications

Oedipus Rex in Albania, *Folk-Lore*, Vol. 60, September 1949, 340–8.
The First Cradle of an Albanian Child, *Man*, May 1950, No. 69, 55–7.
The Unwritten Law In Albania, Cambridge, 1954, 285 pp.

Notes

1. For this information and for much more, I am greatly indebted to Hasluck's niece Jean Bain and great-niece Margaret Woodward, both of whom gave freely of their time and memories of 'Aunt Margaret'. I would also like to acknowledge the kindness and support of Stephanie Schwander-Sievers of the Albanian Studies Programme at the School of Slavonic and East European Studies, London.
2. Helen Waterhouse, *The British School at Athens*, p. 6.
3. F.W. Hasluck, *Letters on Religion and Folklore*, Luzac & Co., 1926 , p. 4. He particularly disliked the 'roorality' of Macedonia, though Margaret suggests his opinion was 'coloured by the sleepless nights he had spent there; he was unfortunate enough to have travelled at the height of the vermin season.' p. 9.
4. This and most other anecdotes were gathered during interviews with people who knew Hasluck. Principal interviewees include: from the BSA, Nicholas Hammond, Frank Stubbings, and Helen Waterhouse; from SOE, Reginald Hibbert and David Smiley; and from Hasluck's family, Jean Bain and Margaret Woodward.
5. Waterhouse, *The British School at Athens*, pp. 24–5
6. M.M. Hasluck (editor) in F.W. Hasluck, *Christianity and Islam Under the Sultans*, Clarendon, 1929, p. viii.
7. F.W. Hasluck, *Letters on Religion and Folklore*, p. 16; in a report dated 11.6.22 to the Wilson Trustees, now in the Marischal Museum, Aberdeen University, she says that she was searching for 'the ancient Macedonians'.
8. Marischal Museum collection, Aberdeen University.
9. Some 1800 of Hasluck's prints are at the Royal Geographical Society, London.
10. Zog's gendarmes had the opportunity, but not the inclination, to contribute to field work. Nicholas Hammond once asked a gendarme how he passed the time in an Albanian village. 'I talk to him,' he said, indicating a translator who spoke almost no English – 'and him,' pointing to his dog.
11. MMH, review in the *Journal of the Royal Geographical Society*, 1937, Vol. 90, p. 469.
12. Report to Wilson Fellows, Marischal Museum, Aberdeen University.
13. She might also have travelled with a wind-up phonograph. One of her photographs in the RGS shows an impeccably dressed Zogist gendarme sitting

cross-legged beside Albanian highlanders in a wattle shelter, with a wind-up phonograph alongside.

14. MMH, *Journal of the Gypsy Lore Society*, October 1938 Vol. XVII, No. 4, p. 111.
15. Ibid, p. 113.
16. Public Records Office, FO 369/3361
17. Ibid.
18. M.E. Durham, review of Hasluck's *English-Albanian Reader* in *Man*, July 1932, No. 212.
19. E. Hoxha, *The Anglo-American Threat to Albania*, 8-Nentori Publishing, 1982, p. 101.
20. MMH's last known letter to her cousin, 7.8.48. A copy was provided to the author by M. Woodward.
21. MMH, letter to *Folk-Lore* Vol. 39, 1928, p. 182, in which she asks that the journal act as a go-between for queries and professional correspondence.
22. A selection is on permanent display at the museum. A letter indicates that she tried to send a complete skeleton from Macedonia to Aberdeen, but was having problems shipping it; a hand-written note on the letter suggests that she may, however, have sent two skulls.
23. In Ms. Myres 19, Western Manuscripts, Bodleian Library, Oxford.
24. A letter to Myres of 15.6.30 begins: 'Can you really do something with the Pope on my behalf about the Catholics of Albania?' His response is not recorded. On 27.6.30 she writes: 'Evidently I misunderstood something you once said about the Pope.'
25. MMH *Journal of the Gypsy Lore Society*, October 1938, Vol. XVII, No. 4, p. 122. Several photos of Hasluck in Albania show her wearing a very military-looking pith helmet.
26. A copy of Hasluck's will was provided to the author by M. Woodward.
27. Zog may have been happy to oblige. Lef Nosi was not in his favour, as evidenced by restrictions on Nosi's travel. And Hasluck was quite capable of making her own enemies. Barely a year before her expulsion she had described Zog as 'an enigmatic personality given . . . to politely deluding his visitors.' *Journal of the Royal Geographical Society*, November 1937, Vol. 90, p. 470.
28. In a post-war letter to Myres, Hasluck says that she began her covert work almost immediately on reaching Athens in April 1939.
29. I am grateful to Frank Stubbings, then at the BSA, for alerting me to this.
30. But then, Manning seemed to dislike most people, unlike her gregarious husband. The following comment is typical: 'Reggie was always welcoming, ready for a discussion about anything under the sun. But Olivia made you feel that the moment you had sense enough to leave she would like to go to bed.' I. Porter, *Operation Autonomous*, Chatto and Windus, 1989, p. 23.
31. Olivia Manning, *Friends and Heroes*, Penguin Books, 1980, p. 39
32. Ibid, pp.231–2.
33. Ibid, p. 337.
34. Hasluck wanted above all Nicholas Hammond, who spoke Albanian fluently, but he was sent to Greece, where he passed on many occasions as a Greek or Vlach shepherd. 'History might have been different if he'd gone my way.' Letter to Myres of 13.1.46.
35. Half a century later the recrimination was still going on. See, for example, R. Hibbert, *Albania's National Liberation Struggle*, Pinter 1991, Chapter 15.

36. 'The lines of the government's policy would meet with our warm approval if we were not at war with the country whose forces now occupy Albania,' she wrote. (PRO, FO 371/43549). Bernd Fischer gives an interesting assessment of the council in *Albania at War 1939-1945*, Purdue 1999.
37. PRO, HS 5/66 and 5/67.
38. Copy of a communication from the Foreign Office provided by Roderick Bailey, who is preparing a doctoral dissertation at the University of Edinburgh on SOE's Albania activities. I am indebted to him for his comments and advice regarding SOE's Albanian operations.
39. The new government turned Hasluck's house into a maternity home. In post-communist times it was handed to a British couple who ran it as an orphanage. It was indirectly in the news during the 1997 breakdown of order in Albania when an SAS troop helicoptered to the orphanage and lifted the Britons and orphans to safety.
40. PRO, FO 369/3361.
41. Letter in Marischal Museum, 14.6.47.
42. PRO, FO 951/1.
43. The tray is part of a small standing exhibition devoted to Hasluck.
44. PRO, FO 372/6302.
45. S. Gjeçov / L. Fox translation, *Kanuni i Lekë Dukagjinit / The Code of Leke Dukagjini*, Gjonlekaj 1989.
46. B. Malinowski, *Crime and Custom in Savage Society*, Routledge and Keagan Paul 1926, p. 9.
47. M.E. Durham, *High Albania*, Virago 1987, p. 41.
48. Curiously, Albanologists seldom ask why the first chapter of a law code used mainly by Moslems is entitled 'The Church'. Sixty years after publication of Gjeçov's canon, the church published another unwritten law (*Kanuni i Skanderbegut*, Editrice La Rosa, 1993). In 1994 a priest in Shkoder involved in that project told the author that he and his colleagues selectively suppressed and upgraded material in the code to support their agenda, particularly regarding the strengthening of family and church. He made no apology for this; in his eyes, he was serving a higher good.
49. MMH, *The Unwritten Law*, p. 12.
50. For examples of modest changes in the canon see Durham, *High Albania*, p. 112 or pp. 153-5; and *The Code of Leke Dukagjini*, Appendix XI. Durham's overall thesis is that north Albania is essentially unchanged for eons, the 'land of the living past'; but her unwritten law has at least some variety and capacity for change. Most of the changes noted in the Franciscan version are very minor; of those changes, many directly reinforce the position of the church, and all could be supported by it.
51. For instance, the punishment of burning homes declined as people shifted from wood and straw homes, which were easily replaced, to stone homes. *The Unwritten Law*, p. 232.
52. B. Malinowski, *Crime and Custom in Savage Society*, pp 125-7.
53. MMH, *The Unwritten Law*, p. 11.
54. I.M. Lewis, *Social Anthropology in Perspective*, Penguin 1976, p. 26.
55. See for example M. Vickers, *The Albanians: A Modern History*, I.B. Tauris 1995; T. Zavalani, *Histori e Shqipnis*, Phoenix 1998; and S. Pollo and A. Puto, *The History of Albania*, Routledge & Kegan Paul 1981 (originally published as *l'Histoire*

de l'Albanie, Horvath). None of these editions mentions Hasluck in the bibliography, or in the text.

56. See her letters to Myres and to Cambridge University Press.

57. C. Lévi-Strauss, *Tristes Tropiques* (John Russell trans.) Atheneum, 1967, p. 314. Early in this book Lévi-Strauss calls travel writers 'auxiliaries who do us nothing but harm' (p. 40). He then proceeds to write a brilliant travel book.

58. MMH, *Journal of the Gypsy Lore Society*, Vol. XVII April 1938, p. 27.

59. J. Morris, Introduction to *The Letters of Gertrude Bell*, Penguin 1987, p. X.

60. A good example is found in a short 1955 item in *Man*. The author clearly identified with Gjeçov, Durham and other 'enlightened patriots' with 'a sense of mission' (his words) to promote a positive national image; Hasluck, by contrast, saw herself as a professional scholar. In attempting to undermine Hasluck's credibility, the author puts forward arguments and anecdotes that are thoroughly inconsistent with other sources. (Q. Kastrati, Some Sources On The Unwritten Law in Albania, *Man*, August 1955, No. 134).

CHAPTER 10

This little digression has interrupted my telling you we passed over the fields of Carlowitz, where, the last great Victory was obtained by Prince Eugene over the Turks. The marks of that Glorious bloody day are yet recent, the fields being strew'd with the Skulls and Carcasses of unbury'd Men, Horses and Camels. I could not look without horror on such numbers of mangled humane bodys, and refflect on the Injustice of War, that makes murther not only necessary but meritorious. Nothing seems to me a plainer proof of the irrationality of Mankind (whatever fine claims we pretend to Reason) than the rage with which they contest for a small spot of Ground. . . .

Lady Mary Montagu Wortley, **Letters During Mr. Wortley's Embassy**, of 1724. Letters from Belgrade to Alexander Pope, 12 February 1717.

Louisa Rayner: An Englishwoman's Experiences in Wartime Yugoslavia

Anne Kay

Louisa Rayner is the pseudonym of Isobel Božić, who wrote *Women in a Village* about her impressions of life in Yugoslavia under German occupation. This was published in London in 1957, and, in translation, in Belgrade in 1986. Excerpts from the book were serialised in the Belgrade daily paper, *Politika*, in November and December 1986.

Louisa Rayner's first visit to Sarajevo in the early 1930s awakened rather than satisfied her curiosity about Yugoslavia. By contrast, her travelling companion thought a return visit:

... would be a sign of sentimental susceptibility quite unworthy of the English tourist. The English tourist should be a connoisseur of views; she should not want to become part of the view herself. (p. 154)*

Louisa Rayner, however, returned to Yugoslavia, and took up a teaching post in Belgrade. There she met her husband, a Bosnian whom she later married, in Sarajevo. Although she is herself dismissive of the suggestion that her interest in Yugoslavia was, at that time, at all unusual, it is worth noting the parallel that Rebecca West's travels took place in 1937, and that her account of them was first published in 1942. When members of the Yugoslav government arrived in exile in London in 1941, they were viewed by the press and their Foreign Office hosts as people from a remote and exotic land. Though Louisa Rayner saw her marriage as an end to her position as an outsider, she remained an acute and perceptive observer of the Yugoslav way of life.

The major part of her book describes the summer of 1944, which she spent as a refugee from the Allied bombing of Belgrade. However, the earlier brief account of the middle-class Belgrade circle which she joined, is also fascinating. Although for most of her friends the Serbian peasant was a near ancestor, their aspirations were cosmopolitan, and the chief influences Viennese and Parisian. The women all had servants, and hence, considerable leisure time. Their interests were largely domestic: staff, cooking, dress-makers, shoe-makers and so on. The men were preoccupied with politics and the prospect of war. Louisa Rayner noted that the absence of an aristocracy meant that the monarchy was supported, somewhat uneasily, by army officers, politicians, industrialists and churchmen, who, to a greater or lesser degree, owed their positions to it. Favours and interventions on behalf of friends were an essential part of the process of social advance and the cafes were the setting both for this and political discussion. When, on rare occasions, her husband brought someone home, she, the Cambridge graduate, waited on them, but was not expected to contribute to the conversation.

Amidst the many detailed military and political accounts of the *coup d'état* of 27 March 1941 and the subsequent German invasion, Louisa Rayner's description provides a useful touchstone:

---

* All quotations in this text are from Louisa Rayner, *Women in a Village: An Englishwoman's experiences and impressions of life in Yugoslavia under German occupation*, London: William Heinemann, 1957, with page references in brackets.

Yet life went on, though there was an increasingly fantastic hunt for food, textiles, shoes and fuel. Still we aired our children in the park; we sat and walked; we talked and knitted–knitted old wool over and over again. (p. 10)

The German occupation was, at first, disciplined and not heavy-handed. Shortages, and the fear of blackmail or betrayal by servants who knew of her English nationality, were the main problems.

Heavy and regular Allied bombing of Belgrade in 1944 caused Louisa Rayner and her husband and daughter to seek safety in a village called Rušanj. Though only a dozen miles from Belgrade, its situation at the end of a long muddy track, away from main lines of communication, made it seem more remote. Her husband felt that there they would be safe from the Germans, the Allied bombing and the Partisans. He estimated that 90 per cent of the two thousand villagers favoured the Chetniks (the non-Communist resistance fighters who supported King Peter). They found lodgings with a grandmother, her two daughters-in-law and four grandchildren. (The two sons were prisoners of war in Germany).

There was never any question of rent. The villagers were unused to house-letting. In a house, they knew, one was hospitable, and a guest would eventually be generous. (p. 23)

Her husband, a fuel merchant, had chosen this household because he had noticed it had a huge stock of wood. Louisa Rayner took to it for quite different reasons. It was not the cleanest or most orderly of households, but the matriarchal Savka intrigued her, as did the very ancient house, unusually situated in a withdrawn position. For six months Louisa Rayner shared this small house and kitchen with Savka and her family. As they cooked, pigs, dogs, hens and cats ran round their feet, and they talked. Savka recalled that in the First World War the household had lost two oxen and two men. 'Such a Homeric scale of values tempted me to further questions.' (p. 25) Louisa Rayner, with her first class Classics degree from Cambridge, found it fascinating to observe rural Serbian life, make comparisons and draw classical allusions.

She describes, in detail, the daily life and its artifacts. Savka's smoky kitchen illumined a passage in Homer's *Odyssey* for her. The level of the mud floor, the door catches, the mattresses, the rugs on the beds, all had their ancestry in, or bore a marked resemblance to, their Homeric forerunners. The social historian can enjoy the details of spinning, washing, baking bread, building houses and local cures. In much of this, the women predominated not only in war-time, when the men were absent, but also in peace-time doing most of the hard work, except ploughing. Fetching water was a major task always performed by women – as was marketing, which meant walking the twelve miles to Belgrade and back. Marriages were arranged and were seen by the bride's family as a sad event, her leaving her home meant the loss of her labour. Her value was reflected in the payment of a deposit to her family, which was then used to equip her with marriage clothes, bedding and bedstead.

Louisa Rayner observed that Savka handled her household with great tact, in six months she never heard an angry word. Politics were never mentioned by Savka, though certainly this was a subject on which her two daughters-in-law differed: one favouring Serbian nationalism, the monarchy, and the Chetniks; the other sympathising with Communism. The former, Vida, had unusually, received four years of schooling, but her family had opposed her attendance at a grammar school in Belgrade, where, in time, it was feared, she would throw over her background, choose her own employment and even choose her own husband. She remained an ardent reader and shocked her family by neglecting her farming to read Louisa Rayner's copy of Virgil in a Serbian translation.

To the historian of war-time military and political matters in Yugoslavia, it is the references to great events, interspersed amongst the details of domestic routine, which are of paramount interest. The microcosm of Rušanj enhances the general picture of events in Serbia. In the village, the metal sign on the Council House had been removed in expectation of a change of regime, but neither Germans nor representatives of the puppet government had ever penetrated the three miles of mud from the main road, and a wooden replica had been erected.

> Rušanj cocked a snook at the German Army, it put out its tongue at the Ministers in Belgrade ... It was in the Kingdom of Yugoslavia–nay, it *was* the Kingdom of Yugoslavia. It was a City State. (p. 80)

The villages knew of the existence of Fascist bands – though no-one ever claimed to have seen any; and of the Partisans, who were far to the west and south-west. Rušanj itself was in the Chetnik common area, whose headquarters were at Ripanj. Though the clerk publicised Chetnik proclamations, he did not run Rušanj in their name. 'Most of the villagers favoured the Chetniks in a rather condescending and uncooperative manner. . . . They might be allies; they would never be subjects.' (p. 81) The villagers clearly managed well, the basis of local government continued to operate, the *gendarmerie* was not missed. Occasional public meetings were held, for the men to discuss a particular matter. Their loyalties were to their land, not the larger community to which they had formerly belonged, and they did not therefore regret its disappearance. It was a village without a priest, a large land-owner, or any important inhabitants; the clerk was the key figure, advising the councillors rather than merely doing their bidding.

Although there was galloping inflation, the people of Rušanj were not severely affected, as they produced little for sale. The refugees, by contrast, found themselves equating former luxuries like a grand piano with three or four pounds of lard. Within the village, some families were a little better off, with more animals or more land than they required for their own needs but all lived in much the same frugal way and worked hard. Without apparent fuss the population of two thousand took in eighteen hundred refugees. Apart from this intrusion in 1944, the War almost passed Rušanj by, though occasionally, the Chetniks came for food. Louisa Rayner observed that they could have measured their falling popularity by noting that the wedges of cheese they were offered grew smaller and smaller. 'It should have been a warning. Armies cannot eat their popularity and have it. The Chetniks ate theirs.' (p. 82)

Louisa Rayner's husband had a nephew, Mirko, who was with the Chetniks 'in the woods'. He recounted how he had taken part in a great service of consecration and blessing on a mountainside, during which a German fighter had circled, looked and flown on. Her husband did not like the sound of this, and liked the accounts of fighting the Partisans even less. 'Like most people we had kinsfolk in every one of the fighting factions. . . . Most people joined the first forces that appeared in their neighbourhood.' (p. 102) Mirko visited them once and told them of his disenchantment, not with General Mihailović, the Chetnik leader, but with the local commanders. Now his tales were not of English parachutists coming to their aid in great numbers with quantities of gold coins, but of leaders who had women brought out in lorries from Belgrade. 'This was not only a shocking lapse from heroic seriousness but implied a shocking collaboration with the authorities.' (p. 103)

Originally the Chetniks' aim was: '. . . to relieve the people and lessen the pain of the giant's oppressiveness, and then to keep

159

alive the old heroic, royalist, Christian tradition . . . against all comers.' (p. 122) They did not expect to defeat the Germans. They found, however, that it was difficult to defend those who had no wish to be defended. In Rušanj, the Germans presented no problem.

> A friendly alliance with the Chetniks was all very well, but to suffer an officious protection against Germans or Partisans and actually to have to make contributions towards such protection seemed to the villagers a quite unnecessary trouble. (pp. 122–33)

One night, unusually, Louisa Rayner and her husband were disturbed by soldiers' voices. 'Clearly some Chetniks had come and were thrashing a number of village youths.' (pp. 123–4) The English Louisa Rayner longed to intervene, but her Yugoslav counterpart realised that they would not listen to a woman, that she would have to be rescued by her husband, and that he in turn would be beaten. The group was led by the Chetnik commandant of a neighbouring district, who had received a report of a meeting between Rušanj boys and a suspected Communist from his own area. As Louisa Rayner noted, the Chetniks '. . . had no firmer ground under their feet than the favour of the people in villages up and down Serbia.' (p. 126) Such heavy-handed tactics were therefore unwise, particularly as covert Communist infiltration was increasingly coming out into the open. On a national scale, for example, the Communists had:

> that solid, respectable, copious, leading, national daily newspaper, the Belgrade *Politika*. All the time when Communism was illegal they had had it, producing a journal in the Serbian Christian, royalist, heroic tradition, so as to have the staff, the machinery and the reading public ready for the moment when the formerly forbidden ideology should be the only one not forbidden. (p. 123)

Locally, the Clerk of the Council provided a parallel. A call-up of one hundred local youths was required by the Chetniks, the Clerk issued the orders. Rifles, cartridges and boots were delivered in readiness. Recruits were to bring three days' food and meet at 3 a.m. This was a good plan, the early departure was exciting, the boots and rifles an incentive. No-one refused to be mobilised. At 9 a.m., after the departure, the villagers found the Council records burned, the safe emptied and the recruits scooped by the Partisans. The Clerk had been the Communist agent for Rušanj.

As the summer of 1944 wore on, Louisa Rayner became aware, even in her isolated village, of a feeling of change in the air. During her stay, the children stopped singing a song about King Peter. Her own position was increasingly dangerous. After the attempt to assassinate Hitler in July 1944, in an atmosphere of irrational fear, the Germans ordered the arrest, in occupied countries, of any remaining women belonging by birth or marriage to Allied states. She was, however, not discovered, as her name was not conspicuously English, and her Serbian was fluent. Soon after, another threat to the family's safety arose. The local Chetnik leader, angered by the loss of his hundred recruits, tried to blame it on the Communist influence of the refugees. The death penalty was ordered for the crime of allowing refugees to stay more than forty-eight hours. Peasants were forbidden to leave their villages, which meant they could neither take refugees to a station nor go to buy winter fodder for their animals. Fortunately, the commander was persuaded to rescind his order. He had, as Louisa Rayner pointedly observed, '. . . the choice of seeming cruel and obstinate or cruel and silly. Both courses led to hatred and failure.' (p. 166)

Late that summer, Rušanj's isolation was threatened. The great wave of Soviet and Partisan troops, heading for Belgrade, was clearly going to pass over it. Immediately in the wake of the Russians on the main road, the Partisans came to Rušanj. The village women were up all night, making bread with their last stocks of flour. The Partisans were ragged, thin and weary, but proud; their officers were remarkably smart. The villagers held back timidly, but Savka rushed forward, her tenderness was what she was storing for her own sons.

> Our offerings were accepted too, but not with much gratitude. In fact the gate remained closed between us as a symbol of a misunderstanding. The men supposed that all that bread and all the trouble of baking it was, if not a tribute to Communism, at least a thank-offering on the part of the villagers for their liberation from the Germans, while the cheese and other little luxuries were a just tax to be paid by fat and lazy Serbia to thin and heroic Bosnia and Lika, which had sacrificed their all to win the war. (p. 197)

The villagers, however, had never felt enslaved and did not feel gratitude for liberation: their gifts were to tired young men-somebody's children.

In this new climate, the people of Rušanj and all Serbia quickly had to make important decisions about whom to support.

Inevitably many flocked to the winning side. Even in those with whom she had lived in such harmony and at such close quarters, Louisa Rayner now notices a changed attitude. One daughter-in-law said.

> You are very clever. Presumably you want the English to win because they are your people; but you never say a single word about it. So that even if anyone wanted to denounce you it would not be possible. (p. 183)

Louisa Rayner's husband was horrified.

> It meant that Vida, the daughter-in-law and no doubt her father too, were no longer supporters of the monarchy and the Chetniks but had veered round to a Partisan point of view. And that point of view, which the simplest peasant could quite well gasp in the autumn of 1944, was that, after the imminent defeat of the Germans, a clear hostility would arise between Russia and her western Allies. It followed that a newly converted Partisan might be able to win the confidence of Russian and other Communists by denouncing someone who had spoken a word in favour of the British. (pp. 183–4)

Although public sentiment now appeared to favour the Partisans, the peasants were not carried away by enthusiasm. Indeed, in their own way, many avoided or discreetly sabotaged Partisan orders. When instructed to provide live meat, Savka sent an ill hen; a villager ordered to go three villages away and transport stores did not refuse, but used a cow which was due to calve at any moment. As anticipated she had to stop to give birth, so he avoided the job. His possession of other more suitable cows was not discovered. Sometimes, however, those who displeased the Partisans did not get away so lightly. A woman who offered bread to a wounded prisoner in a group of captured Chetniks, was shot dead.

Suddenly the sojourn in Rušanj was over. As soon as Belgrade fell, the refugees began returning by cart, anxious to avoid the onslaught of winter in the village. Louisa Rayner had to leave at short notice, her husband had gone on ahead and arranged the transport; the cart had to be back in Belgrade before dark. She had to leave without saying goodbye, as everyone was out in the fields, though she saw Savka's family and other villagers later when they visited Belgrade. As she travelled, she saw slogans in red paint on every possible surface.

The people of Serbia, it has always seemed to me, are rather reserved and ironical in the expression of their enthusiasms. They have little spontaneity in pageantry and public display. Besides, if their feelings this time had burst all reserve and demanded instant expression, whence the red paint? No manufactured commodity in any quantity was available at all in Belgrade at this time. The red paint for all those slogans must have been acquired, hoarded and distributed over a long period, with this very purpose of slogan-painting in view. (p. 220)

The fact that these slogans were not the outward manifestation of spontaneous popular enthusiasm was further emphasised by Louisa Rayner's discovery that:

... the slogans had been stencilled on the walls. If you are sharp enough to see the slogans are stencilled and not painted, and what that implies, you will feel as uncomfortable as a prehistoric fish left over from an earlier age. (p. 221)

That Louisa Rayner's pointed observation was a valid criticism, is indicated by its omission from the recently translated edition of her book.

Communist rule was established and made familiar to people through its open-air meetings and processions. At first harbour workers were organised for the meetings, but then, apparently, someone realised that in a basically agricultural country some peasants ought to be present.

So on the days appointed for demonstrations ... free return tickets to Belgrade were offered to the peasants in the surrounding villages. They came in thousands to sell their milk and cheese privately to their friends; but they were not interested in meetings. (p. 225)

In January 1946 Louisa Rayner left Belgrade after living there for more than a decade. Her summer in Rušanj stood out more clearly than any other time. If the events seemed so significant to her, she thought they might perhaps interest others. 'It is a true story, not a novel ... or rather it is the truth in so far as I was able to grasp it then and can now remember it.' (p. 13)

A feature of her book is the illumination which her classical knowledge and interest lends to her account of everyday things. It is, also, a woman's view: for example, the perception of the Partisan soldiers as someone's tired, hungry children, is probably not an interpretation many men would make. Yet while retaining her stance as an observer, Louisa Rayner clearly adopted the maxim of 'When in Rome'. Her husband, as a Bosnian, was strongly influenced by the Turkish tradition that the man's role was to defend his property and his family, while women were to be obedient and to work, and were privileged to be defended. If no defending was necessary, the men did little or nothing. There is no hint of Louisa Rayner chafing at this situation, though her personal bravery was undoubtedly considerable; for example, when she was sent for by the Partisans to teach at an Adult Education Centre, because she was the only qualified teacher available. Originally the intention had been to give Russian lessons, but the demand for English was so great that she was allowed to teach it instead. She suspects that the Communists were somewhat uneasy – at an early session a soldier sat throughout in the front row with his gun pointing straight at her!

The details of the village way of life which she describes, are what now interest many Yugoslavs. The years since the war have seen such extensive and dramatic change that many now feel they have quite lost touch with their rural antecedents.

Yet at the time of Louisa Rayner's stay, there had been little change for centuries and she found little desire for it. As an outsider, she could see many possible improvements, not only for major matters like health care, but also smaller ones like greater co-ordination of farming efforts. She was, however, well aware that the peasants were contented with their life-style. Greater organisation would have meant some sort of record-keeping, and as most people were neither literate nor numerate, this would have left them open to manipulation by their own clerk. Their priorities remained basic. When Louisa Rayner warned a child against taking the cows to graze near the railway line, because of the danger of stray bullets, the grandmother warned her even more firmly not to run off or leave the cow. Although the child was loved, another cow-minder could be found more easily than another cow. The child – from this basic viewpoint – was a mouth to feed, whereas the cow produced milk and cheese and was used for ploughing, harrowing and carting loads. Louisa Rayner thought veterinary clinics would be a great advance, and would be more likely to be used than health clinics. The peasants rarely visited a doctor, though TB was especially prevalent, and when they did, the disease was usually too far advanced for a cure. The doctors were then blamed for the patient's death, and the belief that they were not worth visiting continued.

Although the main body of her book is concerned with the domestic, the historian of greater events can find information about political and military affairs as they affected one small village, and find too that it elucidates that larger picture. That some of her comments have required – or anyway received – censorship, forty years later, is at least partly a tribute to her perceptiveness (though it is also a comment on the continuing hypersensitivity of Tito's heirs to war-time matters). It is interesting to note, as Louisa Rayner has done in a recent letter, that the excerpts from her book which have been serialised in *Politika* have been subjected to closer scrutiny and censorship than the translation of the book itself. Although the publication of the book in Belgrade was privately funded, the interest generated was sufficient to encourage the state television service to send a film crew to Norfolk to see and film Louisa Rayner. She has recounted, with amusement, her progress round the centre of her local small town, preceded by the swarthy film crew, backing their cameras and microphones into the small shops. Clearly she had taken the whole intrusion in her stride. She is characteristically modest about this renewed attention for her book.

The combination of her education, interest and length of stay has made her observations particularly perceptive. Her account is of great military and political events – including the demise of the Karadjordjević dynasty – as they affected one small village, and the end of a much longer era during which the way of life in that village had been almost unchanged for centuries. The current revival of interest in her book is primarily for its portrayal of social and domestic traditions in a Serbian village, but the Yugoslav reader will also benefit from her account of events in an era of recent history still subject to concealment, misrepresentation and misunderstanding.

CHAPTER 11

Devil's work,
Devil's work, my masters.
Britain, your hands are red!
You may close your heart, but you cannot shirk
This terrible fact: we kept the Turk.
His day was done and we knew his work,
But he played our game, so we kept the Turk;
For our own sake's sake we kept the Turk:
Britain, your hands are red!
Red are the walls and the ways,
And, Britain, your hands are red!
There is blood on the hearth and blood in the well,
And the whole fair land is a red, red hell –
Britain, Your hands are red!

John Oxenford, *The Daily News*, 29 September 1903.

Mercia MacDermott:
A Woman of the Frontier*

Diane Waller

Introduction

Mercia MacDermott is a writer and a historian of the Balkans. Until recently (1989) she lived in Sofia, Bulgaria, where she was a lecturer at the University. She is a foreign correspondent member of the Bulgarian Academy of Sciences and an Honorary Citizen both of the town of Karlovo. This was (the birthplace of the

* Grateful thanks to Mercia MacDermott herself, who has patiently worked through the text with the author. ensuring that the historical details are fairly and accurately presented, and also to Dan Lumley who has read and commented so helpfully on the various drafts.

166

Bulgarian revolutionary Vasil Levsky, the subject of her second book *The Apostle of Freedom*) and of Blagoevgrad, in the Pirin region, where the subjects of her subsequent books were active. There has been a long tradition of Britons who have taken an interest in Bulgarian affairs and who supported the Bulgarians' struggle to free themselves from five hundred years of Ottoman oppression. Among the most prominent of the late nineteenth and early twentieth century were the British prime-minister, William Gladstone, the artist-designer, William Morris, the playwright, Oscar Wilde, and the Viscountess Strangford, whose late husband had been an expert on Eastern Europe and a strong supporter of the Bulgarian struggle.

Dorothy Anderson, in her book *The Balkan Volunteers*, tells the story of the relief funds and voluntary aid organisations which came into existence at the time of the Balkan crisis (1876–78):

> I became aware of the existence of the many fund-raising organisations and of the activities of the volunteers, and also of the paucity of information about this aspect of the Eastern Question, when engaged in research for 'Miss Irby and Her Friends'. Paulina Irby's fund to help the Bosnian refugees was just one of the myriad that existed at the time, and in this book it has been mentioned only as it affected the development of other funds, and to complete the pattern of money subscribed and operations undertaken in the regions of Turkey-in-Europe.[1]

Writing about Lady Strangford's contribution to the medical relief operations in Bulgaria in 1876, following the massacres by the Turks, Anderson said:

> In the years since (her husband's) death, she had devoted herself to nursing and hospital work; she was a Dame Chevaliére of the Order of St John of Jerusalem, and she was on the original committee of the Eastern War Sick and Wounded Fund. Lady Strangford, in making her appeal, asked for £10,000 to re-house the homeless and help the suffering, and she was planning to go out to Bulgaria to administer relief herself.[2]

Britons who have written about Bulgaria include Noel and Charles Rhoden Buxton, whose books deal with the period up to the First World War, and H.N. Brailsford, who headed a relief mission to Macedonia after the War. James Bourchier was a member of the Executive Committee of the Balkan Committee founded in London in 1903, and through his on-the-spot reporting managed to counter much of the anti-Bulgarian propaganda in English newspapers. All the above are still remembered in Bulgaria. In 1960, while Mercia MacDermott was attending a folk festival and taking photographs of women in national costume, one of them remarked, on finding out that she was English: 'We are glad to make the acquaintance of someone from the land of Gladstone.' Although not able to do much in practical terms for the Bulgarians, Gladstone, too, had become a folk hero. As well as being remembered by the people, some of the above have had streets, stations or housing estates named after them.

Mercia MacDermott may fairly be placed within this long and distinguished tradition. This paper is based on a long-standing friendship and appreciation of her approach to historical research, on her published work, and on an interview which Mercia gave with this paper as a focus.

Early Background

Mercia MacDermott was born in Plymouth on 7 April 1927. Her father was a surgeon in the Royal Navy, and her mother had been a teacher. The family travelled extensively as a result of her father's posting to different on-shore hospitals, and one of Mercia's earliest memories is of China, where she went with her parents at the age of eighteen months. They lived on the small island of Wei-Hai-Wei, off Cape Shantung, then a British naval base. For most of the year, they were the only English-speaking family on the island and Mercia learned Mandarin Chinese, which she spoke with her Chinese nurse. She was five when the family left China to return to England, initially to Portsmouth and later to Ditchling in Sussex, which Mercia regards as her home region. Prophetically, in view of her subsequent career, the ship on which they travelled out to China was called 'The Macedonia'.

Mercia attended a 'dame school' in Ditchling for children of the gentry. She described it as: '. . . a very peculiar, rather Victorian type of school, but giving an excellent education.' (Taped text of personal interview with Mercia MacDermott; subsequently T. I.)

In 1938, she won a scholarship to Westonbirt public school in Gloucestershire. Given her family background and early education, it is interesting to ponder on why she developed an interest in 'things Slavonic':

Possibly because in the social circles in which I moved – with my parents and uncles – I only heard ill of the Soviet Union and of Russia. I could never understand why it was that Russia was spoken of as an absolute pariah among nations . . . why people were so suspicious of Russia. And because bad things are often more intriguing than good things to a child, I became intrigued by Russia at an early age. When the Soviet Union became our ally, this latent interest and curiosity blossomed into an absolute passion, and I started to learn Russian on my own when I was about 14 or so. . . . (T.I.)

The headmistress of Westonbirt, Miss Violet Grubb, encouraged her interest and arranged for her to take Russian lessons in Bristol. By that time, her school had been evacuated to Bowood House and Corsham Court, two stately homes near Bath, so she was able to reach Bristol more easily. During the vacations she attended summer schools organised by the School of Slavonic Studies in London, Oxford, and Nottingham. She won a scholarship to St Anne's College, Oxford, to study French and Russian, but dropped French after the first year to concentrate on Russian.

Student Days

In 1946 Mercia got the chance to visit Prague, as a delegate to the Foundation Congress of the International Union of Students and it was there that she had her first encounter with Bulgarians with whom she could converse quite easily through Russian. She renewed her Bulgarian contacts again in the following year, when she went to take part in the building of a youth railway from _abac to Sarajevo in Yugoslavia:

> . . . I put my name down because I wanted to visit a Slavonic country. I went to Yugoslavia which I loved absolutely from the word go. We worked on the railway in Bosnia: our camp was near a village called Nemila, and in the same and neighbouring camps were many nationalities. In one of the camps there was a Bulgarian brigade, which impressed everyone with their enthusiasm. (T.I.)

Like many of the other students in her party, she was keen to visit Bulgaria, and in 1948, joined a brigade of about 50 people to take part in building a dam near the village of Koprivka. The brigade was named after Major Frank Thompson, a British Officer who was parachuted during the War to join the Bulgarian partisans and was killed with them. His heroic stance is remembered by the Bulgarians who named a station on the line from Sofia to northern Bulgaria after him.

In recalling this period of her life, Mercia described the idealism which she and her fellow students shared.

> It was really the most fantastic period when all the young people believed that we were going to turn the world into a paradise in the matter of a decade or so. And so we dug with joy and travelled the world. If you lost your visa it didn't matter: you said: 'I am a student' and perhaps argued a little bit, then they let you through. We hadn't got tickets and we hadn't got visas for various complicated reasons to do with not being able to change money and that sort of thing. (T.I.)

Bulgaria had suffered greatly as a result of the War. For historical reasons the government had taken the German side, although the majority of the Bulgarian people were solidly pro-Russian. As Germany's ally, the country had been severely damaged by British and US bombing raids, and also stripped bare by the Germans. On 9 September 1944, as a result of the Soviet army's support, the growth of a strong partisan movement and the revulsion felt by the Bulgarian people for Fascism, an armed uprising led by the Fatherland Front party overthrew the pro-German government and took Bulgaria onto the Allied side. A daunting task of reconstruction on every level faced the new government. Practical and moral support was desperately needed and thousands of students and workers, both in Bulgaria and abroad responded to the challenge by joining brigades to help in the construction of roads, railways, dams, and other public works.

Mercia recalled that the work in Bulgaria was arduous and the life was harsher and starker than she had experienced the year before in Yugoslavia. But such was the political idealism of the brigadiers who wished to join in not only rebuilding the country but also in building socialism in the Balkans, that they were able to endure grinding hard work.

> We were on a hillside where there was no shade and it was baking hot. We worked with picks, and very primitive spades which resembled the long handled spades which we had used during the War for removing incendiary bombs. You filled the wheelbarrows, then you wheeled them to the dump ... so there was no rest like there was when the trucks went down the line in Yugoslavia. The food seemed to be more monotonous. It was altogether much, much harder. I must admit, I

think at the time I was much more attracted to Yugoslavia. But it was
Bulgaria that really claimed me. I don't think we were very effective
(at) digging. I think probably the most important thing was the contacts
made. Some of the people who went to Bulgaria with that brigade
retained their special interest in Bulgaria forever. (T.I.)

After completing their assigned work, the brigade was given a holiday in Varna, on the coast. Of course, none of the resorts which
have been made so popular by 'Balkantourist' in recent years
existed then, and even Druzhba, the first to be developed, was still
an empty stretch of sand with no hotels at all.

Through a chance meeting in Varna with the wife of the Bulgarian Prime Minister and leader of the Communist Party, Georgi
Dimitrov, Mercia and her colleagues discovered he was on holiday
nearby, in the palace of Evksinograd. They asked their interpreter
if he could fix a meeting and it was duly arranged. Georgi Dimitrov
was a remarkable man who had taken a leading role in the Bulgarian struggle against Fascism. In 1933, he had been arrested in
Germany, following the deliberate burning of the *Reichstag* by the
Nazis. This act had the aim of placing the blame for the fire on the
Communist Party in Germany and worldwide, so that the Nazis
could discredit the Communists and win a reputation for fighting
terror and lawlessness. Dimitrov was the chief defendent at the
Leipzig trial and conducted his own defence, in German, which he
had learned during the several months spent in jail.[3]

> By virtue of his intellect, his ideological conviction and his nerves of
> steel he managed to turn from defendant into prosecutor and to indict
> fascism in its first moral political defeat.

Dimitrov was subsequently freed and went on to exert a major
influence on Bulgaria's post-war socialist development, paying particular attention to the economic structure and especially to the up-
dating of agriculture through improved techniques, new machinery
and co-operative farming.

The British brigade were much honoured by Dimitrov's willingness to meet them. Mercia remembered:

> We were on the beach of what is now Druzhba when the call to meet
> him came. So we put on our old working clothes – all that we had with
> us – and climbed into a lorry, which was the only form of transport
> available. I don't think anyone who visits Bulgaria now has the slight-
> est idea of the backwardness then. There were no asphalted roads in

Bulgaria, except for a couple of kilometres between Varna Station and the Palace. There were paved roads in the centres of towns, but all other roads were just dirt tracks, and this was so up 'till about 1957 or later. The height of luxury was to sit in the back of a lorry. There were few cars or buses and thus we travelled from the beach, covered in sand, in this lorry, to the former Royal Palace, where Georgi Dimitrov received us. (T.I.)

The group spent two hours with him. He answered all their questions and in turn asked if they would remember Bulgaria and tell their fellow countrymen about it when they returned. On receiving ardent promises that they would tell people at home about the good things which they had seen, Dimitrov gently reproved them and insisted that they should present a balanced and critical account, giving credit for the positive but not glossing over the negative. They assured him that they would, and Mercia felt that her lasting commitment to Bulgaria really began with that promise to Dimitrov.

Return to Britain

When Mercia graduated in 1948, the Cold War was already in existence and there was little prospect for Russian specialists to use their knowledge in cultural relations or a similar field. It had not been possible for her to visit Russia as a language student, nor as a tourist. During the period following her return from the Bulgarian brigade, however, she became involved in a number of cultural-political activities connected with Eastern Europe. For a time she was Information Officer for the Society for Cultural Relations with the USSR, and belonged to the 'Balalaika' Dance Group – an amateur group which performed Russian folk dances. Mercia herself felt that she had been drawn towards Russia in the first place by her interest in ethnography, and particularly by the folk music, costume and dance, becoming interested in history, politics and economics later on. Her growing interest in politics and desire to see equal opportunities for all people had led her to join the British Communist Party, and she had found a use for her language skills in teaching English to diplomats and trade representatives at the Soviet, Hungarian, Polish and later, Bulgarian embassies.

In the early 1950s, she joined the Society for Friendship with Bulgaria (now the British Bulgarian Friendship Society), helping to counter the invariably negative vision put forward in the media.

She performed with the Society's dance group for many years, and was elected Chairman of the Society in 1958 – a position which she held until 1973 when she returned to Bulgaria to work for the second time.

In the face of *Perestroika* and the enormous upheavals currently (1990) taking place in Eastern Europe, it is hard to remember what it meant at the height of the Cold War to be actively engaged in organisations associated with the USSR or Eastern Europe – 'the enemy'. Some paid the price for their convictions by finding their employment prospects severely limited or indeed, damaged. Nevertheless, they stuck to their ideals, driven by the desire for peace and for the establishment of humanistic socialism in Britain as well as in Eastern Europe. Mercia herself had to face the reality of the Cold War and the lack of opportunities to work in her field. The likelihood of visiting the USSR was very slight, so, as a result of her growing interest in Bulgaria in the early 1950s, she decided to switch her attention to Bulgarian studies. She enrolled in a two-year Diploma course in Bulgarian Regional Studies at the School of Slavonic Studies in London, studying language, history and economics.

Mercia discovered that although there were many books on Bulgaria available in specialist libraries in universities and in the British Museum, there were very few in the libraries to which most members of the general public had access. Given this shortage of information, and perhaps remembering the promise to Dimitrov, she decided to write about Bulgaria in a way that would be accessible to a wide readership. After completing the Diploma course, she began to prepare an outline of Bulgarian history, using Bulgarian authors as source material.

In the course of writing, the book became far too big, and eventually the central part which dealt with the Turkish yoke was published under the title: *The History of Bulgaria: 1393–1885*, the period from the Turkish Conquest to the reunification of the Bulgarian principality with Eastern Rumelia. (T.I.)

The book was published in 1962. As a result of her research, Mercia had become fascinated by the revolutionary movement of the nineteenth century against Ottoman rule and, in particular, by Vasil Levsky. Mercia said of Levsky:

He was one of the most charismatic revolutionaries in world history–a real-life fairy-tale hero who gains rather than loses when the historians penetrate the legends in search of the truth – and he was also one of the few revolutionaries whose ideas and practices represented in their day an entirely new departure. During the 1860s and 1870s, as a result of his own experiences as a participant in the national liberation movement, Levsky became convinced that revolution could not be imported from outside, neither could it be achieved by the actions of individuals or small groups of conspirators, no matter how brave and self-sacrificing they might be. For Levsky, there was no short cut to revolution. The winning of freedom required the conscious participation of the whole people, led by a disciplined organisation which would gradually prepare them both morally and materially for mass insurrection. To this end, Levsky travelled the country, constantly in danger of arrest, setting up a network of secret revolutionary committees, headed by a central committee and governed by a statute democratically adopted at a clandestine conference. Levsky's goal was not an uprising of the type common enough in Balkan history, namely, an inadequately prepared outburst of popular discontent, doomed to failure from the outset and designed primarily to bring the plight of the oppressed to the attention of world public opinion and the governments of the Great Powers: Levsky remained unconvinced that the latter were in any way motivated by humanitarian considerations, and in his opinion, they were more likely to respond to a demonstration of real strength than to burnt homes and massacred children. (T.I.)

Levsky's insurrection was to be a properly prepared nation-wide seizure of power, a victorious revolution which would sweep away Ottoman tyranny and establish 'freedom and a pure republic' based on 'people's government' and 'brotherhood and complete equality between all nationalities', leading ultimately to some form of Balkan federation. Mercia feels that:

Levsky's total dedication to the people's cause and his premature death on the gallows have ensured that all Bulgarians – no matter how diverse their views may be on other subjects – regard Levsky as a saint and a martyr, and he is adored by old and young alike in a way that has no parallel in Britain. During his own lifetime the Bulgarians began to call him 'the Apostle of Freedom' and even today when a Bulgarian speaks of 'the Apostle' without specifying which, he is not referring to one of the Twelve, but to the one and only Vasil Levsky. (T.I.)

Subsequent to the publication of her first book, Mercia began research into his life and work.

Living and Working in Bulgaria

In order to do full justice to the project, and to have regular access to Bulgarian libraries and archives, Mercia decided that she needed to go and live in Bulgaria. The most straightforward avenue was to obtain a teaching post at the English Language School in Sofia, and in 1963 she went off, intending to stay for a year. There are a number of foreign language schools all over the country. They are secondary schools in which the language is studied intensively in the first year, followed by the ordinary syllabus plus the language and its literature. In the case of the English Language School, many of the other subjects are studied in English and as far as possible are taught by visiting nationals.

During her year at the school, Mercia was delighted by the enthusiasm of the children who she found were eager to participate in her lessons and enchanted by English literature. Less appealing, however, was the style of work.

> The Bulgarian style of work consists of organising everything at the last moment. It will almost always take place, but to an English person who is accustomed to knowing several days in advance, at least, when there is going to be a meeting – if not knowing the programme for the entire year – the Bulgarian propensity for taking last minute decisions and for carrying them out is both amazing and rather unsettling. On the other hand, there were curious things . . . we were expected to produce a programme at the beginning of every term, saying what we were going to teach in every lesson throughout the year, what material, what purpose and the date! This was pure formality because the programme went wrong from the very beginning because the plans were changed. There would be a harvest brigade, or a sport's day, and the whole thing would be thrown out. Eventually we told one of the Inspectors and explained that even if we made a plan the school changed it and you couldn't carry it out. The Inspector very sensibly replied: 'If you can't make a programme and stick to it, then don't!' (T.I.)

Living in Bulgaria and participating in day-to-day activities contributed immensely to Mercia's understanding of Vasil Levsky's life and of his difficulties in persuading the population of the need for organised revolution as opposed to spontaneous or individual action.

The eventual publication of *The Apostle of Freedom* in 1967 had an enormous effect on her life. Although written primarily to inform English-speaking readers, it was also translated into

175

Bulgarian and immediately became a best-seller. The book is scholarly in presentation, but written in a refreshingly lively style, rich with descriptions of the Bulgarian countryside, of everyday life and customs – guaranteed to communicate to the British reader who knew little of Levsky or Bulgaria. But it made an impact in Bulgaria also, which, at the time, Mercia found overwhelming.

> It is very hard for me now to go out in the streets (in Bulgaria) without somebody recognising me and telling me how much they enjoyed my book about Levsky. For the first few years it was, of course, very moving . . . but it means that you are constantly in the public eye. I have appeared on television a number of times and people recognise me, but I think it is perhaps hard for English people to understand this popularity which I have obtained in Bulgaria through Levsky. I got into a tram once and the driver rose and kissed my hand. People give me flowers in the street . . . it is a mirror of their love for Levsky. I don't believe that, if I had written a better book about a less popular hero, this would have happened. (T.I.)

After Levsky

Following the success of *The Apostle of Freedom*, (which was translated into Esperanto and Russian as well as Bulgarian), Mercia found herself considering her next move. There seemed to be two possibilities. The first was to continue to research the history of the revolutionary movement in that part of Bulgaria which had become an independent state as a result of the Treaty of Berlin in 1878, which would have involved writing about Dimiter Blagoev and the Bulgarian Communist Party.[4] The second idea was to pursue research into the development of Levsky's ideas as they had emerged in the revolutionary movement in the areas of Macedonia and Adrianople.

According to the Treaty of San Stefano, signed between Russia and Turkey in 1878 at the end of the war which finally liberated Bulgaria from Ottoman rule, both territories had been included in the resurrected Bulgarian state. This arrangement aroused the opposition of the Western Great Powers, and Britain in particular. Disraeli (Lord Beaconsfield) feared that a strong Bulgarian state would lead to increased Russian influence in the Balkans and Eastern Mediterranean, thus threatening the security of the Suez Canal and Britain's communications with her Indian Empire. At the subsequent Congress of Berlin (to which no Bulgarian representatives were invited) the other Great Powers forced Russia to set aside the Treaty of San Stefano and join them in signing the Treaty of Berlin, which, among other things, divided the lands inhabited by Bulgarians into three, taking account neither of ethnic nor other local considerations. The land between the Danube and the Balkan Range, plus the Sofia Region, gained autonomy as a vassal principality. The area between the Balkan Range and the Rhodope Mountains, i.e. the area which had suffered most in the massacres so eloquently denounced by William Gladstone and others in 1876, became an autonomous province of Turkey, under the name of Eastern Rumelia. (This managed to reunite itself with the Principality in 1885). Macedonia, Aegean Thrace and the Adrianople region were simply left under direct Ottoman rule, with vague promises of reforms.

The motives for this dismemberment of Bulgaria were governed (principally) by the imperialist ambitions of the Great Powers. At no point did the opponents of San Stefano Bulgaria, including Disraeli himself, suggest that the population of Macedonia and the other territories left under Turkish rule were anything other than predominately Bulgarian. Indeed, the official map used at the Congress (Heinrich Kippert's ethnographic map published in Berlin in 1876) in common with virtually every other such map then available, unequivocally confirmed the ethnic justice of the frontiers of San Stefano.[5]

The irony of the situation is that, had the population of San Stefano Bulgaria not been ethnically homogeneous, the Treaty might not have aroused such opposition, since the incorporation of more than one nationality into a single state would have ensured its instability and preoccupation with internal problems and rivalries. It was precisely because Macedonia and the Adrianople region were known to be inhabited predominately by pro-Russian Bulgarians that the Western Great Powers could not countenance their inclusion in a state which could then have become the largest and most influential in the Balkans. Having ensured that the Bulgarians would spend the next fifty years trying to regain their national unity by every means at their disposal, including revolution and war, the Great Powers further fuelled the 'powder-keg' of Europe by allowing Austria to occupy Bosnia and Hercegovina, thus blocking Serbia's political and economic expansion towards the Adriatic, and forcing her to look southwards towards Macedonia and the Aegean. The idea – first mooted at the end of the nineteenth century – that the Slav population of Macedonia constituted a separate nation – was one of several mutually exclusive theories advanced by Serbian nationalists and designed to counter the 'Bulgarian idea' in Macedonia after the population there and the world in general refused to accept the thesis that they were Serbs and not Bulgarians.

James Bourchier, Balkan Correspondent of *The Times* who wrote the entry on 'Macedonia' in the eleventh edition of the *Encyclopaedia Britannica*, summed up the situation in a single sentence: 'The Berlin Treaty, by its artificial division of the Bulgarian race, created the difficult and perplexing, 'Macedonian Question'.'[6]

Despite the complexity of this period and the controversy over the decisions and the outcome from the Congress of Berlin, Mercia decided on this second option for two main reasons: one being her belief that further analysis of the way that Levsky's work had been continued after his death would show the full development of his ideas as well as revealing the man's genius as an organiser and ideologist.

> I decided to pursue this idea. This meant studying the Internal Macedonian and Adrianople Revolutionary Organisation which, led by such men as Dame Gruev, Gotse Delchev and Yane Sandansky, who consciously copied the ideas of Levsky. There are many indications of this in their memoirs where they explicitly state that they decided to renew the struggle against Turkish rule using the principles of Levsky; in other words, to build an Internal Revolutionary Organisation based on a committee network which would prepare the entire people for a victorious internal revolution . . . in fact, in my opinion, anyone who wishes to understand the genius of Levsky as an organiser and ideologist must study the Internal Macedonian and Adrianople Revolutionary Organisation, because here we see the ideas of Levsky in their full development . . . I am interested in revolutionary organisations and not merely historically: I am interested in the lessons which they can have for present-day revolutionary organisations: and the ideas of Levsky are as valid today as they were when he formulated them. I think that all present-day fighters for national independence and social justice, including those who misguidedly practise terror, would be the richer and wiser for learning something of his theories and his example. (T.I.)

The second major reason for choosing this option was that Mercia felt a duty as a British historian to draw attention to Britain's role in the history of the Balkans, and particularly to Disraeli's insistence in Berlin that Bulgaria should be divided. Mercia felt it essential that the British reader should know and understand the connection between Britain and the appalling atrocities which ensued, and not regard the events as 'nothing to do with us'. In the early years of the twentieth century British public opinion was very keenly aware of Britain's responsibility for the suffering in Macedonia, especially the horrors which followed the Ilinden Uprising of 1903. William Gladstone's son, Herbert Gladstone MP, the archaeologist Arthur Evans, the then Archbishop of Canterbury and the delegates to the Trade Union Congress in Leicester were among the more eminent protesters who condemned not only the Turks but also the foreign policies of the British government. One of the protests took the form of the poem on Macedonia, written by John Oxenford and published in the *Daily News* (29 September 1903). Mercia was to use part of it as a motto for *Freedom or Death*, her first book on the Macedonian revolutionary movement (which appears as a motto at the head of this essay).

Mercia decided to focus her book on the life and work of Gotse Delchev, who was a central figure in the formation of the Internal Organisation in Salonika in 1893.

> So I began with the biography of Gotse Delchev, the most famous of all the leaders of the struggle in Macedonia and Adrianople. This book is written in the same way as the one on Levsky – absolutely strictly according to documents, with an element of more literary writing in the descriptions, but I am always extremely careful that even these descriptions are accurate. On the first page I describe Macedonia as a land where the eagles keep watch over the graves of the heroes, and some people may think that this is a poetic metaphor, but it is not. I have actually seen eagles over the grave of Yane Sandansky and I have seen eagles over the place where Pitu Guli, one of the leaders of the Ilinden Uprising was killed.

The Ilinden Uprising, organised by the Internal Organisation took place on the day of St Iliya, 2 August 1903, in Macedonia. For ten days a Republic was established in the highest town in the Balkan Peninsula, Krushevo, until it was brutally crushed by the Bahtiyar Pasha and his army of twenty thousand men. The Internal Organisation also temporarily took power at the other end of its territory on the Black Sea coast and in the Strandzha Mountains.

In 1973, Mercia moved back to Bulgaria, teaching initially at the English Language School again and later at the university. In the process of writing *Freedom or Death* Mercia visited Delchev's birthplace, Kukush (now in Greece, and called Kilkis), Salonika, and Skopje, Yugoslavia, where she faced the still bitter conflicts between Yugoslavia, Greece and Bulgaria concerning the history and current position of Macedonia, and over the issue of ownership of national heroes such as Gotse Delchev and Sandansky. Particularly in Skopje, anyone perceived as pro-Bulgarian, or even trying to maintain a neutral stance on the 'Macedonian Question', was regarded with suspicion or even outright hostility.[7]

Her book was published in 1978, translated into Bulgarian and presented to Sofia University in 1979, when Mercia received a doctorate for the work.

Latest Work

Working on *Freedom and Death* had fired Mercia's interest in the revolutionary movements in Macedonia and Adrianople, so she decided to continue her research with a biography of Yane Sandansky, another leader of the Internal Organisation.

Sandansky is of particular interest because, after the Internal Organisation split in two over tactics, Sandansky headed its left wing, which, under the influence of socialist ideas, gave high priority to working for an immediate improvement in the people's standard of living, culture and education as an essential part of preparing them for revolution. Believing that the problems of the Balkan peoples could best be settled by rapprochement rather than war, he attempted to co-operate with the Young Turks in the hope that the transformation of the Ottoman Empire into a democratic, multinational state could change the whole Balkan peninsula for the better and bring lasting peace to the region.

The title for the book on Sandansky, *For Freedom and Perfection* comes from his most famous words: 'To live means to struggle, the slave for freedom and the free man for perfection'. These words are written on his grave near the Rozhen Monastery in the Pirin Mountains.

Mercia considers this book, published in 1988, to be her greatest contribution to historical science, because in the course of writing it she refers to a very large number of original documents, many of which have never been published, even in Bulgaria. Access to the documents could be extremely difficult, because they were often to be found in distant towns and villages. In order to have more flexible time to visit these, Mercia moved from the English Language School to teaching the period of history which she was researching at Sofia University, and the Teacher Training

Institute in Blagoevgrad, which was near to the essential archival sources in the Pirin region.

Mercia felt that everyone was very co-operative in helping her to obtain documents and references, even to the point of allowing her to take originals to her hotel room – terrified lest anything should happen to them. She usually had to travel to outlying villages by jeeps, borrowed from the army, from the police, or from farmers. Her source material was extremely rich and included recordings from some old people who remembered the revolutionary heroes, and who had even encountered some of Sandansky's 'chetniks' (members of his armed band). But, as Mercia herself admits, she has had a 'real battle' over Sandansky, who is still a controversial figure. Bulgarians who take a special interest in Macedonia usually support one or other of the two rival wings of the long dead Organisation, and therefore either admire Sandansky and revile his opponents or vice versa. Discussion of Sandansky is liable to arouse great passion both for and against, and there are living relatives of some of his enemies who have been known to wish fervently for Mercia's blood! She has had to accept this, and the discomfort and even strong envy which has been aroused as a result of her research – although at times this has caused her considerable personal pain. She feels, however, that she has been more than compensated for this by the love and respect in which she is held by the people of the Pirin region where Sandansky lived and worked.

Mercia was invited to participate in a very expensively produced Bulgarian film *Mera Spored Mera* (Measure for Measure) about the Internal Organisation, made in the early 1980s. She was asked to play the role of Miss Ellen Stone, an American missionary kidnapped by Sandansky in 1901. She decided to refuse, which was just as well for her reputation as a specialist in Macedonian affairs, because the film, both in its original screen version and in its TV adaptation, received a very caustic reception from the ordinary public, especially in the Pirin region. For once, supporters of both wings of the Organisation saw eye to eye, and agreed that the producer had taken unacceptable license with the material and the resulting film was a disgraceful travesty of history. The sole aspect of it which received unequivocal public approval was the role of Miss Stone, played by Christina Bartlett, another longstanding friend of Bulgaria, who has taught in English-language schools there for more than twenty years and is, like Mercia, a former chairman of the British Bulgarian Friendship Society. More recently, Mercia has been asked to write scripts and provide illustrative material for documentary films, including one on Yané Sandansky, and another tracing the activities of his comrades after his death.

The Effects of Mercia's Travels on her Work

Mercia has also appeared frequently on Bulgarian television, and two years ago, during the 150th Anniversary of Levsky's birth, she participated in over 100 meetings, television discussions and interviews, in an exhausting programme of travelling throughout the country.

Mercia MacDermott places great importance on assimilating the atmosphere of the period she is writing about, and the places in which significant events took place. This has led her to travel widely in the Balkans, mostly on local buses, trains and trams, and in lorries and jeeps, with the occasional more comfortable excursion in a private car. As a result of her explorations, and her willingness to experience all aspects of Bulgarian life, she has gained invaluable insight into Bulgaria and Bulgarians, all of which has contributed to the power of her writing and her ability to communicate the history so vividly. No doubt this attention to the 'living history' as well as her meticulous attention to details according to actual documentary evidence, is one of the reasons for the popularity of Mercia's books – in Bulgaria at least, for British interest in things Bulgarian has yet to be developed, thanks to years of adverse media propaganda.

Mercia's love of folklore is incorporated into her work, and in the books about Levsky and Delchev she used proverbs and folk songs as headings for the chapters. When preparing to write about Sandansky, she read over two hundred folk songs collected in his native village to get an idea of the things he may have heard as a child.

> Yané's village, Vlahi, has some horrific folk songs about monsters, blood and revenge, including the frightful revenge taken by men on those who have wronged their sisters. It so happened that Sandansky arranged the killing of his own brother-in-law, who not only supported groups hostile to the Organisation, but also ill-treated Yane's sister. It seems terrible, but when one realises that traditionally a brother had a duty to kill those who insulted his sister, one begins to see it in a new light. (T.I.)

Mercia has lectured in most towns in Bulgaria. She has spoken in schools, universities, factories, libraries and workshops, to soldiers, teenagers, old people, and in villages where most of the population may be Muslim. Speaking in small villages is not always easy:

> because you get such a varied audience, ranging from very small children up to the local intelligentsia, and the Mayor and the Party Secretary. It is a great challenge to make a speech in which there is something for everybody. I have found that I nearly always begin by telling them my name is Mercia, and that it means a frontier, and as a woman's name it means a woman who lives on the frontier between two states. I point out what an appropriate name this is for me, because I travel between Britain and Bulgaria. (T.I.)

A Woman in Bulgaria

Living and working in Bulgaria as a woman on her own, teaching, researching and witnessing a period of rapid change in the lifestyle of Bulgarians, never ceased to inspire Mercia. She felt that being a woman in Bulgaria had several advantages, some of these being: the co-educational nature of all schools which encourage girls to go into science and engineering and medicine (the majority of all doctors are women) and which regard women's careers as being just as important as men's; the strict adherence to equal pay for equal work, which Bulgarians take for granted; the fact that by Western standards Bulgaria is a safe and nonviolent country where women (or men) can feel safe in walking on the streets after dark. It is still probably the case, though, that women take the major share of child-care as well as working, although crèche and nursery provision is much better than that in Britain.

As well as the respect she has earned for her books, her down-to-earth manner, her lack of pretension and genuine love of the country have made Mercia a very popular figure in Bulgaria, and led her to be offered honours not usually accorded to foreigners. She is godmother to brigades of workers in factories and shops. These brigades have the right, if their work is satisfactory, to adopt the name of a national hero and they are entitled to do extra paid work in the name of their patron. Mercia explained:

> I have been invited to be the godmother of several brigades, two of them named after Vasil Levsky and one of them after Gotse Delchev. My first engagement as a godmother was with a team of lorry drivers.

They worked very well and earned the right to have a patron. They chose Gotse Delchev. As the saying goes: 'A hero is always in the ranks', and this brigade proceeded to work in such a way that they obtained the bonuses which were considered to be his contribution to the work. As godmother I had to be present at the naming ceremony, to break a ritual loaf of bread and dip it in honey, and to pronounce a blessing which went: 'You will bear the name of Gotse Delchev. May you bear the name with honour, may your work be as useful as bread, as sweet as honey.' I maintain regular contact with these and other workers to whom I am godmother, and this is one of the many ways in which I have been able to participate in the life of the ordinary Bulgarian. (T.I.)

Conclusion

In this paper I have suggested that Mercia MacDermott warrants a place in the line of distinguished woman travellers to the Balkans. Through her initial interest in the Soviet Union, and her studies of Russian language and literature, she gradually became involved in the history and politics of the Balkans, specialising in Bulgarian studies. Her strong sense of outrage at Britain's role in the decisions made at the Treaty of Berlin, together with her desire to see a fair and just presentation of the events in Bulgaria's history and her contempt for the inaccurate and one-sided view of Bulgaria available to the public through the media, led her to undertake her life's work of scholarly research into Bulgarian history. This research is informed not only through reference to archives and to documents, but by living and experiencing life in Bulgaria at all levels. Her latest book, on the life of Yané Sandansky, *For Freedom and Perfection, is* a brilliant interweaving of presentation and analysis of previously unpublished documents together with insights from folklore, custom and tradition, and from forty years of close relationship with Bulgaria.

As anyone who moves constantly between two countries knows, this is not easy, and can lead to cultural, social and political disorientation. Handled carefully, it can enable one to be both a part of, and at the same time, usefully separate from these societies – to participate, and to observe oneself and one's society from a critical perspective. In order to achieve such a position it is necessary to have a strong sense of self, of one's own identity, yet to be open to experience and prepared to change. Through her willingness to struggle through her early, perhaps slightly romantic idealism towards a real grasp of social and political issues in Bulgaria, Mercia has acquired firm personal boundaries. These have enabled her to deal not only with the excitement but also with the many discomforts of her cross-cultural position. She has determination, enthusiasm and energy, solidly rooted in practical, not dogmatic, socialism. She has an excellent sense of the ridiculous.

Mercia MacDermott is a woman of the frontiers between Britain and Bulgaria – but a woman who manages to cross back and forth over these frontiers. In the summer of 1989 she moved back to Oxford, with her daughter Alexandra, and intends to settle in Worthing, Sussex, and for a time to devote herself to organising her material on Bulgarian folk customs and traditions. Hopefully, a much-needed book will emerge. Her scholarly work on the history of the little-known country of Bulgaria, together with her personal contribution to British-Bulgarian relations, has played its own part in melting the 'Cold War' and is surely a cog in the wheel of European *Perestroika*.

Notes

1. Dorothy Anderson, *The Balkan Volunteers*, London: Hutchinson, 1968, Introduction.
2. *Ibid.*, pp. 13–4.
3. G. Bokov (ed.) *Modern Bulgarian History, Policy, Economy, Culture*, Sofia Press, 1981, p. 94.
4. Blagoev was born in 1856, near Kastoria which is now in northern Greece. He was a student in St. Petersburg where he founded the first Marxist circle in Russia, and in 1891, he founded the Bulgarian Social Democratic Party which was the forerunner of the Communist Party.
5. H.R. Wilkinson, *Maps and Politics. A review of the ethnographic cartography of Macedonia*, Liverpool University Press, 1951.
6. James Bourchier, 'Macedonia', *Encyclopaedia Britannica*, 11th edn,. vol. 17, pp. 216–22. For a similar point, see also G. Bokov *op. cit.*, p. 70.
7. For further information on this issue see D. Kossev et al. (eds) *Macedonia: documents and material*, Sofia: Bulgarian Academy of Sciences, 1978.

Bibliography

Anderson, D. *The Balkan Volunteers*, London: Hutchinson, 1968.
Bokov, G. (ed.) *Modern Bulgaria: history, policy, economy, culture*, Sofia Press, 1981.
Bourchier, J.D. *The Bulgarian Peace Treaty: speeches delivered in the British Parliament*, London: Christophers, 1920.
Brailsford, H.N. *Macedonia: its races and their future*, London: Methuen, 1906.
Buxton, C.R. *Memorandum on Territorial Claims and Self-determination*, London: The Union of Democratic Control, 1919.

Buxton, C.R. *Towards a Lasting Settlement*, London: Allen and Unwin, 1915.

Buxton, C.R. *Turkey in revolution*, London: T. Fisher Unwin, 1909.

Buxton, N.E. and C.R. *The war and the Balkans*, London: Allen and Unwin, 1915.

Buxton, N.E. and Leese, C.L. *Balkan problems and European Peace*, London: Allen and Unwin, 1919.

Buxton, N.E. *Europe and the Turks*, London: John Murray, 1907.

Buxton, N.E. *With the Bulgarian Staff*, London: Smith, Elder and Co., 1913.

Kossev, D. *et. al.* (eds) *Macedonia: documents and material*, Sofia: Bulgarian Academy of Sciences, 1978.

MacDermott, M. *A History of Bulgaria, 1393–1885*, London: Allen and Unwin, 1962.

MacDermott, M. *For Freedom and Perfection. The life of Yané Sandansky*, London: Journeyman Press, 1987.

MacDermott, M. *Freedom or Death. The Life of Gotse Delchev*, London: Journeyman Press, 1978.

MacDermott, M. *The Apostle of Freedom. Biography of Vasil Levsky*, London: Allen AND Unwin, 1967.

Newman, B. *Balkan Background*, London: Robert Hale, 1944.

Wallace, D.M., Bourchier, J. *et al.*, *A short history of Russia and the Balkan states*, London: Encyclopaedia Britannica Co., 1914.

CHAPTER 12

I wonder whether anthropologists always realize that in the course of their fieldwork they can be, and sometimes are, transformed by the people they are making a study of, that in a subtle kind of way and possibly unknown to themselves they have what used to be called 'gone native'. If an anthropologist is a sensitive person it could hardly be otherwise. This is a highly personal matter and I will only say that I learnt from African 'primitives' much more than they learnt from me, much that I was never taught at school, something more of courage, endurance, patience, resignation and forebearance that I had no great understanding of before. Just to give one example: I would say that I learnt more about the nature of God and of our human predicament from the Nuer than I ever learnt at home.

E.E. Evans-Pritchard, from the Appendix 'Some reminiscences and reflection on fieldwork', the 1976 edn of **Witchcraft, Oracles and Magic among the Azande.**

An Anthropologist in the Village

Barbara Kerewsky-Halpern

In the course of ongoing sociocultural research, an American anthropologist has been travelling continuously between the Balkans and the United States for 36 years. This research travel is unusual in the anthropological record, representing an adult lifetime during which she has been moving in two separate worlds – that of her culture of origin and that of a woman maturing in a peasant village. In her own society, life patterns emerged by choice and often overlap: graduate student, wife, researcher, mother, post-doctoral scholar, homemaker, teacher. In the village she is perceived and accepted according to a set of stages which are fixed and irrevocably sequential: bride, wife/woman, mother, 'old woman'. I know. I am that woman.

It is the late 1980s. Once again I am travelling back to the village that has long been my research base. There are other trips to research sites elsewhere in the Balkans, but on this occasion I am returning to 'my' Serbian village. After a segment of efficient highway south from Belgrade to Mladenovac, I negotiate the familiar twisting roads that lead into rolling hill country, past fields fragmented into patches of wheat and corn. Near a wedge of acacias that marks the turnoff to our dirt lane, otherwise so indistinguishable from countless mud-rutted village lanes, I see Milena, an old friend. She is tending a sow. I stop. I part the stalks of Queen Anne's lace and blue chicory blooming along the verge and approach her pasture carefully, seeking drier ridges and matted grass tussocks. Avoiding mud is a village skill. Milena, in brown plaid housedress, apron and rubber boots, raises her eyes below the folds of her kerchief and comes toward me.

'Have you come back?' she says.

'I have come back,' I echo.

Inverting word order, in Serbian as in English, changes an inquiry to an affirmation. In the village, this archetypal linguistic formula provides the means by which one person acknowledges the presence of another. The brief ritual, elegant in its simplicity, also provides the frame from which I leave one realm and enter the other, literally stepping back into the village scene.

Milena and I interact on common ground. The village norms of communication, once I learned them, are the basis of our long interaction. They result in an encounter very different, for example, from one in which I might have tooted the horn, waved, and breezily driven by, American style, or exchanged greetings while seated in the auto with her outside ankle-deep in mud.

'Come,' she says. This means 'Come visit me when you are settled in, come whenever you like. We'll pick up our conversation where we left off last time.'

Right now the condition of the lane is on my mind. Will the car make it down the muddy trail or do I leave it next to the road? Accessibility has always been a problem – not only the crucial political kind but, once granted permission to do field research, the vagaries of the weather as well. I have traversed the potholed road on foot, by oxcart, horse-drawn shay, sleigh, my own vehicles, rickety buses, a tractor, and, once, the open back of a truck (perched on uncovered crates of bottled mineral water). The best way to go down the lane is on foot, and even that is a challenge when, after a good rain, it becomes an unctuous ribbon of mud. In other seasons hail storms and crested snow drifts have all but obliterated its familiar contours.

The infamous mud looks passable this time. I drive down slowly, appreciating the half-buried limestone chips. Periodically villagers shovel broken stone onto the lane, and as frequent users we contribute funds when not around to contribute labour. With a minimum of wheel-spinning the car makes it today, despite recollections of the many times a yoke of cows was needed to haul my car out of the slippery ooze. Past the dip near Stanimir's house, past overhanging blackberry brambles that leave scratch-marks, I put the car in low gear and crosscut wagon-wheel tracks at the edge of the vineyard near the house. Slowly, gently and, finally, home!

And yet – what is this place to me? I pull onto the grass near the collapsing mud and wood barn and get out. The house looks old, with fresh cracks in its once proud whitewashed concrete façade. Mildew has advanced upward above the stone base. On the outside steps leading up to the sleeping rooms, untended geraniums bloom as though by habit in discarded enamel cooking pots. The apricot tree is heavy with fruit that no one has picked. Right here, in this now unkempt grassy patch, my children began to creep and learned to walk. Here is the flat stone they stood on while I gave them sponge baths from a plastic basin. Here is where Grandfather unloaded the hay cart, where Branko brought in fragrant loads of clover, where Grandmother deftly spun wool on her distaff while tending the cows. Here is where Ljubinka and I fed melon rinds and slops to the pigs (was the pigsty once really that close to the house?), where the children scattered corn for the chickens, where they sat on sheepskins and read or made cornhusk dolls.

Two complete families once lived together here, theirs with three generations and for a period with four, and ours eventually with two. Grandfather, Grandmother and Branko are dead. The children of the family are adults in their mid-40s and have long since migrated out of the village. My children, younger, are busy with their own lives; my husband is home in Massachusetts. On this visit that leaves but Ljubinka and me.

A woman strides up from the kitchen two steps below ground level. She wipes her hands on the bib of her dark apron and knots her kerchief securely under her chin, tucking back wisps of curly grey hair. Arms outstretched, she bursts into an agile lope and cries, '*Jao* Babi, have you come back?'

'I have come back,' I whisper, blinking back tears.

We embrace. Hooking her arm in mine this nimble woman of 70 who has been my constant mentor, hostess and friend leads me to an oilcloth-covered table (I bought that grey checkered cloth at least 25 years ago) in the shade under the overhang. From a striped woollen bag hanging on a nail she extracts a rag. The peasant bag was woven by one of my daughters as a young girl. Its colours remain fast, with dyes Aunt Radojka taught her to make from walnut bark and onion skins. The rag is from my husband's old shirt. Ljubinka removes the feathered turkey wing propped behind the nail and tells me to clear away dead flies and wipe the table clean while she goes inside to get *slatko*.

'I've been waiting for you, to welcome and honour you.'

As part of an ancient Balkan rite of welcome, a new arrival, be the newcomer stranger or household member who has been away, is offered a sweet of homemade fruit preserves in heavy syrup. It is served in a small dish with glasses of water and spoons. Ljubinka brings out quince conserve, one of my favourites. With your right hand you take a generous spoonful of the confiture, using the left to shield drips. Then you take a sip of water and place your spoon in the water remaining in the glass. That nicely rinsed the spoon when there were more guests than spoons, and now it is a vestige, a folk aesthetic founded in *kako treba*, the all-important 'right way' to do things.

I get out the coffee beans and sugar I brought, and we take turns grinding the little brass mill for Turkish coffee. Questions begin. One of us is the anthropologist, the other the informant. The roles and interview process are clear: Ljubinka asks in turn, 'How is Djoli (my husband Joel)?'; 'How are the children and their spouses?'; 'How are relations with the in-laws?'; 'What about health?'; 'Are there grandchildren yet?'; ('Babi, you know, you must talk seriously to Lasta. She's not so young anymore.') Her questions on kinship and social structure are similar to many she and the others continuously answer for me.

For this visit I am to be in the house alone. After Branko's death Ljubinka has moved to a small house her son built for her nearer the road. We gather the dishes on an old engraved copper tray and take them into the hot kitchen. She reminds me that I know where everything is, alerts me to pen the sheep when they come up from the meadow and to let them out in the morning. She presses a heavy iron key into my hand. It still has a red and white woollen braid looped through it. Grandmother once told me this amulet keeps the evil eye from the door.

Dusk comes. On the steps I set the minimal gear I have with me (small tape recorder with batteries and blank cassettes, and one duffle bag) and smile as I recall the fluctuating accretions of personal baggage heaped on these crumbling steps during previous arrivals: suitcases of clothing for my family in all seasons, typewriters, typing supplies, manuscripts, books, camera bag, a playpen, diapers, a year's supply of sanitary napkins. . . . Near the wood stump that has always served as doorstop I find my peasant-style rubber shoes. (It does not matter who has been wearing them in the interim.) If it rains during the night and I want to 'go outside' (a village euphemism as well as geographical fact), it is useful to have them dry and at hand. I put them on the threshold before retiring to my room.

Inside, the long trestle table remains where I relocated it near the window. (It is shoved to the centre of the room for the household's annual *slava* feast.) On this table I have compiled notes, written first drafts and changed diapers. The bed is covered with its woven *čilim*, but protruding underneath is a manufactured blanket dating from one of the CARE packages I brought all those decades ago when goods were more important than cash. On the far wall is the enlarged photograph of family patriarch Greatgrandfather Tihomir, the frame set off by a lace-trimmed linen towel. Next to it is a coloured lithograph of Archangel Michael, patron saint of this lineage, with last year's sprig of sweet basil, the holy plant, tucked into its frame. On the same wall, in the same kind of frame, is our own wedding photo. In the narrow cupboard, hand fashioned of oak and painted over with yellow enamel and brown false graining, fitted with shelves and wooden pegs for garments, I find copies of books we have written, well-thumbed in the photo and illustrations sections. There are more dead flies on the painted plank flooring.

It is not scary, but it *is* eerie being here alone with memories. I am a woman in the village but not of the village. Here in this place, in this very room, important parts of my creative life have been spent. I 'know' village life as villagers do, in a way that blurs the usual academic distinctions between emic and etic – that which the folk know to be so versus that which the social scientist observes. An *Amerikanka*, I am an outsider who is nevertheless an insider. I have lectured at the Serbian Academy of Sciences, where my rural vocabulary inadvertently amuses urban colleagues. A chance photograph of me in full folk costume was selected for a Serbian ethnographic publication to illustrate characteristic peasant demeanour and dress of this region. A unit I wrote on village life in Serbia has been adapted for elementary school social studies programmes to introduce children in the United States to anthropological concepts such as social structures and value systems different from their own. And the incongruity deepens. On this visit, I am simultaneously guest and woman of the house, in a house that has long been my family's home yet is not really our home.

In the early 1950s my husband and I were completing studies at Columbia University, he for a doctorate in anthropology and I for a degree at Barnard College. There remained for him the requisite of that academic initiation rite known as fieldwork, to be carried out in Yugoslavia. My own doctoral fieldwork, also village-based, subsequently followed other research directions.

Attempts at language study from books were not fruitful. I did discover other kinds of books. Rebecca West's *Black Lamb and Grey Falcon* seemed like a broad-scale historical novel, and at that early stage I was in no position to differentiate fact from fiction. Edith Durham's *Some Tribal Origins, Laws and Customs of the Balkans* had a certain appeal – if I were not heading off to, say, the South Pacific, at least I was going to a place of blood-feuds, ritual tattooing and sympathetic magic. In fact, I had no real image of the eventual destination. Emily Balch's study of Slavic immigrants to the United States provided photographs (albeit from 1905) of whitewashed peasant houses in peasant villages, and that is the visual notion I carried with me. There was little information on Serbia, or Servia as it was called in her day, but those old photographs were not far off the mark from the contemporary rural reality I was soon to experience.

The initial fieldwork was to be a study of a rural community experiencing accelerated change. This kind of research requires a baseline for measuring 'tradition', with the understanding that varying aspects of a culture change at different rates. The methodology was the intensive endeavour known as participant observation and required harmonious cooperation between each other and with the people among whom we would live.

Yugoslavia at that time was still recovering from the ravages of Axis invasion, a revolution and a bitter civil war. A few years prior, in 1948, Tito had broken with the Cominform. A new political order was in the process of formation. Just before our arrival an abortive attempt to collectivize agriculture had been withdrawn, a significant event in a land where the majority of the population were then peasants.

A small Yugoslav freighter carrying twelve passengers transported us across the Atlantic, into the Mediterranean and up the Adriatic Coast to a Yugoslav port. The voyage took several weeks, during which my ears began to be comfortable with the sounds of the language. The consonant clusters so intimidating in print began to roll off my tongue. *Na vrh brda mrda vrba.* From the flight to Belgrade in a DC-3 I saw the shimmering seacoast give way to bone-white limestone mountains and then to heavy forest before crossing rivers and cultivated plains and alighting at the old dreary Belgrade airport.

The capital appeared grey. Many buildings bore the pockmarks of shrapnel. We took a room in a communal flat, sharing kitchen and WC with three other families. Sharing living space brought me into immediate and constant verbal contact with many people. It certainly augmented language learning.

That month in the city, shuffling letters of introduction at appropriate government bureaus brings back memories of exposure to a hero cult. Tito's likeness was ubiquitous. His portrait billowed from four-story-high red banners hung on public buildings. Meagre displays in shop windows featured his face surrounded by stacks of yellow *keksa* (biscuit) boxes. In yardgoods stores bolts of poor quality dark fabrics unfurled about him. I saw Tito in photos, in bronze, in oils, in wood inlay, in marzipan. Hand-painted on the sides of buildings were red stars and slogans proclaiming 'Long Live Tito!' and 'Long Live the Party!'

Streets were cobbled. Grey-smocked women with twig brooms swept up horse droppings and the debris in pocket parks where bombed-out buildings had stood. Men went unshaven, for razor blades were scarce and so was hot water. Women lifted their skirts in the rear before sitting in trams or on benches in order to prolong the life of the fabric. Workers carried important looking briefcases which turned out to hold slabs of bread and salami. Manufactured goods of all kinds were scarce. An olfactory impression lingers: the particular combination of lignite dust and roasted peppers. That aroma clung in every passageway and corridor, a smell that still means Belgrade to me.

It took a while for administrative tangles to resolve. Eventually permission papers were signed and finalised with a rubber stamp that bristled 'Death to Fascism! Freedom to the People!' The plan was for a year of fieldwork, but our three-month visas had to be renewed at regular intervals, subject to approval. Questionings took place at the headquarters of the Ministry of the Interior, where a dark padded leather door was closed behind me. I recall a large room, bare except for a desk at which a stern-faced questioner sat under an equally stern-faced photo of Tito.

But that year of fieldwork did come about, and it led to many others. All told, I have made some twenty field trips to Serbia, including long ones lasting up to one and a half years and briefer ones over summer months. The work began by selecting the region of Šumadija (Woodlands) in central Serbia because of its ethnic homogeneity. (Later villagers would tell me '. . . and we have the purest air. And the sweetest water. And our speech is the best form of Serbian.' And, from men and women both, 'Our men are the greatest lovers.') Ideally, the village chosen was to have terrain that supported both plow agriculture and small-scale livestock herding; it had to be large enough for a good sample and small enough for us to handle; it had to be far enough away from the city to be free of undue urban influence but within one day's travel to Belgrade in case of emergency. Finally, there had to be some compelling reason why foreigners might be interested precisely in that village. These factors came together in the selection of Orašac as the Serbian village in a United Nations pilot project on the impact of rural electrification. As it happened, the UN project never eventuated in Orašac, but our research, small-scale as it was, did come about. It was a fortuitous choice, with a bonus. In the struggle for liberation from the Turks in the early ninteenth century Orašac had a brief but glorious moment in Serbian history. It was here that the First Revolt against the Turks was organised by Karadjordje, from the nearby hamlet of Topola; his ruse was to gather men as supposed wedding guests under cover of a leafy glen down by the Maričevići. For people as fiercely proud as Serbs, our acquaintance with their village's place in history was enough to justify our presence.

After all the planning and permissions, and apart from the excitement of finally getting to the village, to me it was exhilarating to be out in the countryside. The hills were strips of greens and golds with occasional groves of darker green woods. Life had colour. It was patterned by the natural rhythms of the season and not by the grim dichotomy of pre-war and post-war seasons I had heard all the time in the city. After a train to Mladenovac we switched to a narrow-gauge line that wended its way like a toy through fields of tall corn. Passengers could hop off and walk for a stretch and then rejoin the train.

In Arandjelovac, the market town for Orašac, gender differentiation was made clear to me immediately. After our papers were cleared on the commune level, an Orašac villager returning home from market was induced to give us a lift in his cowcart. I stowed my things in the back, which was lined with straw and inhabited by a pair of newly bartered geese, hissing and cackling at the indignity of being tied together at the feet, and then I climbed up to the plank seat next to the driver.

'You, back there,' he nodded with his head. 'He can sit up here.'

And so I entered Orašac for the first time as a commodity in the rear of a cart along with some poultry. (Grandmother later told me that had this taken place in her ancestral village I would have walked behind the cart.)

It had been decided that we would be put up for the time being at the house of the village council secretary, a man who was literate and politically acceptable; his name was Branko (this arrangement was to last for more than a third of a century). As he walked with us down the slippery mud lane that led to his father's house, Branko explained that the household contained his parents, himself and his wife, and their two young children. A few years before, the *zadruga* or extended family household had divided. His father's brother with wife and children had built a similar house on adjoining land. While I was visualising a kinship diagram my head and thinking how handy it was going to be to observe age and sex roles in both generational and extended family patterns, Branko approached the edge of the orchard. A tall young woman in worn clothes, black knitted stockings and rubber shoes was harvesting plums.

He barked, 'Wife! Come here!'

Ljubinka set down her willow basket and came running, tucking stray brown curls into her kerchief.

'Foreigners,' Branko said. 'They will spend the night.'

Ljubinka was ordered about by both husband and mother-in-law. I tried to follow her example and be a silent, efficient helpmate. Joel picked up the pattern and enjoyed bossing me in public, thinking Branko and Grandfather would approve. Actually they did not even notice, for that was the natural order.

People were addressed according to their role in the household. Lubinka was not referred to by her name but as *snaja* (daughter-in-law), *žena* (wife/woman) and *mama*. Everybody called the older couple Grandfather and Grandmother, and we did too. At first they referred to Joel as 'You (formal form), boy,' an interesting syntactic anomaly, and to me as *mlada*, bride. As the youngest incoming married female, my expected daily responsibility was to wash the rubber boots and the feet of the male members of the household. Ljubinka, ever observant and keenly aware of my shortcomings, explained to Branko that I was not as capable as she and that I would wash dishes while she washed feet.

Women in the village soon began to come to ask me questions. They wanted to know why, since we had been married a year, there was no baby on the way. They explained that they knew *coitus interruptus* was not foolproof, and they wanted to know 'the American way'. For my part, I learned a good deal about village-style abortions. Couples, or rather, households, wanted small families, especially if the first child was a boy. I sensed that the women had many subjects they wanted to talk about but would not in the presence of my husband or their own men, who would tell them to hold their tongues and go about their work.

One autumn day I had bad cramps. I went up to the room to lay down for a while. Ljubinka told Aunt Vida, who hurried through the stubble of the harvested cornfield with an old-style flat ceramic roof tile. They warmed it in the cast iron woodstove and covered it with a rag. It was solicitously brought to me and eased onto my abdomen, with admonitions to me to rest. That situation gave them the opportunity they had been hoping for.

While I lay immobile the room filled with women – Milena, Radojka, Vida, Zorka and many of the women I would later get to know very well. Under the pretext of taking care of me, they opened the cupboard and carefully examined my underwear and other garments. My bra, passed from hand to hand, underwent structural analysis. They spotted a jacket with brass buttons embossed with crowns. That would not do, they explained: signs of the defunct monarchy were dangerous. Off came the offending buttons.

Gradually conversation turned from 'politics' to the serious issues on their minds. 'How do you really avoid getting pregnant in America?'; 'What happens when you are 'unclean'?'; 'Does your husband beat you?'; 'How do you get along with your mother-in-law?' At that time anthropological fieldwork methodologies encouraged researchers to keep their lives and opinions to themselves. I was meticulous in following this guideline on matters of politics, but in personal matters it was not appropriate. The women were as interested in me and my way of doing things as I was in them, and to people as gregarious, hospitable and genuinely inquisitive as Serbian villagers, it seemed to me rude not to answer their questions as openly as they answered mine.

Over weeks and months we came to understand one another as people and not as curious strangers. I learned that what was mine was available to share with others just as they shared everything of theirs with me. Patiently they taught me what they felt I had to know. Then they eased me into village work patterns. They taught me to make soap from tallow, lye and ash, brewed outside in a huge black cauldron and later cooled and cut into serviceable cubes. I learned to boil laundry and spread it to bleach on wattle fences. We hoed in the cornfields and vineyards. The men took wheat to the mill to be ground, and the women made batches of whole-grained dough in long wooden troughs. My job was to patch the holes in the worn-out pans, using grape leaves. The finished loaves, baked in the outdoor mud-brick oven, were expertly thumped on the bottom when pronounced done. Plunked on the table, a fresh crusty loaf was taken by the head of the household and held against his body; drawing the kitchen knife toward himself he apportioned wedges to all. With our daily bread we ate bean soup thickened with a roux of flour and lard and spiced with ground red pepper. In season, garden bounty of scallions, onions, garlic, tomatoes, cucumbers and peppers were placed on the plank table to be dipped in damp salt and eaten raw.

Salt was among the few items purchased in this largely self-sufficient lifestyle. (Others were cooking utensils, nails and kerosene for the lamps.) Daily, women trekked to the well of the area's 'best neighbour', balancing water in buckets suspended from shoulder poles. In our rubber shoes we cut across the pasture, braced ourselves along a dark slippery path through the woods, grabbed hold of saplings to pull ourselves up the other side and eventually entered a field that led to the all important sources of water. I was entrusted to get water for the livestock, dipping it from a waterhole.

Water was precious. Having always taken it for granted I had to learn to recycle it: after washing dishes, it was saved for the men's feet (and then for the women's) and then was dispersed in an economic arc over the kitchen garden; or our personal washing water was saved for household laundry and then used to wet down the floor.

Women were perceived as child-bearing vessels (the term for pelvis is the same as that for vessel; this is so in many languages, although culture concepts of women's roles have altered more rapidly elsewhere). In the early 1960s, back in the village with two small children of my own, my status palpably changed. I was seen as a proper wife/woman fulfilling her destiny.

197

A major change had also taken place on the governmental level. When it had been a tightly centralized federal structure, permission to do fieldwork had had to move down hierarchically from federation to republic to district to commune and finally to the village. Now there was a trend toward decentralisation, which was significant for me because it meant I could simply proceed directly to the village with my family, in my own auto, bypassing all the former elaborate requisites.

During this period, too, a class of new technocrats emerged. Enterprises and small-scale industries in the town evolved, along with the concept of Workers' Self-Management (males exclusively). Joel attended their meetings in the market town while I made observations in the village. The Communist Party had become the League of Communists, and the state a confederation of autonomous republics, in keeping with decentralisation. In Serbia there was a thrust toward more involvement of women. In the village this was manifested by a political meeting where I was the sole female in a roomful of men. A few women huddled about the door, not daring to overstep their societally-determined roles and enter the men's domain.

Before I knew it years added up to decades. I tended to romanticise the daily routine (easy to do since I knew it was not permanent), admiring the villagers' dictum about rising at cock's crow and going to sleep at dusk. Then the area became electrified. Television soon followed and with it TV late shows. One could raise cash for a TV set by selling a heifer or a ram at the livestock market in town. The monthly state tax seemed worth it to the decision-makers in our household. That quashed my vision of the simple life. After chores and supper on most evenings the small kitchen filled with neighbours, and the single window steamed up from the crowding. It was the first television in our lane. A variety show or the sitcom *Ljubav na seoski način* ('Love, Village Style') flickered on the screen while Branko and Grandfather, yawning, soaked their feet in basins of dirty water and, companionably, my sleepy children shared a bucket to soak theirs.

When I returned to the village with a new baby, my peasant friends were preoccupied with modernity and consumerism and could not understand why the baby was nursed when there were modern ways to do things. (Swaddling was going out of style, and this time there was no advice to bind the baby from armpits to toes.)

While I was disappointed at the disappearance of whole-grain bread, they were proud of the soft white bread brought in from town by villagers now working there. Its ultimate virtue was that it was *obogačen* (enriched). And why did not I let my kids drink Pepsi, the 'modern' drink made from famous Bukovićka Banja mineral water right there in Arandjelovac? Healthy bean soup was replaced by foil packets of Argo chicken-noodle soup mix, often enhanced with Vegeta dried vegetable flakes with preservatives.

Villagers took it upon themselves to instruct me as a mother of children of diverse ages on everything they felt I ought to know about child-rearing. Their well-intended ministrations were a catalyst that carried my research into sharper focus. With interest in sociolinguistics and the ethnography of communication I became aware of the abundant resource offered by this traditional oral culture. Serbia has a rich heritage of folk epic, well described and analysed in the academic literature. Its foundation is a characteristic ten-syllable line with marked prosodic features. My more discriminating ear became better tuned to the nuances of everyday and ritual speech, and I started to hear meter and tone as well as meaning. I began to detect this epic pulse in speech acts other than the chanting of epic song. A professional concern with diverse aspects of oral tradition began to take shape. I discovered that many of the features of epic speech can be heard in recollections of genealogies among certain villagers strongly guided by that unconscious epic template, and wrote about it in 'Genealogy as Genre' (see references at end of chapter). Soon it was apparent (although hitherto not acknowledged by most scholars) that some women were endowed with this capacity.

I turned my attention to narrative, to so-called women's themes in epic ('*Udovica Jana . . .*'), to public lament genres at the graveyard ('Text and Context in Ritual Lament'), to the potency of oral charms for healing ('The Power of the Word: Healing Charms as an Oral Genre'), to communicative modes in interactions between practitioners of folk healing and their patients ('Trust, Talk and Touch in Folk Healing') and to the patterned oral transmission of everything villagers deemed worthy of preserving and passing on – injunctions, transmission of recipes and instructions generally, a veritable 'how-to' compendium, all stored in the mind.

By the late 1970s my eldest daughter began to be seen in the village as approaching marriageable age. This evoked yet another difference in villagers' responses to me. Milena, who regretted not having a marriageable son at that time, told me, 'They look on you now as a possible mother-in-law. They look at *her*, at her strong shoulders, the way she builds haystacks and works in the barn. With her industriousness and education she'll make a good daughter-in-law.'

Milena was correct. At a spinning bee I was approached in the traditional way through an intermediary, to negotiate a marriage contract between two families.

No marriage came of this, but scholarly work was abetted. Seeing my daughter as a potential child-bearer in turn elevated my status to that of potential grandmother, or older woman. For years, in my research on aspects of oral tradition I had been trying, unsuccessfully, to elicit information on the transmission of magic and healing charms, either in recitations or as an observer at actual healing rites. The latter was permitted, but the mumbled words were indistinct, and when I asked what they meant invariably I was cryptically put off by the old women practitioners; 'I'll tell you, Babi, when the time is right.'

Now it was clear: they were waiting for me to be recognised as older, as ritually clean. And my semblance of that stage apparently was good enough. The various kinds of data I had been trying to obtain began to flow my way, for in an oral traditional culture there must be receivers as well as transmitters, and the transmitters of Orašac had chosen me to receive their gifts. The women who were skilled in healing with words were effectively practising a form of (folk) psychotherapy, as I explain in my discussion of 'trust, talk and touch'. A more societally based aspect is considered in 'The Complementarity of Women's Ritual Roles in a Patriarchal Society'.

Human lives cycle. Seasons cycle. The government cycled, its policy swinging from decentralisation back to tight central control. This time control was so strong that in 1978, I, who had written that children's textbook on Serbia, was not permitted to continue my fieldwork until the final 30 days of an eight-month international exchange grant. The heightened control bordered on paranoia about national security. But once back in the village, as usual the exigencies of day-to-day living were easier than in the uncomfortably distrustful environment of the city. Home-produced food was abundant, along with the introduction of packaged goods and accompanying plastic and paper trash. Agricultural labor was becoming scarce as villagers migrated to towns or left to become guest-workers in 'Europe'. In our household my older children took over much of the livestock care. Grandmother had died. Grandfather, ailing, spent his days pasturing the milk cow, holding it by its rope tether. When he fell and lacerated his arm we used puff-balls as a styptic. He developed a phlegmy cough, and an expectorant of mullein leaves was brewed. In the spring a tonic was made by boiling stinging nettle leaves.

'It cleanses the blood,' people said.

Once a neighbour was badly burned in an accident, and I saw how ointment was made of St. John's Wort (*Bogorodična trava*, the Holy Mother's grass). The fresh leaves were crushed. The yellow flowers turned red when mashed and released an aroma similar to incense. These were worked into softened wax, forming a balm.

Miniature wild pansies, in the village called 'Day and Night' (*Dan i noć*) were prescribed when my girls started menstruating. This is sympathetic visual mimesis, matching the sunny and dark colours of the petals to day and night to encourage brief duration.

When one of the children developed an abcess, an onion was halved and roasted on the black iron stove top. The inner rings of the onion were removed and the depression filled with warm oil (by now sunflower seed oil was replacing lard). Clamped onto the boil and held in place with clean rags, it soon drew the abcess to a head. It drained and disappeared.

For diarrhoea we gathered mugwort, angelica and tansy leaves (in Serbian *petoprsta* or 'five fingers'), boiled the leaves with vinegar and gave it to the children to drink as a tea. Using mugwort always reminded me of that herb's prominence since medieval times, and probably earlier, when it was known to banish 'demons and venoms'.

The years move forward. The village experiences many changes, and my perceptions continue to alter. What was attentively recorded during the earlier work becomes a personal baseline for assessing new features. One fact never alters. Despite academic degrees, publications and more matronly appearance, to the villagers I am *Babi*, wife to my husband and mother to my children. Increasingly, I am able to delve deeper into the culture, beyond the necessary groundwork of description to the layers of social dynamics below the surface quarrels and animosities and discords and fears that I could not have understood earlier.

In 1986 a Belgrade-based film crew made an hour-long documentary they called *Halpernovi u Orašcu* ('The Halperns in Orašac'). I helped script it, acted in it and also narrated a good part of the Serbian text. The story line of the film depicts decades of change and improvement in the village. In sequences where villagers speak eloquently of their life experiences, their memories are motivated by our interest in those aspects. The resulting film, far from optimal in the art of film-making, had two unexpected spin-offs. One is that it became a visual teaching aid in grade schools in Belgrade, introducing urban children to their cultural heritage in terms of what life was like in their grandparents' day. Another was that in the market town, in the capital and, once, far from Šumadija in a Croatian town where I was en route to the coast, continuously I was approached by people who had seen the film on TV and wanted to talk to me.

When I think back over the cumulative months and years of life in Orašac I recall certain highs that have meaning for my research, and others that I cherish as personal memories, with their visual components, sights and smells. Professionally I recall a rush of excitement when, listening to old Uncle Veljko orally recollect many hundreds of men in his lineage, I came to 'see' the map in his mind, to understand the linear rows and generational nodes that structured his recall, and to understand that in fact it was not merely his lineage he was recreating orally but, rather, that he was preserving these data as history, as his own personal epos.

In one of the remaining old-fashioned wattle-and-daub white-washed cottages, where I was recording unstudied oral genres, an unanticipated event took place. In patterned lines of speech similar to poetry Aunt Zorka was telling me how to make Serbian cheese pie *(gibanica)*.

Daughter-in-law, tomorrow morning get up early,
Get up early and milk the cow.
Boil the milk and save the skin,
Save the skin and salt it down . . .

There was a bang on the door of the storybook cottage. Aunt Zorka was all but pushed aside by two burly young men in long leather coats. 'Police', they announced and proceeded to interrogate me about photographing an old-fashioned house.

'This is a good woman, an honest woman,' Aunt Zorka said.

'Hold your tongue, old woman,' they ordered.

Aunt Zorka set out a generous bottle of *rakija* for them. She busied herself killing roaches by squashing them on the packed earthen floor with a discarded corncob. When she could no longer put up with their questions she stood firmly before them wagging the cob in their faces and intoning:

'O my sons, such nice young men, woe to the mothers who raised you up to be so distrustful.'

Visiting with Granny Mica when she was 87 and too infirm to get about the village, I had the privilege of listening quietly and taping while she explained how the words of healing charms came to her. As I changed cabbage leaf compresses on her aching hips and knees she told me of lore transmitted to her when she was a pre-menstrual girl.

What I remember, I remember. What I don't remember comes to me in the night. (Shades of *Caedmon's Hymn* – oral tradition in process.) But by God I can't remember who visited me this morning.

Granny Mica passed on to me many of her charms: those to remove sties, impotence, impurity in cows milk, the curse of the evil eye. She introduced me to 'the nine winds', those malevolent forces from the netherworld which (even today) lurk in caves and under stones waiting to pounce on unsuspecting victims and make them ill. She recited a colour-coded taxonomy of ill winds and banished them with an archaic litany of names keyed to the winds' capricious qualities:

'*aloviti, šaroviti, plikoviti, orloviti, viloviti . . .*'

Hypnotised by the sound of her own droning inventory Granny Mica fell asleep with her mouth open, and I continued to change the cabbage leaf poultices.

I remember a wintry evening when all of us were packed into the kitchen. Snow piled against the casement window. Under the woodstove the cat dozed in a broken sieve. One of my children was cosy in Grandmother's ample lap. The air was heavy with the smells of wet wool, garlic and unwashed bodies. We sipped Šumadijan tea, made from plum brandy heated with honey. At half the plank table with the oilcloth folded back the elder child of the household was doing homework. We adults were talking at the other end. A kerosene lamp hung on a hand-wrought nail, casting weak light into the room. Grandfather, rolling cigarettes, put a fresh one in his whittled willow holder and peered over his granddaughter's biology lesson.

'Hmmf,' he snorted, 'is that what they teach you in school? A person with only a heart and veins? Is that what Communism teaches? Nonsense! Where is the bone and muscle? I've worked with man and beast for all my years, and I know that this book is wrong.'

The girl explained to her grandfather that it was a lesson on the circulatory system, and the man listened, puffing silently.

As a small boy the son's chore was to pasture the sheep before hiking up to the village school. He was eight or nine then. The early spring morning was raw, and Grandfather removed his own brimless fur hat and placed it on the boy's head where it slipped down over his ears. Imitating his adored grandfather the boy said, 'A man must work,' and took his shepherd's flute and striped bag with its copybooks and slab of bread smeared with melted lard and stoically took off through the tall grass. That boy, today a grown man, sits with me outside the house, along the overhang and recollects the same scene.

'How I loved that man,' he says with fervour. 'I remember the 'old house' with it low ceiling and dirt floor. When I was small I used to curl up in Grandmother's bed to keep warm. *Ej*, everything changes!'

He takes a swig of *rakija* and picks up his accordion.

'I'm going to play *Kolubarska Kolo*. It was Grandfather's favourite.' His eyes mist.

I watched a Millet pastoral painting come to life. I had seen 'The Gleaners' at the Louvre, but here was no *tableau vivant*. This was real life, complete with sweat and calluses. I see a wheat field being harvested. The reaper shifts his weight, bending one knee and rotating his hip as gracefully as a dancer as the great sharp arc of his scythe slices off stalks of wheat. Behind him, paced to his rhythm, follows his wife, her hair bound in a kerchief and her sleeves billowing. She swoops to gather the sheaves, binds them, rests them on the grass. Slash/swoop, bend, rest. It is a ballet of harmony and cooperation danced against the gold of the waning day.

By chance both son and daughter of the household had a child within a year of the birth of my own last child. The three toddlers tumbled together on the patch of chamomile growing wild beside the barn, gambolling like little lambs in the flower-dotted herbs. Their movements crushed the flowerlets and released that pleasant, mildly citron-like aroma that I smell even now, recollecting it.

I recall all those evenings after the children were asleep and the cacophony of bleats and moos came to a stop, indicating that the animals were settled for the night. Branko and Joel carried the plank table outside and we four sat around and talked. The crickets accompanied us, but the rest of the world was silent and the sky was an endless bowl studded with stars. Branko expressed doubts about the tempo of contemporary life. He worried about who would take care of him and Ljubinka when they were truly old, with both their children having left the land and the village. Who would farm? Who would inherit the precious land that had been in the family all those generations? Here in this stillness it was not possible to take notes and call it fieldwork. We were friends listening to friends discuss matters of vital concern.

And the mornings. I recall early mornings when, stirred by the activity of others in the house, we awaited sunrise and with it the walnut leaf shadows dancing on the wall of our room. We lay upon our cornhusk mattress (the husks were stuffed into a coarse linen sacking and had to be reshuffled after each use) and discussed the day's plan. The two older children slept head to foot on a pallet at the base of our bed. The baby slept in a portable playpen fitted with a mattress. Later all three moved to a separate sleeping area, but while they were in the room with us it was tricky to converse and prevent them from awakening. Rarely did a day evolve as planned, and learning to be flexible has been a valuable lesson from the fieldwork enterprise. Difficult days began by picking off biting bed-bugs and wondering what on earth I was doing in this place.

Alone in the room, these are the recollections that flood my memory. On this morning I get up with the dawn, like Udovica Jana and the other women I have met in epic song. During the night it has rained lightly, *rosna kiša*, the 'dewy rain' so good for crops, the kind that Gypsy girls dressed in leaves used to chant and dance for. The last time that ancient ritual was done in the village was the first year I was there. This time the soft rain has fallen on fallow fields. Hay was not mown in time. The apricots will rot soon. Beyond the security of the village, in towns and cities inflation is at an all-time high, and food is expensive. Society is in economic and ethnic ferment.

Here in my room there is no shadow play of walnut leaves on the wall this morning. Outside the leaves flutter damply, green and silver. I pull on a sweater and slip into my rubber shoes. The geraniums thrive in their worn pots. Along the overhang against the outside threshold to the kitchen door are some welcoming presents neighbours have left without my having heard them – a small jar of homemade honey, a green glass wine bottle filled with fresh milk and stoppered with a trimmed corncob, and, wrapped in yesterday's *Politika*, a round loaf of warm black bread. (In the natural cycle of things some villagers will return to healthy food.)

Chores first. I exit from the gate in the chickenwire fence put up 20 years ago to pen in my creeping baby so that the chickens could roam free, and step through the wet grass to the sheep hutch. The weathered wooden bolt is hard to slide. Finally, it gives way, and I prop the stave against the hutch.

'Prrssiko! prrss! prrss!' I trill, summoning the sheep out to pasture.

Then, folding an old rag-rug on the stone steps, for I don't want the ill winds to catch me, I sit down to eat my bread and honey, and I know why I am here.

Later, back in Massachusetts, in that most mundane of settings – the parking lot of my local supermarket – I am approached by a foreign graduate student at my university who asks in Serbian,

'Excuse me, Mrs, but aren't you, well, that woman from Orašac?'

Bibliography

A Serbian Village in Historical Perspective, Case Studies in Cultural Anthropology series, New York: Holt, Rinehart and Winston, 1972. Revised and updated edn, Prospect Heights, Illinois: Waveland Press, 1986 (with J. Halpern).

'The People of Serbia' in *People in States*, TABA Social Science Program for Grades 4–6, Menlo Park, California: Addison-Wesley Publishing Co., 1972.

Selected papers on a Serbian Village: Social Structure as Reflected by History, Demography and Oral Tradition, Amherst: University of Massachusetts Research Report No. 17, 1976.

'"Udovica Jana": A Case Study of Oral performance,' *Slavonic and East European Review*, XIV, 1: 11–23, 1976 (with J. Foley).

'The Power of the Word: Healing Charms as an Oral Genre,' *Journal of American Folklore*, 91, 362: 903–24, 1978 (with J. Foley).

'Changing Perceptions of Husbands and Wives in Five Yugoslav Villages', in *Europe as a Culture Area*, J. Cuisinier, ed., The Hague: Mouton, 159–72, 1979.

'Genealogy as Genre in Rural Serbia', in *Oral Traditional Literatures*, J. Foley, ed., Columbus, Ohio: Slavica Press: 301–21, 1981.

'Text and Context in Serbian Ritual Lament', *Canadian-American Slavic Studies*, special edn 15, 1: 52–60, 1981.

'Watch Out for Snakes! Ethnosemantic Interpretations and Misrepresentation', *Anthropological Linguistics*, Bloomington, Indiana: Fall 1983: 309–25.

'Rakija as Ritual', *East European Quarterly*, XVIII, 4: 481–94, 1985.

'Trust, Talk and Touch in Folk Healing', *Social Science & Medicine*, 21, 3: 319–25, 1985.

'Trećina veka u proušavanju srpskog sela: Zašto?' *Zbornik Radova Desetog Savetovnja Etnološkog Društva SR Srbije*, Belgrade: Sveska V 11: 144–55, 11985 (with J. Halpern).

'Complementarity of Women's Ritual Roles in a Patriarchal Society', *Balkanologische Veröffentlichungen*, Weisbaden, Band 12 (Berlin): 79–98, 1987.

'Dugoroćna istraživanja u Orašcu', *Pregled*, Belgrade, 237: 84–94 (with J. Halpern) 1987.

'Healing with Mother Metaphors', in *Women as Healers: a Cross-Cultural Perspective*, C. McLean, ed., Rutgers: The University Press: 115–33, 1989.

CHAPTER 13

Give me, 0 indulgent fate!
Give me yet, before I die,
A sweet, but absolute retreat,
'Mongst paths so lost, and trees so high,
That the world may ne'er invade
Through such windings and such shade
My unshaken liberty.

Anne, Countess of Winchelsea, ***Petition for Absolute Retreat***.

Bucks Brides, and Useless Baggage: Women's Quest for a Role in their Balkan Travels

Dea Birkett

'There is a peculiar pleasure in riding out into the unknown,' wrote Edith Durham on leaving Scutari one May dawn, heading for the mountains.[1] For women who left behind the comfort of home for the uncertainty of Balkan travel, the unknown into which they leapt was more than geographic. From Edith Durham's 1903 winding Albanian journey to Barbara Kerewsky-Halpern's first field trip to a Serbian village in the early 1950s, the unknown was also the role in which they would be incorporated into these foreign societies. How would they explain themselves? How far would they have to assume a new set of values, even a new identity? How far would they *want* to? Would they be accepted? And if so, as *what*?[2] For many this uncertainty was itself a motive for their journeys, especially for those Victorian and Edwardian women who found their home life unfulfilling. The lure of a new purpose, a new identity, had launched them out into a wider world. Perhaps, in these lands so far from their own, they might not only explore and unravel an exotic society but something new, exciting and rewarding in themselves.

For the last century and more, women have travelled to the Balkans for this spiritual as well as physical exploration. Yet the focus of their travels has varied enormously. Simple wanderlust propelled Winifred Gordon and her husband on their journey.

Many happy memories of distant lands – Korea, Mexico, Uganda; East Africa ... Zanzibar; a purpled star-lit night on an Arab roof with the murmuring ocean below; the dry swish of palm-trees by the Blue Nile – had only deepened our love for the more primitive lands and the adventurous paths of the world.[3]

Others simply ventured forth from 'curiosity'.[4]

The decade in which they travelled, their aims and objectives, and the length of their visits varied widely. Edith Durham was a forerunner of those who pursued anthropological studies. 'I explained that I wished only to note things characteristically Servian, such as the costumes of the peasants, the houses, and so forth,' she claimed setting out in 1902. 'In short,' said a gentleman, 'you are making geo-ethnographical studies'.[5]

With the development of anthropology as a discipline and fieldwork as its main means of research, women travelled to the Balkans for more well-defined, professional purposes, often settling for long periods or returning to the same village over decades. Ernestine Friedl went to live in and examine a Greek peasant community in 1955. Diane Freedman visited Romania in the early 1970s to study folk dance.

Whether they settled in one village or wandered, whether they were wives, sisters or travelled alone, also affected the women travellers' place as foreigners within Balkan societies. But the common thread in these very different women's experiences is the painful process of incorporation into a society at once enticing and intimidating in its foreignness.

As the woman traveller bent down through a low arched stone doorway and entered her first Albanian home, or adjusted her eyes to the unaccustomed smoke of the *han*, or unpacked her crates in her rented half of a family home, she did so as an honoured guest. She would be toasted with thimblefuls of coffee and plied with glasses of fruit brandy as polite enquiries were made as to how she came to reach such a remote spot. As strangers, the women were unsure how to act. When they misunderstood, their hosts showed enormous patience in explaining the eating and sleeping arrangements. If they strayed from the behaviour expected of them as guests, they were coaxed back into acting in accordance with their honoured position in the household. Rose Wilder Lane spent her very first night in an Albanian home waiting anxiously for the food to arrive. It was past midnight, Lane and her friends had been on horseback all day without a break, and the pre-dinner pleasantries seemed endless. But their guide warned: 'In Albania it is not polite to care about food!' and directed the two women to inquire about the local spirits and listen attentively to their host's stories. 'It is the custom, when strangers come, to talk to them,' he explained. Dinner eventually appeared at half past two in the morning.[6]

For a woman travelling alone, the status of honoured guest was further enhanced by her dubious gender. Although it was clear to her hosts that she was physically female, the fact that she was foreign and acting outside the parameters deemed fit for feminine behaviour (both in her own and the host society) meant she could be considered as if male, a privilege not enjoyed by women journeying with a husband. But, as Durham found on her Albanian travels, this advantage could not be relied upon. No sooner had she sat to eat with the men while the women withdrew to a respectful distance. ('I am always classed with the buck herd', she confidently recorded.) An 'Albanian virgin' treated the traveller 'with the contempt she appeared to think all petticoats deserved – turned her back on me, and exchanged cigarettes with the men, with whom she was hail-fellow-well-met.'[7] When night came, there was often a debate amongst her hosts as to whether Durham should sleep in the male or female quarters.

For some women travellers, the privileged and undemanding position of honoured guest was all they sought. Although inheriting the use of Durham's guide Marko Shantoya, Winifred Gordon wanted no more than a superficial acquaintance with Balkan societies, and that mostly of the upper classes. She enjoyed the curiosity she stirred up as an outsider, never seeking to assimilate. 'English women travelling in the Balkans are still a not too frequent sight, and the people of these countries – with the exception of Turkey – display a great, though quite polite, interest in their appearance and doings,' she noted, submitting to her wrist watch, her fur coat, and her earrings being fingered in public places.[8]

To Durham, the distance between herself and those amongst whom she travelled served to bolster her claims as a pioneering traveller and anthropologist. 'I was said to the be the first, foreign female and the first female dressed *alla franga* in Vuthaj,' she boasted. 'And the first foreigner of any sort that had come right into Vuthaj'.[9]

Many more found the limitations of being treated as an outsider frustrating. The village officials courteously tried to accommodate Diane Freedman and her husband's wish to film the local dance. But, Freedman records, they viewed:

> our interest in customs and folklore as equivalent to that of tourists. They acted as though all we required was to participate minimally in a colourful event and to have our participation dutifully recorded on film so that we could take the photo home as a souvenir. Clearly, this kind of participation in village society posed no threat.[10]

The precise degree of Ernestine Friedl's incorporation into her Greek rural community was also regulated. Although the villagers allowed her to wear warm boots and heavy jackets, which contradicted her status as a professor and anthropologist, she was frowned upon for tying a standard village woman's kerchief around her head to guard against the sun. 'That was clearly a symbol of the rural woman who works in the fields, and I was allowed only partially to simulate the position of village women', she writes.[11]

To get to know and speak with authority about Balkan societies, the women travellers felt that they must be involved beyond the limits which the distanced role of stranger and honoured guest allowed. They must somehow try to assimilate. But both to the women themselves and the people amongst whom they travelled, the nagging question was – 'As what?' Only three weeks into her 1910s travels through Albania, Montenegro, Serbia, Romania and Bulgaria with her brother, who was compiling a report for the Turkish government, Demetra Vaka was already beginning to ask what that role might be. If her life had made sense at home in nearby Greece, it was being increasingly questioned by those she met on her journey:

> My last hostess, in perplexity over the reason for my existence, turned to her husband and asked:
> 'Master Nikita, can you imagine this young girl ever giving sturdy sons to her husband?'
> The husband caressed with his two hands the belt which carried his many weapons and shook his head doubtfully.

'That is why the Greeks are of no account nowadays,' he replied.
'They pamper their women, and they school them as if they were
boys. . . .'

And so much did they marvel at my slenderness and smallness that
I began to wonder myself if I were not really a pretty useless baggage.[12]

As a Greek woman allied through her brother to the Turkish
government, Vaka may have been more severely censured than a
traveller from further away. But the closer she came to living with
the people – moving out of her tent and into their homes – the
more her incorporation into a role perceived as fit for the host
society was demanded, and the more peculiar her deviations from
these norms were deemed to be. Her continual requests to wash
were greeted by one hostess with astonishment. Kyria Melitza had
reluctantly supplied hot water on the day of her arrival, but refused
to do so again, wanting to know, reported Vaka, 'why in the name
of Mount Olympus I needed so much washing? Was I a leper?'[13]

Yet while Vaka chafed against such unpleasant aspects of her
travelling life, that such conformity was being demanded was a
sign of her acceptance. The lady of the house where she stayed in
Cetinje called her not by a polite title for stranger or guest, but 'my
dear child' a form of incorporation far more open to female than
male travellers. This inclusion into the family circle meant, however, that Vaka must act as her hosts acted, and was forbidden to
take a rest when she arrived in town, even after a whole day in the
saddle, because, said her hostess, 'people don't lie down in the
daytime unless they are sick.'[14] 'After a few days in Montenegro I
learned not to speak of lying down. No matter how tired I felt,'
Vaka wrote.[15]

The closest and most engulfing way in which the travelling
women could be invited to become part of their host societies was
not as a 'child' but as a wife. They were not short of proposals.
Vaka was asked by the wild and handsome Albanian guide
Acheron to be his 'eagle woman' and fly back to the mountains
with him. 'I cannot go back to the mountains with you, Acheron,'
she replied, 'for I am not an eagle.' 'I can teach you to be an eagle,'
was Acheron's rejoinder, clearly inviting her to intimately partake
in his world. But Vaka further explained:

You have been seeing me now on my holidays, Acheron, when for a little time I could do many things, such as ride all day, sleep in tents, eat
black bread, and above all, live without books – and those things I cannot do always.[16]

212

For women who travelled with a husband, these awkward situations did not arise. As wives, their position was more readily understood and they could be included in the married women's social circles and activities. Barbara Kerewsky-Halpern recalls that people in her Serbian household were not referred to by their name but by their role. As a married woman, she was addressed as *mlada* (bride).[17] The fact that she had children ameliorated still further her path of acceptance into village life.

> Despite academic degrees, publications and more matronly appearance, to the villagers I am Babi, wife to my husband and mother to my children. Increasingly, I am able to delve deeper into the culture. . . .[18]

But as a woman traveller was drawn closer into village life as a child, wife or mother, she would also be expected to conform more and more to the behaviour expected of a woman in that world. Transgressions of acceptable behaviour would not be tolerated as they were when she had been a stranger and honoured guest. Diane Freedman was advised that her husband should wash the clothes – if he would *insist* on doing it himself – inside their house, and she should hang them outside. Otherwise her reputation as a good wife would suffer.[19]

While Freedman was prepared to conform in these matters of outward propriety, including attending the local Romanian Orthodox church although a Jew, in situations of deep emotional trauma she found herself unable to be so compliant. When her husband died and she returned to the field recently widowed, the women of the village were shocked that she had cropped her hair. On her first stay with her husband, she had tied her hair in a *conci*, a braided knot worn by married women. At her husband's death in America, she had cut her hair to symbolise, to herself, a new stage in her life. But the village women were horrified:

> Why had I cut my hair? Didn't I realize that the period of mourning would soon be over? Surely, I would marry again soon. What of my hair when I remarried'? Wasn't I sorry that I had done such a thing? And so on. The consensus seemed to be that by this act I had further removed myself from village custom. Since I could no longer look like a village woman, my actual identity as an outsider, a 'lady' from the city, was more evident.[20]

As a young widow, the behaviour expected of her by the villagers was very different from that as a bride, and far less amenable to

Freedman. After the period of mourning, she was expected to marry as soon as possible. 'Why shouldn't I marry a man from the village? Village men are handsome. Village men are strong. Village men are hardworking,' she was continually reminded.[21] Freedman's refusal to remarry – to do the very thing that every other Transylvanian villager in a similar situation would have done-led her to be reprimanded. Whereas a foreigner new to the village could be forgiven for acting outside the normal patterns of behaviour, someone who had been incorporated into village life could not be excused such abnormalities. Freedman's everyday actions – talking to men in the street or on the bus, or even exchanging a smile – became the subject of village gossip. The privileges of an outsider had been lost. Once women were incorporated into a female role within their host societies, they were also expected to conform to appropriate feminine behaviour.

For many this was an impossible task. They had, after all, left their homes precisely because of the uncomfortable conformity it expected of them as women. Durham, as a spinster daughter responsible for an ailing parent, described how her travels 'made the endless vista of grey imprisonment at home the more intolerable. And a bullet would have been a short way out.'[22] Yet despite a close sympathy with the Albanian people, she stoutly refused to be incorporated into the feminine role. While in no way disguising her sex, Durham attempted to preserve male status on her travels – firing off guns with glee at every invitation and exchanging quips with local dignitaries, man to man:

> The tale had gone round that I was sister to the King of England . . . The Bariaktar's son said they did not want the King of England, or any king, interfering in Luria. Luria is a free country. If he thought I was really the King's sister, he would cut off my head at once. He asked if I were afraid. I, entering into his pleasantry, replied that if some one would lend me a revolver I should be very pleased to shoot him. This is the sort of joke they like.[23]

With all her assumed gallantry, Durham still gives the impression of acting a part, uncomfortable with her masculine role yet unable to find another which would allow her the independence she so cherished.

For later women anthropologists in the Balkans, being social scientists and members of the host society was often an awkward and irreconcilable combination of roles. What happened to the carefully nurtured objectivity of the observer when she was incorporated into village life? Durham could at the same time write that she was an 'outsider', yet also insist 'one must live the life of the people' to really know and understand them.[24]

Barbara Kerewsky-Halpern recalls; 'I am a woman in the village but not of the village . . . I am simultaneously guest and woman of the house, in a house that has long been my family's home yet is not really our home.'[25]

Many women found, and still find it attractive to embrace a new identity in their Balkan homes. Yet they are understandably unable to entirely surrender their allegiances, cultural and personal, to the land of their birth. A few, like Durham, became less and less able to resolve the conflict between their assumed role in the Balkans and their home life. Growing old and isolated in England, she became more and more enraged at the misplaced demands placed upon her by her adopted Albanian homeland. On her final visit in 1921, she found herself unable any longer to fulfil the role of 'the Balkan Englishwoman, the friend of the Montenegrins'.[26] When the heads of the Kastrati and Hoti petitioned for her support, she recorded in her diary, 'Said I was powerless. They would not believe me. Said in vain I was now old and tired. They persisted until I promised to "write something" . . . God knows what.' The next day's entry reads: 'Must get away at all costs.'[27]

Yet for others these conflicting roles themselves were attractive, allowing them two lives and all the multifarious attendant experiences – one life more than women who stayed at home and resided in only one culture. But for many, the key to these increased opportunities was to maintain a slight distance between themselves and their host society. As an adopted child, wife or political saviour, the women travellers inherited a fresh set of unwelcome constrictions in their newly discovered role.

Notes

1. Edith Durham, *High Albania*, London: Edward Arnold, 1909, p. 39.
2. Much of this discussion was stimulated by Jean Briggs' 'Kapluna Daughter' in Peggy Golde (ed.), *Women in the Field: Anthropological Experiences*, 2nd edn, Berkeley: University of California Press, 1986, pp. 19-44.
3. Mrs Will Gordon, *A Woman in the Balkans*, London: Hutchinson, 1916, p. 1.
4. Omer Hadžiselimović, 'Two Victorian Ladies and Bosnian Realities, 1862-1875', p. 2.
5. John Hodgson, 'Edith Durham, Traveller and Publicist', p.14.
6. Rose Wilder Lane, *The Peaks of Shala. Being the Record of Certain Wanderings among the Hill Tribes of Albania*, New York: Harper and Brothers, 1923.

7. Durham, *High Albania*, pp. 64 and 80.
8. Gordon, *A Woman in the Balkans*, p. 63.
9. Durham, *High Albania*, p. 138.
10. Diane Freedman, 'Wife, Widow, Woman: Roles of an Anthropologist in a Transylvanian Village', in Golde, *Women in the Field*, p. 345.
11. Ernestine Friedl, 'Field Work in a Greek Village', in *ibid.*, p. 214.
12. Demetra Vaka, *The Heart of the Balkans*, Boston and New York: Houghton Mifflin and Co. 1917, pp. 111–12.
13. *Ibid.*, p. 27.
14. *Ibid.*, pp. 68–9.
15. *Ibid.*, p. 77.
16. *Ibid.*, pp. 98 and 100.
17. Barbara Kerewsky-Halpern, 'Anthropologist in the Village', p. 152.
18. *Ibid.*, p 120.
19. Freedman, 'Wife, Widow, Woman', p. 345.
20. *Ibid.*, p. 350.
21. *Ibid.*, p. 355.
22. Edith Durham, *Twenty Years of Balkan Tangle*, London: George, Allen and Unwin, 1920, p. 81.
23. Durham, *High Albania*, p. 315.
24. *Ibid.*, preface and p. 20.
25. Kerewsky-Halpern, 'Anthropologist in the Village', p. 191.
26. Durham, *High Albania*, p. 254.
27. John Hodgson, 'Edith Durham, Traveller and Publicist', p. 25.

CHAPTER 14

Travelling is the ruin of all happiness!
There's no looking at a building here
after seeing Italy.

Fanny Burney, **Cecilia**, IV, Chp. 2

In France they were among friends.
Italy, which they crossed next day,
seemed the end of the known world.

Olivia Manning, **Fortunes of War**, Vol. 1, Chp. 1.

Constructing the 'Balkans'*

John B. Allcock

One of the central tasks which this volume addresses is to trace the process by which a particular image of the Balkan region has come to be largely accepted in the English-speaking world. To tell this story in anything approaching completeness would be an enormous undertaking, quite beyond the scope of one essay. The scale of such an endeavour could perhaps be measured by comparison with the scholarly effort that has already been expended on a parallel project, namely, the exploration of European perceptions of Islam. Norman Daniel's impressive efforts in this direction have resulted in a monograph of more than six hundred pages, which its author modestly calls a 'long essay rather than a comprehensive record'.[1] The brief discussion offered here hardly bears comparison with Daniel's scholarship. This is simply a thumb-nail sketch which might be developed later into a portrait. It is an

* I would like to acknowledge gratefully the critical observations on an earlier draft of this essay made by Angela Phelps and Neal Robinson. A version of it was read to the VIe. Congrès International d'Etudes du Sud-Est Européen in Sofia, September 1989. The helpful comment of participants on that occasion is also recognised.

attempt to suggest some hypotheses, and not a digest of the conclusions achieved after extensive investigation.

The problem of how and why an image of the Balkan region has come to be constructed in the English-speaking world is an interesting one. The area does have the capacity to grip the imagination and engage the affection of outsiders in a remarkable way, and to an extent which might appear to be out of all proportion to its real historical or cultural importance.

This long process of image creation has not been done disinterestedly, however: the writers whose work has contributed to it have always had their own reasons. The encounter with the Balkans has played its own part in the development of their personal projects and identities. The point of this particular essay, however, is not to explore that inter-penetration of character and experience. We are concerned on this occasion more immediately with the fact that they all wrote about their experiences, and this writing has come to provide a very significant contribution to the formation of generally current perceptions of the region and its peoples.

The Construction of Images

The process by which one group of people comes to know – or to imagine that they know – another must be one of the most important problems for modern social scientists. A glance at any daily newspaper will demonstrate beyond doubt the power of such images in the world. The 'Christian' countries are mesmerised by the rise of so-called 'Islamic fundamentalism'; the progress of political and economic unification in Europe is bedevilled by English fixed ideas about the French – which appear to be reciprocated. The importance of representations of this kind is revealed dramatically when they are challenged by events. American perceptions of the threat posed by 'Communism in their own back yard' are reduced to confusion when confronted by Mr Gorbachev's efforts to promote *glasnost* and *perestroika*.

How do groups, peoples or cultures come to perceive each other? How is it that these collective preconceptions have such power over us? Social scientists have devoted a good deal of effort to this problem in the past but along a regrettably narrow front of enquiry. The issue for a long time came to be defined in terms of 'prejudice'. Prejudice, however, is an attribute of individuals: the term refers to the fixed manner in which attitudes or beliefs are held, so that they are resistant to change in the face of evidence which challenges them.

The limitations of a framework of explanation which remains at this level can be shown easily by reference to the two specific historical problems which were principally responsible for stimulating research in these areas – the rise of anti-semitism associated with the coming to power of Nazism in Germany, and the struggle for equality of the black population of the United States of America.

Although no social explanation which sets aside entirely individuals can be said to command much intellectual respect, both of these complex configurations of events clearly demand that factors other than simple individual prejudices be taken into account, for two reasons. In each case the bigotry of the dominating, discriminating and oppressing group goes well beyond the incidental irrationalities of individuals and takes on a highly organised, patterned and definitely institutional form. Furthermore, sociologists and psychologists looking at the history of race relations have repeatedly come up against the need to explain why, on the one hand, some prejudiced individuals refrain in practice from discrimination and the open display of racial hostility, and on the other hand, why some of the people who do actively engage in discriminatory behaviour show little or no sign of rooted personal prejudice.

'Prejudice', then, can only be at best a part of the story. We need to find another strand, and one which takes up the account of how these images accumulate over time, how they develop their organised character, and how they become rooted in the institutions of society. In order to meet these demands, social scientists in recent years have turned their attention more to the idea that inter-group images need to be looked at as processes of 'construction'. The belief that our knowledge of the world ought to be looked at in terms of a process of construction was popularised by Peter Berger and Thomas Luckmann more than twenty years ago, in their book *The Social Construction Reality*.[2] In essence, however, the idea is much older and can be traced back to the early days of sociology.

Emile Durkheim, for example, writing during the last quarter of the nineteenth century, insisted that the process which he called 'collective representation' must be central to our understanding of social life. The business of knowing the world (Durkheim argued) has to be a shared endeavour. We actively share our experiences with each other, or in his terms, we represent the world to each other; so that the experiences which each of us has are made sense of by being placed in a framework which we learn from others. We each help in the general process of knowing the world, not only by having more and more experiences to throw into the pool, but more significantly, by reinforcing and transmitting to others the whole scheme of ideas into which the fragments of life can be fitted.

The idea of construction is as interesting as it is ambiguous. It seems to refer to both something going on in the heads of the observers, and something which actually happens to the people who are being observed. That ambiguity is actually an asset in this case; because what social scientists are trying to convey through the term is precisely that these two things are intimately linked. The observers who are constructing the world in that they are finding out 'what construction can be placed on events' (making sense of these events) are at the same time imparting a kind of fixity and definition to their experiences when they come to communicate these socially.

In recent years this way of looking at knowledge as a social construction has been applied fruitfully to several problems, one of the most vigorous of which has been the study of gender. Feminists have devoted a great deal of attention to illuminating the ways in which all kinds of agencies in our society – families, the state, schools, employers, churches, the media of mass communication, groups of friends and so on – all appear to be engaged in some gigantic conspiracy to construct women from their very earliest moments as certain kinds of people – particularly as subordinated to men and as relatively disadvantaged in most aspects of life.

Whatever else social scientists are in disagreement about, they are of one mind about the flexibility and adaptability of human beings. We can become a bewilderingly wide variety of types of people. The big puzzle, however, hangs over the problem of explaining why it is that in spite of that general openness to possibility which is inherent in our species, it is so very difficult to rework those processes of construction once they are set in motion. This difficulty seems to hinge on the intimate link which we have already noted between the 'objective' and the 'subjective' aspects of the construction process. Where do you begin to change the world if the oppressed or disadvantaged – the victims of misconstruction in any way – have themselves internalised (that is, learned to define themselves) as necessarily made in the way represented by their oppressors?

Constructing the Orient

Within the context of our present interest in this book, the idea of the social construction of reality takes on a special significance in relation to the ways in which particular regions of the world come to be represented as having specific kinds of identity. (How did the Balkans come to be seen as 'Balkan'?) Sadly, relatively little good work has been done in the social sciences on this type of question – although it is of obvious importance for a great range of issues, including the impact which these representations or images may have for world peace.[3]

In spite of this relative indifference to a very significant set of questions, one widely read and highly stimulating study has been written which provides us with a point of departure. It is by Edward W. Said, whose controversial discussion of Orientalism tackles the way in which 'The Orient' has come to be constructed in the West.[4] The Orient, he insists, 'is not an inert fact of nature. It is not merely there, just as the Occident is not just there either.' The starting point for Said's discussion is the configuration of ideas which have come to shape our perception of things Eastern–especially the Arab world. He stresses, however, that Orientalism can not be defined solely in relation to ideas.[5]

> ... ideas, cultures and histories cannot seriously be understood or studied without their force, or more precisely their configurations of power, also being studied. To believe that the Orient was created – or as I call it, 'Orientalized' – and to believe that such things happen simply as a necessity of the imagination, is to be disingenuous. The relationship between the Occident and the Orient is a relationship of power, of domination, of varying degrees of complex hegemony. ...
>
> The Orient was Orientalized not only because it was discovered to be 'Oriental' in all those ways considered commonplace by the average nineteenth century European, but also because it could be – that is submitted to being made Oriental.

The contrast which the author draws here between 'discovering' and 'making' the Orient captures precisely the notion of 'construction' to which we have already referred, by which the Balkans became 'Balkanised'.

Said is not offering us an interpretation of the development of this aspect of Western thought which hinges on some notion of a crude conspiracy to misrepresent the East to the West, and thus facilitate the task of holding it down economically and politically.

221

His long, complex and wide-ranging investigation dwells rather on the largely unconscious and unrecognised process by which Western European writers in a wide variety of disciplines and contexts in the eighteenth and nineteenth centuries began to weave together that intricate blend of fact and prejudice which was to become Orientalism.

The extraordinary continuity in these images over time is due in large measure, he argues, to the way in which they have not only been created but sustained with particular authority by the fact of their origin within the canon of scholarly and scientific work. The process has been supported, however, by the political ambitions of Western statesmen, especially in Britain and France but more recently in the USA, who needed to justify the imperial aspirations and expansion of their own countries towards 'the Orient'. Even so, it was not simply a 'political' process, in the narrower sense of that word.

For Said, Orientalism means that a picture of the East was constructed which demonstrated that the movement towards the subordination of Orientals was not merely excusable but inevitable and necessary. Orientals were shown conclusively to be without the capacity to create great civilisations, or even to think logically. They were trapped within cultures which were structurally incapable of growth, constrained within a mental life shaped by languages which are intrinsically inferior as modes of grasping the world or communicating about it, and so on. The West came to know that the East was like this because scholars of tremendous learning, travellers of wide experience and statesmen of great authority, affirmed that things were indeed like that.

Little of this complex process of constructing the Orient depends crucially upon the personal bigotry or prejudice of the scholars, travellers or statesmen involved. Indeed, Said's appreciation of the grandeur, range and imaginative power of the work of the great figures in the growth of Orientalism, such as Sir Richard Burton, Gustave Flaubert, Sir Hamilton Gibb, Louis Massignon, or Ernest Renan, is rarely stinted.[6] His argument is not that their construction of the Oriental reflects the distortion of their own minds. Nevertheless, out of this unhappy wedding of scholarship and politics has emerged a set of images through which one significant part of the world is now represented to another; and so natural and inevitable do these constructions now seem that it is hard to recognise their arbitrary and constructed status, let alone to shake our minds free of them. Just as the differences between men and women which our culture accepts confront us with the sure authority of common sense or human nature, so the differences between East and West seem to be rooted in the very nature of things. We are no longer able to recognise them as chance constructions of the human mind.

Edward Said's work is valuable as a pioneering effort in the study of the mutual construction of peoples – a process which is central to all culture. As such, it provides a useful focus for our own interest in the development of an image of the Balkans. It has its limitations, nonetheless, and it is worth pausing for a moment to consider some of these, as reflecting on them will point us in the direction of matters of real interest and value in our own material. Before moving on to a consideration of the Balkans, therefore, it will be useful to engage with Said briefly on his own ground – the Orient.

Reconstructing Edward Said

A detailed appraisal of Said's study would be out of place here – this has been done authoritatively by others but two critical observations are in order.[7] Said makes two specific claims about the ways in which Orientals come to be constructed by Occidentals which are not necessarily wrong, but in which he does overstate his case. Easterners are always shown in a negative light: and they are never allowed to speak for themselves. Anyone who delves at first hand into the material which Said has made his own will discover relatively quickly that neither of these claims is strictly true. These are not trivial attempts to score points over Said. Taken together they suggest a more fundamental issue to which his work needs to give deeper consideration.

Said's argument makes much of Edward Lane's *Manners and Customs of the Modern Egyptians*, published in 1836. He is represented as a significant contributor to the development of a negative view of the Orient, with his:

> propensity for sadomasochistic colossal tidbits: the self-mutilation of dervishes, the cruelty of judges, the blending of religion with licentiousness among Muslims, the excess of libidinous passions, and so on.[8]

An interesting account of the Orient of which Said appears to be unaware, however, is provided by D. Urquhart, whose book *The Spirit of the East* appeared in 1838 – two years later than Lane's.

Urquhart, although he freely pays his respects to Lane's intimate knowledge of the East, sets out to attack precisely this prejudicial view of native life, fostered by Orientalists.

> We have been deprived of the means of appreciating what is good; we have exaggerated that which is bad.
> Having dwelt so much on the difficulties that stand in the way of a correct estimate of the East, I must observe, that these difficulties *reside solely in a European's preconceived opinions.* (Urquhart's emphasis.)[9]

Indeed, his Introduction could be recommended to modern students of the social sciences as a homily on the evils of ethnocentrism.

This is not to say that there are no problems in relation to Urquhart's account of the East – especially his understanding of Islam. There is no doubt, however, that he cannot be accused of fostering antipathy to Muslims. He stands rather more in danger of being accused of having 'gone native' during his stay in Turkey, and of a lack of critical detachment. Of course he is engaged in precisely that process of constructing the Orient which concerns Said: that is inevitable. In that task, however, his work is if anything apologetic rather than denigratory, reductive or patronising.

Are the natives able to speak for themselves? Said has been criticised elsewhere for the one-sidedness of his discussion of this point.[10] It is certainly remarkable that he has no word of recognition for the work of Franz Fanon, to mention only one outstanding counter-case. One other case closer to our own interests will serve to establish the point.

In 1819, as a part of the reordering of Europe following the defeat of Napoleon, the southern Albanian village of Parga was sold to the Vizir of Jannina by the High Commissioner for the Ionian Isles, Thomas Maitland. The villagers, 'preferring exile to the Mahommedan yoke', fled taking with them all that they could having first burned the bones of their ancestors in the village square. Travelling at first to Corfu, then to Trieste, some ended their journey in Switzerland. A child of that experience later became well-known as the writer, La Comtesse Dora d'Istria. Her book *Les Femmes en Orient* was published in Zurich in 1859, making her a contemporary of Ernest Renan, depicted by Said as a pivotal figure in the emergence of Orientalism. The Comtesse's work shows her to be a woman of erudition who was certainly familiar with the central figures in the formation of Said's Orientalism. More than this, however, her interest and authority stems from the fact that, as a native speaker of at least one of the region's languages, who in spite of her marriage into a European noble family never forgot her own origins, she was eminently able to write as 'an Oriental'.

There is room for a good deal of argument about the nature and significance of Dora d'Istria's book. To what extent, for example, did she internalise Western definitions of the Orient, in spite of her own background? One thing is certain, however, and that is that in spite of the outward adoption of the Orientalist frame of reference in her title, her book is shot through with a keen sense of the cultural diversity of the region about which she writes. She is as devoid of sympathy for 'The Turk' as any of Said's subjects: but she is adamant that the Orient is not exhausted by its Ottoman rulers, or by their Islamic faith.

None of this is to say that Said is simply wrong. The point is that the representation of the Orient in European literature is rather more complex and certainly less unanimous than he gives us to believe. His case, that a certain construction of the East has emerged as clearly dominant in Western thought, is not in doubt. It is necessary to stress, nevertheless, that in this process it was certainly contested. The story is more subtle and its outcome less certain than Said is prepared to admit.

Surely this point should not be surprising. After all, if any phrase comes readily to mind as capturing the essence of the Orient it is 'the mysterious East'. If what everybody knows about the Orient is that it is essentially mysterious, then ambiguity is built into the heart of that construction just as much, if not more so, than any statement about definite attributes which the East may have. In the words of the philosopher W. Bryce Gallie, the concept of the Orient is 'essentially contested' rather than neatly packaged.[11] This supposed 'mysterious' quality of things Eastern is, of course, the seat of their fascination for us. It is typically things which are obscure and requiring illumination which excite our curiosity. After all, 'the North' of England is fundamentally uninteresting to Londoners precisely because they have such a clear and emphatic image of it; they already know (or think that they know, which is more to the point) exactly what 'the North' is like. It seems more likely, therefore, that 'the Orient' remained of such overriding interest to Western Europeans, and elicited such a flood of expert writing about itself, precisely because its essential character was constantly contested in European thought, and not because there was massive homogeneity in our representation of it.

Constructing the Balkans

Our interest is in the Balkans; and indeed we find here another construction which can be compared with Said's 'Orient'. Certainly many aspects of his study of Orientalism ring very true with respect to the process by which this region and its peoples have come to be constructed by and for non-Balkan peoples. There are differences, however, which are important. In particular, we can not escape the obligation to recognise from the very outset the importance of contrasting, or even contradictory, elements which are worked together into that construction.

The generally derogatory associations which are typically carried by the word 'Balkan' in the English language are suggested by the definition which Collins *English Dictionary* gives for its derivative, 'Balkanise': 'to divide (a territory) into small warring states'. So fundamental is the perception of disunity to the region, that the naming of it as a geographical entity only dates from 1889, and the work of the German geographer Zeune. Indeed, his term remained hotly contested until the publication in 1918 of that landmark of regional geography, *La Peninsule Balkanique*, by Jovan Cvijić.[12]

Charles and Barbara Jelavich, introducing a volume specifically dedicated to studying the 'unity in its historical, social, economic, political and cultural development', admit that 'history has nurtured a tradition of emphasis upon diversity and conflict'.[13] Their own discussion of the area then tends to identify it in terms of its multiple marginality. So powerful is this association with fragmentation that John C. Campbell, writing in the same volume, asks (as it turns out, with remarkable prescience): 'Will the Communist empire absorb the Balkans, or will the Balkans absorb and 'Balkanize' communism?'[14]

It might seem that this repeated emphasis on fractionalisation would preclude the emergence of any coherent process of image construction in relation to the Balkans. Perhaps all we have is a mosaic composed from the overlapping edges of other, different regional constructions. It is, however, precisely this characteristic which provides the key to our understanding of how the peoples of the peninsula have come to be perceived, and even to perceive themselves. Three quite separate clusters of ideas can be identified as central to the historical image of the Balkans.

In the first place, one of the most influential factors which seem to have shaped our image of the Balkans is its marginal position with respect to 'the Orient'. If the East is by definition 'mysterious', then the Balkan peninsula has been even more so, as it has been shown to be peripherally, or incompletely 'Oriental' – 'Oriental', but not quite so.

The second idea which provides a focus for constructing the Balkans is the Classical World. Our region and its people are depicted as the heirs to the ancient civilisations upon which Western Culture has come to rest. They are, in fact, quintessentially the very embodiment of wisdom and civility.

Finally, the inhabitants of the area are depicted as, first and foremost, peasant peoples, and their representation centres on notions of 'folk' culture and the virtues which are said to be embodied in a life shaped both by tradition and closeness to Nature.

i) 'In' the Orient, but not 'of' the Orient

The Balkan peninsula was for a long time – between the fourteenth and the nineteenth centuries – largely a part of the Ottoman Empire, and this aspect of its history enables us to look at the image of the Balkans as a sub-theme to Said's study. Dora d'Istria had no obvious doubts about including the entire Balkan peninsula in her *Les Femmes en Orient*, and it is the Turkish presence which dominates the perceptions of many people.

'The Turk' is typically associated in writing about the Balkans with barbarity and the rule of force. This is spelled out in no uncertain terms by W.E. Gladstone, in the Preface which he contributed to *Travels in the Slavonic Provinces of Turkey-in-Europe*, by Georgina Muir Mackenzie and Adeline Irby.[15]

> Other conquerors, such as the Greek or the Roman, have relied, along with force, upon intellectual superiority, and upon the communication of benefits to the conquered. The Ottoman Turk, with his satellites, has relied upon force alone. Whatever intellect he has at any time displayed, and it has not always been small, has been intellect addressed to the organisation and application of force.

Gladstone qualifies the severity of his remarks by the admission that 'there are two distinct phases of existence for the subject races of Turkey: the ordinary, and the exceptional', and recognises that the exceptional use of force is only called forth by those 'rare occasions, when oppression is felt to be absolutely intolerable, and the downtrodden rayahs, appealing to force, seek to obtain their rights'. The direct use of force may be 'exceptional': but clearly the oppression is 'ordinary'.

There is a broad unanimity among Western Europeans of this period, however, about the essential unfitness of the Turks to rule, in spite of (or perhaps because of) the way in which they are represented as necessarily oppressing their Christian subjects, and about the inevitability of their eventual expulsion from Europe. They themselves, therefore, are decadent, and the most important feature of their legacy to their former lands, or those lands over which they retain a control which is portrayed as ever more precarious, is an enforced backwardness.[16]

The parallel themes of Turkish oppression and Turkish decadence run throughout the writing of many of the figures who are the subject of our collection. Edith Durham's reports of her encounters with Albanian and Slav peasants repeatedly chronicle their complaints.

> What has the Turkish government ever done for us? There is not a road in the country. Give us a just government. We are poor and ignorant. The Turks will do nothing except for bribes. . . . All Turkish government had been bad, and this would be also.[17]

Although her significant, but rather forgotten contribution to Balkan scholarship is not the subject of a particular essay here, the dedication of Lucy Garnett's *Greek Folk Songs* (1885) sums up the sense of oppression in a phrase: 'To the Hellenes of enslaved Greece.'[18]

The theme of Turkish decadence is nowhere conveyed with more force or more vividly than by Rebecca West. Her visits to Yugoslavia took place nearly a quarter of a century after the effective ejection of Ottoman government from the area, so that the completeness of her condemnation is the more remarkable. The following cameo recounts Rebecca West's encounter with the *danseuse du ventre* to whom she gives the name Astra.[19]

> It was very disagreeable, her occupation. She did not state explicitly what it included, but we took it for granted. It was not so bad in Greece or Bulgaria or in the North of Yugoslavia, in all of which places she had often worked, but of late she had got jobs only in South Serbia, in night clubs where the clients were for the most part Turks. She clapped her hand to her brow and shook her head and said, 'Vous ne savez pas, madame, à quel point les Turcs sont idiots.' Her complaint when I investigated it, was just what it sounds. She was distressed because her Turkish visitors had no conversation. Her coat frock fell back across her knee and showed snow-white cambric underclothing and flesh scrubbed clean as the cleanest cook's kitchen table, and not more

sensuous. She was all decency and good sense, and she was pronouncing sound judgement.

The judgement was appalling. The Turks in South Serbia are not like the Slav Moslems of Sarajevo, they are truly Turks. They are Turks who settled there after the battle of Kossovo, who have remained what the Ataturk would not permit Turks to be any longer. They are what a people must become if it suspends all intellectual life and concentrates on the idea of conquest. It knows victory, but there is a limit to possible victories; what has been gained cannot be maintained for that requires the use of the intellect, which has been removed. So there is decay, the long humiliation of decay. At one time the forces of Selim and Suleiman covered half a continent with the precise and ferocious ballet of perfect warfare, the sensuality of the sultans and the viziers searched for fresh refinements and made their discoveries the starting points for further search, fountains played in courtyards and walled gardens where there had been until then austere barbarism. At the end an ageing cabaret dancer, the homely and decent vanishing point of voluptuousness, sits on a bed and says with dreadful justice: 'Vous ne savez pas, madame, à quel point les Turcs sont idiots.'

This passage, which shows Rebecca West to be a true mistress of English style, is so complex and subtle in its blend of innuendo, understatement, interplay of homely parable and high political theory, that an essay could be written on what it tells us about her own 'Orientalism'. In spite of her disclaimer about Ataturk the old imagery of the sensuous and cruel Oriental is displayed here in its quintessential form. Said himself cites no more compelling illustration of his own case. Yet all this is heavily underscored by her own scathing imagery of 'the long humiliation of decay'.

Even after the Empire has gone, then, the shadow of Ottoman Orientalism lies over the Balkans: but always in oppositional form. The Turks are guilty of imposing on their former subject peoples the grimness of 'the long Turkish night': but it is clear that burdensome as that legacy has been, there was always something else there, waiting for the dawn in order to bloom again. The Balkans are Oriental: but they are never entirely so. They can be constructed within the imagery of Orientalism : but this can only ever convey a part of the truth. Other truths – other constructions – are constantly contending for a hearing.

ii) *The Balkans as heirs to the Ancient World*

Alongside, and closely related to, the construction of the Balkans in terms of their location on the decaying fringes of the Orient stands another and competing set of images. These are equally complex, evocative and deeply rooted in history. This is the notion that its peoples are the heirs to the Classical World, and their lands the home of great civilisations. Sir Thomas Jackson describes the Dinaric mountains as having 'fenced out the Turk from the Adriatic, and stayed the tide of Moslem conquest in the south': and even though the inhabitants of the peninsula may have been reduced for a time to subjugation under 'the Turk', they are nevertheless, picturesquely, the 'waifs and strays of the Roman Empire'.[20] As a Western European, therefore, one goes to the Balkans, not to marvel at its otherness – its 'savagery' or its backwardness – but to renew one's contact with the roots of those great traditions from which the whole of European civilisation has grown.

There are several strands to this argument; and the first of these is architectural. The role of architecture is a factor in the process of image construction which Said never considers. His own analysis is dominated by language and religion. In the case of the Balkans, however, their claim to embody ancient civilisation are substantially and visibly met in their heritage of ancient buildings. What is more, the task of constructing the region to a Western European readership was shouldered in large measure by historians of art and architecture. Jackson gives us an account of his own long intellectual pedigree in this respect.[21]

> George Wheeler visited Spalato in 1675, and has left us the earliest description of the ruins of Diocletian's palace; Robert Adam's account of that building, published in 1764, is still the best; the antiquities of Pola were explored by Stuart in 1750, and splendidly illustrated in the fourth volume of the great work that goes by his name; Sir Gardner Wilkinson in 1848 published an excellent general account of Dalmatia, Montenegro and part of Herzegovina; Mr Paton's book followed; more recently Professor Freeman has published some brief sketches of the earlier architecture of some of the maritime towns; while the well-known researches of Mr. Arthur Evans in the interior of Bosnia and Herzegovina have introduced us to a part of Europe till then unknown.

Adam, of course, was even more influential than Jackson in the development of British architecture. 'When we look at a façade in Portman Square or a doorway in Portland Place,' wrote Rebecca West, in tribute to that influence, 'We are looking at Roman Dalmatia'.[22] The architecture of Dalmatia dominates also Oona Ball's book, published in 1932. Dalmatia is defined for her by its ancient urban settlements Split, Zadar, Šibenik and (above all) Dubrovnik. She is, indeed, a self-confessed disciple of Jackson.[23]

> 'No one', says Mr Horace Brown, 'who goes to Dalmatia can afford not to have read Sir Thomas Jackson's *Dalmatia and the Quarneiro.*' This is a true saying.

By the time her own book was written, as we have already noticed, tourism was developing rapidly along the Adriatic coast, and she addressed herself principally to the educated upper middle class visitors such as Mr and Mrs Henry Andrews (Rebecca West and her husband). To be a tourist and to travel along the coast in the Austria-Lloyd steamers consisted, above all, of a pilgrimage from one beautiful old building, one artistic treasure, one venerable piazza, to another. In each 'sight' the tourists reaffirmed the essential civility of the places they visited, and through the discovery of their capacity to appreciate its beauty, affirmed their own right to be considered the inheritors of its civilisation.

The theme of the Balkans as the repository of civilisation has other strands as well as the architectural. For many visitors the secrets of the region are unlocked by the image of 'Illyria' (the old Roman name for the lands along the Eastern shore of the Adriatic). Arthur Evans entitles a collection of his letters, published in 1877, *Illyrian Letters*;[24] and as his intended readership was a general audience of educated people and not his fellow archaeologists, we may assume that this was not an 'in joke' for his professional circle.

Oona Ball, also, appeals to the notion of 'Illyria' in her search for an image which will convey the independent-mindedness which she sees as characteristic of the inhabitants. She finds the symbol she is looking for in Bishop Gregory of Nona, the subject of the monumental statue by Meštrović, formerly housed within the walls of Diocletian's palace in Split. The Bishop, she tells us, was the only ecclesiastic at the Synod of Split, in 1099, to defend actively the continuing use of the indigenous 'Illyrian liturgy' in the face of the advocates of Latin uniformity.[25]

Lucy Garnett and her collaborator J.S. Stuart-Glennie, in similar vein, take great pains to develop the theme of the profound continuities in Hellenic culture.[26] With specific reference to the Greek language, their Preface to her translation of *Greek Folk Songs*, of 1885 insists that:

> The Originals are in a patois of which some of the characteristics will presently be noted. But it is important first, to point out that, as spoken

by an educated contemporary Greek, the Language, of which this patois is a rustic dialect, differs less, in its grammatical forms, from that of the Homeric Rhapsodists of nearly three millenniums ago, than the Language of an educated contemporary Englishman differs from that of Chaucer, only half a millennium ago ... the reader will be most readily enabled to understand, and hence realise the fact that, while Italian, for instance, differs from Latin, as a new Language, or a new genus, Modern differs from Classical Greek as but a new Dialect, or new species.

The weight which they attach to this specifically linguistic point becomes clear in the context of the very general claim which provides a guiding thread throughout most of Lucy Garnett's Hellenic studies. The main butt of her attack is Sir Edward Tylor's 'animistic', or 'spiritualistic' theory of the origins of religion. The central idea of this theory – which was very influential throughout the nineteenth and early twentieth centuries, although modern anthropology is reluctant to engage in such speculative endeavours – stated that the seed out of which religion grows is belief in the existence of a spirit or soul. Tylor's views are summed up concisely by E.E. Evans-Pritchard, in his survey of 'theories of primitive religion'.[27]

> Primitive man's reflections on such experiences as death, diseases, trances, visions, and above all dreams, led him to the conclusion that they are to be accounted for by the presence or absence of some immaterial entity, the soul. Primitive man then transferred this idea of soul to other creatures in some ways like himself, and even to inanimate objects which aroused interest. The soul, being detachable from whatever it lodged in, could be thought of as independent of its material home, whence arose the idea of spiritual beings, whose supposed existence constituted Tylor's minimum definition of religion; and these finally developed into gods, being vastly superior to man and in control of his destiny.

Lucy Garnett and her collaborator set out to discredit systematically this view through an intimate study of Greek folk sayings, songs, stories and poetry. The theory which they came to on the basis of their researches is that the view of nature contained in this folk material – and which they believed to be very ancient in its origins – was far closer to a scientific than a religious conception?.[28]

> ... the primitive Folk-conception of Nature is a notion of it made up of mutually influencing powers; a notion, therefore, of the predictableness

of the events, and controllableness of the forces of Nature by knowledge of these Powers; and hence a notion of the very antithesis of that
derived from a belief in Spiritual Beings whose action on Nature is wil-
ful and arbitrary, or, in a word, Supernatural.

They quote with approval, in this respect, Aristotle: 'Nature is not
episodic in its phenomena, like a bad tragedy.' Supernaturalism,
therefore, is alien to traditional Greek culture.[29]

And the Semitic conception of a Creator-God outside and independent
of Nature, becoming 500 years later the intellectual core of Aryan Chris-
tianism, such an antagonism was set up between the fundamental con-
ceptions of Religion and of Science as to this day endures.

Edward Said, of course, would have been intrigued to find them
defining their problem in terms so obviously related to his own
analysis of Orientalism.

The relevance of the insistence on the continuity of the Greek
language becomes clear in this context. It serves to buttress the
view that Greek folk culture is not some 'primitive' residue, but the
repository of a system of sophisticated beliefs about the natural
world which place the bearers of this culture in direct line with the
wisdom of the ancients, whose language is still – to all intents and
purposes – spoken by the Greek people. From this line they have
only been deflected temporarily and superficially by the imposition
of an essentially alien (Semitic-Oriental) theology.

A similar theme is developed, although with less persistence,
erudition and display of scholarship, by Sir Thomas Jackson, who
contends that the language and culture in general of the Dalmatians is Latin-based, but specifically distinguishes this from Italian,
insisting that they have resisted strongly the encroachments of
Venice throughout the ages.

Among the writers considered in this collection, the tendency to
see in Balkan societies the still living tradition of the Classical
World is commonplace. Rose Wilder Lane and Edith Durham,
reflecting on the origins of the Albanians, repeat the story of their
antiquity as a people – and in particular the belief in the link
between Albania and the family of Alexander the Great. (A similar
view is presented by Dora d'Istria.)[30] It is immaterial to their argument as to whether 'Lek' was indeed Alexander: the important factor is that the sense of continuity moves powerfully in those who
make this claim to them.

Louisa Rayner – trained as a classicist – sees the entirety of her enforced residence among 'women in a village' in relation to the ancient world. The kitchen of her hostess, Savka, becomes 'The Hall of Penelope'. The artifacts of daily life, and even the deportment and language of the Serbian villager, are made sense of by placing them in relation to classical references.[31]

> The iron lid used for baking interested me. Cato had used a *testu*, a crock of some kind, on the hearth for this purpose, and I cannot help thinking that something of this sort was what Aristophanes meant by the word *pnigeus*; in the Clouds, 'The heavens are a *pnigeus* and we are the embers.' Everyone supposes that, whatever the 'stifler' was, it was a stifler in respect of the embers. But the heavens being a 'stifler' in respect of men on earth is hardly an idea of Aristophanic elegance. Savka's iron lid was a 'stifler' in respect of the dough, but it hung unchanging over the embers which danced and crackled and went out beneath it.

In another passage:[32]

> Then with a sudden passionate movement Ivka crushed the jacket together between her hands and pressed it to her nose. 'Ah, my Mila!' she cried. 'It has got her smell still!' Just as you cannot reproduce in pastels the luminous and simple splendour of a stained glass window, so my English phrases will not convey to the reader the terse, bold beauty of Ivka's natural rhetoric. Only an actress reciting Sophocles with loving sincerity has given me something of the same impression.

The daily life of the villagers illuminates and clarifies passages from classical authors: but equally, these experiences are somehow validated and given significance by being recognised as 'classical'.

iii) The Balkans as the home of 'folk cultures'

Alongside the 'Orientalist' construction of the Balkans, and the competing construction of the area and its peoples in terms of their inheritance of the great civilisations of antiquity, there stands a third. This is intricately related to the other two (just as they are enmeshed with each other) but nevertheless is sufficiently distinct in its content to be treated as a separate configuration. A clue to its character is contained in the title given by the correspondent of the *Westminster Gazette*, Henry de Windt, to the account of his travels in the period just prior to the First World War *Through Savage Europe*. The central term here is 'savage'. The notion of 'savagery' is quite different from the 'backwardness' or decadence associated with the Ottoman legacy. Perhaps 'primitive' would be a more apt expression.

In the dead of night on 9 June 1903, a group of Serbian officers forced their way into the Royal Palace in Belgrade. They were intent upon regicide. After several hours of search, King Alexander Obrenović and his Queen Draga were finally located, hidden in a tiny dressing room. Riddled with bullets, their bodies were then mutilated with sabres, and thrown into the courtyard from a balcony. Shortly before 4.00 on the morning of 10 June, the regicides proclaimed the end of the dynasty, and the accession of Peter Karadjordjević.

It was not the fact of the assassination itself that shocked the outside world, as the preceding months had seen many rumours of plots against the Obrenović dynasty. The aspect of events which was most effective in shaping public awareness was the brutality with which the murders were accomplished. Edith Durham, known for the unsentimental directness of both her speech and writing, later tried to convey something of this response.[33]

> According to current report the assassins, drunk with wine and blood, fell on the bodies and defiled them most filthily, even cutting off portions of Draga's skin, which they dried and preserved as trophies. An officer later showed a friend of mine a bit which he kept in his pocket book.
>
> Alexander was a degenerate. His removal may have been desirable. But not even in Dahomey could it have been accomplished with more repulsive savagery.

Later in the same book the unfortunate inhabitants of West Africa are the subjects of a similar comparison, as she suggests that the murders were no isolated incidents which could be attributable to the idiosyncratic brutality of the officers concerned. The deaths of Alexander and Draga (even to the bizarre details of their execution) could almost be considered typically Balkan.[34]

> West Europe was, in 1903, quite ignorant of the state of primitive savagery from which the South Slavs were but beginning to rise. Distinguished scientists travelled far afield and recorded the head hunters of New Guinea. But the ballads of Grand Vojvoda Mirko – King Nikola of Montenegro's father gloating over slaughter, telling of the piles of severed heads, of the triumph with which they were carried home on stakes and set around the village, and the best reserved as an offering

to Nikola himself for the adornment of Cetinje; and the stripping and mutilating of the dead foe – give us a vivid picture of life resembiing rather that of Dahomey, than Europe in 1860. In the breast of every human being there is a wolf. It may sleep for several generations. But it wakes at last and howls for blood. In the breast of the South Slav, both Serb and Montenegrin, it has not yet even thought of slumbering.

This preoccupation with primitiveness appears frequently in Edith Durham's writing (not only in relation to the South Slavs: the first chapter of her *High Albania* describes the region as 'The Land of the Living Past'). Her frequent contributions to the ethnographic journal *Man* during the twenties included a piece on head-hunting and nose-taking in the Balkans (the most recent case she records is 1912). She also wrote several articles on bird symbolism in the region (especially falcons and eagles) in a manner which strongly suggests links with totemism, although she herself does not make that link explicit.[35]

Concerns of this kind, on the part of writers about the Balkans, show that their understanding of 'primitiveness' is not confined by any means to the bloodthirstier side of human behaviour. If anything, it seems that (as in Edith Durham's use of the 'wolf' metaphor in the passage we have just quoted) this kind of savagery is seen as only one instance of a more generally 'elemental' quality of human life in the Balkans. She suggests that the letting of blood is entirely natural, much as we find it abhorrent. It is just that in the case of more civilised peoples, this part of our nature sleeps. Her frequent discussions of folk medicine have precisely the same kind of ambivalence. Her Anglo-Saxon scepticism about the efficacy of some of these is balanced by, not only an acceptance of the view that perhaps some of them do work, but also by a deeper sense that a real wisdom about Nature infuses this supposedly primitive set of practices.

The elemental quality of the life of the folk of the Balkan peninsula, and their greater proximity to Nature, is celebrated in one way or another throughout the work of the writers considered in this book.

This kind of representation is most highly developed in Rebecca West's *Black Lamb and Grey Falcon*. It is a characteristic of her book that, no matter how incidental are her characters or their settings to the development of the story, each seems to carry a half-explicit symbolic freight rendering them larger than life.

Possibly the high point of the whole book, measured in terms of its literary and dramatic power, is the account of her visit to the

Macedonian area of Ovče Polje. Here she is a witness to several folk rituals which were traditionally performed on St George's Eve. Their great antiquity is suggested by the fact that, although nominally a Christian saint, 'St George' is celebrated in their several ways by Muslims, Orthodox Christians and Gypsies.

Two of these events move her very profoundly. The first involves Muslim women who are experiencing difficulty in conceiving, and who in order to promote their fertility embrace a large black stone. The second rite (from which a part of her title is drawn) is the sacrificial slaughter of a black lamb by a group of Gypsies, in thanksgiving for the birth of a child. The length of these passages makes it difficult to cite them here, although that would be ideal, for only in the detailed texture of her prose does the intensity of Rebecca West's engagement with her material become fully visible. The following paragraphs will have to serve, in this context, to convey her central concerns.[36]

> All I had seen the night before was not discreditable to humanity. I had not found anything being done which was likely to give children to women who were barren for physiological reasons; but I had seen ritual actions that were likely to evoke the power of love, which is not irrelevant to these matters. When the Moslem women in the Tekiya put out their arms to embrace the black stone and dropped their heads to kiss it, they made a gesture of the same nature, though not so absolute, as that which men and women make when they bend down to kiss the cloth which lies instead of Christ on the holy table at Easter. Such a gesture is an imitation by the body of the gesture made by the soul in loving. It says, 'I will pour myself in devotion to you, I will empty myself without hoping for return, and I can do this serenely, for I know that as I empty myself I shall be filled again.' Human beings cannot remind themselves too often that they are capable of performing this miracle, the existence of which cannot be proved by logic.
>
> But the rite of the Sheep's Field was purely shameful. It was a huge and dirty lie. There is a possibility that barrenness due to the mind could be aided by a rite that evoked love and broke down peevish desires to be separate and alone, or that animated a fatigued nature by refreshment from its hidden sources. But this could do nothing that it promised. Women do not get children by adding to the normal act of copulation the slaughter of a lamb, the breaking of a jar, the decapitation of a cock, the stretching of wool through blood and grease. If there was a woman whose womb could be unsealed by witnessing a petty and pointless act of violence, by seeing a jet of blood fall from a lamb's throat on a rock wet with stale and stinking blood, her fertility would be the reverse of motherhood, she would have children for the purpose of hating them.

At first sight it may seem that the author's response to these two experiences is quite different: the one she warms to, in spite of its obvious irrationality, while she abhors the other. At a deeper level, however, there is a common theme which is played with variations in each case. In fact, she is highly ambivalent towards both of the ceremonies which she records. Her own scepticism regarding the efficacy of the black stone is never concealed: she reports that she and her husband had both kissed it – but it may as well have been the Blarney Stone for all the real meaning it contained for them. In the passage quoted above, it is clear that in comparison with the Easter rites of an English church, what she has witnessed is inferior even in its own terms, as a celebration of love.

The contrast with her treatment of the sacrificial rock is remarkable. It seems that she cannot express strongly enough her opprobrium for it and everything associated with it: and yet, strangely, her identification with the occasion shines through powerfully.[37]

> It would have been pleasant to turn round and run back to the car and drive away as quickly as possible, but the place had enormous authority. It was the body of our death, it was the seed of the sin that is in us, it was the forge where the sword was wrought that shall slay us.
> I knew this rock well. I had lived under the shadow of it all my life.

Far from being the epitome of all that is alien, it is in this place that she recognises more vividly than any other the grosser side of her own nature. Here is Edith Durham's 'wolf' which sleeps in all of us. Love/creation and hate/destruction are equally acknowledged as part of the human condition.

The world of folk belief which is discovered and displayed in the works of these travellers is indeed, in Edith Durham's phrase, 'the land of the living past'; it is a world which has not yet undergone the process which Max Weber called 'disenchantment'. Here, magic and ceremony live on, not as relics of superstition or the invincible evidence of backwardness, but as visible signs of the continuing victory of the imagination, which, however grotesquely, continues to wrestle with the mysteries of our place in Nature and the Cosmos. The rock of sacrifice (and the outlandish practices of Edith Durham's folk healers) are a world removed from the 'decadence' attributed to the Turks, and as such they are presented to us as aspects of a universal humanity rather than as traits of an Orient enduring the 'long humiliation of decay'.

Women Travellers and Image-Construction in the Balkans

In an essay as brief as this we cannot hope to match the coverage of the process of image construction given to us by Edward Said in his study of 'Orientalism'. In taking on the task of reviewing how 'the Balkans' have come to be constructed, then, our aim has been a much less ambitious one: we will be content if we have managed to get discussion of the problem under way.

An important part of our undertaking has been the desire to demonstrate that the history of this imagery has been a story of ambiguity and even contradiction, in which a braid of partly complementary and partly incompatible and contradictory ideas about the region and its peoples has been plaited together. The resulting ambivalence and sense of mystery is not a sign of the lack of any form or coherence in the image: it is one of its essential characteristics. The fact that this imagery has achieved such general currency, and has been so influential in shaping the way in which the Balkans are seen today, is a tribute to the commitment to, and identification with, the region and its peoples of the women whose lives and writing are the subject of this collection of essays.

Notes

1. Norman Daniel, *Islam, Europe and Empire*, Edinburgh: The University Press, 1966, p. xiii.
2. Peter L. Berger and Thomas Luckmann, *The Social Construction of Reality*, London: Allen Lane, The Penguin Press, 1967.
3. One of the few areas in which this issue has been addressed is that of the study of images of destination among tourists.
4. Edward W. Said, *Orientalism*, London: Peregrine Books, 1985.
5. *Ibid.*, pp. 5–6.
6. The noteworthy exception to this is probably Edward Lane, whose contribution to linguistic knowledge passes unrecognised in Said's discussion, and whose ethnographic work seems, to me, to be seriously underrated by the latter when one bears in mind the fact that it was undertaken almost a century before the practice of fieldwork became established in anthropology.
7. For some critical discussions of Said's book, see: Norman Daniel, 'Edward Said and the Orientalists', *Mélanges de l'institut dominican orientales du Caire*, Vol. 15, 1982, pp. 211–22; Maxime Rodinson, *La fascination de l'Islam*, Paris: Librarie François Maspero, 'Introduction'; review by Ernest Wilson, *Journal of Palestine Studies*, Vol.10, No. 2, 1981, pp. 59 69.
8. Said, *op. cit.*, p. 162.
9. D. Urquhart, *The Spirit of the East. Illustrated in a Journal of his Travels Through Roumeli during an Eventful Period*, London: Henry Colburn, 1838, pp.

xv and xxix. Surprise might be registered similarly at the absence from Said's book of any mention of the work of Ami Boué. See, *La Turquie d'Europe*, Paris: 1840, and, *Receuil d'itineraires dans la Turquie*, Vienna: 1854.

10. See Wilson, *op. cit.*

11. W.B. Gallie, *History and the Philosophical Understanding*, London: Chatto and Windus, 1964, Chap. 8.

12. The early use of the term 'Balkan' as a geographical concept is discussed in: F.W Carter, 'Introduction to the Balkan Scene', F.W. Carter (ed.), *An Historical Geography of the Balkans*, London: Academic Press, 1977.

13. Charles and Barbara Jelavich (eds), *The Balkans in Transition: Essays on the development of Balkan life and politics since the eighteenth century*, Berkeley and Los Angeles: University of California Press, 1963.

14. *Op. cit.*; John C. Campbell, 'The Balkans: heritage and continuity'. The quotation is from p. 396.

15. G. Muir Mackenzie and A.P. Irby, *Travels in the Slavonic Provinces of Turkey-in-Europe*, London: Daidy, Isbister and Co., 1877, p. x.

16. Norman Daniel, in his *Islam, Europe and Empire*, (*op. cit.*) documents this thesis very fully.

17. Edith Durham, *High Albania*, London: Virago Press, 1985, pp. 155 and 263. (First published, Edward Arnold, 1909.)

18. Lucy M.J. Garnett, *Greek Folk Songs*, London: David Nun, 1885.

19. Rebecca West, *Black Lamb and Grey Falcon*, London: Macmillan, 1967, Vol. I, pp. 314–5.

20. Sir Thomas Jackson, *Dalmatia, the Quarniero and Istria*, Oxford: The Clarendon Press, (III vols.) 1887, Vol.I, p. viii.

21. *Ibid.*, pp. vii–viii.

22. *Op. cit.*, Vol. I, p. 142.

23. Oona H. Ball, *Dalmatia*, London: Faber and Faber, 1932, p. 188.

24. Arthur.J. Evans, *Illyrian Letters*, London: Longmans, Green and Co., 1878.

25. *Op. cit.*, pp. 32–3. The imagery of 'Illyria' has been remarkably persistent. See also, Dymphna Cusack, *Illyria Reborn*, London: Heinemann, 1964.

26. *Op. cit.*, pp. xxiii–xxiv.

27. E.E. Evans-Pritchard, *Theories of Primitive Religion*, Oxford: The Clarendon Press, 1965, p. 25.

28. Lucy M.J. Garnett, *Greek Folk Poesy*, London: David Nun, 1896, (II vols.), Vol. II, pp. 513–4.

29. *Ibid.*, p. 518.

30. Rose Wilder Lane, *Peaks of Shala*, New York: Harper, 1923; Edith Durham, *op. cit.*

31. Louisa Rayner, *Women in a Village*, London: William Heinemann Ltd., 1957, Chap. Six, esp. p. 58.

32. *Ibid.*, p. 71.

33. Edith Durham, *Twenty Years of Balkan Tangle*, London: George Allen and Unwin, 1920, p. 74.

34. *Ibid.*, pp. 79–80.

35. See, M. Edith Durham, 'A bird tradition in the west of the Balkan peninsula', *Man*, Nos. 32–33, April 1923, pp. 55–61; 'Some Balkan embroidery patterns', *Man*, Nos. 39–40, May 1923, pp. 69–72; 'The seclusion of maidens front the light of the sun, and a further note on the Bird tradition in the Balkans', *Man*, No. 61, July 1923, pp. 102–3.

36. *Op. cit.*, Vol. II, pp. 203–4.

37. *Ibid.*, pp. 201 and 205.

CHAPTER 15

Altho' in some particulars we may perhaps be incompetent observers,
we have seen enough to convince us that very little is known in England
concerning these districts.

Adeline Irby, in a letter to the British Consul; in Crete, 9 April 1863

Women Travellers in the Balkans: A Bibliographical Guide

Jennifer Finder

This bibliographical guide aims to reflect the wide range and diverse nature of the writings of English-speaking women on the Balkans. In that respect it ranges rather more widely than the works of 'women travellers', more narrowly defined, and acknowledging the large areas of overlap between the interests of readers whose approach to this field may well be from women's studies, or a number of academic disciplines.

Many of the works referred to in the collection are repeated here, together with other material from books and periodicals, in an attempt to coordinate the writings in this field. Personal diaries and archive material have not been researched except where also published, but it is hoped that the material selected gives a reasonably representative review of the available literature in the English language.

Travellers' Experiences

Published accounts of women travellers in the Balkans are many and varied, as shown by the papers in the collection.

Nora Alexander in her book *Wanderings in Yugoslavia*, London: Skeffington, 1936, recorded her travels, 'mostly on foot and mostly among the byways' in Yugoslavia, describing along the way the country, its festivals and people.

Dorothy Anderson, herself a writer and historian of the Balkans, wrote *Miss Irby and her Friends*, London: Hutchinson, 1966, about Adeline Pauline Irby, Georgina Muir Mackenzie and Priscilla Johnston, who travelled extensively in Europe, first as tourists then as students and observers.

Miss Irby first travelled in 1859 with Georgina Muir Mackenzie, and made more journeys across the Balkan lands, later joined by Priscilla Johnston, with whom she worked for three years among Bosnian refugees in Austria. Miss Irby became a champion of the South Slav cause, also working in education and housing.

Among the articles she wrote are:
'Bosnia in 1875', *Victorian Magazine*, November 1875.
'Work Among the Bosnian Fugitives', *Good Words*, September 1875, pp. 638–42.
'Bosnia and its Land Tenure', *Contemporary Review*, July 1889, pp. 28–40.
'Ischia in June', *Nineteenth Century and After*, July 1904, pp. 119–25.

Among Georgina Muir Mackenzie's writings with Miss Irby are:
Travels in the Slavonic Provinces of Turkey-in-Europe, London: Daldy, Isbister, 1867, or 2nd edn. with an introduction by W. Gladstone, 2 vols., London: Daldy, Isbister, 1877.
Across the Carpathians, London: Macmillan, 1862.
'Christmas in Montenegro', *Vacation Tourists and Notes of Travel in 1861*, ed.
F. Galton, London: Macmillan, 1862.
Notes on the South Slavonic Countries in Austria and Turkey-in-Europe, Containing Historical and Political Information, ed. H. Sandwich, Edinburgh: Blackwood, 1865.

Articles which appeared in *Good Words* include
'Notes on the Balkan: The Church in Bulgaria', March 1865, pp. 197–205.
'Pilgrimage to Old Serbia: Ancient Churches and Modern Schools', June 1865, pp. 429–35.
'The Condition of the Christians Under the Turks', November 1866, pp. 762–6.

Oona H. Ball wrote *Dalmatia*, London: Faber, 1932, covering both the geography and history of the area, with photographs, but as a tourist informing the educated visitor.

Anne Bridge wrote two novels, one set in Dubrovnik: *Illyrian Spring*, Boston: Little Brown, 1935; and one in the northern Albanian mountains, *Singing Waters*, New York: Macmillan, 1946. In the latter, her 'Miss Glanfield' is a thinly-disguised Edith Durham. She later wrote *Facts and Fictions: some literary recollections*, New York: McGraw-Hilll, 1968.

Fanny S. Copeland used stories, poems and illustrations to describe her wanderings in the Alpine region of Slovenia in her book, *Beautiful Mountains: in the Yugoslav Alps*, Split: Jugoslav Bureau, 1931.

A more recent account based on five trips to Yugoslavia between 1976 and 1983, written from her personal diary, is L. Grace Dibble's *Return Tickets to Yugoslavia*, Ilfracombe: Stockwell, 1984.

Dymphna Cusack describes a journey in 1964 through Albania, at the invitation of the government, during the time of the country's deepest diplomatic isolation, in *Illyria Reborn*, London: Heinemann, 1966, and Agim Neza and Miranda Hanka's *Travellers' Guide to Albania*, Aylesbury, Bucks: ACO UK, 1993, claims to be a 'true and impartial view of [the country]', looking at the cultures and traditions of the people, with photos.

Mary Edith Durham's contribution to literature on the Balkans is considerable, and covers the fields of history, anthropology, ethnology, religion, politics, folklore and traditions. She travelled regularly for over 20 years, from her first journey in 1900, taken for health reasons and to sketch in a new country – 'Thus fate led me to the Balkans'. The books she wrote about her travels and about the relief work she was later involved in are:

Through the Lands of the Serb, London: E. Arnold, 1904.

The Burden of the Balkans, London: E. Arnold, 1905.

High Albania, London: E. Arnold, 1909.

The Struggle for Scutari, London: E. Arnold, 1914.

Twenty Years of Balkan Tangle, London: Allen and Unwin, 1920, which was also translated into German and Italian.

The Sarajevo Crime, London: Edward Arnold, 1925.

Some Tribal Origins, Laws and Customs of the Balkans, London: Allen and Unwin, 1928.

Several of the contributions to *Some Tribal Origins* had originally appeared in the periodical *Man*, in 1923, as follows:

February, pp. 19–21, 'Head-hunting in the Balkans'.
March, pp. 39–42, 'Dardania and some Balkan place-names'.
April, pp. 55–61, 'A bird tradition in the West of the Balkan Peninsula'.
May, pp. 69–72, 'Some Balkan embroidery patterns'.
June, pp. 83–5, 'Some Balkan taboos'.
July, pp. 102–3, 'The seclusion of maidens from the light of the sun'.
September, pp. 131–5, 'Some Balkan remedies for disease'.
December, pp. 189–91, 'Of magic, witches and vampires in The Balkans'.

Grace M. Ellison wrote her guide, *Yugoslavia*, London: Lane, 1933.
Cora J. Gordon travelled with her husband Jan Gordon, and together they wrote and illustrated very different accounts:
The Luck of Thirteen: Wanderings and Flight through Montenegro and Serbia, London: Smith Elder, 1916, in which Cora's experiences of medical and relief work are recorded.

Two more light-hearted post-war accounts, illustrated by the authors themselves, are given in: *Two Vagabonds in the Balkans*, London: Lane, 1925, and *Two Vagabonds in Albania*, New York: Dodd Mead and Co., 1927.

Winifred Gordon wrote *A Woman in the Balkans*, London: Hutchinson, 1916. She wrote, mainly for the upper classes, of her experiences, enjoying the curiosity she attracted as an outsider on her travels.

A contemporary of Mrs Gordon was Agnes E. Conway, whose account of her journey with a companion, Evelyn Radford, on the eve of the First World War, covers almost the entire Balkan region, *A ride through the Balkans: on classic ground with a camera*, London: Robert Scott, 1917. The journey began as an expedition to record the antiquities of Athens and Constantinople, but soon turned into 'an orgy of wandering and brisk adventure'. (The title the authors originally considered was 'Two Archaeologists on Strike').

Maude M. Holbach was fascinated by Yugoslavia and its people, and gave her impressions of the land and the people, their history and conditions, in two books: *Dalmatia: the Land where East meets West*, London: John Lane, 1908, and *Bosnia and Herzegovina: Some Wayside Wanderings*, London: John Lane, 1910. Both are well illustrated, the second also with photographs and maps.

The view of a more casual traveller, with a more romantic view of the area, is given in Frances Kinsley Hutchinson, *Motoring in the Balkans: along the Highways of Dalmatia, Montenegro, the Hercegovina and Bosnia*, London: Hodder and Stoughton, 1910.

Anne Kindersley lived for three years in Belgrade when her husband was on the staff of the British Embassy there. She travelled all over Yugoslavia, which she has revisited often. In her account of her journeys, *The Mountains of Serbia: Travels through Inland Yugoslavia*, she gives a sympathetic view, with details on history and the landscape (Newton Abbot: Readers' Union', 1977.

Milla Z. Logan visited her mother's native village in 1948 and wrote an affectionate and humorous account in *Cousins and Commissars: an Intimate Visit to Tito's Yugoslavia*, New York: Scribner's Sons, 1949.

Another sympathetic work, describing the beauty of the country, was by an American writer, Dorothea Orr, *Portrait of a People: Croatia Today*, New York: Funk and Wagnalls, 1936.

Viscountess Strangford (Emily Anne Beaufort) travelled briefly in southern Albania on horseback and wrote about her journey in *The Eastern Shores of the Adriatic in 1863 with a Visit to Montenegro*, London: Bentley, 1864.

Demetra Vaka travelled with her brother to Albania, Montenegro, Serbia, Romania and Bulgaria, and wrote of her experiences in *In the Shadow of Islam*, New York: Houghton Mifflin, 1911, and *The Heart of the Balkans*, New York: Houghton Mifflin, 1917.

Three other accounts are given in:

Mary Adelaide Walker, *Through Macedonia to the Albanian Lands*, London: Chapman, 1864

Barbara M. Ward, *Hitler's Route to Bagdad*, London: Fabian Society, 1939.

Lily F. Waring, *Serbia*, London: Williams and Norgate, 1917.

Rebecca West's book *Black Lamb and Grey Falcon: the Record of a Journey through Yugoslavia in 1937*, 2 vols, London: Macmillan, 1942, is still one of the best general introductions to the country and its people, in which she explores the history, culture and customs which she encountered on her journey. The original two-volume edition is illustrated with a number of photographs, which did not appear in the single-volume edition of 1981.

Linda White, Peter and Andrea Dawson have produced an updated and expanded edition of an earlier work by the Dawsons,

Albania: a guide and illustrated journal, Chalfont St Peter: Bradt
Publication, 2nd edn, 1995.
   Mrs E.R. [Mary Janet] Whitwell's book *Through Bosnia and
Herzegovina*, London: Dresser, 1909, is more of a general travel-
ogue, though with some interesting observations.
   Rose Wilder Lane visited the north of Albania in 1921 with two
women friends, and describes the customs and folklore in *Peaks of
Shala*, London: Chapman and Dodd, 1923. Other works include
Discovery of Freedom, New York: John Day, 1943, and *Diverging
Roads*, New York: Century, 1919. She has also written a number of
short stories relating to the Balkans:
   'Padre Luigi of Kir', *Harper's Magazine*, Vol. 147, June 1923.
   'Edelweiss on Chafa Shalit', *Harper's Magazine*, Vol. 147,
      November 1923.
   'The Blue Bead', *Harper's Magazine*, Vol. 151, June 1925.
   'Nice Old Lady', *Saturday Evening Post*, 6th July 1935.
   'Song without Words', *Ladies' Home Journal*, Vol. 54, August
      1937.

   She and Helen Dore Boylston wrote *Travels with Zenobia: Paris to
Albania by Model T Ford. A Journal by Rose Wilder Lane and Helen
Dore Boylston*, ed. by William Holtz, Columbia/London: University
of Missouri Press, 1983, describing the journey, the landscape, and
the changes taking place.
   Antonia Young has written an article about Rose Wilder Lane, in
Albanian Life, Vol. 40, No. 3, 1987, pp. 10-7, and has also edited
*Albania and the surrounding world: papers from the British-
Albanian colloquium, South East European Studies Association,
held at Pembroke College, Cambridge, 29th-31st March 1994*, Brad-
ford: Research Unit in South East European Studies, University of
Bradford, 1995 (Studies on South Eastern Europe, Occasional Paper
No. 2). This volume contains two papers concerned with British
travellers in Albania, one by Valentina Duka 'Albania as viewed by
British travellers of the 19th century' (pp.6-13), and Harry
Hodgkinson's 'Edith Durham and the formation of the Albanian
state' (pp. 14–33).
   Other general works on women travellers which are of interest
are:
   Dea Birkett, *Spinsters Abroad: Victorian Lady Explorers*, Oxford:
      Blackwell, 1989.
   Dea Birkett and Sara Wheeler, eds, *Amazonian: the Penguin
      Book of Women's Travel Writing*, London: Penguin, 1998,

which contains a chapter on Bosnia by Mary Russell, 'Mirror Images', pp. 122–53.

Dorothy Middleton, 'Women in travel and exploration', in: H. Delpar (ed.), *The Discoverers: an Encyclopaedia of Explorers and Exploration*, New York, London: McGraw-Hill, 1980.

Dorothy Middleton, *Victorian Lady Travellers*, London: Routledge, 1965.

Jane Robinson, *Unsuitable for Ladies: an Anthology of Women Travellers*, Oxford: Oxford University Press, 1994, which includes a section on Eastern Europe, the Balkans, Greece and Turkey.

Jane Robinson, *Wayward Women: a Guide to Women travellers*, Oxford: Oxford University Press, 1990, is an invaluable reference source. She has compiled an enormous mine of information in this annotated bibliography, the scope of which is far wider than the Balkans.

Experiences of War: World War I and Before

Many women have been involved in the Balkans in times of trouble, caught up in the action of war themselves, or been directly involved in relief work, and there have been many accounts of their experiences.

An account of the principal women's units formed to work in Serbia in 1914 is given in Monica Krippner's book, *The Quality of Mercy: Women at War, Serbia 1915-18*, Newton Abbot: David and Charles, 1980. This book traces the work of the Scottish Women's Hospitals, the Serbian Relief fund, and the Anglo-Serbian Hospital.

Olive M. Aldridge went to Serbia as a member of the 3rd Serbian Relief Unit to work at one of the village dispensaries, and was then on the road with the Serbian soldiers as they retreated; and wrote *The Retreat from Serbia through Montenegro and Albania*, London: Minerva, 1916, and Alice and Claude Askew wrote *The Stricken Land: Serbia as we saw it*, London: Eveleigh Nash, 1916.

Lady Frances May Dickinson Berry and Sir James Berry wrote two books on the area, *The Story of a Red Cross Unit in Serbia*, London: Churchill, 1916, and *Austria-Hungary and her Slav Subjects*, London: Allen and Unwin, 1918.

Elsie C. Corbett arrived in Serbia in 1915 with Kathleen Dillan to join a British Red Cross Unit. Elsie Corbett wrote *Red Cross in*

Serbia, Banbury: Cheney, 1964, comprising her own memories of events and excerpts from Kathleen's diary.

Jessie Mabel Dearmer died in Kragujevac, but her work was recorded in her *Letters from a Field Hospital*, London: Macmillan, 1915. Her husband had been appointed as chaplain to the British units in Serbia and, rather than be left at home alone, she worked as a hospital orderly until she contracted typhoid and pneumonia from which she died in 1915.

Ruth S. Farnam wrote of her experiences in *A nation at bay: what an American woman saw and did in suffering Serbia*, Indianapolis: Bobbs-Merrill, 1918.

L.E. Fraser's experiences were published as 'Diary of a dresser in the Serbian unit of the Scottish Women's Hospitals', *Blackwood's Magazine*, June, 1915.

Lady Hutton (Dr Isabel Emslie) served as a doctor in Serbia, and was one of only a few women to be invested with Serbia's highest Order, the Order of the White Eagle, for her work. She wrote two books on her experiences: *With a Women's Unit in Serbia, Salonika and Sebastopol*, London: Williams and Norgate, 1928, and *Memories of a Doctor in War and Peace*, London: Heinemann, 1960.

Dr Elsie Inglis also had the Order of the White Eagle conferred upon her for her extensive work, particularly in founding the Scottish Women's Hospitals for Foreign Service. Books written about her life and work are:

Lady Frances Balfour, *Dr Elsie Inglis*, London: Hodder, 1919.

Margot Lawrence, *Shadow of Swords: a Biography of Elsie Inglis*, London: Joseph, 1971.

Eva S. McLaren, *A History of the Scottish Women's Hospitals*, London: Hodder, 1919, and

Elsie Inglis: the Woman with the Torch, London: S.P.C.K., 1920.

Caroline Matthews wrote her *Experiences of a Woman Doctor in Serbia*, London: Mills and Boon, 1916.

Florence Maw's work with Mrs Stobart's unit is recounted in a book by Una P. Moffet and Lena A. Yovitchitch, *Florence Maw: the Chronicle of her Lifework in Serbia*, Edinburgh: Gray, 1957 (privately printed for Nellie Hooker of Lee Green, London). Marion I. Newbigin wrote *Geographical Aspects of Balkan Problems in Their Relation to the Great European War*, New York: Putnam, 1915.

Lady Louisa Leila Paget served in Skopje as the head of the first and second Serbian Relief Fund units from 1914, and she remained with her staff and their Serbian patients when the Bulgarians occupied the city. She wrote *With our Serbian Allies*, London: Serbian Relief Fund, 1915.

Jess Dixon introduces the diary of Isobel Ross, who served with the Scottish Women's Hospitals in Serbia: *Little Grey Partridge*, Aberdeen: the University Press, 1988.

In an earlier crisis, Emma M. Pearson and Louisa E. MacLaughlin responded to an appeal from Lady Strangford for experienced nurses to help with relief work in 1876. Their account of the work is recorded in *Service in Serbia under the Red Cross*, London: Tinsley, 1877.

Flora Sandes served first as a V.A.D. in Serbia, but later joined the Serbian army, with which she saw active service and was wounded and was later awarded the Karadjordje Star for bravery in action. Her autobiography has been published as *An English Woman-Sergeant in the Serbian Army*, London: Hodder and Stoughton, 1916, and *The Autobiography of a Woman Soldier: a Brief Record of Adventure with the Serbian Army, 1916–1919*, London: H.F. and G. Witherby, 1927. A book about her life has also been written by Alan Burgess, *The Lovely Sergeant: the Life of Flora Sandes*, London: Heinemann, 1963, and an article about her by J. Wheelwright 'Flora Sandes – military maid', *History Today*, March 1989, pp. 42–8, and also in her book, *Amazons and Military Maids*, London: Pandora Press, 1989.

Monica M. Stanley served as chief cook with the Stobart unit in Serbia, and wrote *My Diary in Serbia, April 1, 1915 – November 1, 1915*, London: Simpkin, 1916.

Mabel St Clair Stobart was administrator of the Third Serbian Relief Fund unit from 1915, formed her 'flying field hospital', and eventually retreated with her unit through Albania. She wrote *The Flaming Sword in Serbia and Elsewhere*, London: Hodder, 1916, and *Miracles and Adventures: an Autobiography*, London: Rider, 1935.

Viscountess Strangford (Emily Anne Beaufort) wrote of her work in *Report on the Bulgarian Peasant Relief Fund, with a Statement of Distribution and Expenditure*, London: Hardwicke and Bogue, 1877.

Francesca M. Wilson was renowned for her relief work during two world wars, and wrote several books: *On the Margins of Chaos: Recollections of Relief Work in and between the Wars*, London: Murray, 1944.

Portraits and Sketches of Serbia, London: Swarthmore Press, 1920.

Yugoslav Macedonia, London: Women's International League, 1930.

Aftermath: France, Germany, Austria, Yugoslavia, 1945 and 1946, West Drayton: Penguin, 1947.

Experiences of War: World War II

Anne Dacie gave her personal reactions to events in *Instead of the Brier: concerning Yugoslavs*, London: Harvill Press, 1949. She also wrote *Yugoslav Refugees in Italy: The Story of a Transit Camp*, London: V. Gollancz, 1945.

Irene Grunbaum has written of her experiences in *Escape through the Balkans: the Autobiography of Irene Grunbaum*, translated and edited with an introduction by Katherine Morris, London: University of Nebraska Press, 1996.

Barbara Jancar-Webster's *Women and Revolution in Yugoslavia, 1941–1945*, Denver: Arden, 1990, is a well-researched book dealing with the participation of women throughout Yugoslavia in the army, the Yugoslav Communist Party and the national liberation movement against the Germans, and the consequences of the changed status of women.

Flavia Kingscote wrote *Balkan Exit*, London: Bles, 1942, about her travels through Croatia, Bosnia and Montenegro from 1939 to her escape in 1942, including some social observations on occupied Yugoslavia.

Olivia Manning used her own experiences of war as the basis for her fictional works, *The Great Fortune*, London: Heinemann, 1960, *The Spoilt City*, London: Heinemann, 1962, and *Friends and Heroes*, London: Heinemann, 1965. These were published as a single volume edition, *The Balkan Trilogy*, London: Penguin Books, 1981.

A woman's view of the Second World War is given in Louisa Rayner's *Women in a Village: an Englishwoman's Experiences of Life in Yugoslavia under German Occupation*, London: Heinemann, 1957, which was also published in translation in Belgrade in 1986. She vividly describes the summer of 1944 when she was a refugee from the bombing of Belgrade, giving details of village life, not only in domestic affairs, but also in political and military affairs as they affected a small village community.

Lena A. Yovitchitch, daughter of the former Serbian *chargé d'affaires* in London, wrote about civilian life during German occupation in the Second World War, in *Within Closed Frontiers: a Woman in Wartime Yugoslavia*, London: Chambers, 1956. She also wrote *Pages From Here and There in Serbia*, Belgrade: S.B. Cvijanovich, 1926, *Yugoslavia* (in the Peeps at Many Lands series), London: Black, 1928, and *The Biography of a Serbian Diplomat (Alexander Zdravko Yovitchitch)*, London: Epworth Press, 1939.

Women and the Writing of Balkan History

Several women historians have written about certain periods of Balkan history. They include the following:

Phyllis Auty, *Yugoslavia*, London: Thames and Hudson, 1965, and her contribution on Yugoslavia appears in Warriner, D. (ed.), *Contrasts in Emerging Societies: Readings in the Social and Economic History of South Eastern Europe in the Nineteenth Century*, London: Athlone Press, 1967. She also wrote *Tito: a Biography*, London: Longman, 1970, and with Clogg, R. (eds), *British Policy Towards Wartime Resistance in Yugoslavia and Greece*, London: Macmillan, 1975.

Elizabeth Barker, *British Policy in south-eastern Europe in the Second World War*, London: Macmillan, 1976.

Elinor Murray Despalatović, *Ljudevit Gaj and the Illyrian Movement*, Boulder, Colorado: East European Monographs, 1975.

Barbara Jelavich, *History of the Balkans*, Vol. 1. 18th and 19th Centuries, Vol. 2. 20th Century, Cambridge: Cambridge University Press, 1983, and *The Balkans in Transition*, (with Charles Jelavich), Berkeley: University of California Press, 1963.

Mercia Macdermott, *A History of Bulgaria, 1393-1885*, London: Allen and Unwin, 1962. *The Apostle of Freedom: a Portrait of Vasil Levsky against a background of Nineteenth Century Bulgaria*, London: Allen and Unwin, 1967. *Freedom or Death: the Life of Gotse Delchev*, London: Journeyman Press, 1978. *For Freedom and Perfection: the Life of Yane Sandansky*, London: Journeyman Press, 1988.

Alice Mead, *Journey to Kosova*, Maine: Loose Cannon Press, 1995. In her own words Alice Mead went to Kosovo 'as a Quaker, writer, and children's rights advocate, I decided to make myself a primary source of information, a first-hand observer, a witness for peace.' N.B. She has chosen to spell Kosova with an 'a' although that is not the accepted international spelling. She has also written a novel, *Adam's Cross*, New York: Farrar Strauss Giroux, 1996.

Mary Motes, *Kosova Kosovo: Prelude to War 1966–1999*: Redland Press, Homestead, Florida, 1998. Mary Motes lived for five years in Prishtina, much of the time as British Council lector, from the mid-1960s, maintaining good relations with her Serbian friends in Belgrade. She was in Kosovo for Tito's first visit there when he declared that 'Kosovo belongs to the people who live and work there'. She returned in the 1980s. Motes gives a unique, often amusing account of the province over several decades.

Gwen Robyns, *Geraldine of the Albanians: the authorised biography*, London: Muller, Bland and White, 1987.

Miranda Vickers, *Between Serb and Albanian: a history of Kosovo*, London: Hurst, 1998. She first visited in 1985, talking to the people about their experiences and knowledge of the region. The first half describes the history from the 15th century up to 1945; the second half deals in depth with the post-1945 periods. An historian of the Albanian people, and of Kosovo in particular, she has written other books, including: *The Albanians: a modern history*, London: Tauris, 1995; *Albania: from anarchy to a Balkan identity* (with James Pettifer), London: Hurst, 1997.

Doreen Warriner edited and contributed to *Contrasts in Emerging Societies: readings in the social and economic history of southeastern Europe in the nineteenth century*, London: Athlone Press, 1965.

Elizabeth Wiskemann, *Prologue to War*, London: Constable, 1939.

Karen Offen *et al Writing Women's history: international perspectives*, London: Macmillan, 1991 contains a chapter by Andrea Feldman, 'Women's history in Yugoslavia', and one by Efi Ardela, 'The 'History of Women' in Greece'.

Maria Todorova, who was raised in the Balkans, uses a mixture of travel and diplomatic accounts, academic and journalistic contributions, to explain the development of the 'image' of the Balkans, and 'to trace the relationship between the reality and the invention' in her book *Imagining the Balkans*, Oxford: Oxford University Press., 1997.

Anthropological Studies

A number of women have chosen the Balkans as an area in which to pursue anthropological or sociological studies as either specialists or general observers.

Emily Greene Balch spent the year of 1905 travelling and doing field research as the basis for her comprehensive and observant study on the Slavs, *Our Slavic Fellow Citizens*, New York: Charities Publications Committee, 1910. She had also written a journal article 'A week in Hercegovina and Bosnia', *The Bryn Mawr Alumnae Quarterly*, Vol. 2, 1908, p. 5. A biography has also been written about her, by M.M. Randall, *Improper Bostonian: Emily Greene Balch*, New York: Twayne, 1964.

In 1986–88 Tone Bringa conducted anthropological research in Bosnia. She has followed the disintegration of the community she was studying over the following years, returning in 1993 to assist in the making of a Granada TV documentary, and writing *Being Muslim the Bosnian way: identity and community in a central Bosnian village*, Princeton, N.J.: Princeton University Press, 1995.

Clarissa de Waal wrote an article on the privatisation of cooperative land in Albania after the changes of 1991, entitled 'Decollectivisation and total scarcity in High Albania', first published in *Cambridge Anthropology*, Vol. 18, No. 1, 1995, pp. 1–24, and later included in *After socialism: land reform and social change in Eastern Europe*, edited by Ray Abrahams, Oxford: Berghahn Books, 1996, p. 169–92.

Emanuela Del Re wrote the text for a catalogue produced for an exhibition in 1993 entitled 'Bread, salt and heart' (photographs by Franz Gustincich) which presented the importance of cultural support between the nations (here Italy and Albania): *Bread, salt and heart: the Kanun of Lek Dukagjini among the people of the Albanian mountains*, Lecce: Argo, 1993.

Of Bette S. Denitch's several contributions, a good example is her article on rural women in families that have migrated to towns, 'Urbanization and Women's roles in Yugoslavia', *Anthropological Quarterly*, vol. 49, 1976, pp. 11–19.

Ann Christine Eek, a photographer with the University Ethnographic Museum in Oslo, worked with the anthropologist Berit Backer on an exhibition on Albanian traditions in 1990, and produced a book for that exhibition, *Albanske Tradisjoner*, published jointly by Universitetets Etnografiske Museum in Oslo and Institutii Kultures Popullore, Tirana, 1991.

Her love of music opened many doors for June Emerson, who wrote *Albania: the search for the eagle's song*, Studley: Brewin Books, 1990.

One of the most frequently cited studies of Greek rural life is Ernestine Friedl's study of Greek village life contained in *Vasilika: a Village in Modern Greece*, Chicago: Holt, Reinhart and Winston, 1962. See also Friedl's contribution: 'Field work in a Greek village' in Golde, P. (ed.), *Women in the field: anthropological experiences*, 2nd edn., Berkeley: University of California Press, 1986 – a volume which also contains Diane Freedman's contribution: 'Wife, widow, woman: roles of an anthropologist in a Transylvanian village'. A brief biography of Ernestine Friedl is found in U.F.E. Gacs *et al* (eds), *Woman Anthropologists: Selected Biographies*, Urbana: University of Illinois, 1989.

Lucy M.J. Garnett writes about the Albanians, Bulgarians and Balkan Greeks and their daily lives, ceremonies and superstitions in *Balkan Home-Life*, London: Methuen, 1917.

Margaret Hasluck lived in Albania for thirteen years. Her study, which became an important ethnographic source, was published posthumously, edited by J.H. Hutton: *The Unwritten Law of Albania*, Cambridge: the University Press, 1954. Margaret Hasluck also wrote a 3-part series of articles on the gypsies of Albania in the *Journal of the Gypsy Lore Society*, 1938:

(Third Series)	No. 2 (April 1983), pp. 49–61
	No. 3 (July 1983), pp. 18–30
	No. 4 (Oct 1983), pp. 110–22.

Barbara Kerewsky-Halpern, with her husband Joel M. Halpern, has had extensive experience of field work in Serbia, particularly in the village of Orašac, and they have recorded their observations in: *A Serbian Village in Historical Perspective*, New York: Rinehart & Winston, 1972; *Selected Papers on a Serbian Village: social structure as reflected by history, demography and oral tradition*, Amherst, Mass.: University of Massachusetts, Dept. of Anthropology, 1977; and *Papers on a Serbian Village*, Amherst: 1986. Other works by her alone include: 'Genealogy as genre in rural Serbia', *Oral Traditional Literatures* (Festchrift in honor of Albert B Lord), ed. J. Foley, Columbus : Slavica Press, 1981, pp. 301-21; 'Text and context in ritual lament', in *Slavic Studies*, 1981, v.15(1), p. 52-60; 'Bulgarian oral tradition: context, continuity and change' in *Culture and History of the Bulgarian People, their Bulgarian and*

American parallels, ed. W.W. Kolar, Pittsburgh: Duquesne University, Tamburitzan Inst. Folk Arts, 1982; and (with J.M. Foley) 'The power of the word: healing charms as an oral genre', *Journal of American Folklore*, 1978, v.91(362), pp. 903-24.

Phyllis Kemp based her investigation of folk medicine on her observations throughout Yugoslavia, in *Healing Ritual: South Slav Traditions and Folk-Belief in the Field of Medicine*, London: Faber, 1935.

Olive Clare Lodge first travelled to Yugoslavia in 1919, visiting remote villages and valleys, and her observations on family life and customs of pre-war Yugoslavia are in *Peasant Life in Yugoslavia*, London: Seeley Service, 1942. Many of the chapters had previously appeared as articles in periodicals.

Marcia McDermott covers Bulgarian traditions, beliefs and lifestyles in her volume *Bulgarian Folk Customs*, London: Jessica Kingsley, 1998.

Susan E. Pritchett Post moved to Albania in 1994 when her husband went to work there for the U.S. Agency for International Development, and wanted to give a balanced presentation of Albanian women and tell their story, which resulted in her book *Women in Modern Albania: firsthand account of culture and conditions from over 200 interviews*, London: McFarland, 1998.

Stephanie Schwander wrote about the 'Albanians' in *Encyclopedia of world cultures*, vol. 4, *Europe (Central, Western and Southeastern Europe)*, edited by Linda A Bennet, Boston, Mass.: G.K.Hall & Co., 1992, pp. 3-8.

Marjorie Senechal's *Long life to your children! A portrait of High Albania*, Amherst, Mass.: University of Massachusetts Press, 1996, is a portrayal of the life and customs of the people of Northern Albania intended to create awareness of the country, and she also pays tribute in the book to Edith Durham.

Carol Silverman's work on Bulgaria includes: 'The politics of folklore in Bulgaria', *Anthropological Quarterly*, Vol. 56, 1983, pp. 55-61.

Ruth Trouton's *Peasant Renaissance in Yugoslavia, 1900-1950: A Study of the Development of Yugoslav Peasant Society as Affected by Education*, London: Routledge, 1952, has not been superseded, and deservedly remains in print.

Another anthropologist who studied village life in Slovenia, living in a household in that village, is Irene Winner. Her major work is *A Slovenian Village: Zerovnica*, Providence, Rhode Island: Brown University Press, 1971.

Although this guide is of necessity selective, the items listed reflect a remarkable diversity of approach: contributions have ranged from the amateur to the professional, the general to the scholarly, subjective to objective, patronising to respectful, but what they all have in common is an underlying enthusiasm for the field. Collectively, they and their offshoots form a corpus of writing which is of significance to both Women's Studies and Balkan Studies.

Bibliography

For further information on the literature of the countries covered consult the Clio Press, World Bibliographical Series.

Cathie Carmichael, *Slovenia*, Oxford: Clio, 1996, and *Croatia*, Oxford: Clio, 1999.

John J. Horton, *Yugoslavia*, rev.edn., Oxford: Clio, 1990.

Peter and Mary Siani-Davies, *Romania*, Oxford: Clio, 1998.

Antonia, Young, *Albania*. rev. edn., Oxford: Clio, 1997.

Also of interest:

Sava Peić, and Magda, Szkuta, comp. *The Balkan Crisis, 1990 –
: Catalogue, Part 1.*
London: British Library, Slavonic and East Europe Collections, 1997.

Notes on Contributors

John B. ALLCOCK has been involved in the study of Yugoslavia and its successor states for more than thirty years, and teaches sociology at the University of Bradford. Currently he is head of the Research Unit in South East European Studies at Bradford. His contributions to books and journals have appeared in America, Canada, France, Germany, Hungary, Poland and Yugoslavia as well as in Britain. The most recent of these is *Conflict in the Former Yugoslavia: An Encyclopedia*, which he edited together with Marko Milivojević and John Horton (1998). His *Explaining Yugoslavia* will appear in 2000. He has also broadcast regularly on the affairs of the region, and is a member of the editorial advisory board of *Balkanologie*. His interest in this project emerges from a former research programme into the development of tourism in Yugoslavia. John Allcock's engagement with the Balkans is far from being a solely academic affair, and extends into his activities as cook, mountaineer, painter and writer of fiction.

Dea BIRKETT is a writer on women and travel for the *Guardian* and the *Sunday Tribune*, the *Scotsman* and *Women,'s Review*. She is a contributor to *Half the Earth: Women's Experiences of Travel Worldwide (1986)*. Her book on Victorian women travellers, *Spinsters Abroad*, the result of five years of work in the area of the history of women travellers, was published in 1989. Her doctoral thesis dealt with the life and work of the Victorian traveller and political activist Mary Henrietta Kingsley. In addition to her writing, Dea Birkett has undertaken several broadcasting engagements for the BBC and independent TV production companies. Her travels in connection with the study of women travellers have taken her to many parts of the globe.

MARC CLARK is a freelance scientific journalist and researcher, formerly attached to the International Institute for Applied Systems Analysis, at Laxenberg, Austria. A Canadian citizen, he has travelled extensively in the Balkans, and has been resident in

Vienna since 1990. He holds an honorary visiting fellowship, attached to the Albanian Studies programme, at the School of Slavonic & East European Studies in London.

Elinor Murray DESPALATOVIĆ is Brigada Pacchiani Ardenghi Professor of History at Connecticut College in New London, CT. She holds a BA from Barnard College, and an MA and PhD from Columbia University. Her area of research is South Slav history in the nineteenth and twentieth centuries. She is author of: *Ljudevit Gqi and the Illyrian Movement (1975)*, co-editor with Joel Halpern of *How the People Live (1981)*, and author of a number of articles on Croatian and Yugoslav political and social history. Elinor Despalatovid has spent every sabbatical year in Yugoslavia since *1960*, and almost every summer since 1992 in Croatia. She is currently completing a study of Croatian rural life between *1880* and *1914*.

Jennifer FINDER has been the Librarian of the Management Centre at the University of Bradford since September *1989*. Previously as Readers' Services Librarian at the University's J.B. Priestley Library she had subject responsibility for Women's Studies. She graduated in Librarianship from the Leeds Polytechnic and completed her Master's degree in European Studies at the University of Bradford.

Omer HADŽISELIMOVIĆ graduated in English from the University of Sarajevo in 1970, and took an MA in American Studies at Oberlin College, Ohio, in 1972. His doctoral dissertation on the American social novel and its reception in Yugoslavia between 1918 and 1941 was published by Svjetlost (Sarajevo) in 1980. In 1989 he edited a collection of British travel writing on Bosnia and Hercegovina entitled *At the Gates of the East* (Veselin Masleća, Sarajevo). He taught at the University of Sarajevo between 1972 and 1994, and currently teaches at Earlham College and Indiana University, East Richmond, Indiana.

Joel HALPERN since 1992 has been Professor Emeritus of Anthropology at the University of Massachusetts at Amherst. His Ph.D. at Columbia included Soviet Studies at the Russian Institute. He has also been an Associate of the Russian Research Centre at Harvard University. From 1993 he has been a Visiting Professor and Senior Researcher at the Institute of Southeast European Studies at the

University of Graz. His field researches include work on the former Yugoslavia and its successor states, Bulgaria and Albania, the Canadian arctic, and (as a diplomat) with the US aid Committee in Laos and the UN Mekong Committee. His publications include (with Barbara Kerewsky-Halpern) *A Serbian Village in Historical Perspective* (1977 and 1982); monographs on Laos; an English translation of *How the People Live,* by the Croatian economist Rudolf Bišanić (with Elinor Murray Despalatović).

June HILL is the Keeper of Costume and Textiles for Calderdale Leisure Services. Based at the Bankfield Museum, Halifax, she is responsible for the extensive textile collections held there, including the Durham Collection of costume and embroideries. An Open University graduate and holder of the Museums Diploma, June has worked for Calderdale Museums since 1974 in the Social History and Textile Departments, and is interested in interpreting textiles in their social, historical industrial and artistic context.

John HODGSON is a professional translator and teacher of English. He has worked in Austria, Sweden, the GDR and Russia, and taught English language and literature at Priština University in Kosovo from 1980 to 1984, and at Tirana University in Albania from 1992 to 1995. He has published translations from Albanian of books by Ismail Kadare and Fatos Lubonja.

Anne KAY graduated in history from Southampton University, and Library Studies from University College, London. She has written her doctoral thesis on the subject of the British attitude to the Yugoslav government-in-exile, on which she continues her research. A good deal of her energies are also taken up with the running of a smallholding in Suffolk.

Barbara KEREWSKY-HALPERN studied at Barnard College and the University of Massachusetts, from which she gained her PhD in 1979. She worked for several years for the American Museum of Natural History, as a specialist on ethnographic materials relating to Yugoslavia and Laos, before taking up an academic appointment at the University of Massachusetts at Amherst. She has also worked as cartographer and illustrator and has experience in broadcasting. Although anthropological research has taken her to many countries in Europe and Asia, she retains a special interest in the Balkans. Both independently and with her husband she has written extensively in this field, specialising in studies of oral tradition and in medical anthropology.

Monica KRIPPNER, although born and educated in Australia, has spent most of her working life in Europe. She has travelled extensively in the Balkans, particularly in the course of her journalistic work as a special correspondent for the *Daily Herald* (between 1951 and 1956) and more recently as special correspondent for the *Guardian*, based in Vienna (where she also worked for the Australian Broadcasting Commission). From 1960 she was employed by the UN International Atomic Energy Agency, as English editor in its Division of Publications, and remained there until her retirement in 1984. She is the author of several guides and travel books and, in 1980 completed *The Quality of Mercy*, a study of the work of British medical women in Serbia during the First World War. She lives in Vienna and retains a deep interest in, and concern for, all the regions of the former Yugoslavia.

Felicity ROSSLYN studied at the University of Cambridge between 1969 and 1978, from which she completed her doctorate in English literature Since that date she has taught in the Departments of Literature at the Universities of Lancaster and Leicester. After a period of research in Yugoslavia, she has published numerous articles both in Britain and Yugoslavia on the work of Ivo Andrid. Felicity Rosslyn was awarded the Andrid Prize in 1982.

Diane WALLER studied Fine Art and Art History at the Ruskin School of Drawing in the University of Oxford, and went on to do an MA by research at the Royal College of Art subsequently obtaining her doctorate. She was awarded a Leverhulme European Scholarship and spent a year in Bulgaria and southern Yugoslavia, researching the effects of a rapidly changing society on the folk arts, and on art education. On her return, she trained in art therapy and psychotherapy and initiated postgraduate training in art therapy at the University of London, Goldsmith's College where she now leads the Unit of Psychotherapeutic Studies. Diane Waller is a consultant with the World Health Organisation for a project to develop art therapy within the Bulgarian health service, and regularly visits Bulgaria and Yugoslavia to maintain her involvement with the folk arts, and with recent developments in the visual arts generally. She is a member of the Vasil Levsky Bulgarian folkdance ensemble in London.

Julie WHEELWRIGHT is the author of *Amazons and Military Maidens*, a book about historical examples of women soldiers (Pandora Press, 1989). A freelance writer and journalist, she previously developed a script on the life of Isabelle Gunn, *The Orkney lad*, which is currently being considered for production as a feature film in Canada. Her current film work includes a documentary on the life of Flora Sandes, *Madame Captain*, with Flashback Television Ltd. She has an MA in history from the University of Sussex, and has written for several publications in Canada and the UK.

Antonia YOUNG graduated in anthropology from the University of California, Berkeley. She has studied, travelled and worked in a variety of capacities in several Balkan countries over many years, and has a special familiarity with Yugoslavia. She has had substantial organisational and administrative experience, particularly in the field of peace education, in Norway, Great Britain, and the USA, where she is now resident. Alongside working on this book, Antonia Young conducted a group research trip to the northern Albanian mountains, visiting some of the remote villages which these earlier women travellers described in their writing and is planning future such trips.

Index

Aberdeen 132; 134; 142
Aberdeen University 129; 141
Abinger, Lord 85
Abortion 59
Abrams, Euphemia Murray 47–52; 55;
   60–64
Acheron 212
Across the Carpathians 2
Adam, Robert 230
Addams, Jane 44
Adler, Felix 44
Adrianople (see, IMRO)
Adriatic xxii; xxiv; 48; 177; 193
Africa 187
African campaign, North 140
Alaska 62
Albania xiii; xvi; xxiii; xxix; 2; 10;
   11–31; 33–35; 71; 79; 84; 93;
   100–110; 128–154; 208–215
   independence 23–24; 27; 101;
     108–109; 134
   retreat through 79
Albanian(s) 10; 133; 134; 135; 136;
   142; 144; 145
Autocephalous Orthodox Church 27
   independence 18; 26; 101
   language 17; 101
   national idea 18
   origins of 106; 233
   resistance leaders 137
   Section (See, SOE) 'telegraph' 104
   tribes 20; 102–108
   virgin 105, 136; 210
Alexander, Miss 102
Alexander the Great 106; 233
Alexandra, Queen 95
Allcock, John B. xxxiii
Allen, W. E. D. xiii
Allies, Allies 90; 93; 157; 162
   offensive 83
Amazons and Military Maids xv
Ambasssadors' Conference 23; 35; 101
Ambler, Eric xxxii
America 44–46; 50–51; 54; 59; 62–63;
   129; 213; 219

American(s), Amerikanka 40–43; 52;
   60; 62; 64; 99; 105; 106; 108;
   134; 181; 187; 191; 196; 218
   Civil War (1863–4) 42–43
   Economic Association 43
   School in Paris 44
   Slavic immigrants 39–40; 45–64
   Unit (SWH) 81–83
Anatolia 129
Ancient World 229–234 (See also,
   Classical World)
Anderson, Dorothy 3; 167
Anderson, William 105
Andrews, Henry Maxwell 116–117; 119;
   125–126; 231
Andrijevica 16
Anglo-Albanian Association 26
Anglo-American Threat to Albania,
   The 10
Animism 232
Anthropology, Anthropological,
   Anthropologist 141; 146; 187;
   192; 196; 209; 214
Anthropometry 132
Anti-Communism xxviii; 65; 140
Anti-Partisan 141
Anti-semitism 219
Anti-Slavery Movement 42
Apostle of Freedom 167; 175; 176
Apalachia 57
Arab, Arabia 100; 221
Aranjelovac 194; 199
Arbuthnot, Lt. xxvii
Archangel 83
Archangel Michael 191
Architecture 230–231
Aristophanes 234
Aristotle 106; 233
Armenia 100
Arno 114
Asia 5; 100
Astra 228–229
As You Like It 90
Ataturk 229
Athens 128; 130; 131; 137; 138; 139

Atlantic 193
Augustine, St. 114
Aunt Agatha 119
Aus Dalmatien xxiv
Australia(n) 73; 81; 86; 92; 94; 129; 138
Austria(n) 5; 28; 35; 54; 114; 177
 Lloyds steamers xxv
Austria-Hungary (Austro-Hungarian)
  40; 46; 50-52; 55; 62-63; 64;
  101; 231
Austro-Italian treaty 61
Auty, Phyllis xxxii
Axis 66; 138; 192

Babuna Pass 83
Baedeker (guides) xxvii; 11
Bahtiyar Pasha 179
Bajna Bašta 85
Bajraktar 21; 214
Balaclava 74
Balalaika Dance Group 172
Balch, Emily Greene xxv; xxviii;
  39-70; 192
Balch, John 42
Balch, Joseph 42
Balkan Committee 167
Balkan as a geographical concept 226
Balkan States Exhibition, Earls Court
  (1907) 12; 37
Balkan Wars (See, War)
Balkan Home Life 32
Balkan Tangle xxv
Balkantourist 171
Balkan Volunteers 167
Ball, Oona 230; 231
Banja Luka 5; 6; 63
Bankfield Museum (Halifax) 33; 36; 37
Barker, Elizabeth xxxii
Barnard College 192
Bartlett, Christina 181
Bath 169
Beaconsfield, Lord (see, Disraeli)
Beaufort, Emily Anne (see, Strangford)
Bebel, F. A. 45
Beethoven, Ludwig van 120
Bektashi 131; 133
Belgians 176
Belgrade (Beograd) xxvii; 2; 5; 10; 15;
  27; 77; 78; 84; 85; 97; 116; 119;
  126; 155-161; 163; 165; 188;
  193; 201-202; 235
Bell, Gertrude 147
Beloff, Nora xxxii
Bennett, Dr. Agnes 81; 83
Berat 35
Berger, Peter 219

Berlin 119
 Congress of 136
 Treaty of 136; 177; 184
 University of 45
Berry James 80
Berry Unit 75
Besa 21; 103
Beverly 42
Bible, The, bibles 17; 29
Biggs, Mrs. Elspeth 86
Bird, Isabella 91
Birkett, Dea xiv
Birth control 196
Bitola (See, Monastir)
Bizerta 81; 95
Black Lamb and Grey Falcon xxvi;
  xxviii; xxxi; 29; 32; 113-127;
  192; 236-238
Black Sea xxii
Blagoev, Dimiter 176
Blagoevgrad 167; 181
Blair, Dr. Mary 81
Blarney Stone 238
Bled xxvii
Blood feud 21; 103-105; 107; 192
Blue Bead 99; 102
Blue Nile 209
Boka Kotorska (Bocche) 51; 61
Booth, Charles 44
Bora 61
Bosanska Gradiška 5; 6; 7
Bosnia and Hercegovina, Bosnian(s)
  1; 2-7; 19; 33; 47-48; 50; 51; 60;
  63-64; 82; 161; 167; 169; 177
Boston (USA) 41; 43-45
'Boston Brahmins' 41; 47
Bourchier, James 167; 178
Bowood House 169
Boylston, Helen Dore 108-109
Bozšic, Isobel (See, Rayner)
Bradshaw's *Continental Guide* 7
Braga-Mati 22
Brailsford, H. N. 16; 167
Brigades (See, Youth Brigades)
Brighton 126
Brindisi 79; 109
Brindley, Dorothy 85
Bringa, Tone xxxii
Bristol 169
Britain, British 72; 79; 81-86; 84; 108;
  109; 110; 137; 138; 139; 140; 141;
  167; 172; 174; 176; 179; 183; 222
 diplomatic representation 92; 176
 forces 78
British-Bulgarian Friendship Society
  172; 181

Council 114
Diplomatic Representation
    Expeditionary Force 92
Forces 81
and Foreign Bible Society 17
Intelligence 130; 137
Legation 130
Museum 173
Press 91; 94
School at Athens (BSA) 129; 137;
    138; 140; 142
(See, British Red Cross)
Brod 8
Brontë, Charlotte 9
Brontë, Emily xxi; 9
Brown, Horace 231
Brusa 142
Bryn Mawr (Quaker women's college) 43
    Alumnae Quarterly 63
Budapest 120
Bulgaria(n), Bulgar xiii; xxi; 16; 32;
    33; 51; 76-79; 101; 166; 186
Academy of Sciences 167
Burden of the Balkans 16
Burma 117
Burney, Fanny 217
Burton, Sir Richard 222
Bush, George 43
Buxton, Noel and Charles Rhoden 167
Byron, Lord xxxii
Byzantium, Byzantine 125; 129

Cairo 139; 140; 142
Cambridge Natural History 11
Cambridge University 81; 129
Campbell, John C. 226
Canada 73
Canterbury, Archbishop of 73; 179
Cape Shantung 168
Carline, George, Hilda, and Sidney 37
Carlowitz 155
Carnavon, Lady 84
Carniola 47; 51; 55
Carter, April xxxii
Carter, Frank xxxii
Carthaginian 115
Catholic(s) 106-107; 129; 134; 135;
    144; 145
Cato 234
Çeausescu, Nikolae xxiii
Cetinje xxv; xxvii; 10; 11; 18; 20; 48;
    51; 62; 212; 236
Chafa Bishkasit 103
Chaucer, Geoffrey 232
Chernembl 55
Chesney, Dr. Lilian 83

Chetniks (See also, Sandansky)
    158-162; 181
China 168
Christ, Jesus 122; 237
Christian(s), Christianity, Christendom
    xxiii; 3-5; 17; 34; 64; 129; 130;
    160; 218; 228; 233
Christian Socialists 44; 65
*Christianity and Islam under the
    Sultans* 130
Christie, Agatha xxxii
Churchill, W. 128
Cicero 106
Čilim 191
City of God, The
Clark, Mark xvi
Clark, Walter Ernest 47
Classical World 227; 230; 233
Clouds, The 234
Cold War xxiii; 172; 173
Colorado 40; 62
Columbia University 192
Comintern 124; 125
Communism, Communist(s),
        Communist Party xxiii; xxviii;
        125; 140; 141; 160; 161; 163;
        164; 171; 172; 203; 218
'Complimentarity of Women's Ritual
    Roles in a Patriarchal Society'
    200
Conant, Katerine 44
'Constantine' (See, Vinaver)
Constantinople xxxi, 17
Contemporary Review 27
Contraception 196
Corfu 79; 80-91; 224
Corsica 81; 85
Costume 13; 17; 24; 33-38; 48; 53; 55;
    64; 125-126; 158; 192
Council of Ambassadors (See,
    Ambassadors' Conference)
Counihan, Joan xxxiii
Court and the Castle xxix
Crna Gora (See, Montenegro)
Croatia(n), Croats 1; 33; 41; 49; 50; 52;
    58; 59; 61; 125; 202
    Military Frontier 47; 56; 58
Croatia-Slovonia (See, Slavonia)
Croato-Serbian (See, Serbo-Croatian)
    48
Cross-dressing 95
Čurcin, Dr. 79
Cvetkovski, Prof. 86
Cvijić, Jovan 226
Cyprus 141; 142
Czechoslovakia, Czechs 46; 124; 141; 142

Dahomey
Daily News, The 166; 179
Dakota 99; 129
Dalmatia(n) 11; 33; 47; 49; 50; 51; 52; 55; 56; 60; 61; 63; 64; 129; 230; 233
Dalmatia, the Quarnero and Istria 231
Daniel, Norman 217
Dante 114
Danube 77; 177
Danzig 28
Davies, Miranda xiv
Dearmer, Jessie Mabel 75
Dečani 15
Decourt, M. Gaston 103
Dedinje Railway Hospital 84
Dehmel 119–120
Delchev, Gotse 178–179; 180; 182–183; 184
De Smet, Missouri 100
De Windt, Harry xxi; 234
Dimitrov, Georgi 171–173
Dinaric Mountains 230
Diocletian's palace 60; 230; 231
Discovery of Freedom 106
Disraeli (Lord Beaconsfield) 176–177; 178
D'Istria, La Comtesse Dora 224; 225; 227; 33
Ditchling 168
Dobrujdja Front 82–83
Doda, Prenk Bib 20
Dole, Charles Fletcher 42–43
Douglas, Norman 114
Draga, Queen (see, Obrenović)
Drangojt 108
Drumblade 129
Druzba 171
Dublin 142
Dubrovnik 2; 48; 51; 60; 85; 231
Dunabin, Tom 138
Dunlop, Mr. Graham xxvi
Durazzo (See, Durrës)
Durham, Mary Edith xvii; xx; xxii; xxv; xxvi; xxvii; xxviii; 131; 33–38; 91; 101; 102; 104; 105; 108; 129; 131; 134; 136; 144; 145; 146; 192; 208–209; 210; 224; 215; 228; 122; 124; 127; 128; 233; 238; 239
Durham Collection 33–38
Düringsfeld, Ida xxiv
Durkheim, Emile 219
Durrës 24; 78–79; 106

Earls Court Exhibition (See, Balkan State Exhibition)
East, The (See Orient)
Easter 121–123; 237

Eastern Europe(an) 39; 40; 50; 66
Eastern Question xxiii; 147
Eastern Rumelia 173; 174
Eastern War Sick and Wounded Fund 167
Edinburgh 73; 81; 83
Education 18; 43; 50; 53; 89; 91; 101; 102; 164; 175; 183; 202
Egypt, Egyptian 22; 100; 106
Elbasan 79; 133; 136; 141; 146
Elgin 129
Eliot, Sir Charles (President of Harvard) ('Odysseus') 15; 46
Elizabeth, Empress of Austria 119
Ellis, William 11
Elsie Inglis Unit 83
Emerson, R. W. 42
Emigrants, emigrate, emigration 51; 53; 54; 58; 59; 61; 62
Emslie, Dr. Isobel 83; 85
Encyclopaedia Britannica 19; 178
England, English, Englishman, Englishwoman 1; 2; 3; 5; 6; 7; 73; 75; 79; 85; 93; 94; 124; 134; 155; 156; 162; 168; 175; 176; 188; 210; 115; 232
press (See British press)
Esperanto 176
Ethnography of communication 199
Europe, European 7; 15; 35; 39; 40; 46; 49; 60; 66; 107; 109; 116; 123; 129; 131; 133; 144; 147; 167; 173; 177; 185; 200; 217; 225; 230
Powers (See, Great Powers)
Evans, Sir Arthur 73; 179; 231
Evans-Pritchard, E. E. 187; 232
Evil eye 190
Evksinograd 171

Fabians 44; 45; 65
Fairfield, Cicily 115
Fanon, Franz 224
Fascists, Fascism xxiii; 66; 158; 170–171; 193
Federal Labour Union 45
Feminists, Feminism xv
Femmes en Orient, Les 224; 227
Fermor, Patrick Leigh xxxi
Ferri, Enrico 45
Ferris, Lorna 75
Fertility rite 237
Finder, Jennifer xvii; xxiv
Finland, Finnish 113; 114
First Aid Nursing Yeomanry 139
First World War (See, War)
Fis 145

Fisher, Dorothy Canfield 44
Fiske, John 46
Fiume (See, Rijeka)
Fjalor Enciklopedik Shqiptar (Albanian
    Encyclopaedic Dictionary) 10
Flaubert, Gustave 222
Florence 114
'Flower of the Road' 105
Folk costume (See, Costume)
Folk cultures, Folk custom, Folk lore,
    Folk healers, Folk psychotherapy
    108; 130; 134; 136; 190; 200;
    227; 233; 238
Folklore Society 134; 135
Foreign Affairs 27
Foreign Office 24; 26; 28; 29; 137; 141;
    156
For Freedom and Perfection 180; 184
Forster, E. M. 11
Fortunes of War 217
France, French 44; 73; 80; 81; 82–83;
    94; 106
Franciscan 144; 145
Franco-Prussian War (See also, War)
    xxix
Franklin, Miles 86
Freedman, Diane 209; 213; 214
Freedom or Death 179; 180
Freeman, Prof. 230
French, Field Marshal Lord 81
Friedl, Ernestine 211
Friends and Heroes 138; 139
'Friends of Albania' 29
Frontiers (See also, Croatian Military
    Frontier)

Gallie, W. Bryce 225
Gallipoli campaign 72
Galveston 40
Garnett, Lucy 32; 228; 232
Genčić, Col 78
Gendarmerie 159
Gender 90; 210 (See also, Women's
    roles)
Geneva 65; 66
George Watson's Ladies College 115
Gerbaud 119–120
Gerda 113–120
Germany, German(s) 4; 28; 40; 47; 54;
    64; 72; 80; 85; 116; 137; 140;
    155; 156; 157; 158; 159; 160;
    161; 170–171
    Army 158
Gerth, Hans 158
Gibb, Sir Hamilton 222
Giddings, Franklin H. 43; 44; 46

Girton and Newnham Unit (SWH) 81;
    82; 84
Giubba 33
Gjeçov, S., Gjeçovian 144; 145
Gladstone, Herbert 179
Gladstone, William Ewart xxiii; 3; 167;
    168; 177; 179; 227
Glasgow Herald, The 95
Glasnost 218
Gooch, G. P. 29
Gorbachev, Mihail 218
Gordon, Jan and Cora 78; 85
Gordon, Winifred 209; 210
Gorski Kotar 55
Gospić 59
Gradiška (See Bosanska Gradiška)
Gramsci, Antonio 97
Grand Tour xxvi
Graphic, The xxii; 71; 95
Great Powers 164; 176;–177; 179; 209;
    212
Great War (See, War)
Greece, Greek(s) xiii; xxi; xxvi; xxix; 2; 24;
    35; 60; 71; 82; 100; 103; 106; 133;
    134; 139; 148; 227; 231; 232; 233
Greek Folk Songs 228; 231
Greenwich Settlement House (NY) 47
Gregory, Bishop of Nona 231
Grey, Sir Edward 92; 94
'griners' (Slovenes) 54
Grouitch, Madam Mabel's Red Cross
    Unit (See also, Grujić) 92
Gruev, Dame 178
Grujić, Mabel and Slavko 73
Guardian, The, Manchester Guardian
    xxi; 29
Guli, Pitu 179
Gursi 22
Gypsy, Gypsies 133; 136; 146; 147; 237

Hadžiselimović, Omer xxvii
Haiti 66
Halifax 33; 36
Halifax Museums, 37
Halley's Comet 22
'Halperns in Orašac, The' 201
Hammond, Nicholas 132
Han (khan) 209
Hardie, John 129
Hardie, Kier 45
Hardy Frances 100; 101
Harley, Mrs. 81; 82
Harper's Monthly Magazine 99
Harvard Annex 45
Harvard University 43; 45; 46; 109
Hasluck Frederick 130; 133; 142

Hasluck, Margaret xvi;
Hassolel, Doamna xxii
Haverfield, Hon. Mrs. Evelina 77; 78;
    85; 86
Hawthorne, Nathaniel 43
Hellenes, Hellenic 232 (See also, Greek)
Herbal remedies 201–203
Herbert, Aubrey 26
Hercegovina, Herzegovina,
    Hercegovinians 33; 51; 230 (See
    also, Bosnia)
Herriot School 81
Hibbert, Reginald 139
High Albania 21; 146; 236
Hill, June xvi–xvii
Hill 1212
History of Bulgaria, The 173
Hitler, Adolf 115; 161
Hodgson, John xxv; 105
Hodgson, T. R. 17
Holloway, Dr. Edith 77; 80
Holmes, O. W. 43
Holtz, William 109
Home library programme Homeric
    xxix; 62; 157; 232
Honour 13; 17; 103; 104; 105; 184; 190
Hospitality 21; 22; 103; 104; 157;
    190–191; 210–211
Hoti 23; 25; 215
How the Other Half Lives 44
Hoxha, Enver xiii; 10; 30
Hrnetić
Hull House 39; 44
Hungary, Hungarian 47; 59; 80; 124;
    172
Hunter, Col. 76
Hutchinson, Dr. Alice 77; 80
Hutchinson, Francis Kinsley 40
Hutton, Dr. Isabel Emslie 93
Hutton, Lt. Gen. Sir Thomas 84
Hyderabad 129
Hygeine 4; 45; 46; 74; 84; 108; 157; 212

Ilenden (Ilyen den) Uprising 16
Illiteracy 59
Illyria 23
Illyrian Letters 231
Illyrian Liturgy 231
Imagining the Balkans
    xivImmigrant(s), immigration
    44; 45; 46; 50; 51; 52
Immigration History Institute,
    Philadelpia 39
Immigration Restriction League 46
Independence (See, Albanian
    independence)

India 73; 81; 177
Ingalls family 100
Inglis, Dr. Elsie 73–86
Internal Macedonian–Adrianople
    Revolutionary Organisation
    (IMRO) 124; 178–179
International Congress of Women at
    the Hague 39
International Socialist and Labour
    Congress 45
International Union of Students
Ionian Isles 224
Irby, Adeline Paulina xxvi–xxvii; 1–8;
    20; 167; 227
Ireland 73
Islam, Islamic fundamentalism xxiii,
    217; 218 (See also, Muslim)
Istanbul 139
Istria 47; 48; 54; 55
Italy, Italian(s) 10; 27; 44; 48; 100; 101;
    137; 139
Ivens, Dr. Frances 73

Jackson, Sir Thomas 230; 231; 233
Jajce 63
Jambol 71
James, William 46
Jansz, Natasha xiv
Jannina, Vizier of 224
Japanese–Americans 66
Japang 33
Jelavich, Charles and Barbara 226
Jelek 34; 35
Jew(s), Jewish 47; 53; 124; 213
Jewell, H. H. 130
Johnston, Priscilla 1; 4
Jovanović, Ljuba 27
Jugoslavia (See, Yugoslavia)
Junaštvo 16

Kajmakćalan, Battle of 82
Kalemegdan 77
Kansas City 100
Karadjordje 194
Karadjordjević dynasty 165; 235
Karlovac 54; 55
Karlovo 165
Karlstadt 41
Kastrati (tribe) 215
Kay, Anne xxix; xxxi
Kellogg–Briand Pact 66
Kemal, Ismail Bey 101
Kerewsky-Halpern, Barbara xvi; xxxi;
    208; 213; 215
Kahn 46
Kilkes (See Kukush)

King, Olive Kelso 84; 85
Kingsbury, Mary 45
Kingsley, Charles 44
Kingsley, Mary 91
Kippert, Heinrich 177
Kirk-Kilisse 76
Kiseljak 6
Konia 130
Koprivka 168
Korça (Korcha) 35
Korea
Kosovo, Kossovo, Kosova xiii; 2; 22;
    79; 101; 102; 134
  Battle of 115
Kozani 131
Kragujevac 73-80; 85
Kralice e malesorëvit 22
Kraljevo 79; 80
Kransler 119-120
Kriegschuldfrage, Die 28
Krippner, Monica xxix
Kršnjavi, Herr K. 49
Krushevo 179
Kukush 179

Labour Movement 45
Ladysmith 12
'Land of the living past' 236; 238
Landmines 72; 75
Lane, Edward 223
Lane, Rose Wilder xxvii; xxviii; 20;
    99-112; 136; 143; 233
Latin 231; 233
Law, Bonar 73
Lawrence, D. H. 114-115
Lazar, Tsar 115
Lazarevac 77; 80
League of Communists 198
League of Nations 26; 65; 102
Leake, Major Philip 140
Lear, Edward 130
Leeds Library xxx
Liepzig 171
Lek, Laws of, Canon of 103; 107; 145; 233
Leninism 65
Letters During Mr. Wortley's Embassy
    xxiv; 155
Levasseur, Emile 44
Leverhulme Fellowship 136
Lévi-Strauss 146
Levsky, Vasil 167; 173-176; 182-183
Liebknecht, Karl 45
Life and Labour of the People of
    London 44
Lika 161
Lik-krbava 51; 57; 59

Little House on the Prairie, The 99
Little Russians 54
Liverpool 24
Ljubljana 49; 51
Lodge, Olive xxxii, 81; 85
Lodge, Senator Hanry Cabot 46
London, Londoners 10; 15; 36; 72; 91;
    101; 128; 130; 134; 138; 141;
    142; 156; 225
London Globe, The 95
  Gondon Graphic (See *Graphic*)
Longfellow, H. W. 43
Lotos Eaters, The 12
Lowell, A. Lawrence 43
Luckmann, Thomas 219
Lulash, Chief 105
Luria

McCarthy era MacDermott, Mercia
    xxv; xxviii; xxxi; 166-186
MacDonald, Ramsay 27
Macedonia, Macedonian xxiii; xxix; 2;
    16; 34; 75; 77; 81; 82-83; 86; 93;
    106; 116; 120; 121; 124; 128;
    131; 133; 134; 136; 145; 148;
    167; 168; 176-177; 178-179;
    180-181; 237
'Macedonia', The 168
Macedonian Relief Committee 16
Macedonian Revolutionary Movement
    (See, Internal Macedonian
    Revolutionary Organisation
    [IMRO])
McGregor, Dr. Beatrice 77, 80
McIlroy, Dr. Louise 81; 84
Mackensen, General 80
Mackenzie, Georgina Muir xxvi, xxviii;
    1-8; 227
Macmillan 29; 81
Macphail, Dr. Katherine 85; 86; 97
Macphail, Dr. Matilda 81
Mafeking 12
Magic 121-124; 187; 192; 236
Mahommedan (See Muslim)
Maitland, Thomas 224
Mali Sharit 107
Malinowski, Bronislaw 144
Man 135
Manchester Guardian (See, *Guardian*) 29
Manchuria, Manchurian Crisis 65; 66
Manners and Customs of the Modern
    Egyptians 223
Manning, Olivia xxxii; 138; 217
Mansfield, Missouri 99; 110
Marginality xxi-xxiv
Maričevići 194

Marischal Museum, Aberdeen 134
Markagjoni, John 135
Marquis, Annette 108
Marriage 103–105; 107; 110; 158;
    199–200; 213–214
Marseilles 73
Marx, Karl, Marxism 65; 118; 125
Massachusetts 42; 44; 189; 206
Massachusetts Institute of Technology
    (MIT) 45
Massignon, Louis 222
Mat (place and tribe) 27
Mati, River 22
Matthews, Ronald 132
Maw, Florence 85
Medical relief 22
    Army medical corps, Royal 76; 78
Mediterranean 176; 193
Mera sporet Mera (Measure for
    Measure) 187
Meštrović, Ivan 231
Meta, Rexh 102; 110
Migration 39–70 (See also, emigration,
    immigration)
Mihailović, Gen. Draža 124; 159
Michigan 40
Mijatović, Čedomilj 3
Milenkovitch,Deborah xxxii
Military Frontier (See Croatian Military
    Frontier)
Mill, John Stuart 11
Mills, C. Wright xxiii
Milošević, S. xiii
Mirage, The 25
Mirdita 135
Mirdite 20
Mirko, Grand Vojvoda 235
Miss Irby and her Friends 3; 167
Miss Ireland's School 43
Mladenovac 77; 80; 86; 188; 194
Modruš-Rijeka 41; 51; 57
Moglena Mountains 82
Mohammedan (See, Muslim)
Monastir 33; 79; 82; 85; 93; 95; 142
Montenegro, Montenegrin xxix; 2; 10;
    11; 12; 15; 16; 18; 22; 23; 26; 33;
    34; 37; 48; 51; 55; 62; 78–79;
    101; 102; 211; 212; 215; 230
Morality 42–43; 53; 58–59; 61; 106; 159
Morris, Jan
Morris, William 125; 147; 167
Morrison, Dr. 74
Mostar 2; 4; 51; 63
Mozart 120
*Murray's Handbook for Travellers in
    Turkey* 7

Murray, Lord John 47
Museum of Mankind 35
Muslim(s), Moslem(s), Mussulman(s)
    5; 34; 35; 63; 64; 106; 131; 135;
    145; 183; 223; 224; 229; 237
My Brilliant Career 86
Myres, John 134; 135; 136; 142

National costume (See, Costume)
'National Rebirth' 18
Nationalism 53; 103
Nazism, Nazi(s) 28; 219; 171
Near East 94
Near East Association 28
Near East Relief 100
Nevinson, H. W. 22; 23; 35
Newburyport 42; 60
Newcastle 83
New England, New Englanders 42; 43; 45
New Europe 84
New York 40; 46; 47
New Zealand 73; 81
Nightingale, Florence 84
Nikola, Prince/King of Montenegro 18;
    26; 235–236
Nikolai, Bishop 121–123
Nikolić, Dr. 92
Niš, Nish 79; 83; 85; 92
Njegoš, Prince Njegož Petar Petrović
    xxvii; 1
Njeguš 17
Nobel Laureate 39
Nobel Peace Prize 39; 66
Noli, Fan 26–27; 29; 102
Nopcsa, Baron Franz 35
Nosi, Lef 133; 134; 136; 137; 140; 141
*Notes on the South Slavonic Countries
    of Turkey in Europe* 2; 4; 7
Noyes, Ellen Maria 42
Nuer 187
Nurses 70–90
    Nursing Yeomanry, Ladies' 91

'Object Matrimony' 110
Obrenović, King Alexander and Queen
    Draga 235
Odessa 83
'Odysseus' (See, Eliot)
Odyssey xxix; 59; 257
Oedipus Rex in Albania 142
Ohrid, Lake 124
Olympus, Mount 131
Omer Pasha and the Christian Rebels
    xxvii
Opatija xxvii
Ora, oreads 1

Orašac 194; 195; 202; 206
Orient, Oriental(s), Orientalism xxii;
    63; 221; 221; 223; 224; 225; 226;
    229; 234; 238–239
Orthodox 3; 23; 121; 134; 213; 238–239
    Bosnian Church 33 (See also,
    Albanian Authcephalous
    Orthodox Church)
Osijek 52
Osmanlis (See, Ottoman)
Ostrovo, Lake Ostrovo 81; 82; 136; 137
Otočac 57
Ottoman Empire, Ottoman(s) 4; 15; 17;
    18; 63; 134; 167; 174; 176; 180;
    227; 219; 233
Our Slavic Fellow Citizens 40; 46; 54;
    63
Ovče Polje 237
Oxford 134; 142; 185
Ozarks 99

Pacifism 65
Paget, Lady 73–75; 78; 80; 84
Paget, Sir Ralph 78
Parga 224
Paris(ian) 44; 55; 100; 104; 108; 156
Partisans 30; 140; 141; 158; 159; 160; 161
Peace Pledge Union 115
Peace worker 39
Peaks of Shala 101; 103; 107; 108
Pearl Harbour 65
Peasant(s) 52–53; 55–56; 63; 59; 94;
    125; 162; 164; 191–192; 228
Peasant Life in Yugoslavia 85
Peć, Pejë, Ipek 15; 34; 79; 107
Pejović, Krsto 18; 19–20
Peninsule Balkanique 226
Pennsylvania 41; 43
Perestroika 173; 185; 218
Perlant, A. xiii
Perolli, Rrok 102; 107
Peter, King of Yugoslavia 79; 157; 161;
    235
Philip II of Macedonia 106
Pick, Hella xxxii
'Pie Supper' 110
Pirin Mountains 167; 180–181
Pirot 14
Pitt-Rivers Museum 36
Pittsburgh 62
Plymouth 168
Plymouth, Massachusetts
    (See, Massachusetts)
Pnigeus 234
Podgorica 23
Pog 107

Pola (Pula) 230
Poland, Polish 137; 172
Politika 155; 160; 165; 205
Poppleton, Yorkshire 91
Port Said 24
Portsmouth 168
Poverty 19; 34; 36; 44–46; 57–60; 228
Power xxviii; 114; 221; 227
'Power of the Word: Healing Charms as
    an Oral Genre' 199
Prague 7; 168
Prejudice 218–219; 222
Primitiveness 235–236
Prisoner, The xxi
Prizren 79
Protestant 47
Public Assistance of the Poor in France 44
Public opinion xxxii
Pultit 105; 107
    Catholic Bishop of 106
Putnik, Vojvoda 79
Pyrenees 24

Quaker(s) 40; 42; 43; 66
'Queen of the Mountain People/
    Highlanders' 105

Radcliffe College (See Harvard Annex)
Ragusa Comittee 1
Railways 52; 60; 169
Raki, Rakija 12
Ramadan 131; 145
Randall, Mercedes 39
Rankin, Sister Jean 85
Rayner, Louisa (Isobel Božić) xxix;
    xxxi; 19; 155–165; 233
Red Cross xxix; 25; 71; 77; 78; 80; 90;
    94; 100
'Red Scare' (See, Anti-Communism)
Refugee(s) 1; 22; 24; 66; 102; 161; 162;
    167
Reichstag fire 171
Religious persecution 42
Renan, Ernest 222; 224
Rhodope Mountains 177
Riis, Jacob 44
Rijeka 41; 49; 51
Rimbaud, Arthur 114–115
Ripanj 158
Rome, Roman(s), xxii; 106; 227; 230; 231
Romania, Romanian xxiii; 80; 82; 209;
    211
Romanticism xxvii; 12; 18; 21; 41; 110;
    184
Room with a View 11
Ross, Dr. Elizabeth 75

Rossetti, Christina 25
Rosslyn, Felicity xxviii
Roth, Ling 37
Rowbotham, Sheila xxxii
Royal Anthropological Institute 11; 26; 37
Royal Command 95
Royal Free Hospital 75–76
Royal Institute of International Affairs 28
Royaumont 73
Royce, Josiah 46
Rozhen Monastery 180
Runciman, Sir Stephen xxxii
Rusanj 158; 160; 161; 162; 163
Ruskin, John 125
Russia, Russian 80; 82–83; 85; 95; 114;
 162; 164; 169; 170; 172;
 176–177; 185

Šabac 169
Sabor 61
Said, Edward W. xi; xv; 221; 223–225;
 226; 229; 239
St. Anne's College, Oxford 169
St. Augustine (See, Augustine)
St. George's Eve 115; 237
St. John's Day 20
St. John's wort (*borgorodić na trava*) 201
St. Nicholas 54
Salem 60
Sallanches 81
Salonika, Salonique xxix; 73; 76; 81;
 82; 84; 86; 93; 131; 142; 179
Sandansky, Yane 178–179; 180–181;
 182; 184
Sandansky's Chetniks 181
Sanders, Irwin xxxii
Sandes, Flora xxviii; xxix; 73–775; 79;
 81; 82; 85; 90–98
Sandes, Re.Sandwith, Humphrey 2
San Francisco 100
San Francisco Bulletin, The 100
San Stafano, Treaty of 176; 177
Sarajevo xxvii; 2; 4; 6; 7; 20; 28; 48;
 51; 83; 155; 156; 169; 229
 Assassination at 24; 27
Sarajevo Crime, The 27
Sargent, Sir Orme 124
Sava, River 5; 7; 15
Savagery 230; 234–235, 236
Savka 157; 158; 161; 162
Saywell, Shelley xxviii; xxxi
Schmoller, Gustav 45
School of Slavonic Studies 169; 173
Scotland, Scottish, Scotch 47; 73; 77;
 136; 142
Scott, Charlotte Angus 43

Scottish Women's Hospitals for Foreign
 Service (SWH) xxix; 73–86
Scudder, Vida 44
Scutari (See Shkodër) 208
Second World War (See War)
Semite(s) (See, Jewish)
Senj 48; 56; 60
Serbia, Serbian(s), Serb(s) xxix; xxxi;
 10; 12; 13; 14; 24; 25; 27; 50; 51;
 52; 72–86; 90–97; 102; 120; 124;
 125; 157; 158; 160; 161; 163;
 165; 177; 178; 188; 191; 194;
 196; 208; 211; 235
 Academy of Sciences 191
 Joan of Arc 94
 Relief Fund 72–74; 76; 79; 81;
 82–83; 85
Serbo-Croatian 64
Servia (See, Serbia)
Seton Watson, R. W. 19; 28; 72–74; 84
Seton-Watsons, the xxxii
Shakespeare, William 27; 90
Shala guide 103
Shantoya, Marko 210
Shkodër, Skodra, Scutari 14; 18; 20; 22;
 23; 24; 25; 33; 35; 100; 132; 143
Shoshi 102; 103
Šibenik 231
Simmel, Georg 45
Simmonds, Emily 73–75; 92
Sinas, Konstantin 17; 18
Singleton, Fred xxxii
Skanderbeg Square xiii
Skopje 15; 74–77; 78; 81; 83; 85; 180
Slav(s) 46; 48; 51; 52; 60; 61; 177; 179;
 236
Slavic, Slavonic xxviii; 52; 53; 64;
 168–169
 immigrants xxix; 40; 46; 50; 54
Slavonia(n), Croatia-Slovania 49; 51;
 52; 54; 56; 57; 58; 59
Slovaks 61
Slovenia, Slovene(s) 50; 51; 54; 55; 82;
 125
Smallpox
Smiley, David 142
Social Construction of Reality, The 219
Socialist(s), Socialism xxiii; xxviii; 45;
 64; 170; 173; 180; 185
Social work 45
Society for Cultural relations with the
 USSR 172
Society for Friendship with Bulgaria
 (See, British-Bulgarian
 Friendship Society) Society of
 Friends (See, Quakers)

Sofia 167; 170; 175; 177
  University 180
Soltau, Dr. Eleanor 74–75; 77
Some Tribal Origins, Laws and Customs
  of the Balkans 19; 28; 192
Sons of the Eagles 132
Sophie, Archduchess 119
Sorbonne 44
Soviet Union, Soviet xiii; xxii; 140;
  161; 169; 170; 172–173; 184
Spalato (See, Split)
Spain 66
Special Operations Executive (SOE)
  128; 139; 140; 142
Spencer, Stanley 37
Spinsters Abroad xiv
Spirit of the East, The 223
Split 51; 60; 230; 231
Sremska Kamenica 85; 86
Stahl, Henri xxxii
Stalin(ism) xxiii; 125
Stanzas 9
Stjipanjica 35
Stobart, Mrs. St. Clair 78; 85
Stone, Miss Ellen 181
Stoney, Edith 81
Strandzha mountains 179
Strangford, Lady 167
Struga 79
Struggle for Scutari 23
Struma 83
Stuart-Glennie, J. S. 23
Stubbings, Frank 142
Sublime Porte xxiv
Suez Canal 176
Suffragettes 73; 91
Šumadija 194; 202
Summer School for Applied Ethics
Summers, Lieut. Col. 76
Sumner, Sen. Charles 42
Swire, J. 26
Switzerland 81; 141; 224
Sworn virgin (See, Albanian Virgin)
Synod of Split 231

Taylor Institution of Modern Languages
  142
Tekiya 237
Tennyson, Alfred Lord 12; 25
Testu 234
'Text and Context in Ritual Lament' 199
Thethi 105
Thinking Reed, The 113; 119
Thomas, Carey 43
Thompson, Major Frank 169
Thoreau, Henry D. 43

Thrace 179
Through Savage Europe 234
Through the Lands of the Serb 14
Times, The 17; 148; 178
Tirana xiii; 25; 30; 105; 109; 132
Tito, Josip Broz 125; 193; 194
Todorova xiv; xv
Tolstoy, Count Leo
Topola
Toptani, Essat ('Tyrant of Tirana') 24
Totemism (See, Magic)
Tourism, tourist(s) xxi; xxvi; 12–13;
  42; 156; 171; 172
Trade Union Congress 179
Transylvania 214
Travels in the Slavonic Provinces of
  Turkey in Europe 2; 227
Trepča Mine 124
Tribe(s), Tribesmen 18; 21; 102; 106;
  143 (See also, Hoti, Kastrati,
  Mati, Mirdite, Shoshi)
Trieste xxv; 47; 49; 51; 54; 224
Trijepča, Battle of 13
Troubridge, Vice-Admiral 77
'Trust, Talk and Touch in Folk Healing'
  199
Tunis 94
Turkey, Turkey-in-Europe, Turk(s),
  Turkish xiii; 3; 4; 5; 6; 7; 10; 13;
  14; 15; 16; 22; 23; 24; 33; 56;
  63; 106; 155; 173; 177–179; 180;
  190; 210–211; 212; 227; 228; 229;
  230; 238
  government 4–6; 17; 22; 23; 177;
    211; 228
Two Vagabonds in Albania 85
Two Vagabonds in the Balkans 85
Tylor, Sir Edward 232
Typhus 1; 72; 74–77; 79

Union of Soviet Socialist Republics
  (See, Soviet Union)
Unitarian(s), Unitarianism 40; 42
United Nations 194
United States of America 29; 45; 48;
  54; 84; 100; 109; 187; 222
  (See also, America)
University of Berlin 45
University of Birmingham 74
University of Bradford xxiv
University of Chicago 45
University of Nevada 47
University of Skopje 86
Unwritten Law of Albania, The 127;
  127; 141; 143; 144; 145; 146; 147
Urquhart, David 224

Vacation Tourists and Notes of Travels in 1861 2
Vaka, Demetra 103; 211; 212
Valjevo 76–77; 80
Valona (See, Vlorë) 79
Varaždin 51
Vardar 82–83
Varna 171
Veles 83
Venice 233
Verein 45
Victorian 1
Vida (daughter-in-law) 158
Vidević, Vaso 6
Vienna, Viennese 47; 48; 156
Vilayet 14
Vinaver, Stanislav ('Constantine') 116
Vinodol 40
Virgil 158
Vlah 134
Vlahi 182
Vlorë 22; 24; 79; 101
Voluntary Aid Detachment (VAD) 73; 92
Vranje 78; 83; 85
Vrnjačka Banja 76; 77; 80
Vuthaj 211

Wagner, Adolph 45
Wales 73
Wall Street Crash 119
Waller, Dianne xxxi
War(s), Wartime xiv; xxix; 103; 127;
    139–140; 142; 148; 155–165;
    170; 192
    American Civil 42
    Balkan xxvii; 23; 24; 26; 34; 76
    First World, Great War xxviii; 10; 23;
        28; 65; 71; 86; 91; 94; 101; 128;
        167; 234
    Franco-Prussian xxix
    Second World xxix; 66; 118;
        126–127; 129–154; 169; 192
War Office 73; 83; 91
Warner, Sam Bass jr. 411; 46
Warriner, Doreen xxxii
Warsaw 107
Waterhouse, Lady Helen 128; 138
Wayward Women xiv
Weber, Max 238
Wei-hai-wei 168
Wellesley College 45; 46; 65
West, Rebecca; xxv; xxvii; xxxi; 9; 29;
    32; 40; 113–127; 156; 192; 228;
    229; 230; 231; 236
Western Union 100
Westminster Gazette, The 234
Westonbirt Public School 169

West Virginia 41
Wheeler, George 230
Wheelwright, Julie xv; xxix
'White Plague' 59
Whittier, J. G. 43
Wilde, Oscar 167
Wilder, Laura Ingalls 99; 100; 109
    Home Association 110
Wilkinson, Sir Gardner 230
Wilson, Edmond 43
Wilson, Francesca M. 81
Wilson Travelling Fellowships 131
Wilson Woodrow 43
Wimbourne Unit 75
Winchelsea, Anne, Countess of 208
Witchcraft, Oracles and Magic among the Azande 187
Women in a Village 155
Women Travel xiv
Women's International League for Peace
    and Freedom (WILPF) 65; 66
'Women's place is in the Home' 110
Women's rights 45; 59; 183
Women's Sick and Wounded Convoy
    Corps 76
Women's writing xxx–xxxi
Woods, Robert A. 46
Worker's rights 45
Workers' self-management 198
World War (See, War)
Wortley, Lady Mary Montagu xxiv; 155
'Wounded Allies' 77

Yale University 43
'Young Farmers' 77
Young Men's Christian Association
    (YMCA) 24–25
'Young Turks'; 'Young Turk'
    Constitution 20; 22
Youth Brigades 169–172
Yugoslavia, Yugoslav xiii; xxi; xxxi; 9;
    71; 82–83; 100; 102; 113; 114;
    115; 119; 124; 125; 126; 140;
    155–165; 170–171; 179; 193; 228

Zadar 11; 231
Zadruga 57; 58; 195
Zagorje, Croatian 57
Zagreb 47; 48; 51; 59; 62
Zaptie (policeman) 6
Zemun 77
Zeune 225
Zog, Zogu, King Ahmet 27; 29; 102;
    105; 108; 109; 110; 132; 137
Zukin, Sharon xxxii
Zurich 224
Zu Wied, Wilhelm 23–24

Lightning Source UK Ltd.
Milton Keynes UK
UKOW03f0406171213

223148UK00003B/128/P